Yagyu Ninja Scrolls

Scrolls

Revenge of the Hori Clan

ORIGINAL STORY BY FŪTARO YAMADA
MANGA BY MASAKI SEGAWA

TRANSLATED AND ADAPTED BY MINI EDA
LETTERED BY B. HAN

2

BALLANTINE BOOKS • NEW YORK

The Yagyu Ninjas Scrolls: Revenge of the Hori Clan volume 2 is a work of fiction. Names, characters, places, and incidents are the products of the author's imagination or are used fictitiously. Any resemblance to actual events, locales, or persons, living or dead, is entirely coincidental.

A Del Rey Manga/Kodansha Trade Paperback Original

Published in the United States by Del Rey Books, an imprint of The Random House Publishing Group, a division of Random House, Inc., New York.

Del Rey is a registered trademark and the Del Rey colophon is a trademark of Random House, Inc.

Publication rights arranged through Kodansha Ltd.

First published in Japan in 2005 by Kodansha Ltd., Tokyo

ISBN 978-0-345-50120-2

Printed in the United States of America

www.delreymanga.com

9 8 7 6 5 4 3 2 1

Translator/adapter: Mini Eda
Letterer: B. Han

Honorifics Explained

Throughout the Del Rey Manga books, you will find Japanese honorifics left intact in the translations. For those not familiar with how the Japanese use honorifics and, more important, how they differ from American honorifics, we present this brief overview.

Politeness has always been a critical facet of Japanese culture. Ever since the feudal era, when Japan was a highly stratified society, use of honorifics—which can be defined as polite speech that indicates relationship or status—has played an essential role in the Japanese language. When addressing someone in Japanese, an honorific usually takes the form of a suffix attached to one's name (example: "Asuna-san"), is used as a title at the end of one's name, or appears in place of the name itself (example: "Negi-sensei," or simply "Sensei!").

Honorifics can be expressions of respect or endearment. In the context of manga and anime, honorifics give insight into the nature of the relationship between characters. Many English translations leave out these important honorifics and therefore distort the feel of the original Japanese. Because Japanese honorifics contain nuances that English honorifics lack, it is our policy at Del Rey not to translate them. Here, instead, is a guide to some of the honorifics you may encounter in Del Rey Manga.

-SAN: This is the most common honorific and is equivalent to Mr., Miss, Ms., or Mrs. It is the all-purpose honorific and can be used in any situation where politeness is required.

-SAMA: This is one level higher than "-san" and is used to confer great respect.

-DONO: This comes from the word "tono," which means "lord." It is an even higher level than "-sama" and confers utmost respect.

-KUN: This suffix is used at the end of boys' names to express familiarity or endearment. It is also sometimes used by men among friends, or when addressing someone younger or of a lower station.

-CHAN: This is used to express endearment, mostly toward girls. It is also used for little boys, pets, and even among lovers. It gives a sense of childish cuteness.

BOZU: This is an informal way to refer to a boy, similar to the English terms "kid" and "squirt."

SEMPAI/
SENPAI: This title suggests that the addressee is one's senior in a group or organization. It is most often used in a school setting, where underclassmen refer to their upperclassmen as "sempai." It can also be used in the workplace, such as when a newer employee addresses an employee who has seniority in the company.

KOHAI: This is the opposite of "sempai" and is used toward underclassmen in school or newcomers in the workplace. It connotes that the addressee is of a lower station.

SENSEI: Literally meaning "one who has come before," this title is used for teachers, doctors, or masters of any profession or art.

-[BLANK]: This is usually forgotten in these lists, but it is perhaps the most significant difference between Japanese and English. The lack of honorific means that the speaker has permission to address the person in a very intimate way. Usually, only family, spouses, or very close friends have this kind of permission. Known as *yobisute,* it can be gratifying when someone who has earned the intimacy starts to call one by one's name without an honorific. But when that intimacy hasn't been earned, it can be very insulting.

The Yagyu Ninja Scrolls

2

ORIGINAL STORY BY
FŪTARO YAMADA

MANGA BY
MASAKI SEGAWA

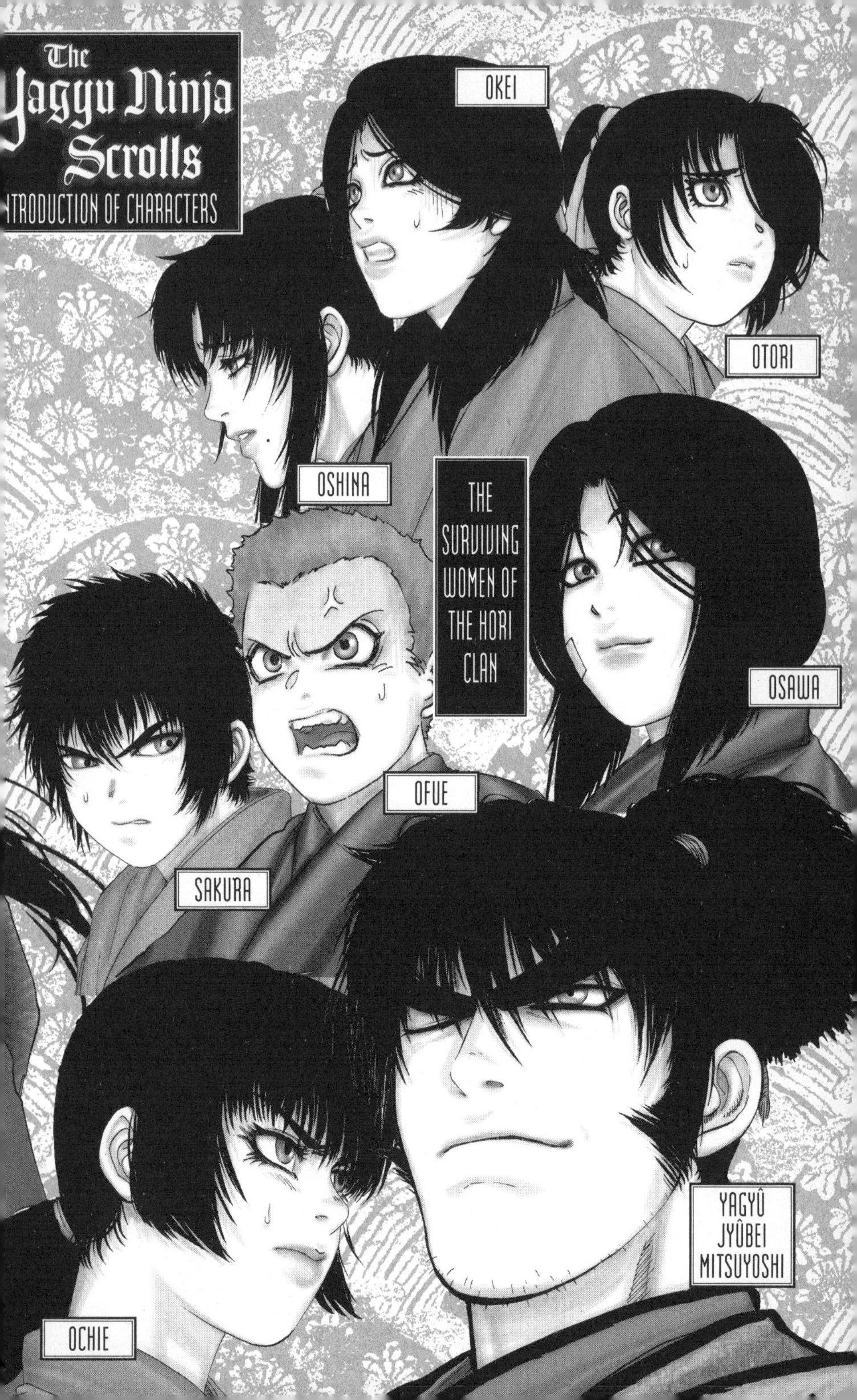
The Yagyu Ninja Scrolls
ITRODUCTION OF CHARACTERS
OKEI
OTORI
OSHINA
THE SURVIVING WOMEN OF THE HORI CLAN
OSAWA
OFUE
SAKURA
YAGYÛ JYÛBEI MITSUYOSHI
OCHIE

SYNOPSIS: THE REBEL MEMBERS OF THE HORI CLAN HAVE BEEN BRUTALLY EXECUTED BY THE AIZU SEVEN SPEARS, WHO SERVE UNDER THE MURDEROUS AIZU CLAN HEAD, KATÔ AKINARI. SEEKING REVENGE, OCHIE AND THE SURVIVING WOMEN OF THE HORI FAMILY ENLIST THE HELP OF YAGYÛ JYÛBEI MITSUYOSHI AS THEIR FIGHTING ARTS INSTRUCTOR. JYÛBEI AGREES TO INSTRUCT THEM, ON THE CONDITION THAT THEY ARE PREPARED TO LOSE THEIR LIVES AND THEIR "CHASTITY." TO DEFEAT THE POWERFUL SEVEN SPEARS, THEY WILL NEED TO ENDURE GRUELING LESSONS, WILL NEED JYÛBEI'S CUNNING, AND A LOT OF LUCK. WHICH OF THE SEVEN SPEARS WILL JYÛBEI SET HIS SIGHTS ON FIRST?

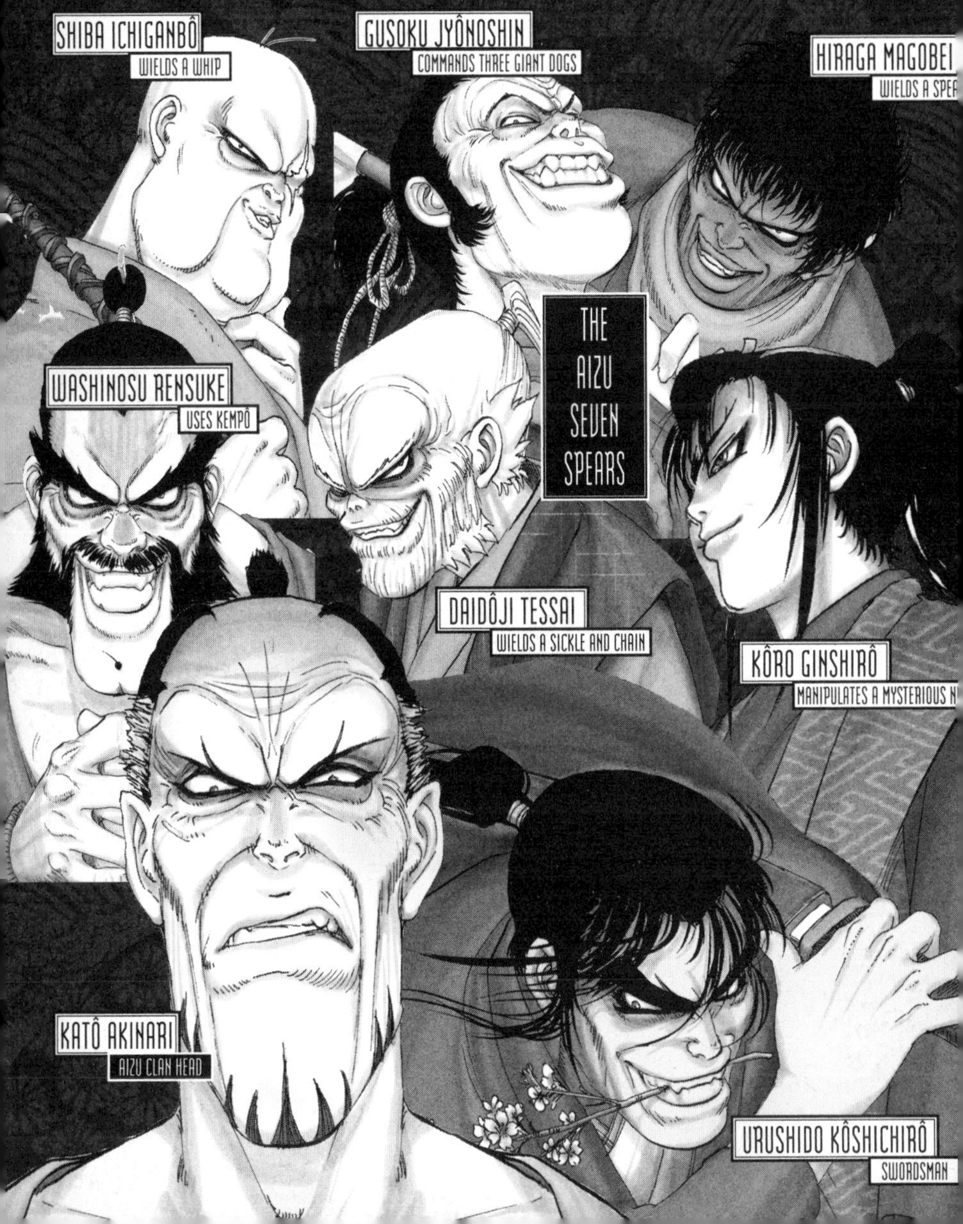

HIRAGA MAGOBEI
WIELDS A SPEA
GUSOKU JYÔNOSHIN
COMMANDS THREE GIANT DOGS
SHIBA ICHIGANBÔ
WIELDS A WHIP
THE AIZU SEVEN SPEARS
WASHINOSU RENSUKE
USES KEMPÔ
DAIDÔJI TESSAI
WIELDS A SICKLE AND CHAIN
KÔRO GINSHIRÔ
MANIPULATES A MYSTERIOUS N
KATÔ AKINARI
AIZU CLAN HEAD
URUSHIDO KÔSHICHIRÔ
SWORDSMAN

CONTENTS

The Yagyu Ninja Scrolls 2

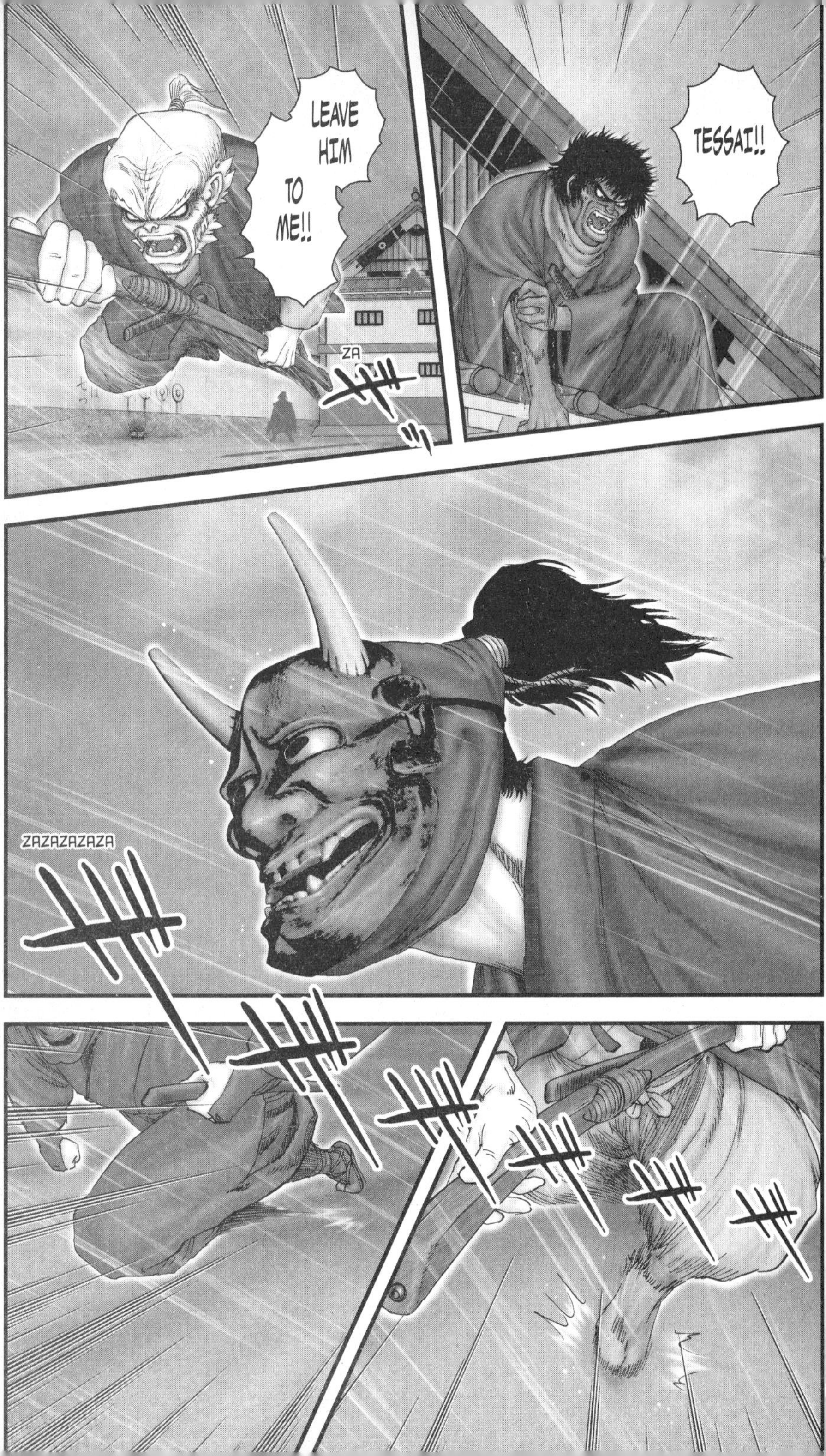
TESSAI!!
LEAVE HIM TO ME!!
ZA
ZAZAZAZAZA

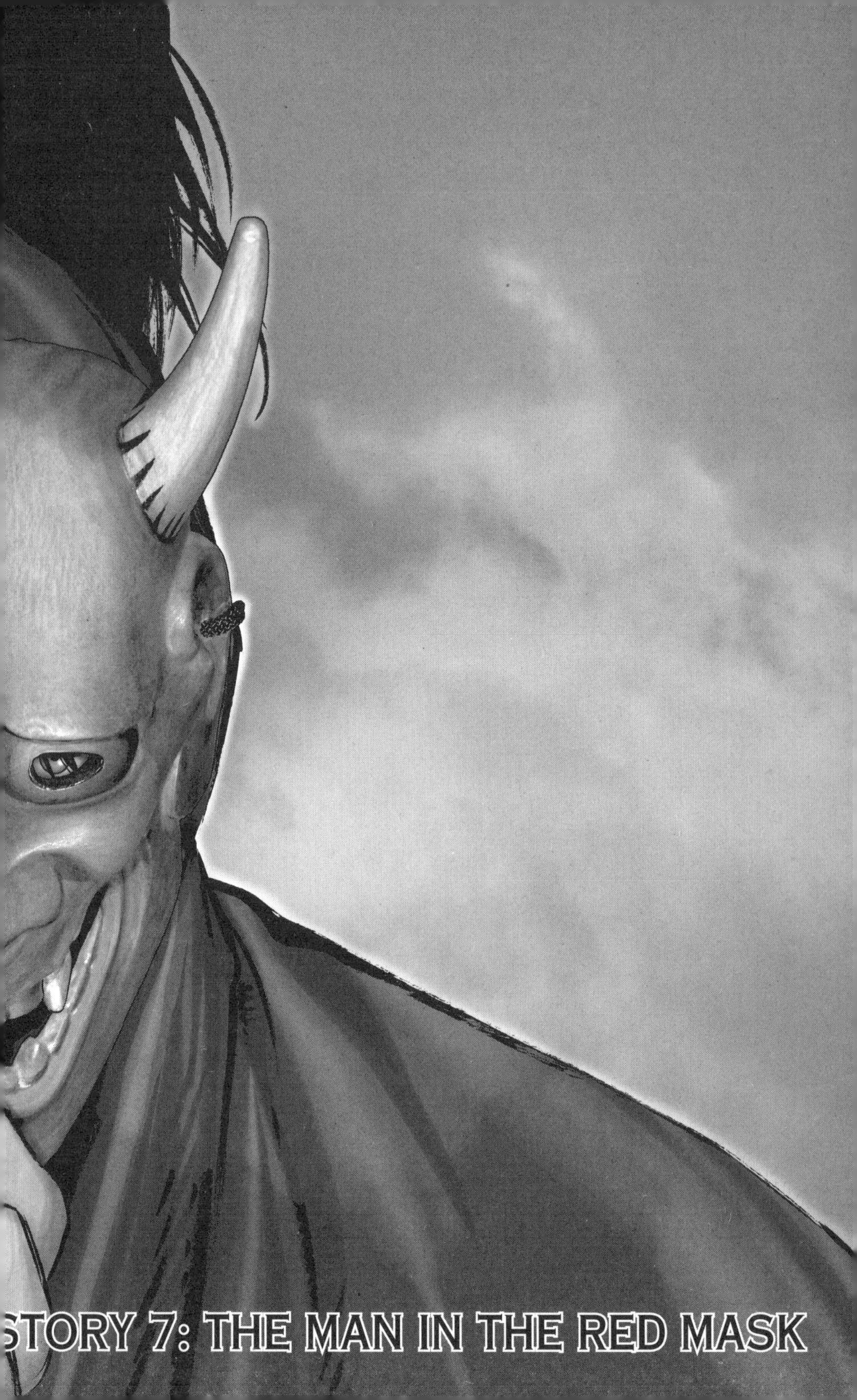

STORY 7: THE MAN IN THE RED MASK

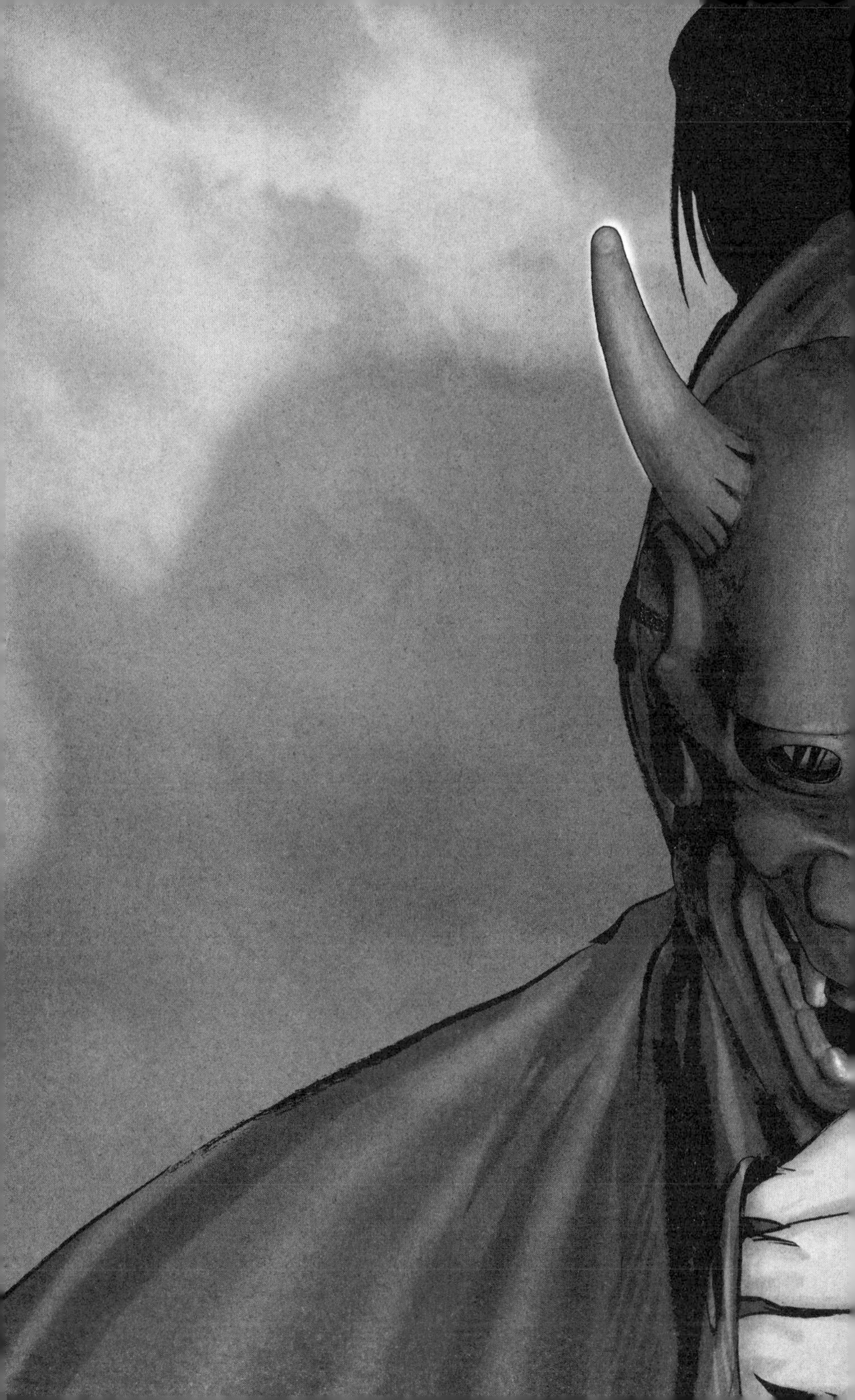

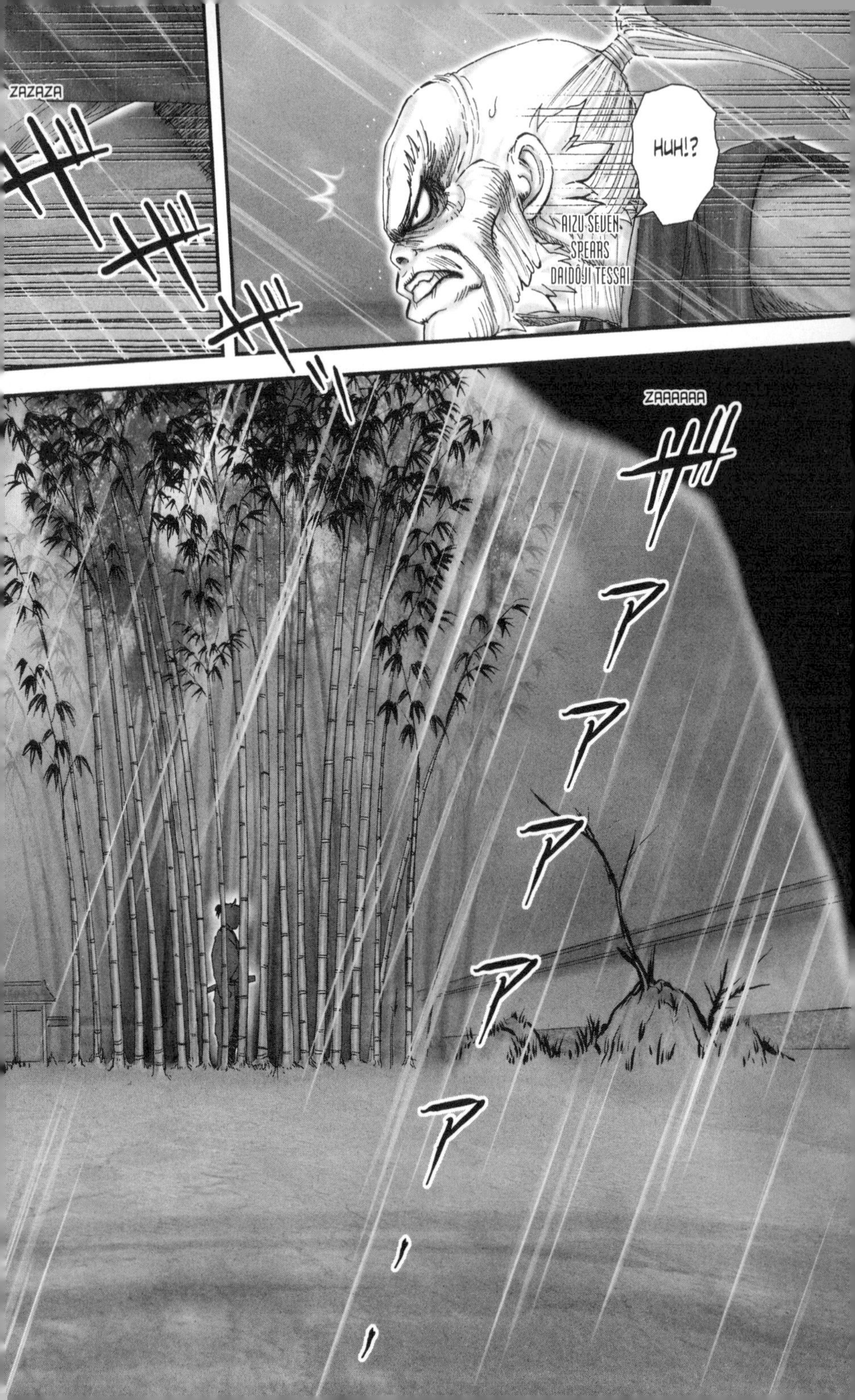
HUH!?
AIZU SEVEN SPEARS DAIDÔJI TESSAI
ZAZAZA
ZAAAAAA

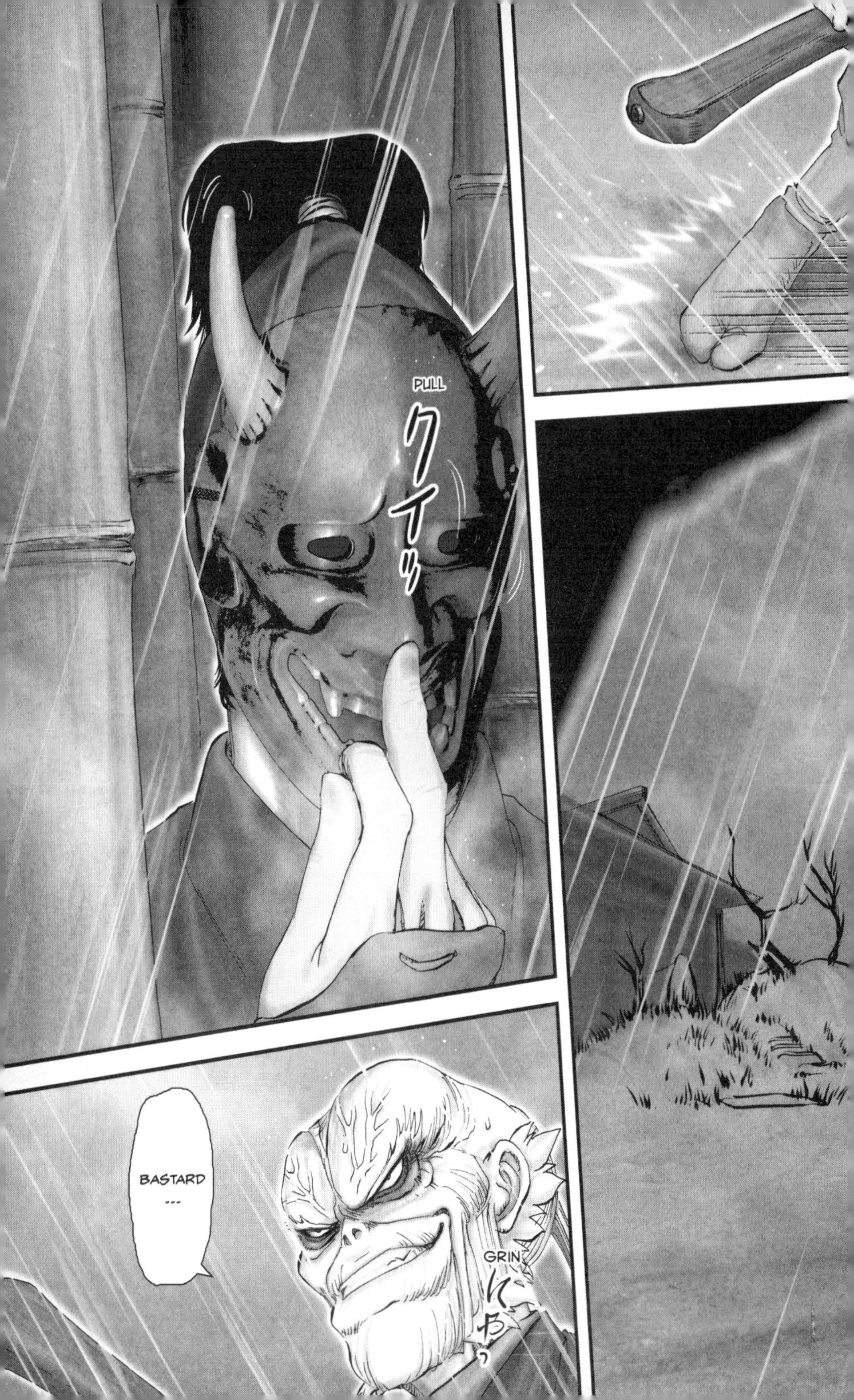
PULL
クイッ
BASTARD ---
GRIN
にやっ

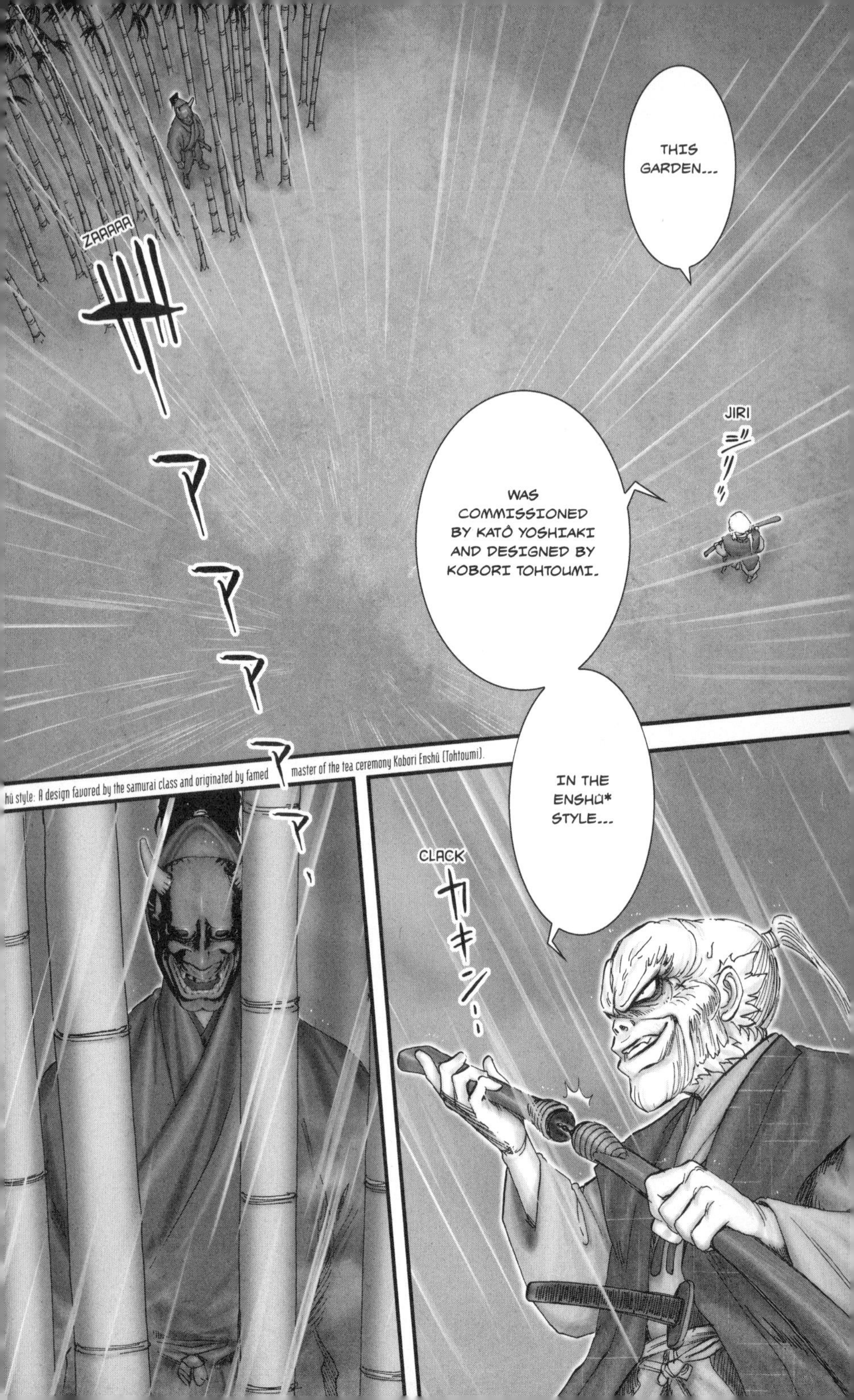
THIS GARDEN...
JIRI
WAS COMMISSIONED BY KATÔ YOSHIAKI AND DESIGNED BY KOBORI TOHTOUMI.
ZAAAAA
IN THE ENSHÛ* STYLE...
CLACK

hû style: A design favored by the samurai class and originated by famed master of the tea ceremony Kobori Enshû (Tohtoumi).

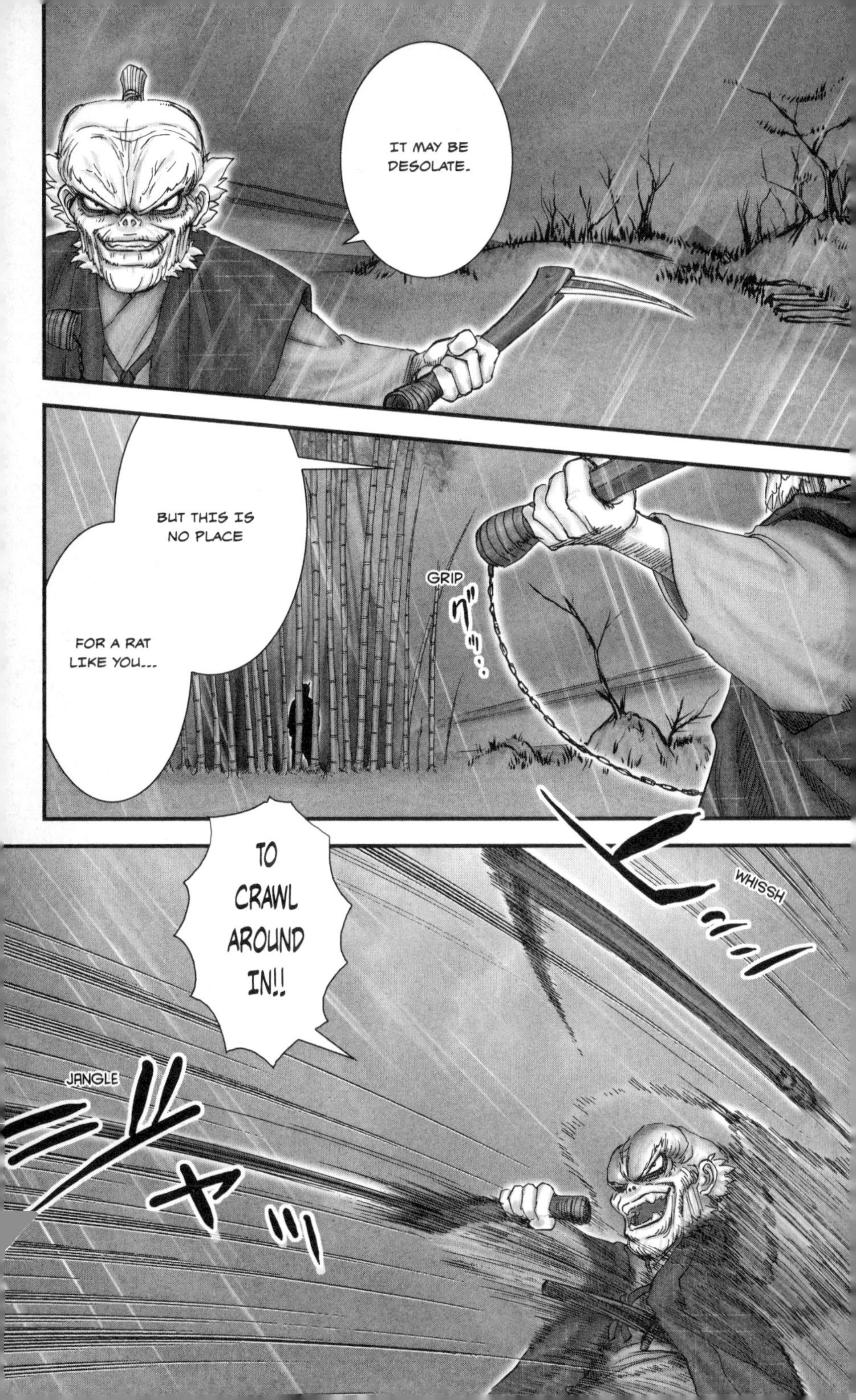
IT MAY BE DESOLATE.
BUT THIS IS NO PLACE
GRIP
ｸﾞｯ
FOR A RAT LIKE YOU...
TO CRAWL AROUND IN!!
WHISSH
JANGLE

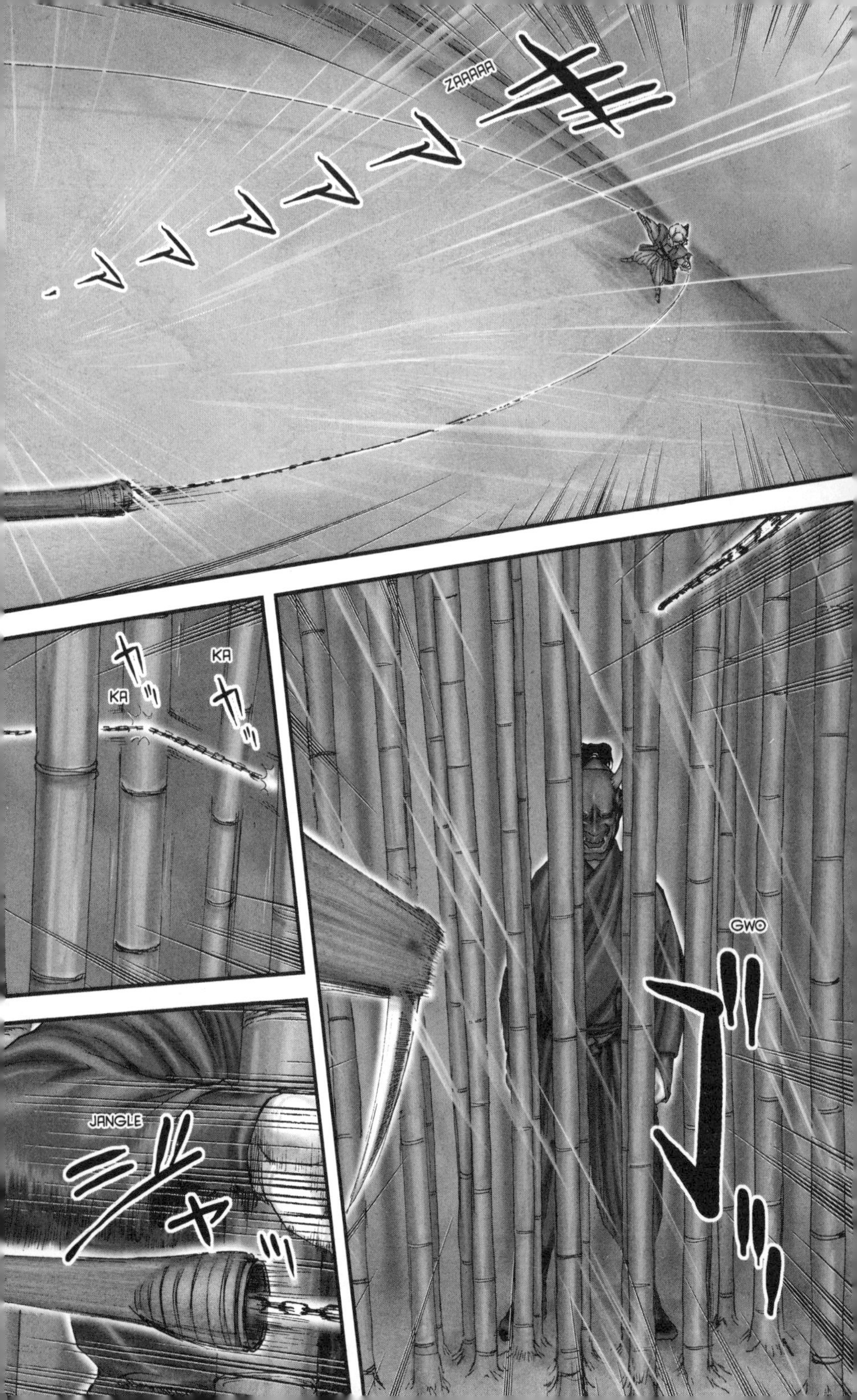
ZAAAAA
GWO
KA
KA
JANGLE

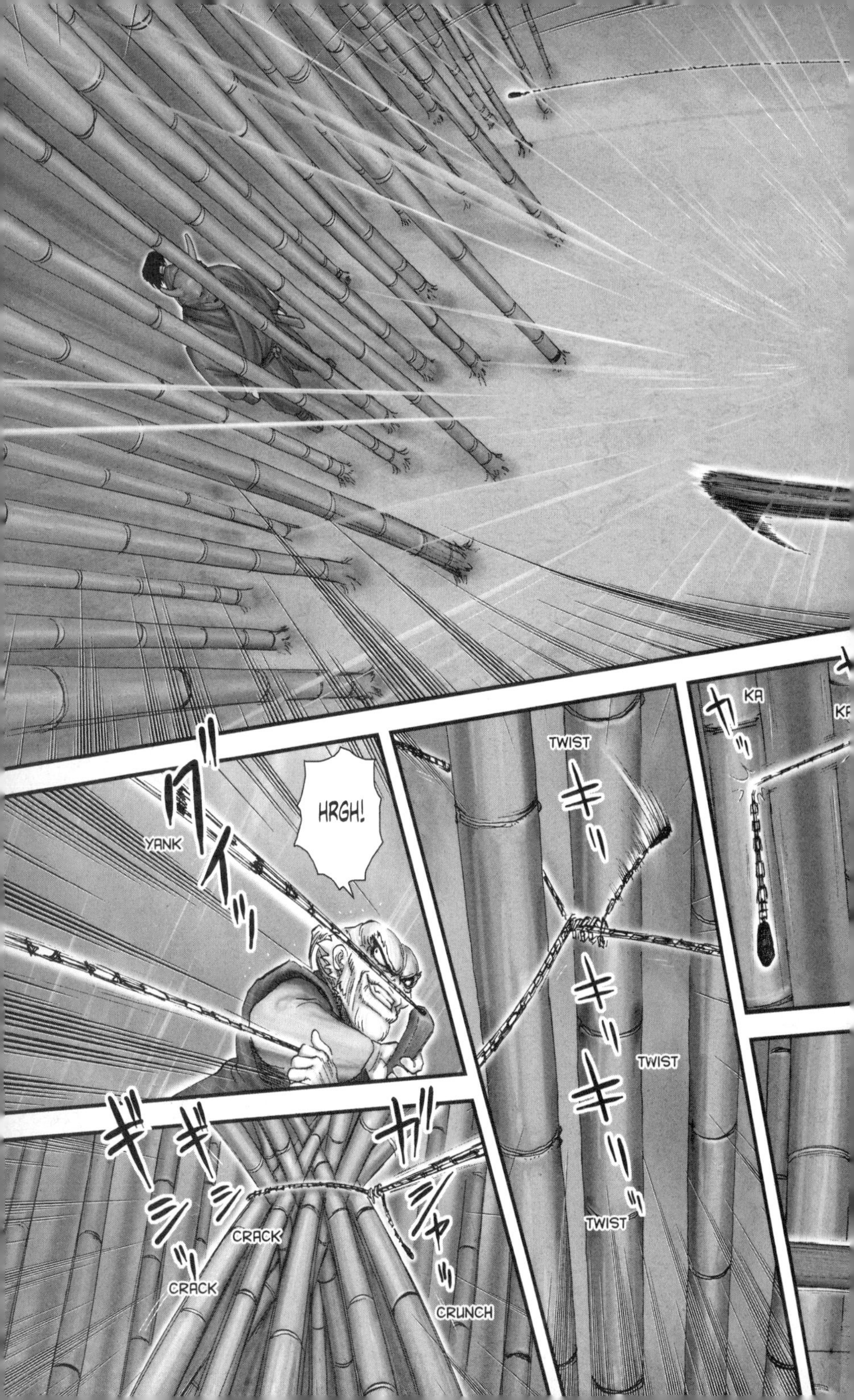
KA
TWIST
TWIST
TWIST
HRGH!
YANK
CRACK
CRACK
CRUNCH

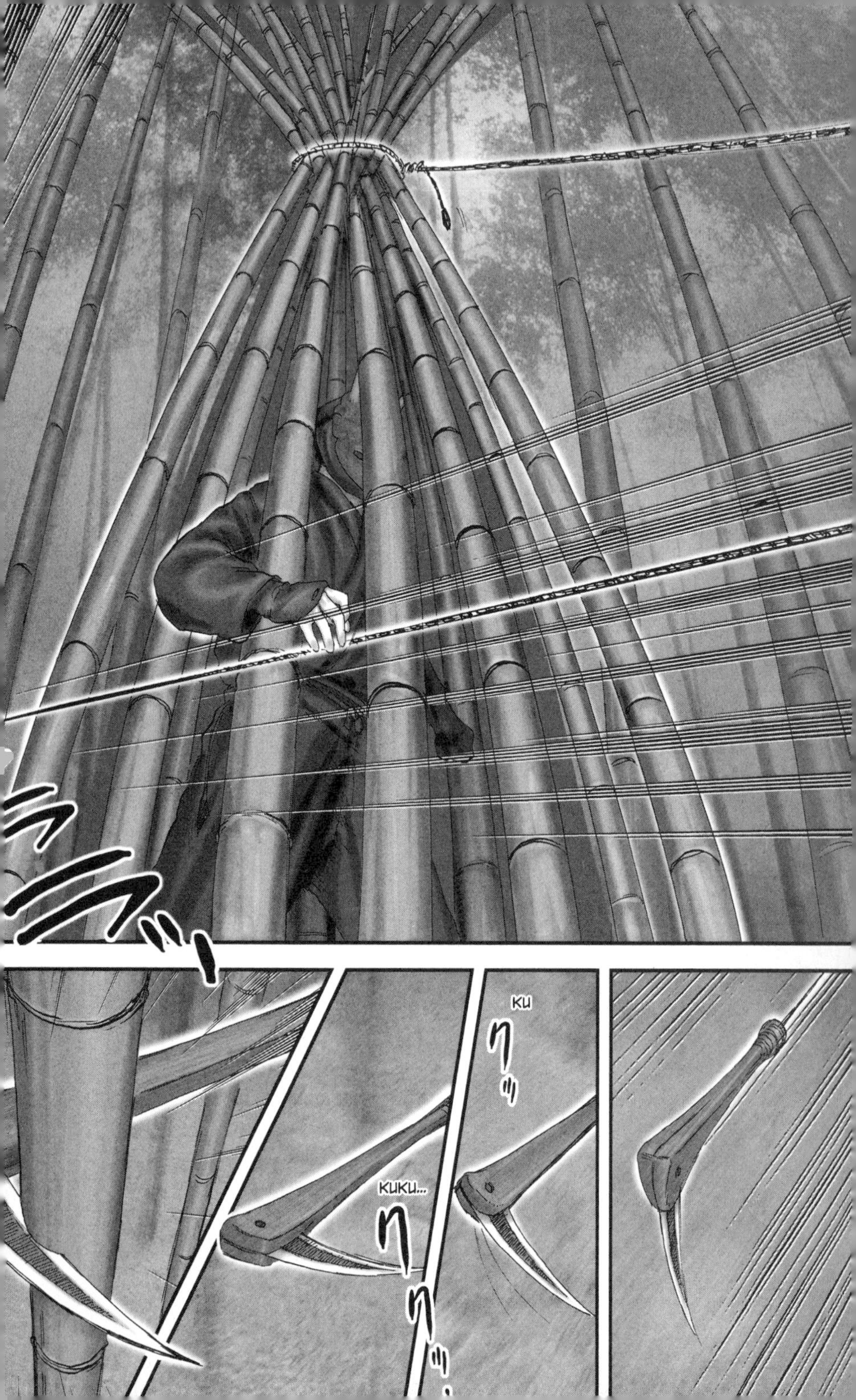
KU
クッ
KUKU...
ククッ

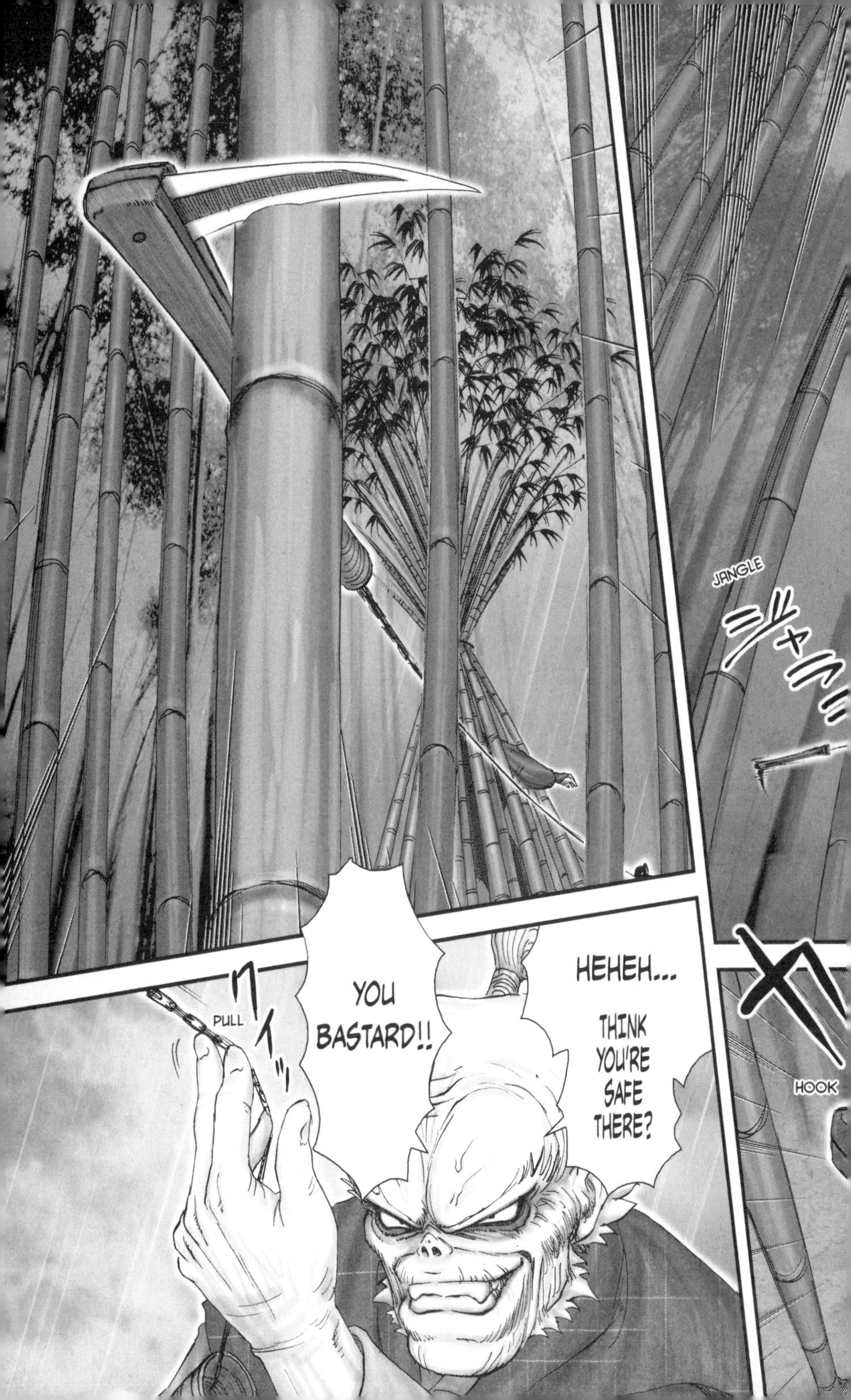
JANGLE
HOOK
HEHEH...
THINK YOU'RE SAFE THERE?
YOU BASTARD!!
PULL

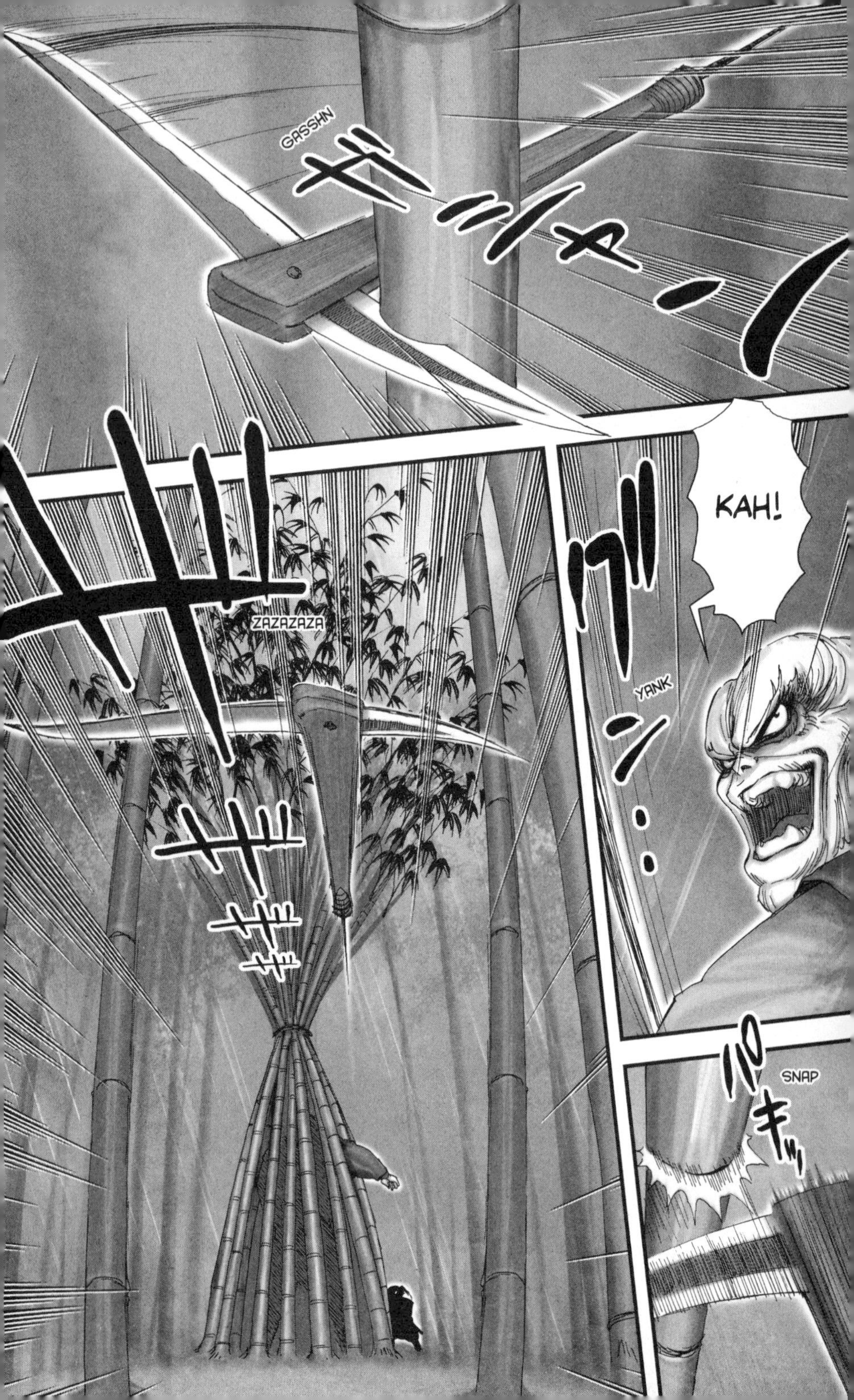
GASSHN
KAH!
YANK
SNAP
ZAZAZAZA

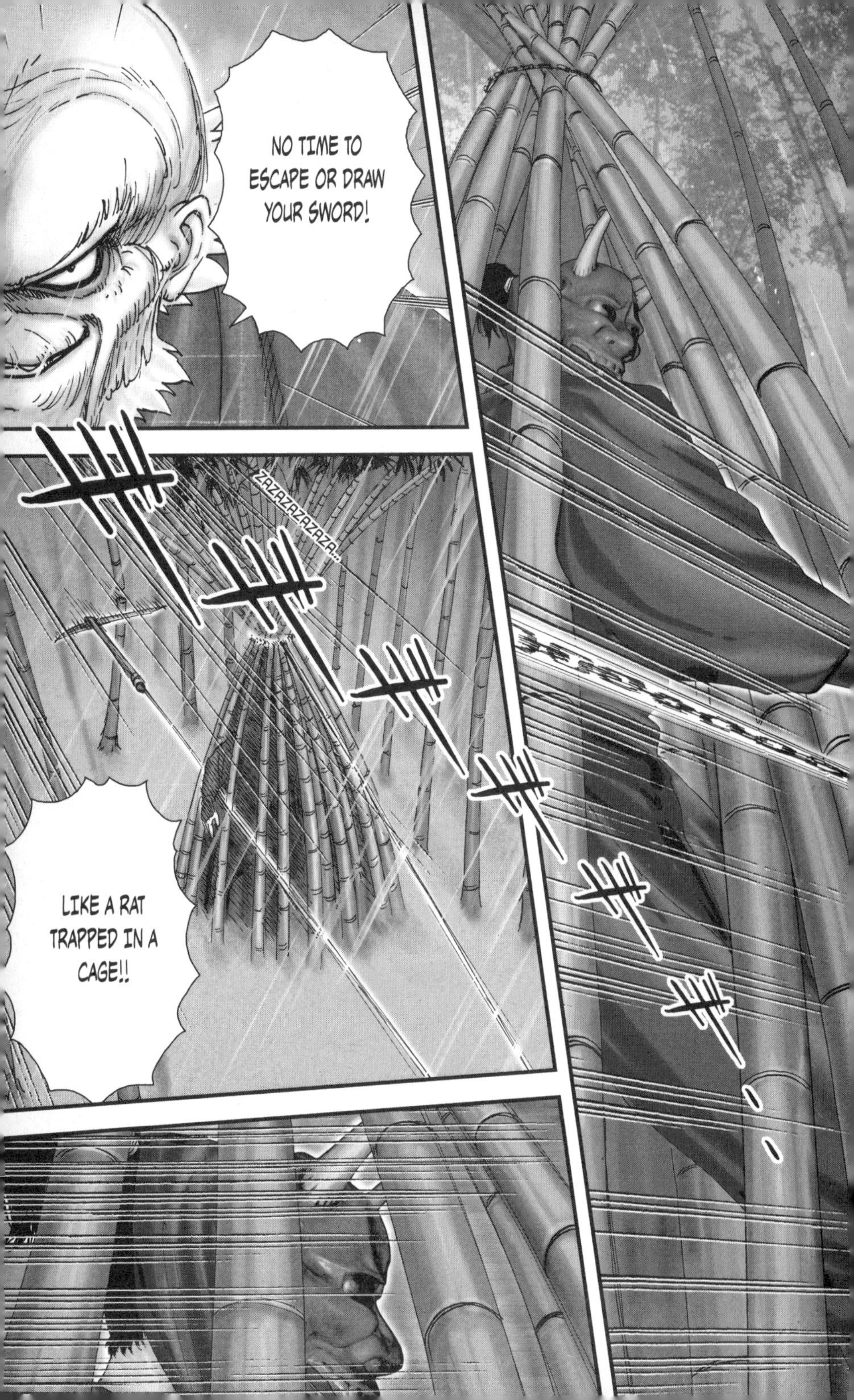
NO TIME TO ESCAPE OR DRAW YOUR SWORD!
ZAZAZAZAZAZAZA...
LIKE A RAT TRAPPED IN A CAGE!!

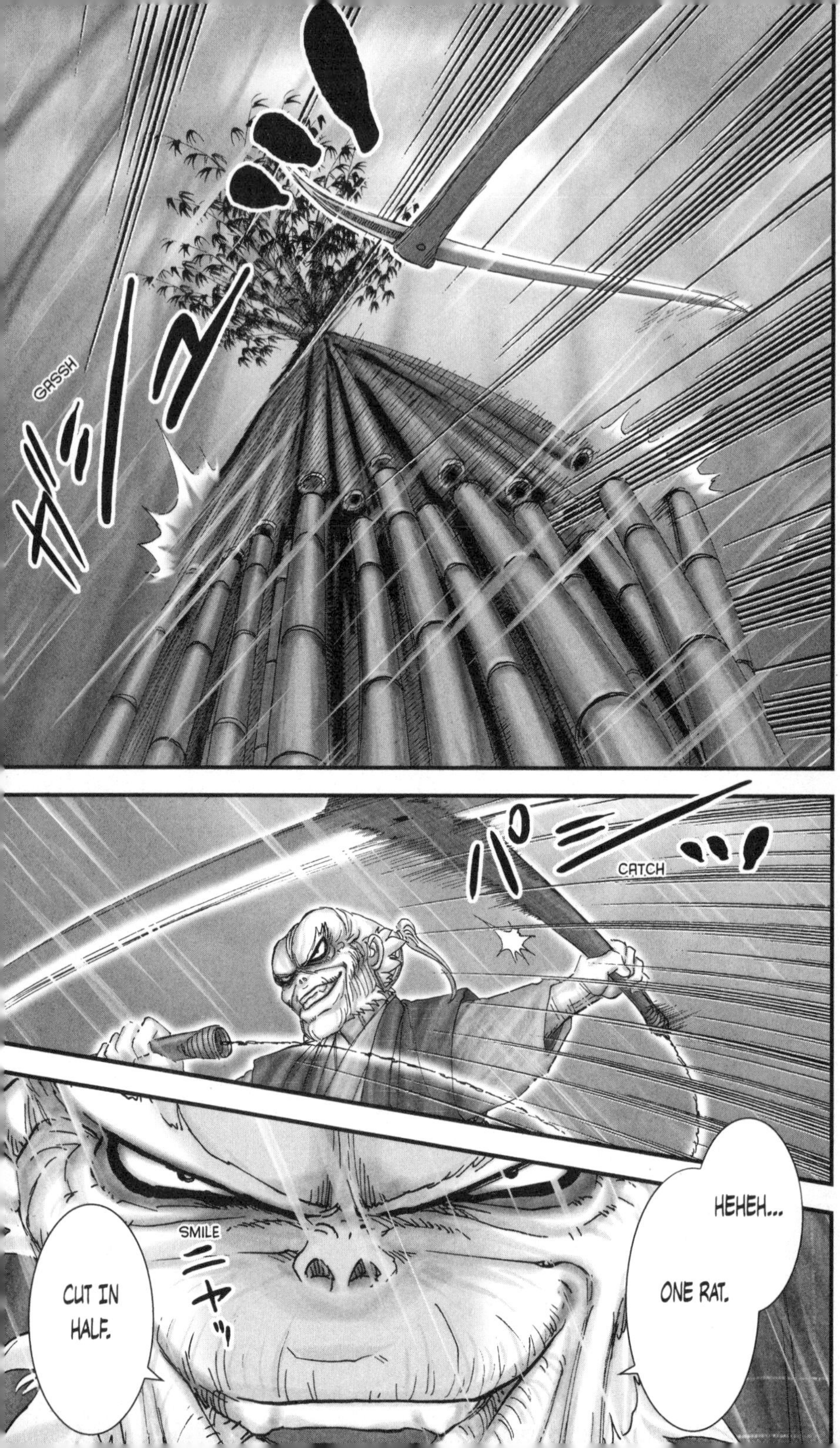
GASSH
CATCH
HEHEH...
ONE RAT.
SMILE
CUT IN HALF.

ZAAAA...
ザァァァァ
HUH?
THONK
ボト
THUD
ゴトッ

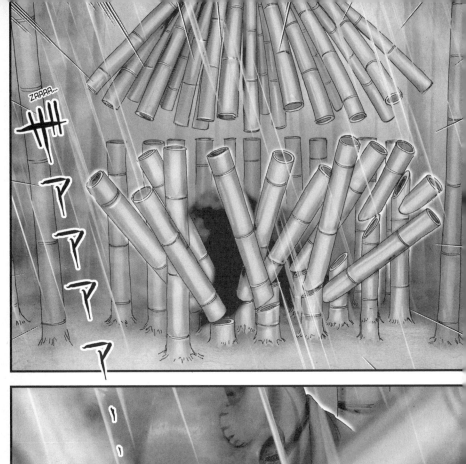

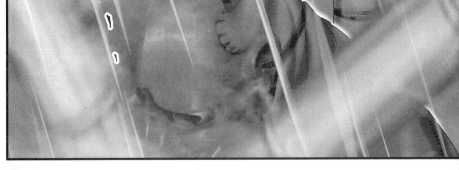

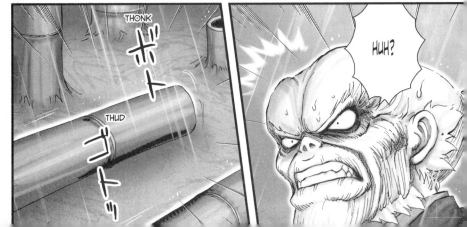

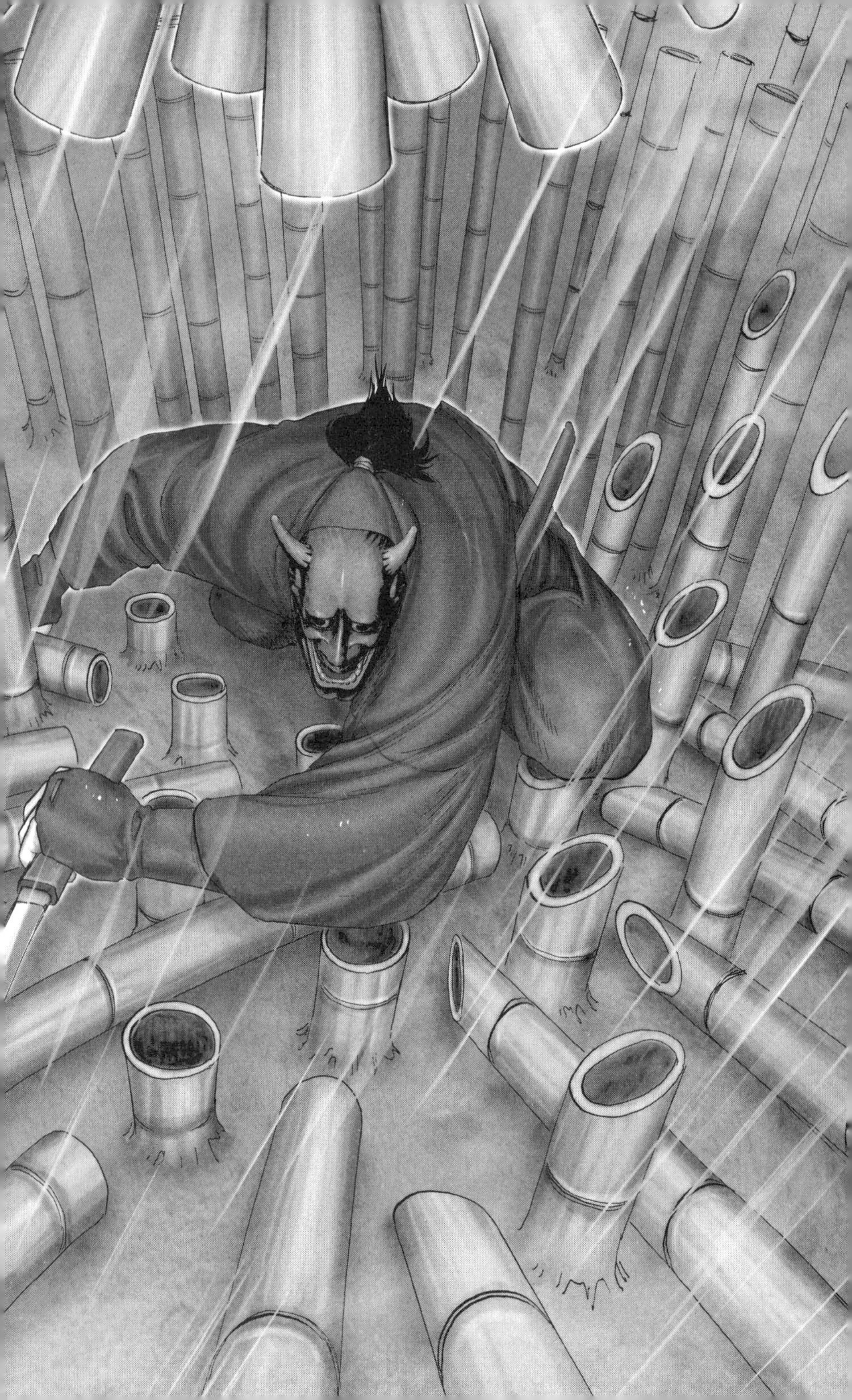

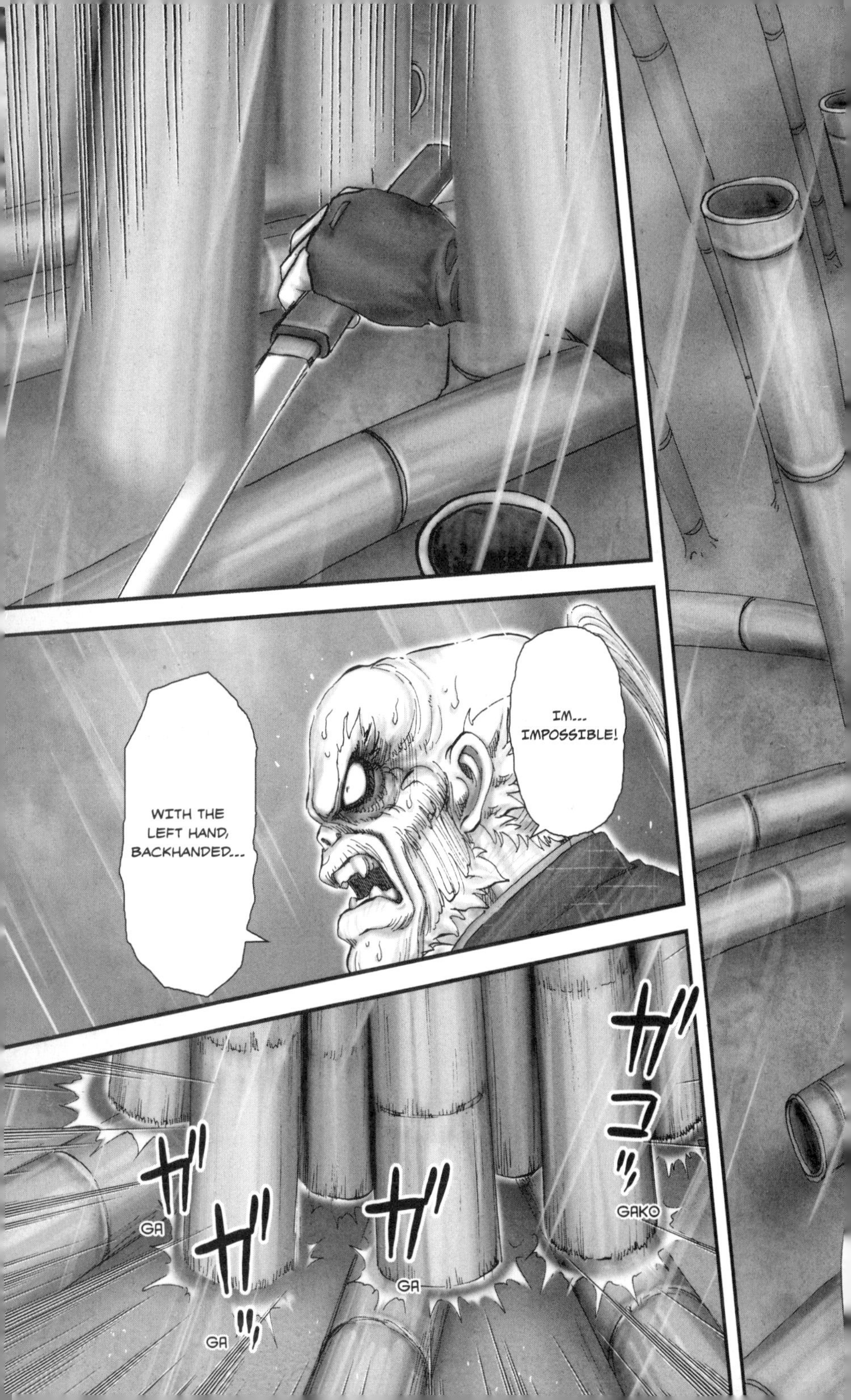
IM... IMPOSSIBLE!
WITH THE LEFT HAND, BACKHANDED...
ガコッ
GAKO
ガ
GA
ガ
GA
ガッ
GA

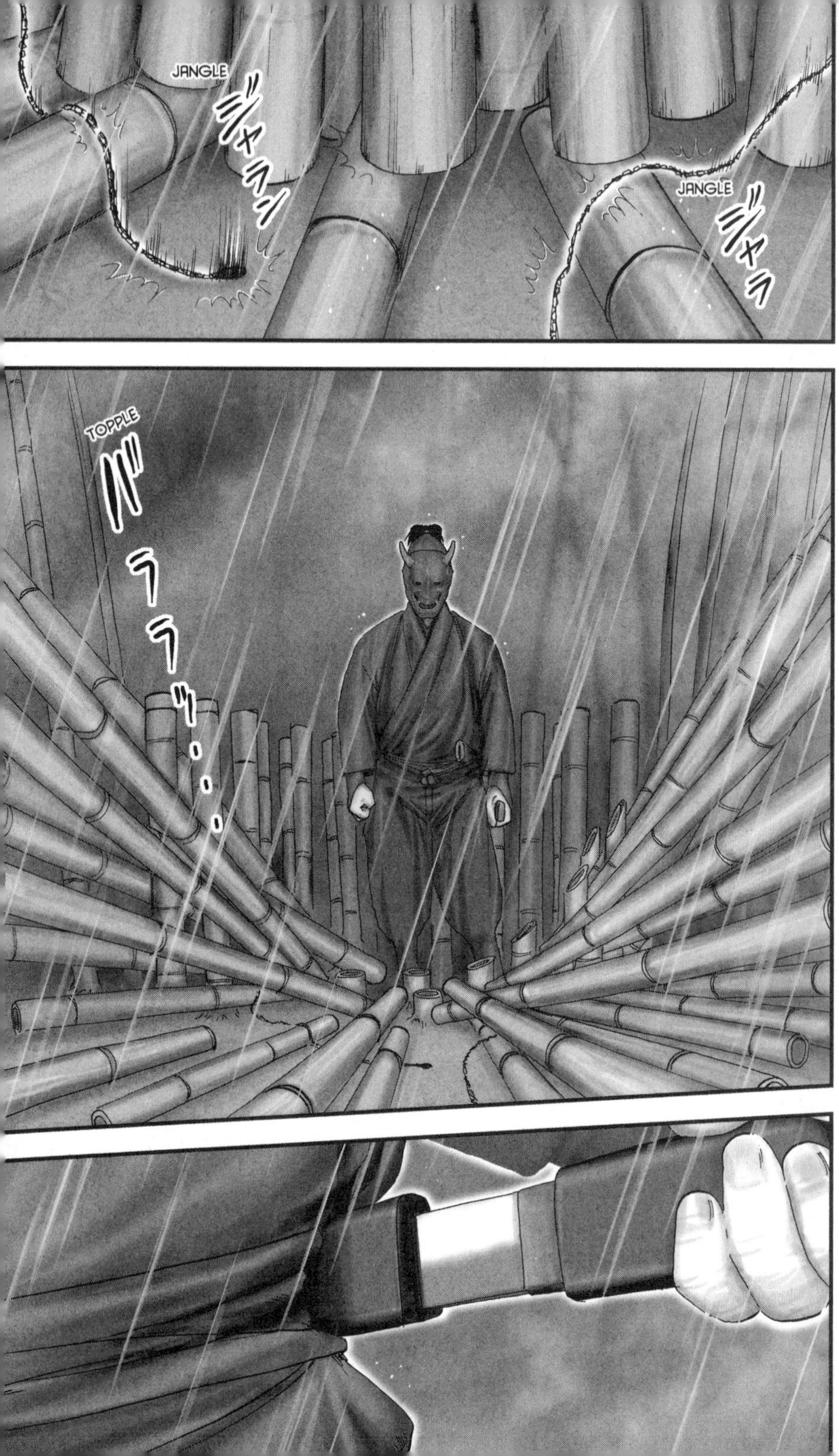
JANGLE
ジャラ
JANGLE
ジャラッ
TOPPLE
バララッ...

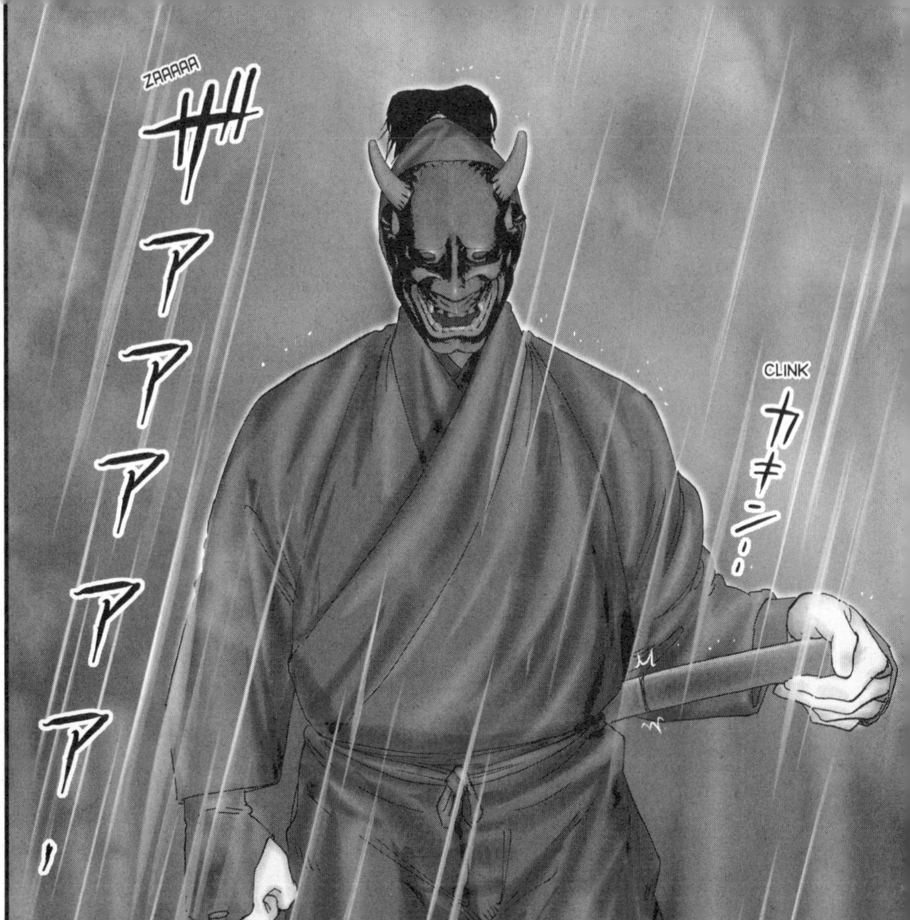
ZAAAAAA
ザァァァァァ、
CLINK
カキン…
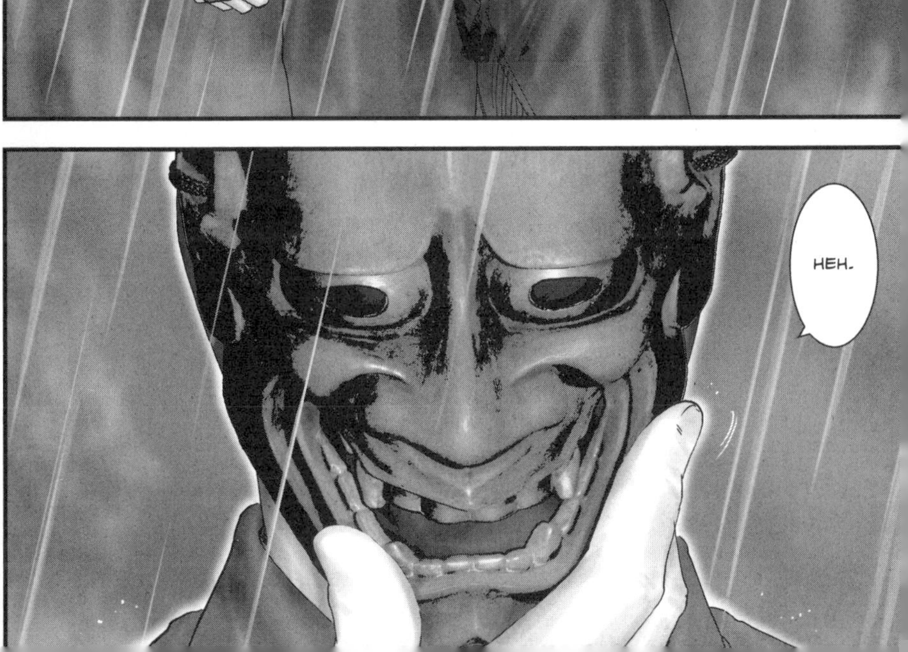
HEH.

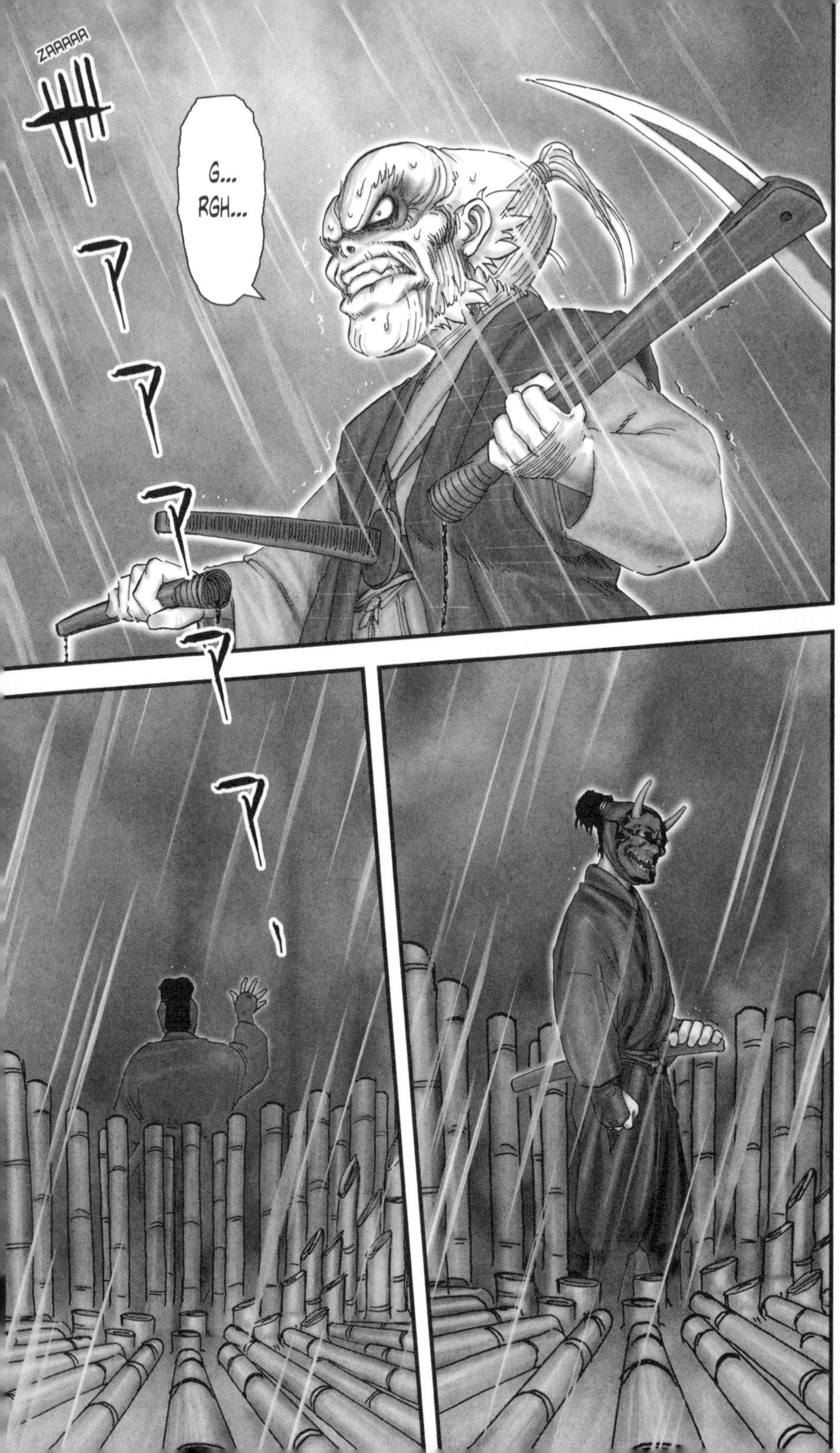
G...
RGH...
ZAAAAAA
ザァァァァァァ

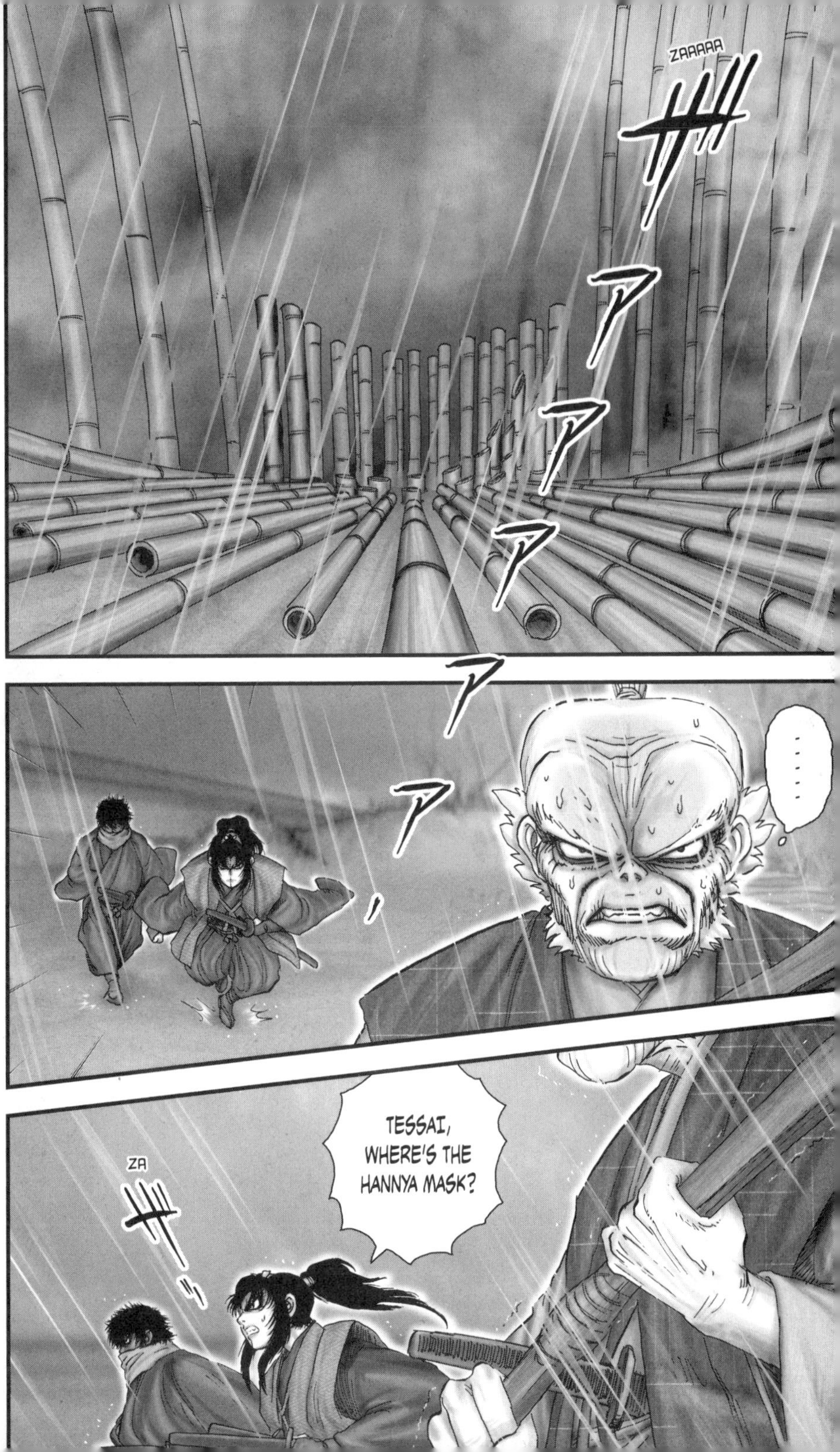
ZAAAAA
. . . . .
TESSAI, WHERE'S THE HANNYA MASK?
ZA

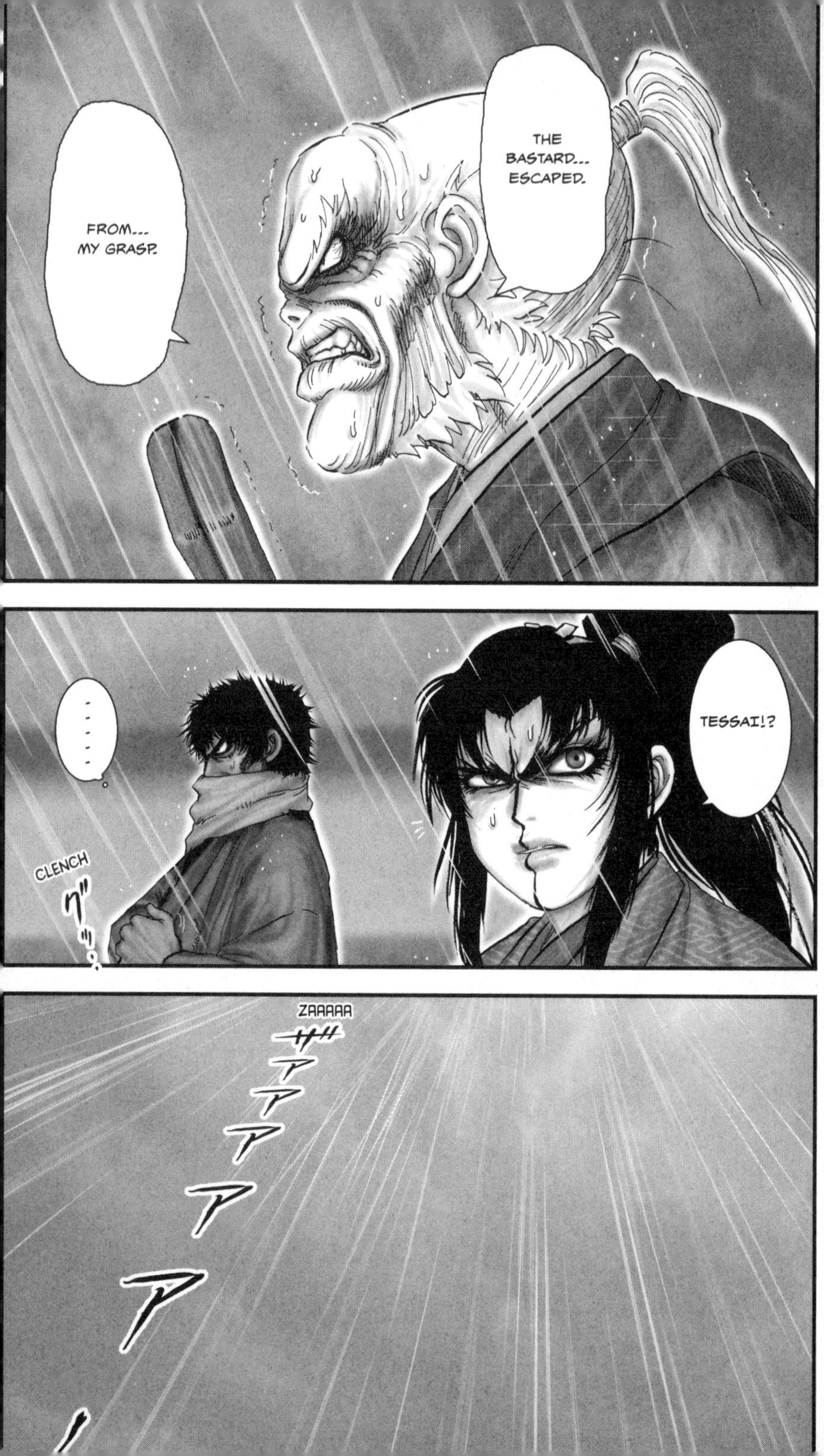
THE BASTARD... ESCAPED.
FROM... MY GRASP.
TESSAI!?
......
CLENCH
ZAAAAA

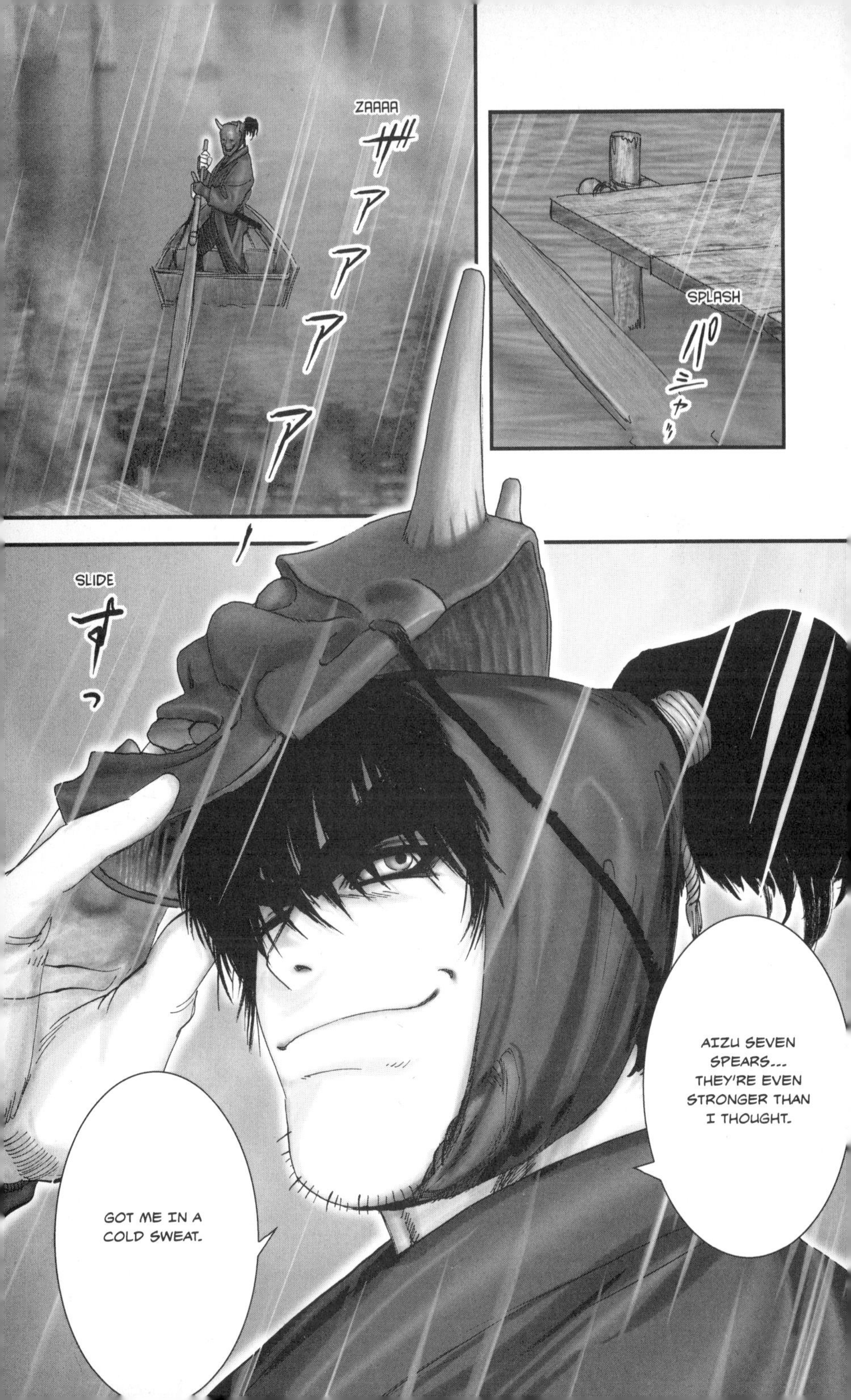
SPLASH
パシャッ
ZAAAA
ザァァァァ！
SLIDE
すっ
AIZU SEVEN SPEARS... THEY'RE EVEN STRONGER THAN I THOUGHT.
GOT ME IN A COLD SWEAT.

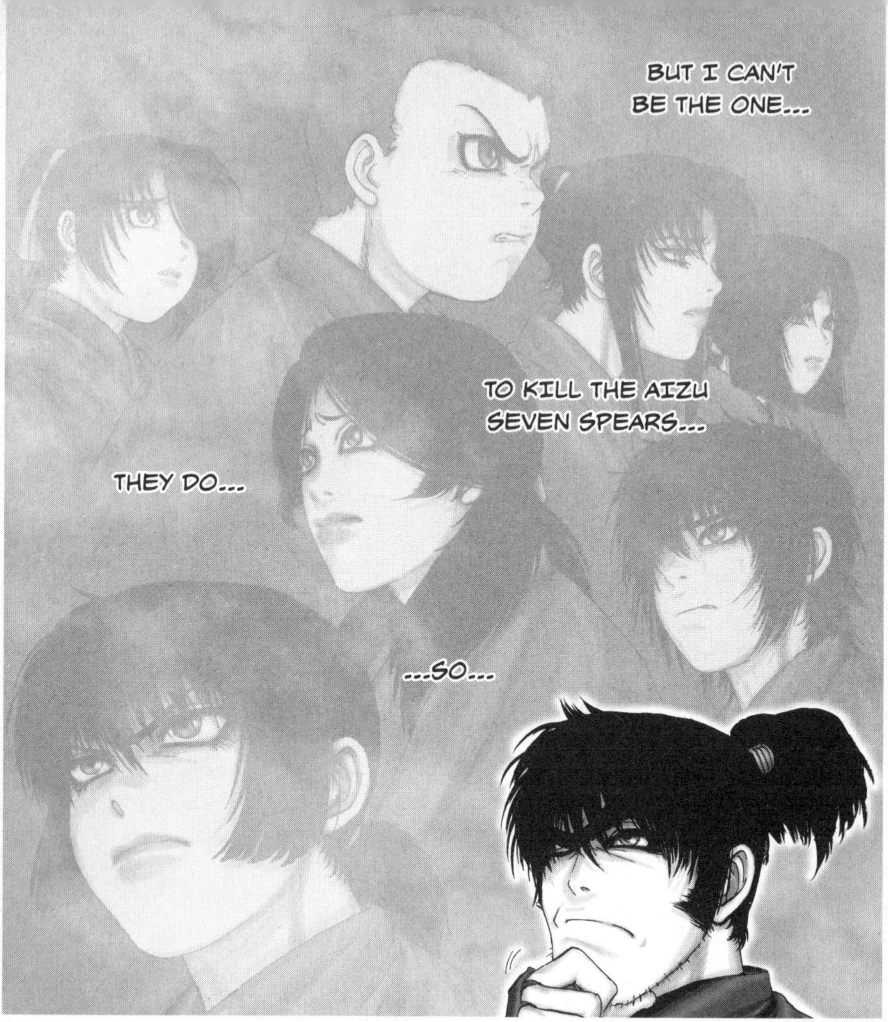
BUT I CAN'T BE THE ONE...
TO KILL THE AIZU SEVEN SPEARS...
THEY DO...
...SO...
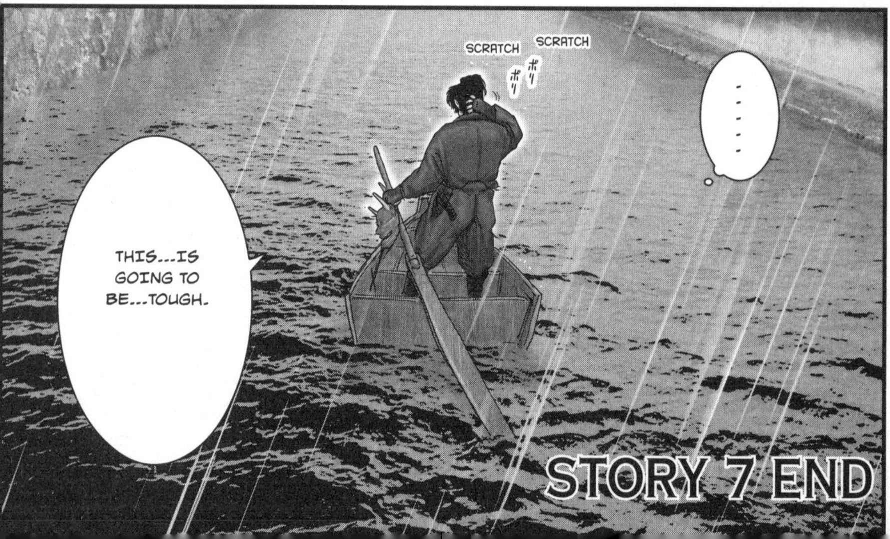
SCRATCH SCRATCH
ボリ ボリ
......
THIS...IS GOING TO BE...TOUGH.
STORY 7 END

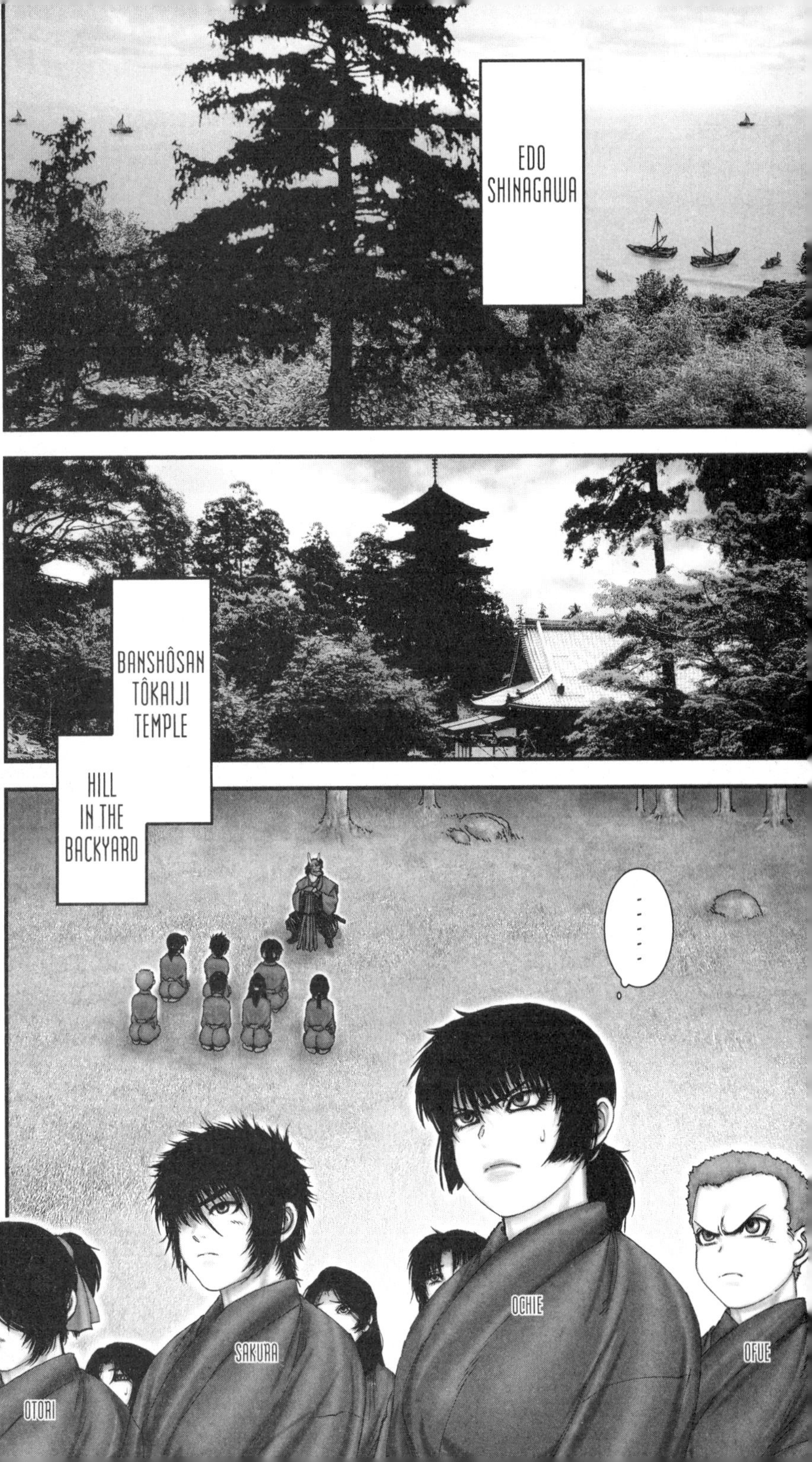
EDO SHINAGAWA
BANSHÔSAN TÔKAIJI TEMPLE
HILL IN THE BACKYARD
......
OFUE
OCHIE
SAKURA
OTORI

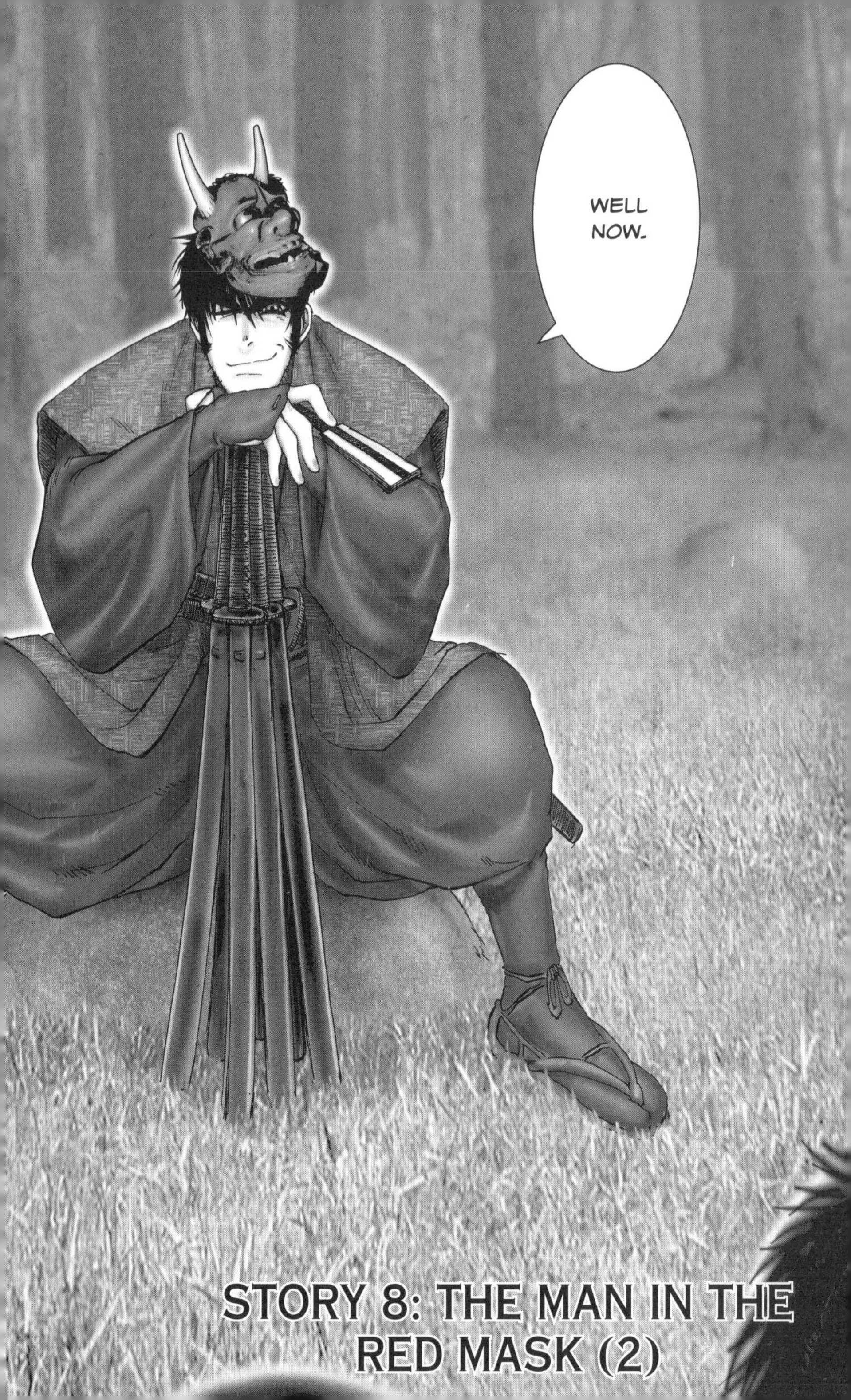
WELL NOW..
STORY 8: THE MAN IN THE RED MASK (2)

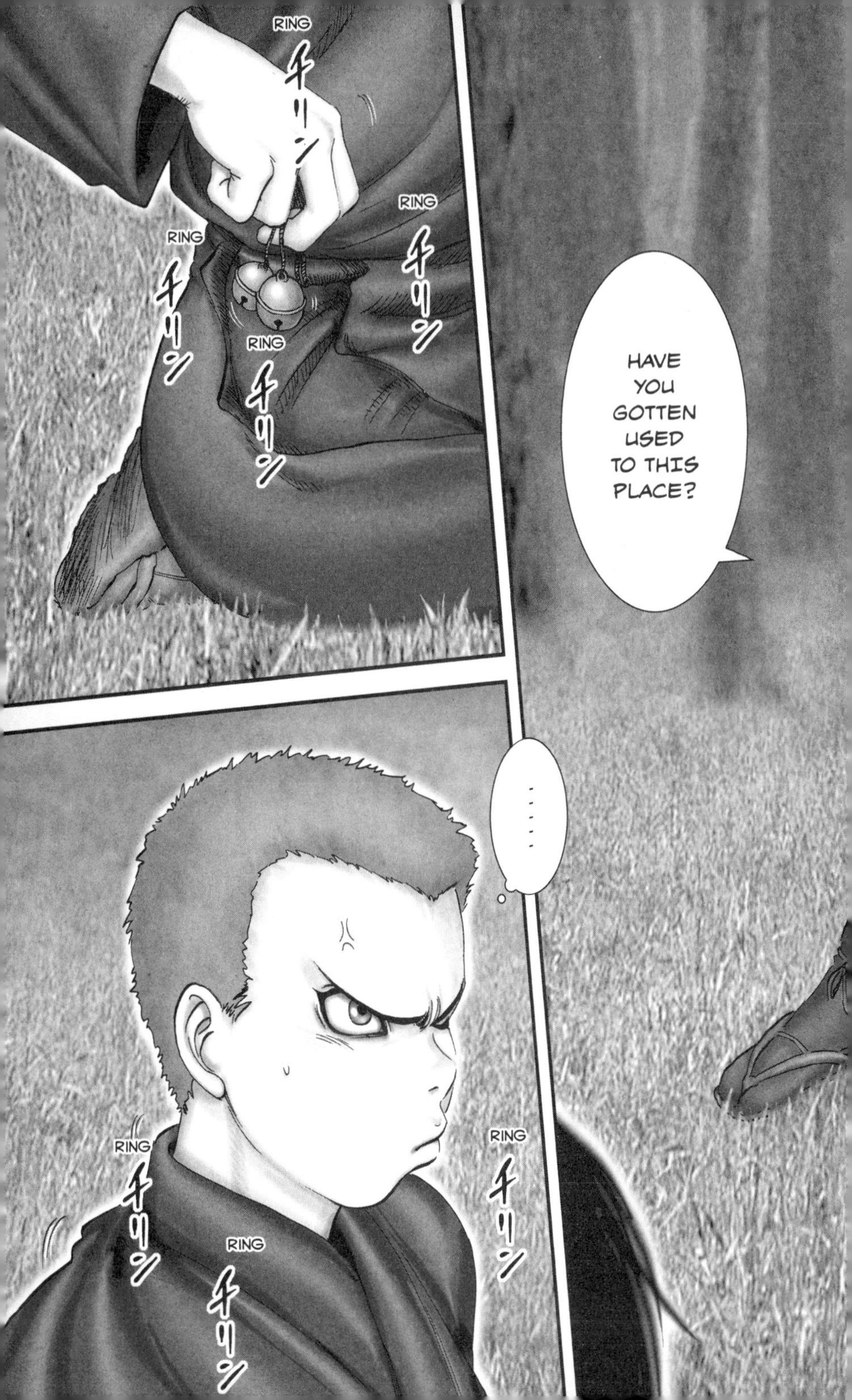
HAVE YOU GOTTEN USED TO THIS PLACE?
RING
チリン
RING
チリン
RING
チリン
RING
チリン
......
RING
チリン
RING
チリン
RING
チリン

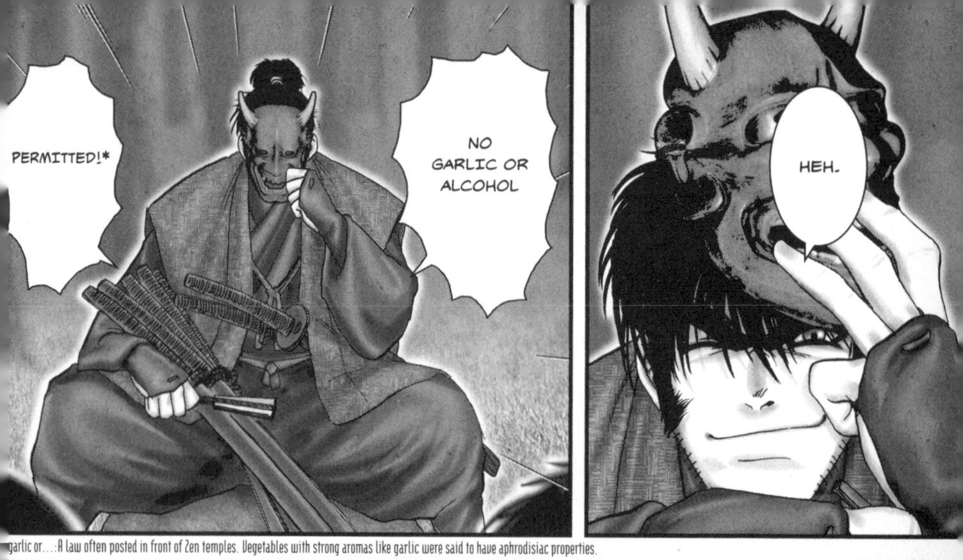
HEH.
NO GARLIC OR ALCOHOL
PERMITTED!*

*garlic or...: A law often posted in front of Zen temples. Vegetables with strong aromas like garlic were said to have aphrodisiac properties.

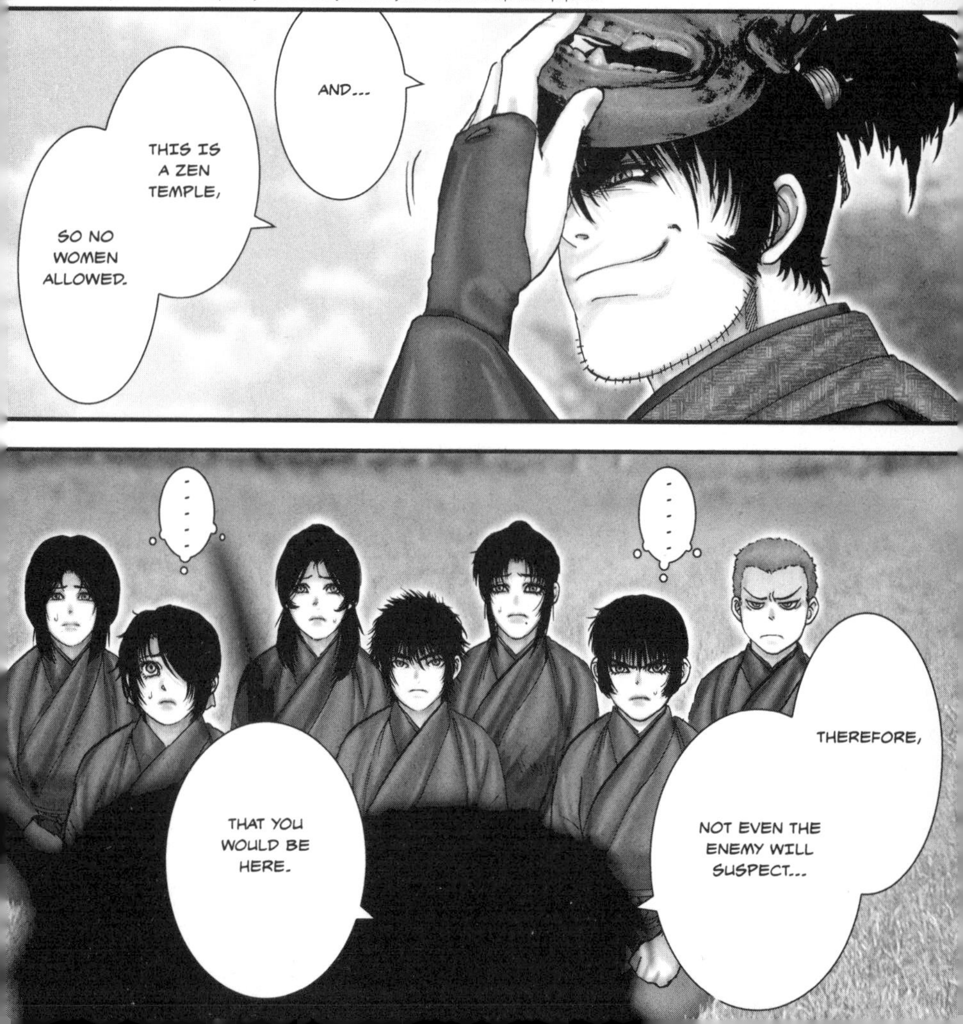
AND...
THIS IS A ZEN TEMPLE,
SO NO WOMEN ALLOWED.
......
......
THEREFORE,
NOT EVEN THE ENEMY WILL SUSPECT...
THAT YOU WOULD BE HERE.

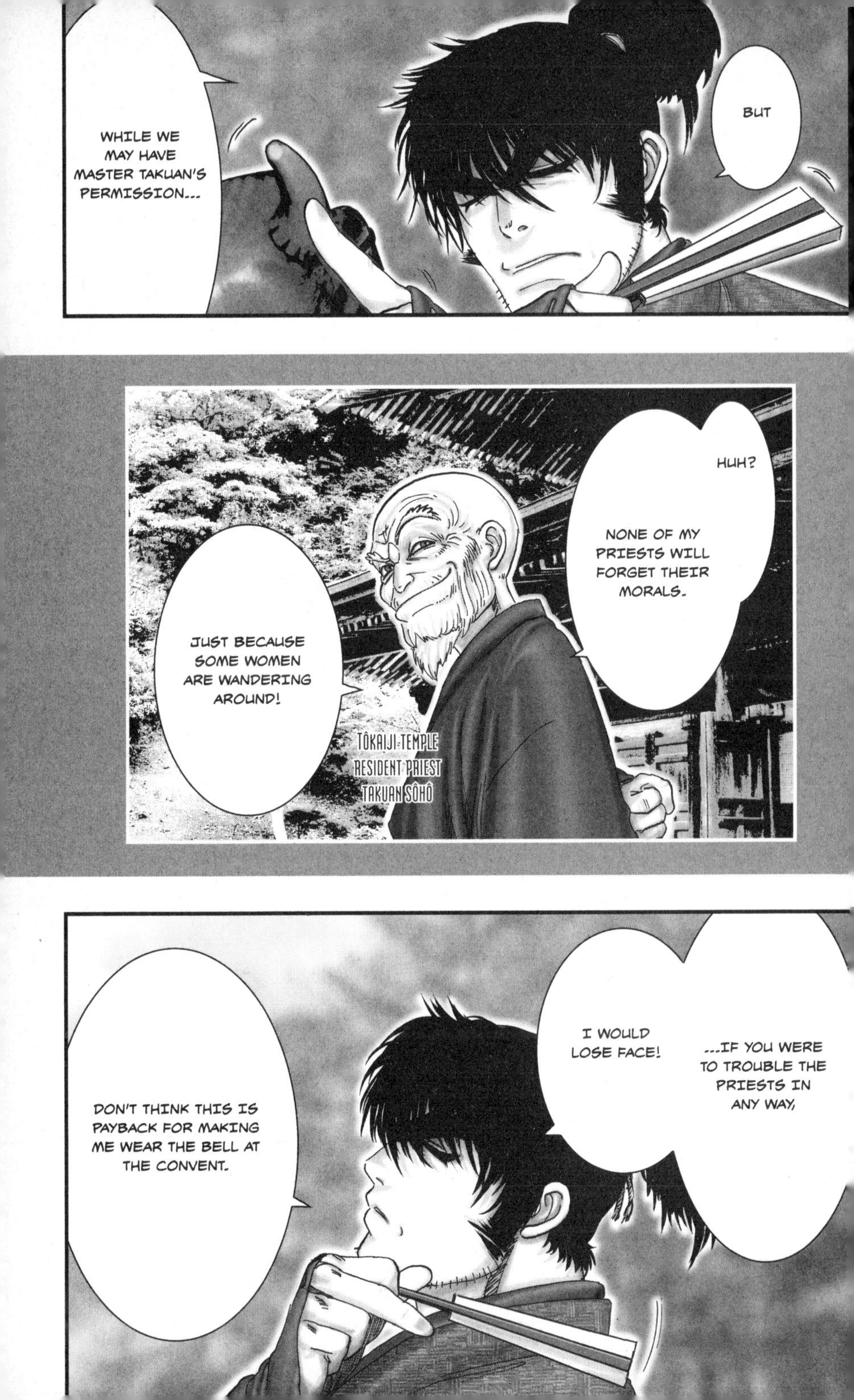
WHILE WE MAY HAVE MASTER TAKUAN'S PERMISSION...
BUT
HUH?
NONE OF MY PRIESTS WILL FORGET THEIR MORALS.
JUST BECAUSE SOME WOMEN ARE WANDERING AROUND!
TÔKAIJI TEMPLE RESIDENT PRIEST TAKUAN SÔHÔ
...IF YOU WERE TO TROUBLE THE PRIESTS IN ANY WAY,
I WOULD LOSE FACE!
DON'T THINK THIS IS PAYBACK FOR MAKING ME WEAR THE BELL AT THE CONVENT.

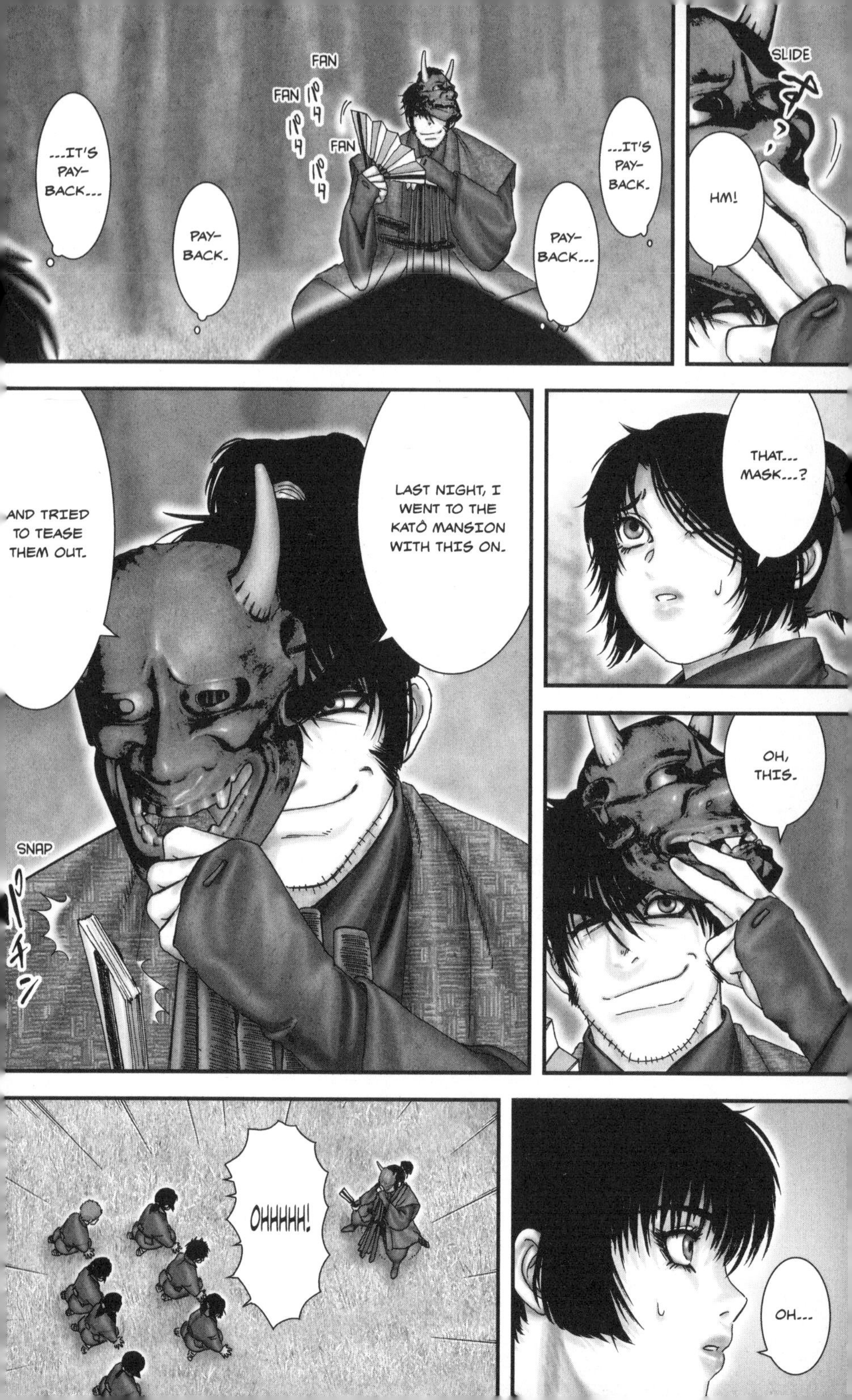
SLIDE
HM!
...IT'S PAY-BACK.
PAY-BACK...
FAN
FAN
FAN
PAY-BACK.
...IT'S PAY-BACK...
THAT... MASK...?
OH, THIS.
LAST NIGHT, I WENT TO THE KATÔ MANSION WITH THIS ON.
AND TRIED TO TEASE THEM OUT.
SNAP
OH...
OHHHHH!

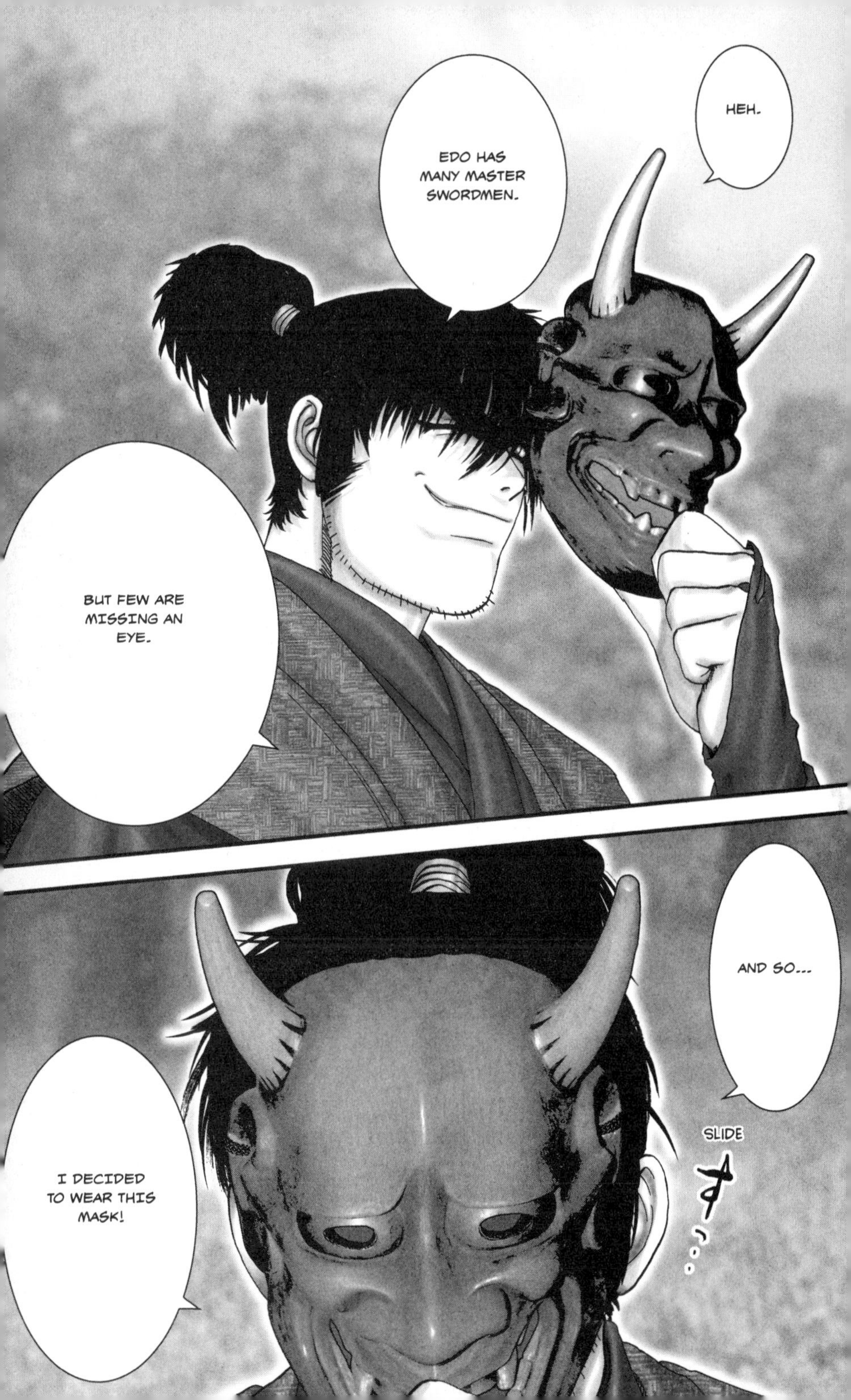
HEH.
EDO HAS MANY MASTER SWORDMEN.
BUT FEW ARE MISSING AN EYE.
AND SO...
SLIDE
す
I DECIDED TO WEAR THIS MASK!

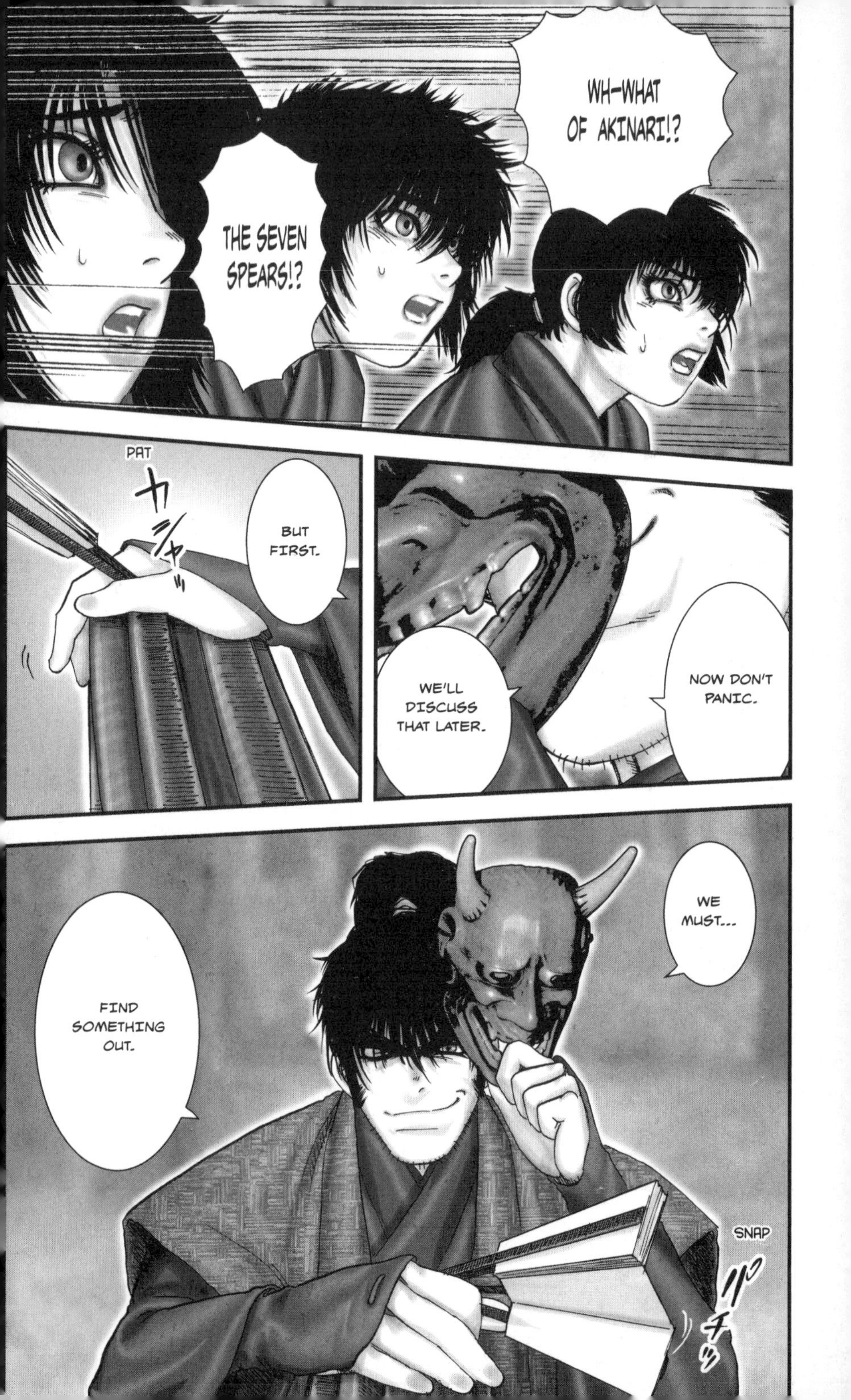
WH-WHAT OF AKINARI!?
THE SEVEN SPEARS!?
NOW DON'T PANIC.
WE'LL DISCUSS THAT LATER.
PAT
BUT FIRST.
WE MUST...
FIND SOMETHING OUT.
SNAP

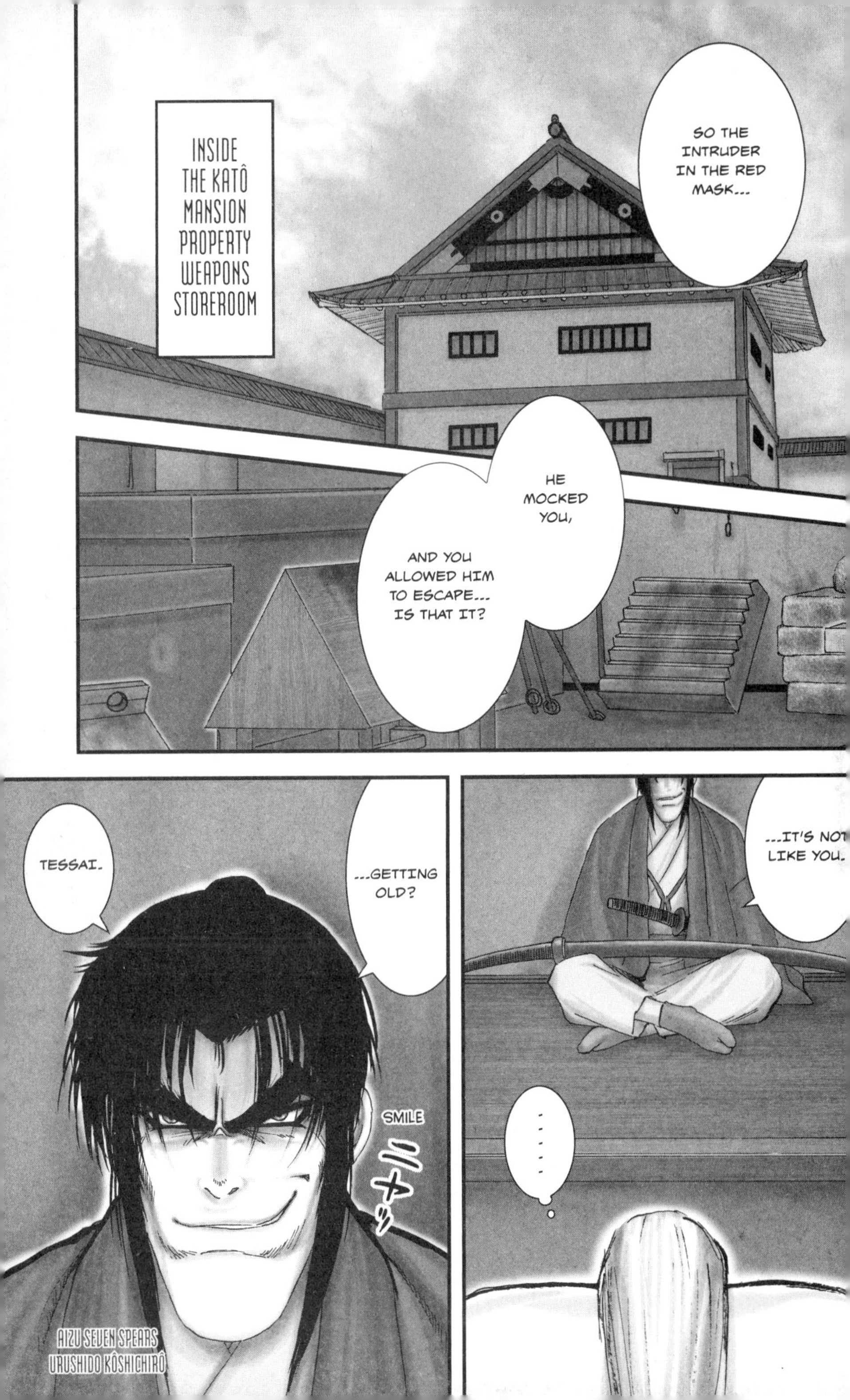
SO THE INTRUDER IN THE RED MASK...
INSIDE THE KATÔ MANSION PROPERTY WEAPONS STOREROOM
HE MOCKED YOU,
AND YOU ALLOWED HIM TO ESCAPE... IS THAT IT?
...IT'S NOT LIKE YOU.
......
...GETTING OLD?
TESSAI.
SMILE
AIZU SEVEN SPEARS
URUSHIDO KÔSHICHIRÔ

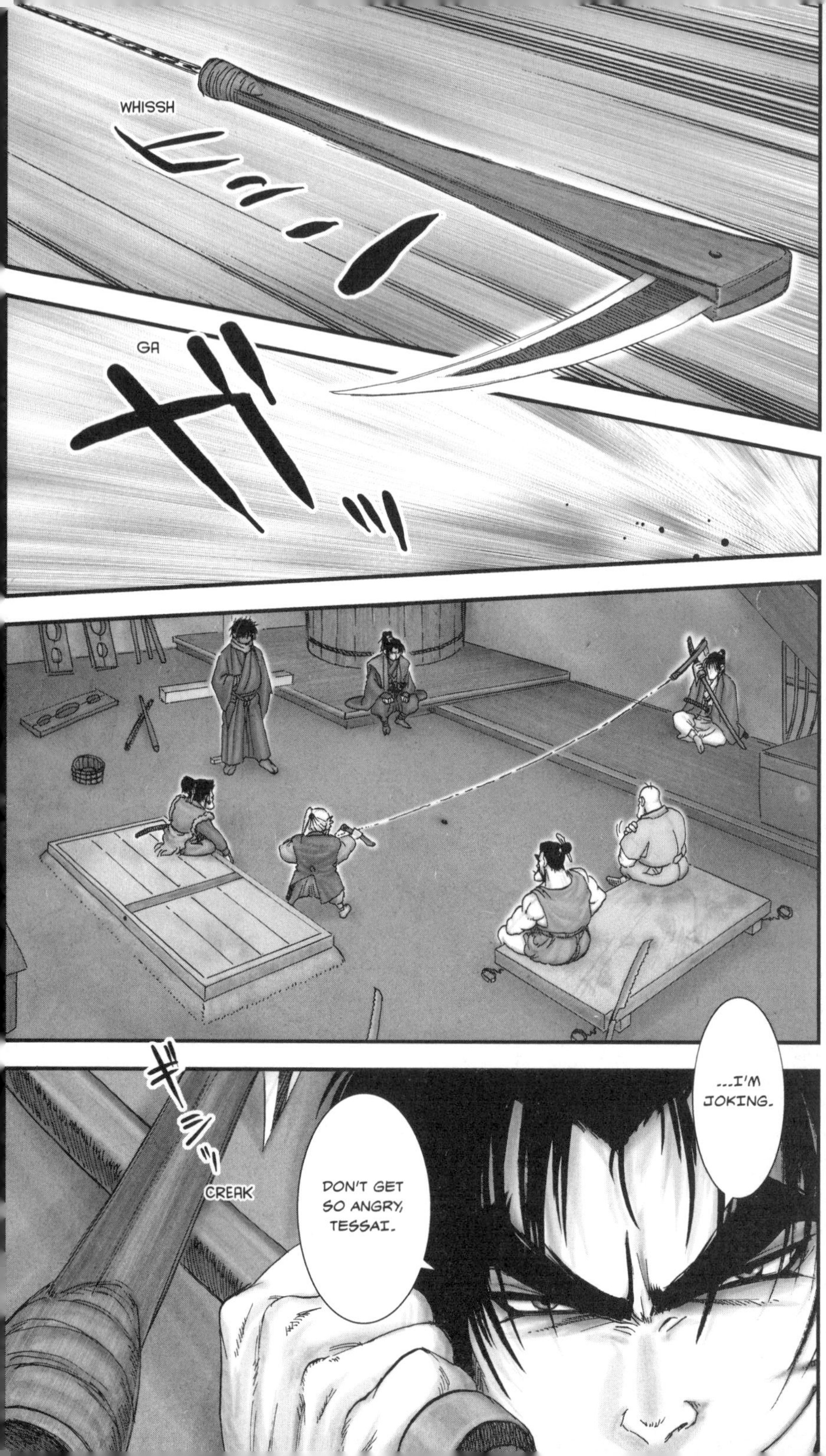
WHISSH
GA
...I'M JOKING.
DON'T GET SO ANGRY, TESSAI.
CREAK

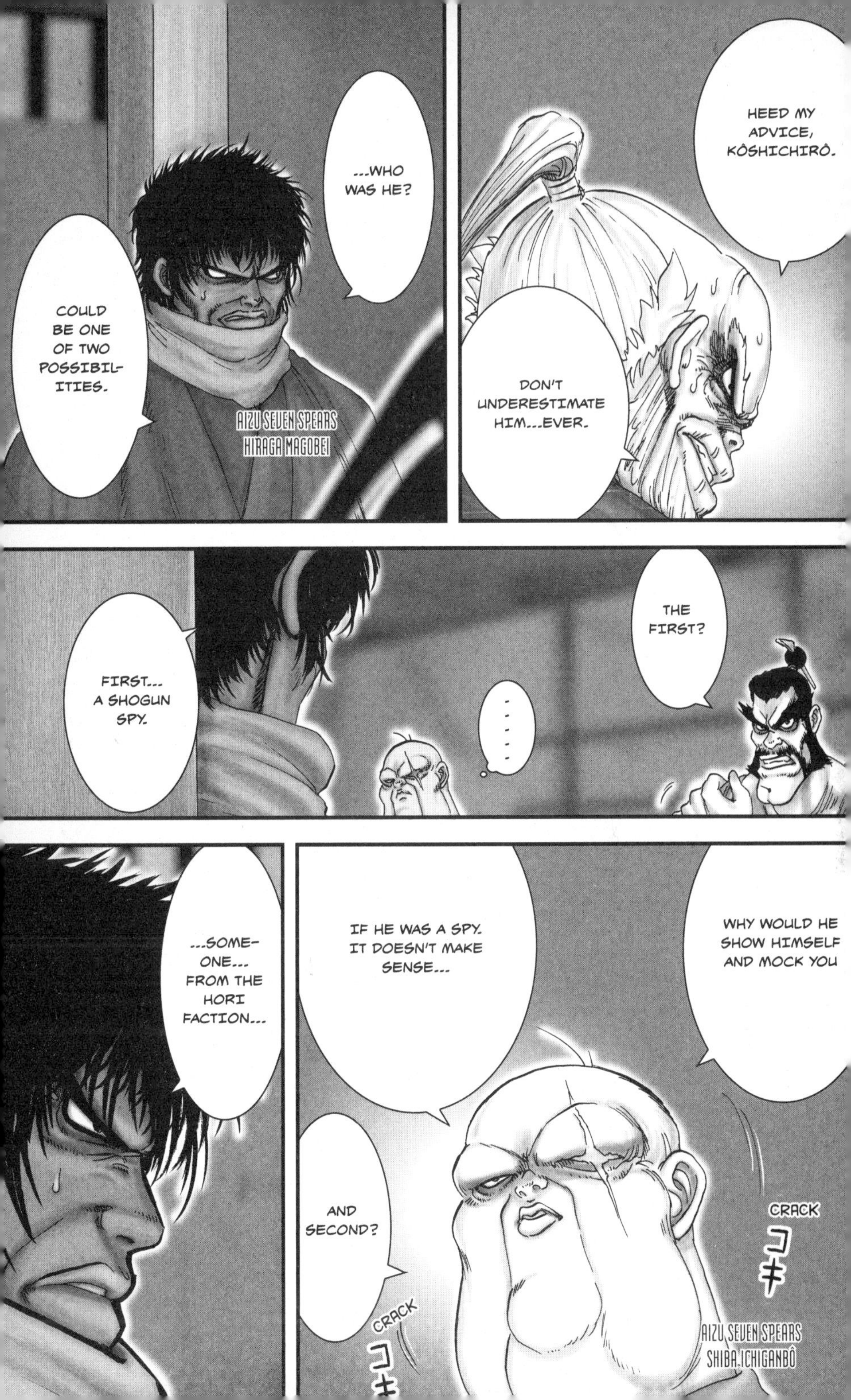
HEED MY ADVICE, KÔSHICHIRÔ.
DON'T UNDERESTIMATE HIM...EVER.
...WHO WAS HE?
COULD BE ONE OF TWO POSSIBIL-ITIES.
AIZU SEVEN SPEARS HIRAGA MAGOBEI
THE FIRST?
......
FIRST... A SHOGUN SPY.
WHY WOULD HE SHOW HIMSELF AND MOCK YOU
IF HE WAS A SPY. IT DOESN'T MAKE SENSE...
CRACK
AND SECOND?
CRACK
AIZU SEVEN SPEARS SHIBA ICHIGANBÔ
...SOME-ONE... FROM THE HORI FACTION...

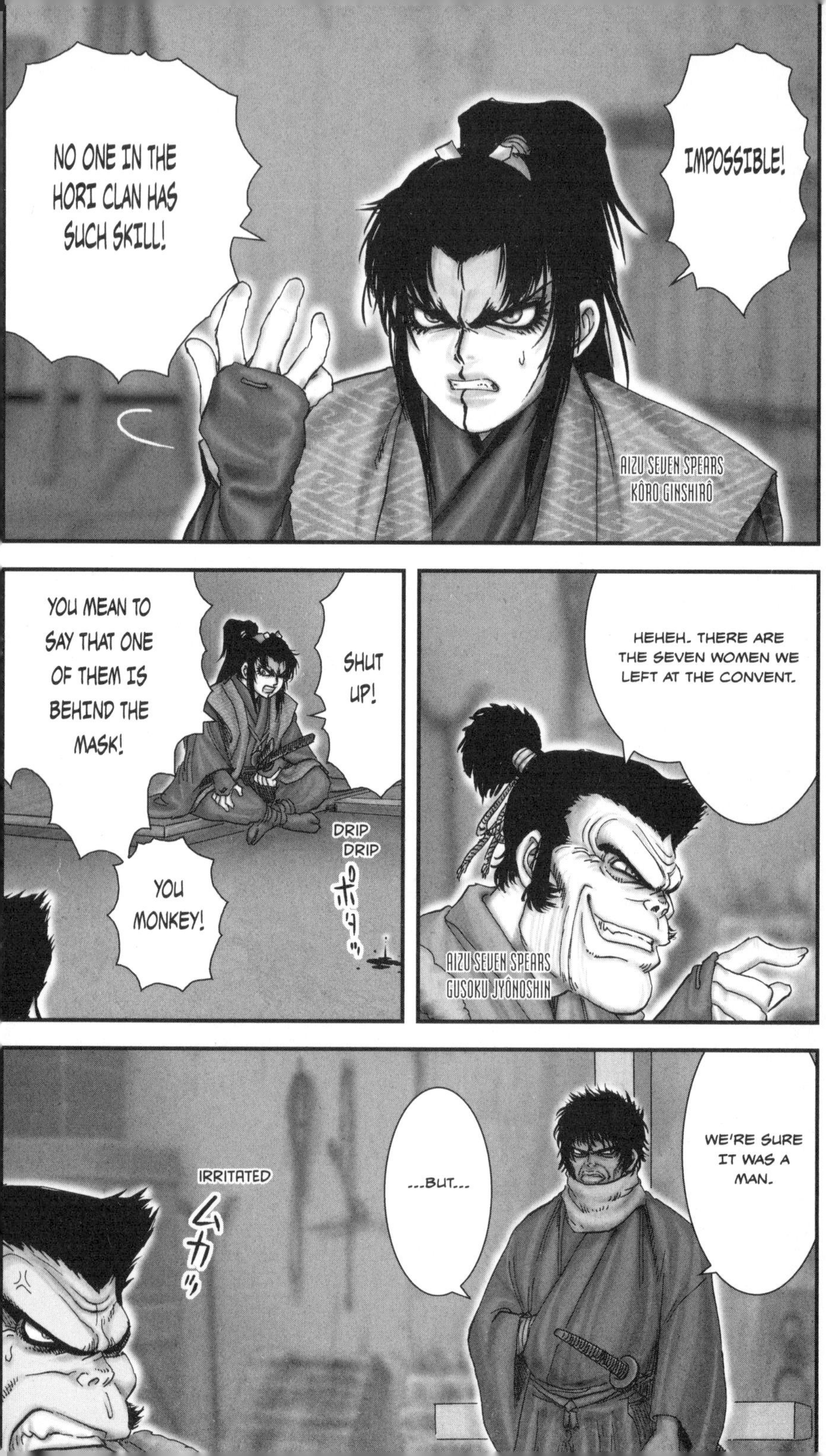
IMPOSSIBLE!
NO ONE IN THE HORI CLAN HAS SUCH SKILL!
AIZU SEVEN SPEARS KÔRO GINSHIRÔ
HEHEH. THERE ARE THE SEVEN WOMEN WE LEFT AT THE CONVENT.
AIZU SEVEN SPEARS GUSOKU JYÔNOSHIN
SHUT UP!
YOU MEAN TO SAY THAT ONE OF THEM IS BEHIND THE MASK!
DRIP DRIP
ポタッ
YOU MONKEY!
WE'RE SURE IT WAS A MAN.
...BUT...
IRRITATED
ムカッ

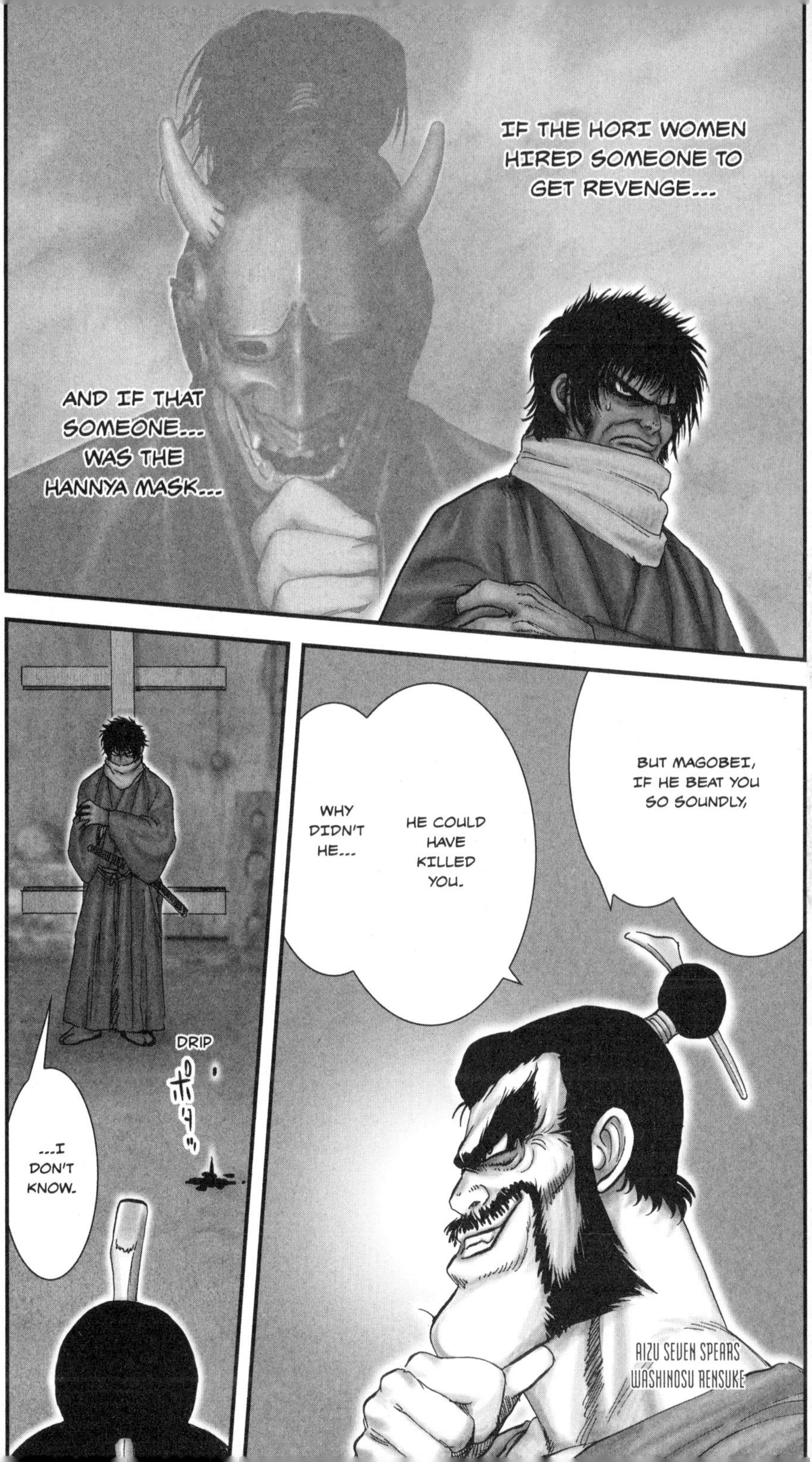

IF THE HORI WOMEN HIRED SOMEONE TO GET REVENGE...
AND IF THAT SOMEONE... WAS THE HANNYA MASK...
BUT MAGOBEI, IF HE BEAT YOU SO SOUNDLY,
HE COULD HAVE KILLED YOU.
WHY DIDN'T HE...
AIZU SEVEN SPEARS WASHINOSU RENSUKE
DRIP
...I DON'T KNOW.

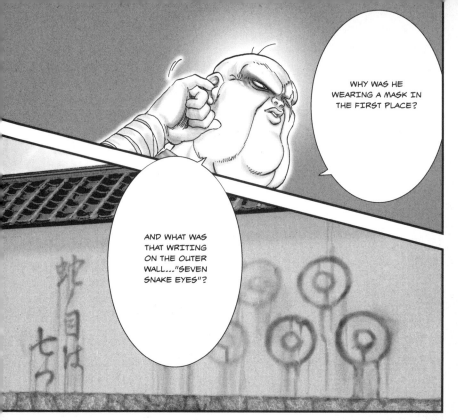

WHY WAS HE WEARING A MASK IN THE FIRST PLACE?

AND WHAT WAS THAT WRITING ON THE OUTER WALL...."SEVEN SNAKE EYES"?

ENOUGH!

WE'RE GETTING NOWHERE HERE!

I DON'T KNOW.

DRIP

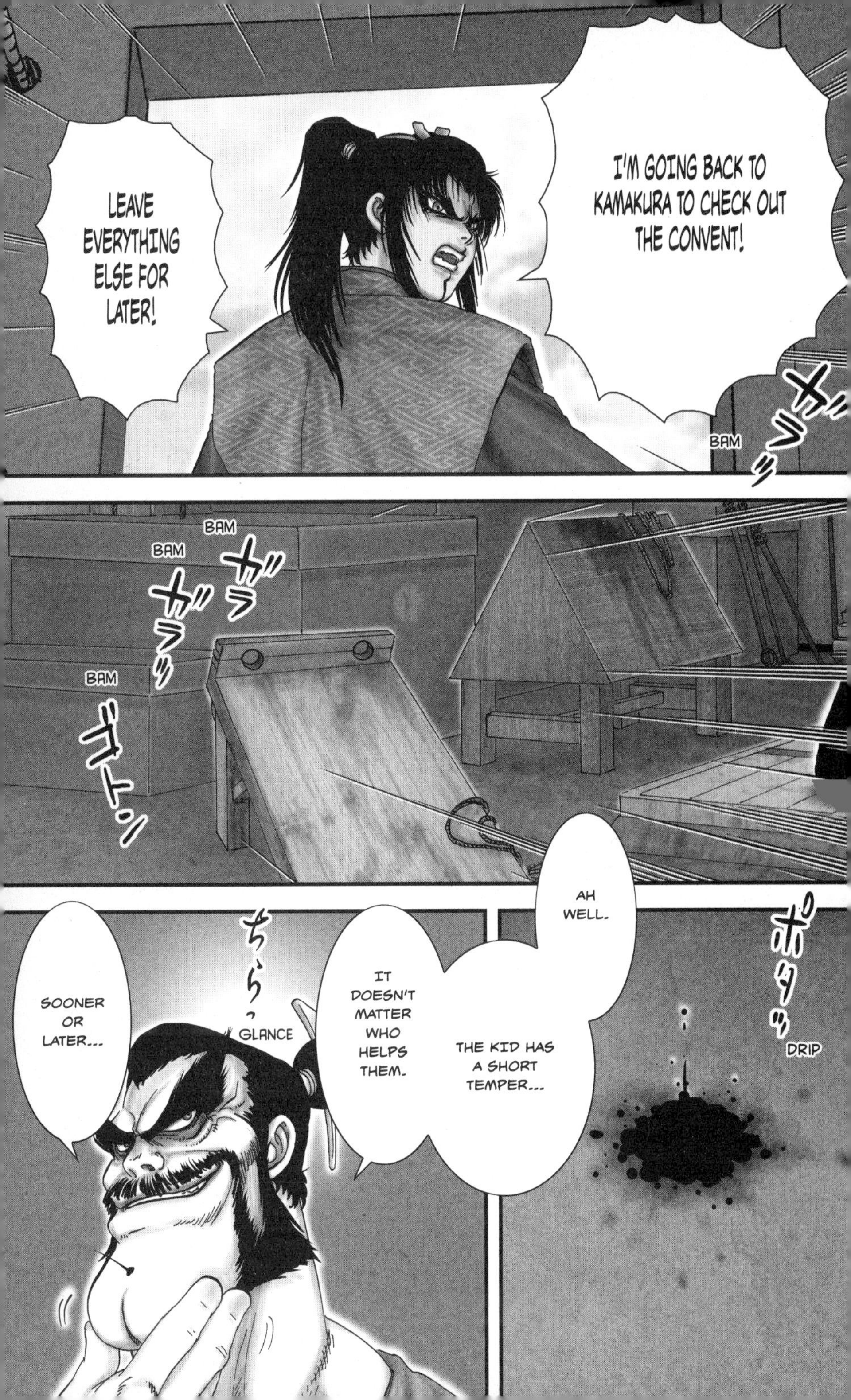
I'M GOING BACK TO KAMAKURA TO CHECK OUT THE CONVENT!
LEAVE EVERYTHING ELSE FOR LATER!
BAM
ガラ
BAM
ガラッ
BAM
BAM
ゴトッ
ポタッ
DRIP
AH WELL.
THE KID HAS A SHORT TEMPER...
IT DOESN'T MATTER WHO HELPS THEM.
ちらっ
GLANCE
SOONER OR LATER...

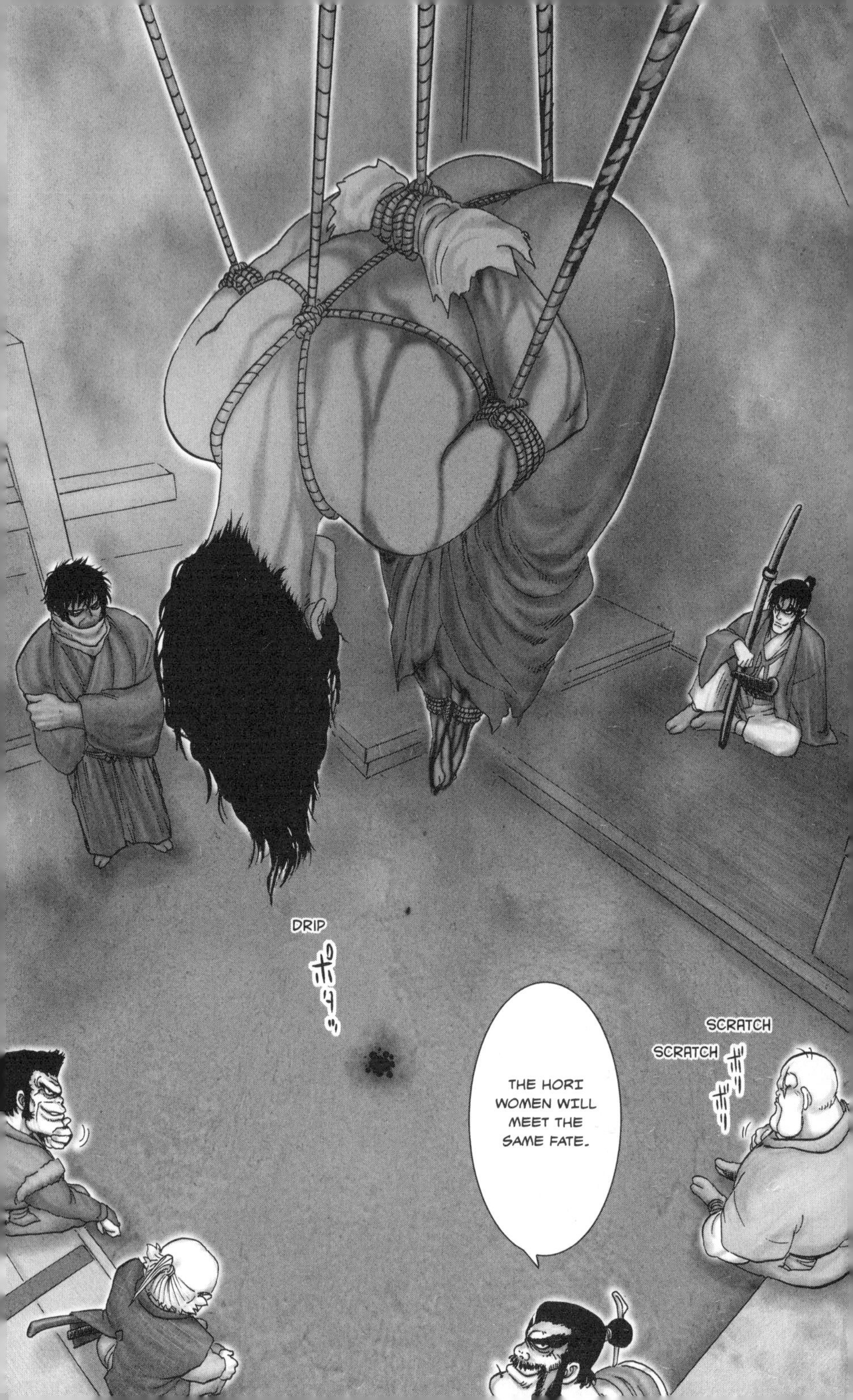
DRIP
ポタッ
THE HORI WOMEN WILL MEET THE SAME FATE.
SCRATCH
SCRATCH
ボリボリ

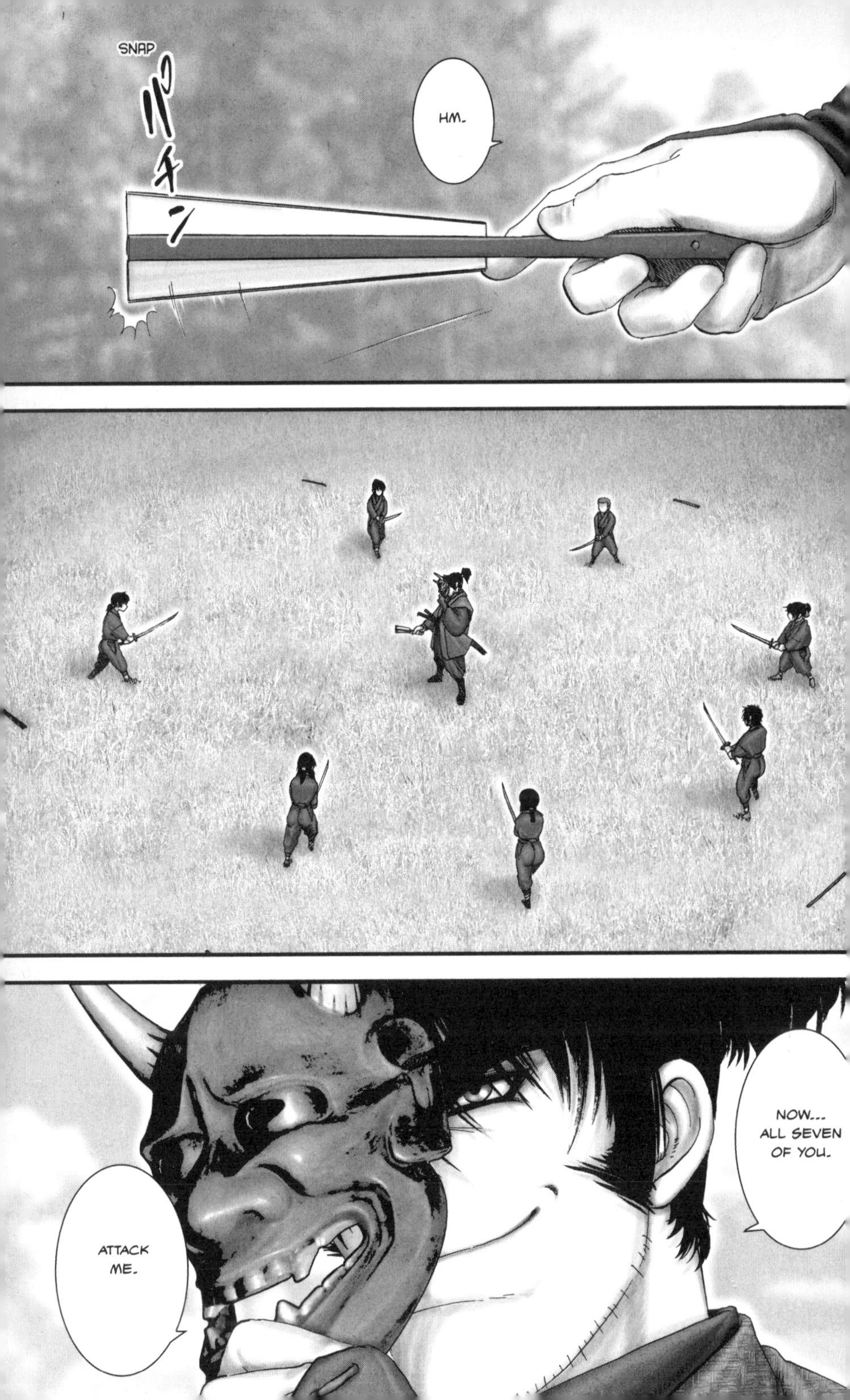
HM.
SNAP
パチン
NOW... ALL SEVEN OF YOU.
ATTACK ME.

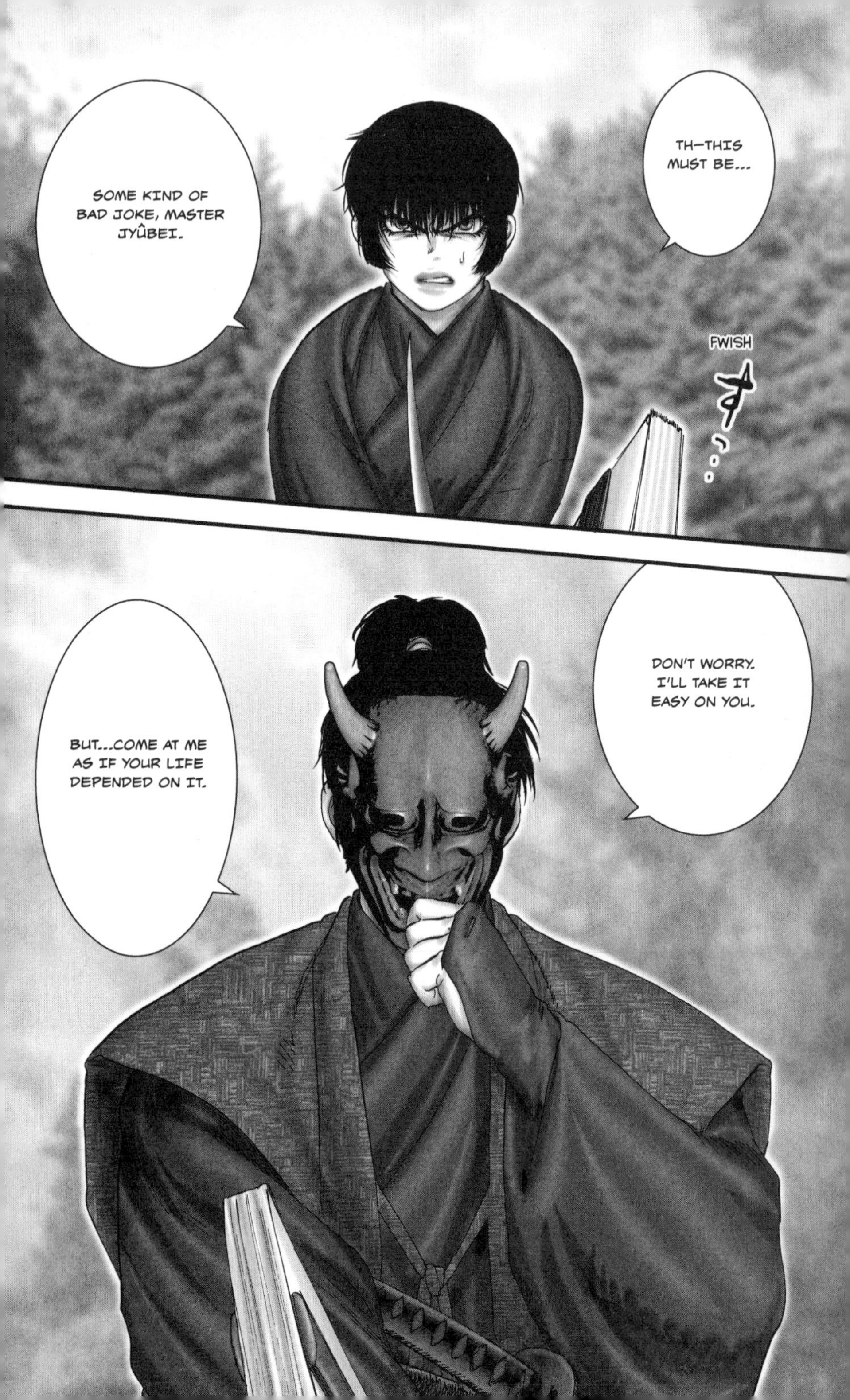
TH—THIS MUST BE...
SOME KIND OF BAD JOKE, MASTER JYÛBEI.
FWISH
DON'T WORRY. I'LL TAKE IT EASY ON YOU.
BUT...COME AT ME AS IF YOUR LIFE DEPENDED ON IT.

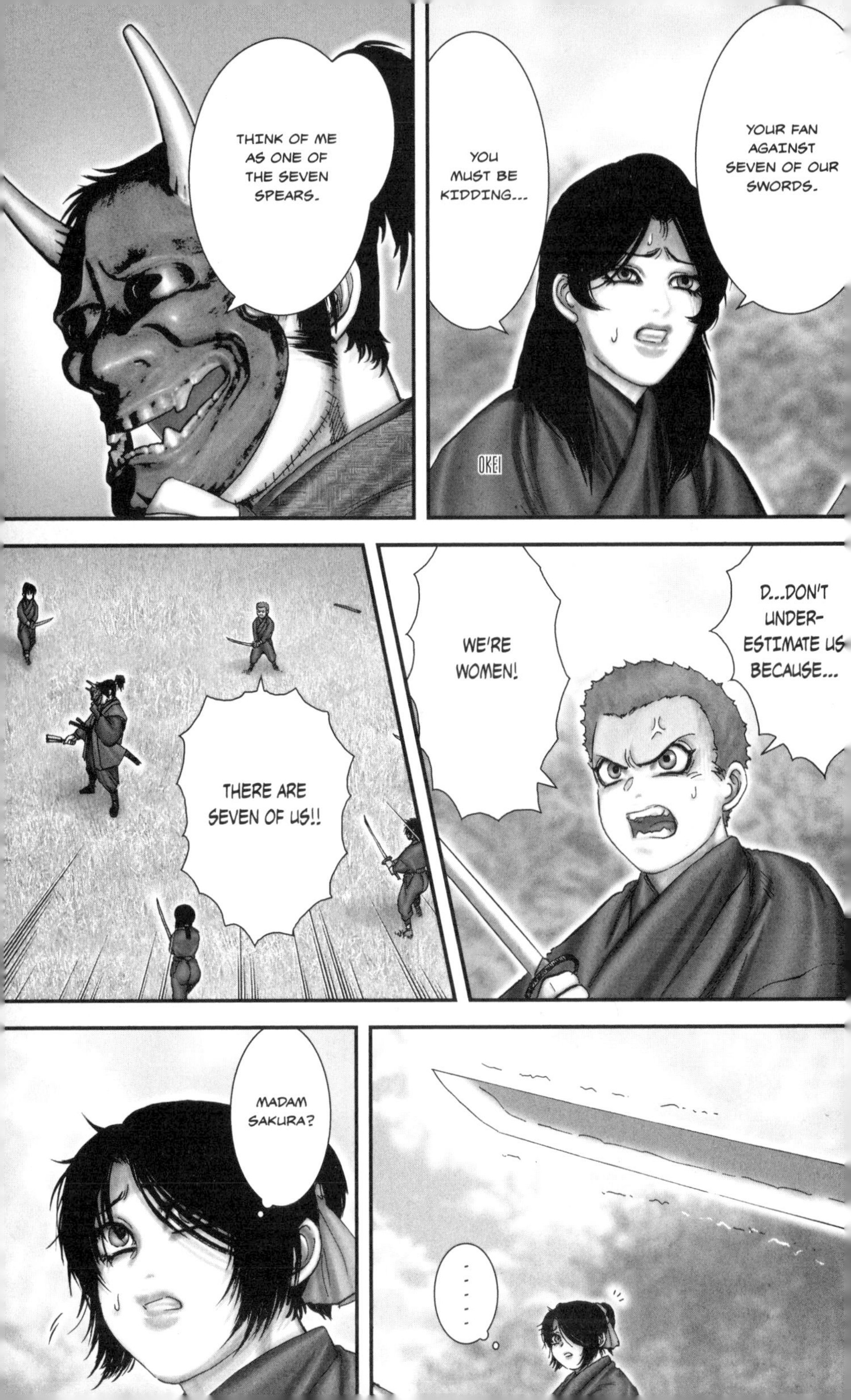
YOUR FAN AGAINST SEVEN OF OUR SWORDS.
YOU MUST BE KIDDING...
OKEI
THINK OF ME AS ONE OF THE SEVEN SPEARS.
D...DON'T UNDER-ESTIMATE US BECAUSE...
WE'RE WOMEN!
THERE ARE SEVEN OF US!!
......
MADAM SAKURA?

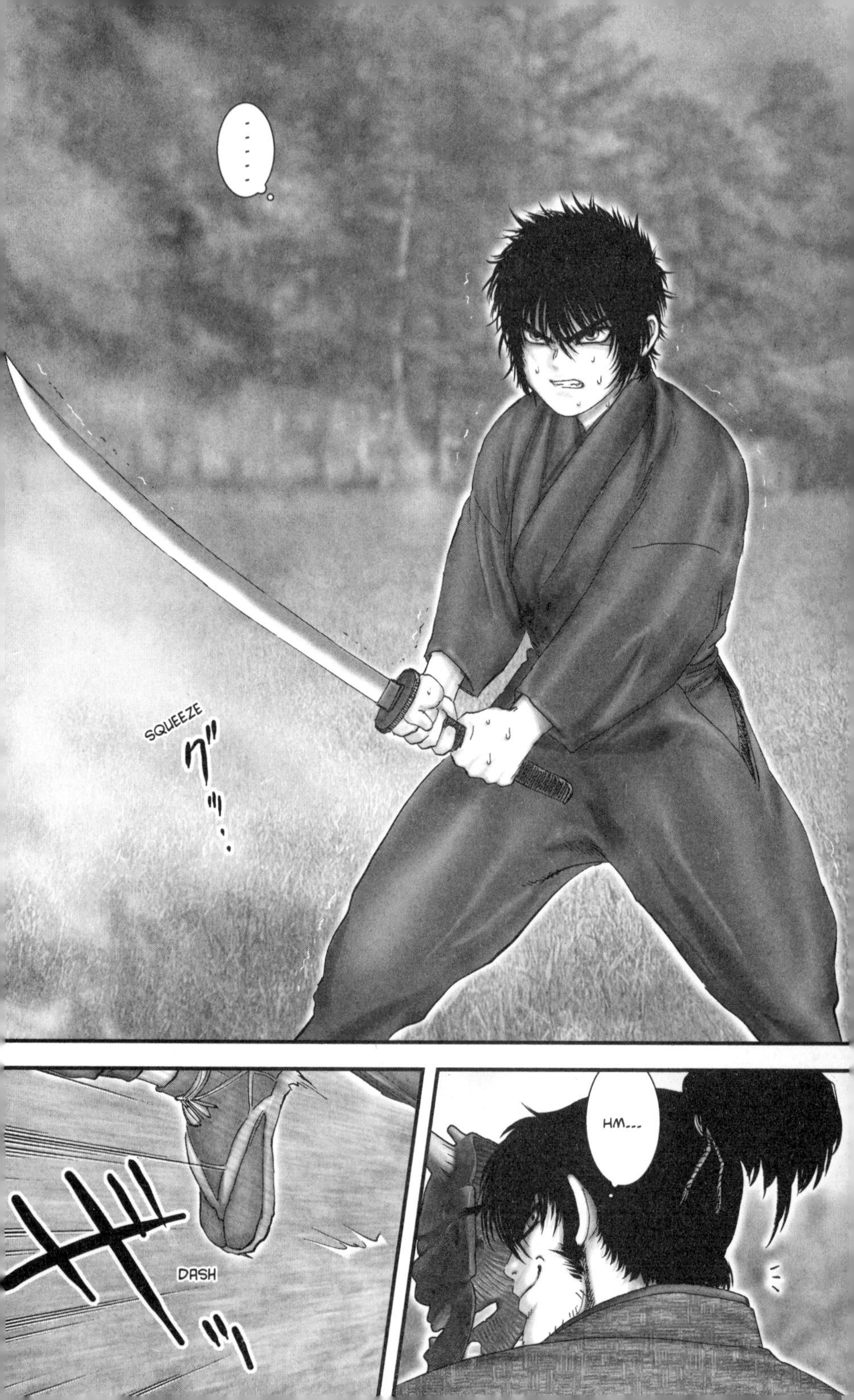
......
SQUEEZE
HM...
DASH

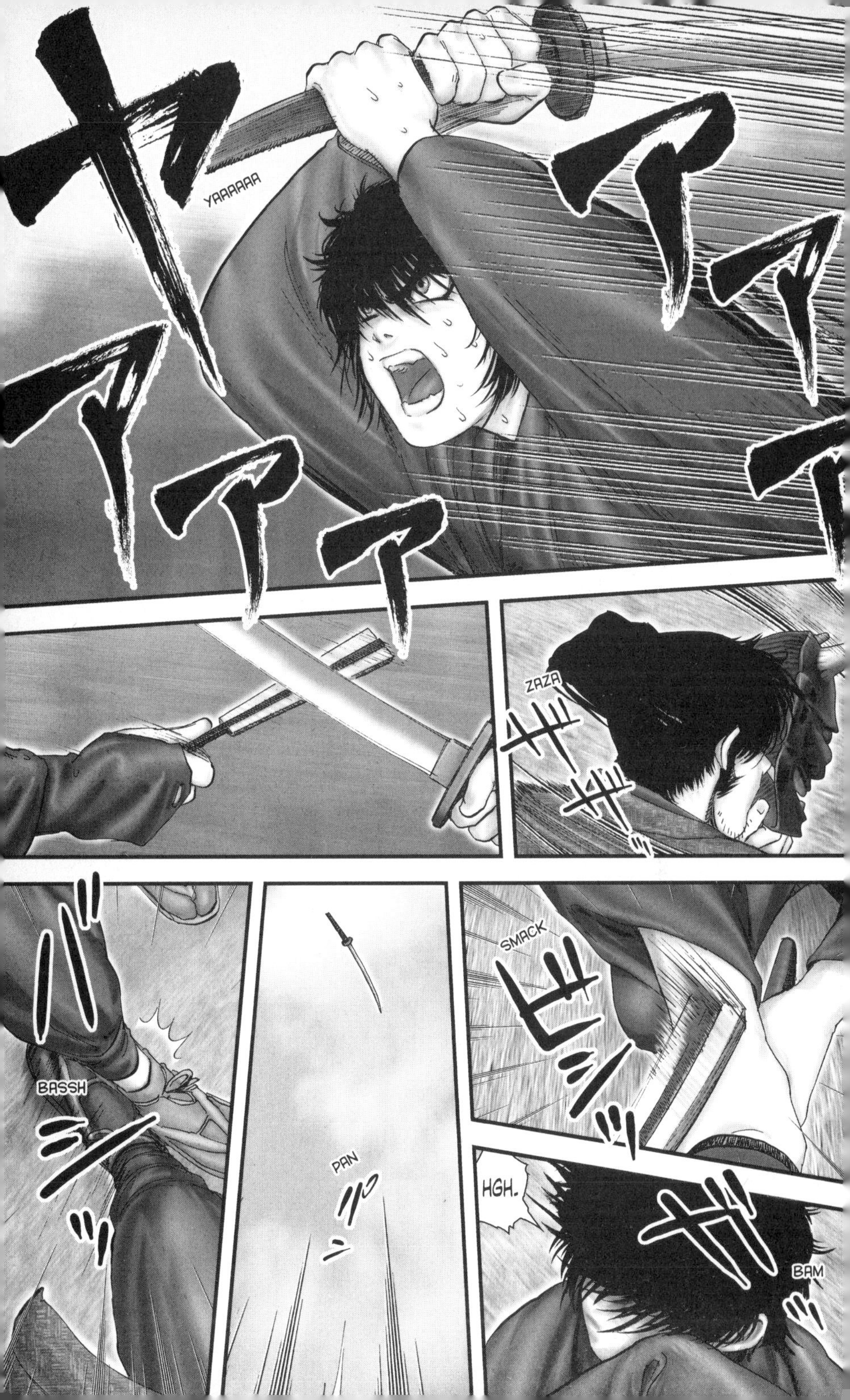

YAAAAAA
ZAZA
SMACK
HGH.
BAM
PAN
BASSH

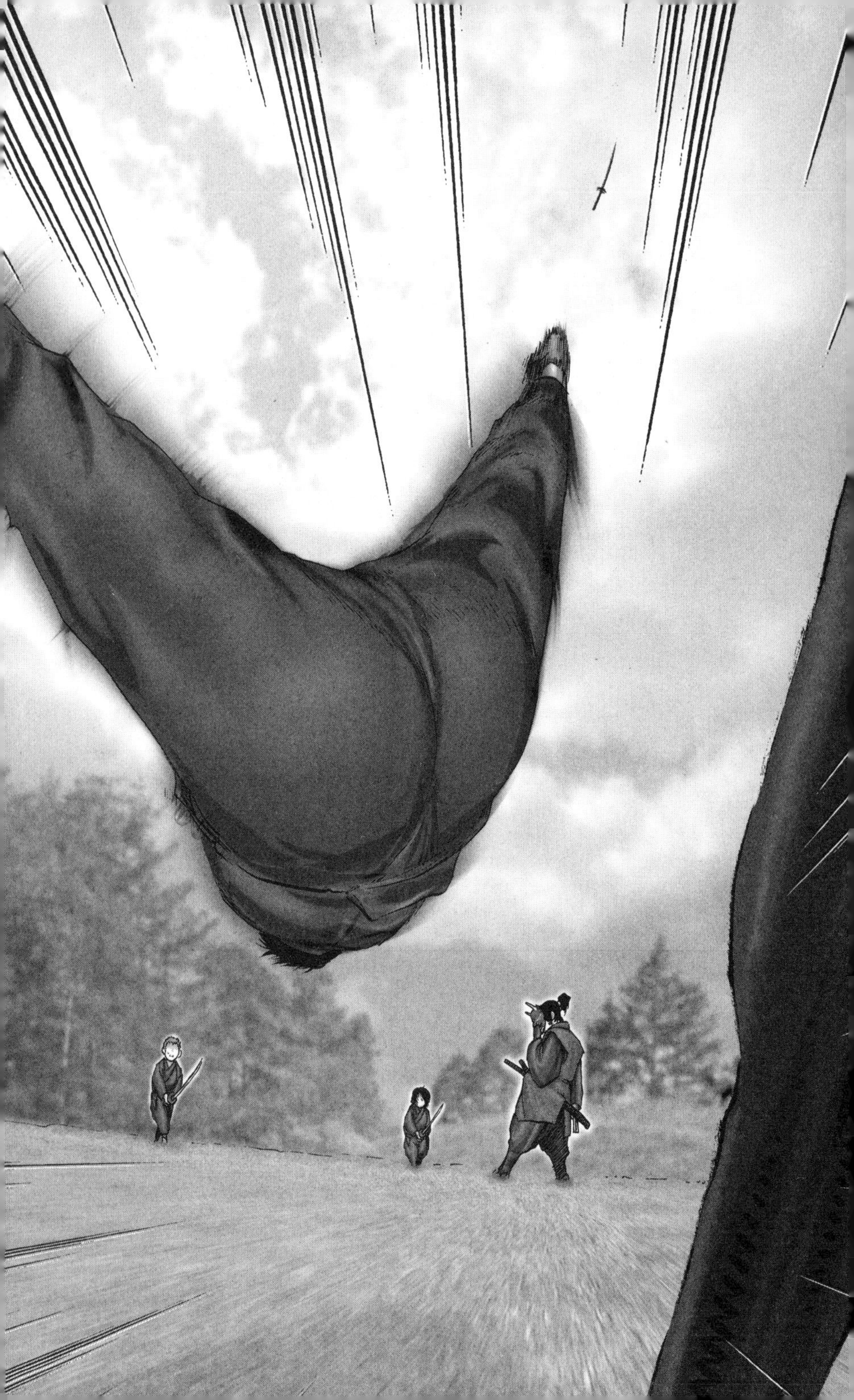

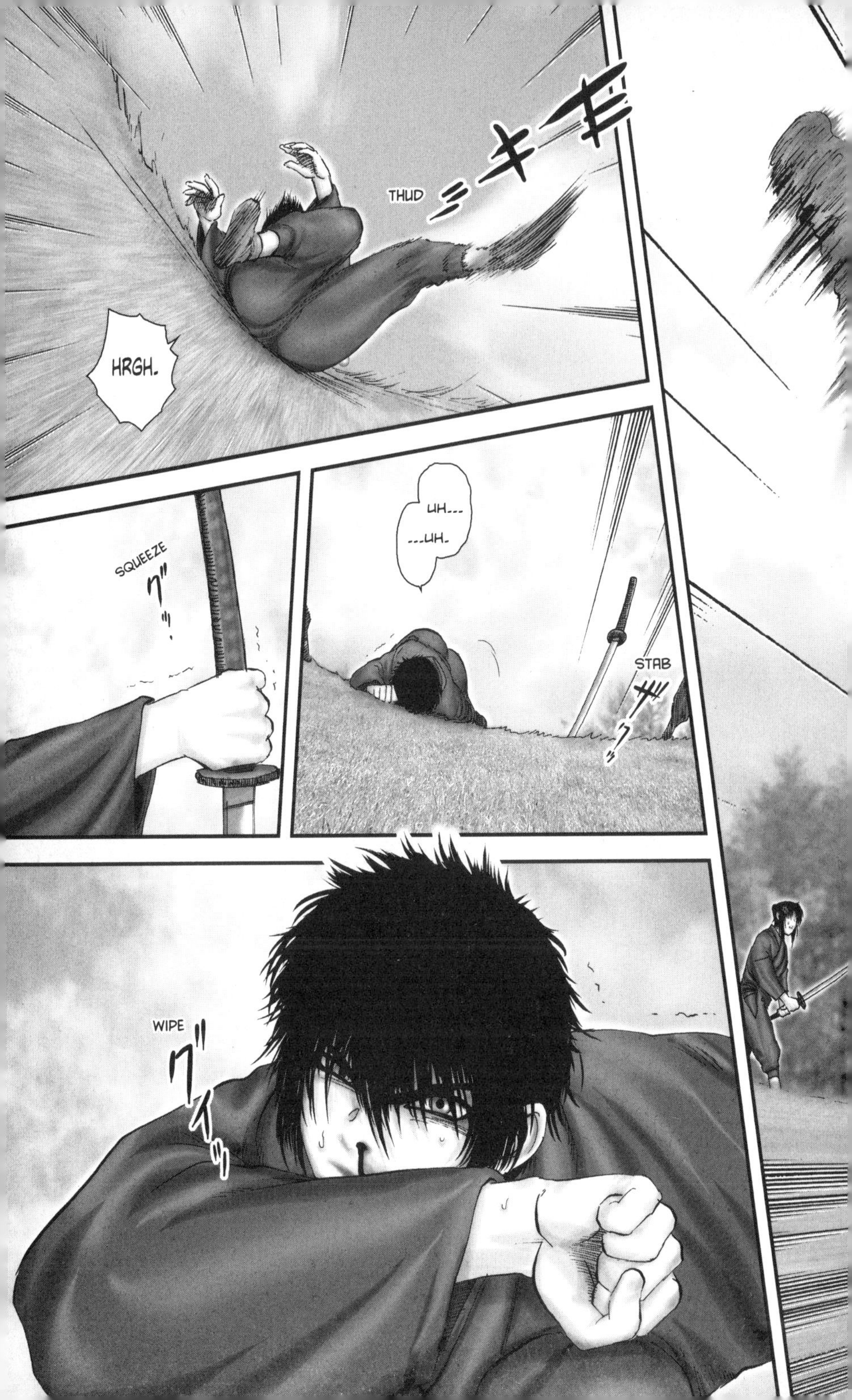
THUD
HRGH.
UH...
...UH.
STAB
SQUEEZE
WIPE

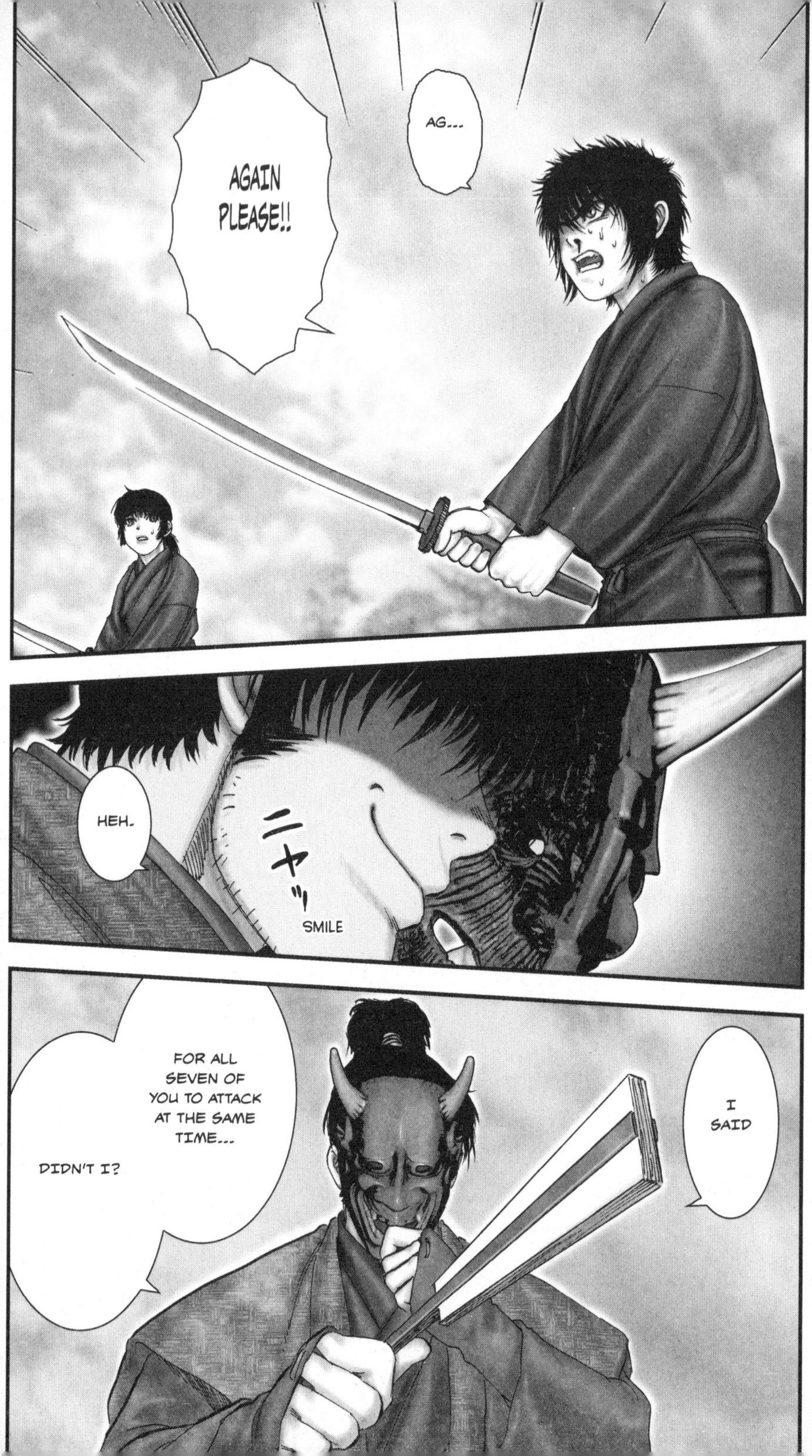
AG...
AGAIN PLEASE!!
HEH.
ニヤッ
SMILE
I SAID
FOR ALL SEVEN OF YOU TO ATTACK AT THE SAME TIME...
DIDN'T I?

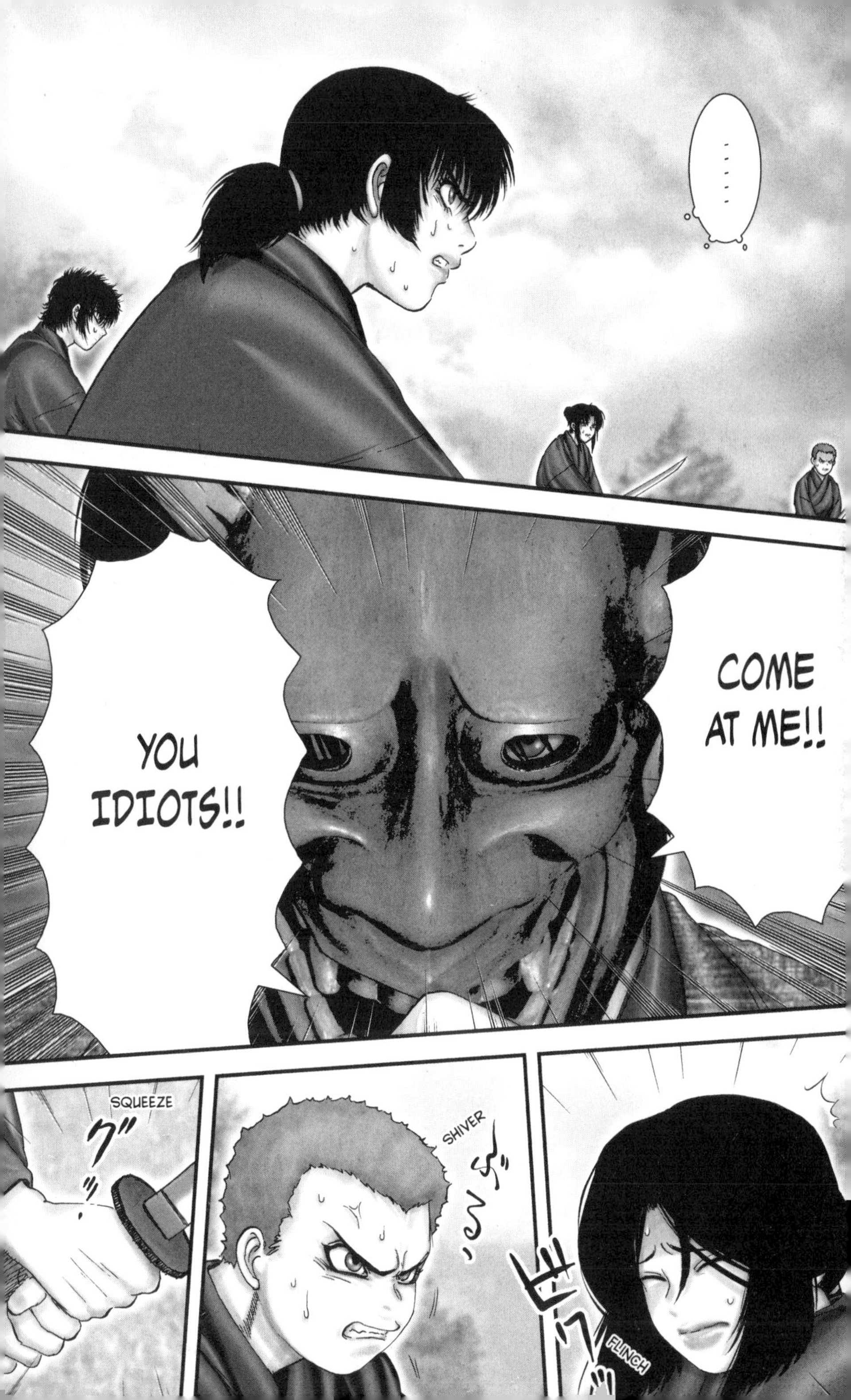
……
COME AT ME!!
YOU IDIOTS!!
FLINCH
SHIVER
SQUEEZE

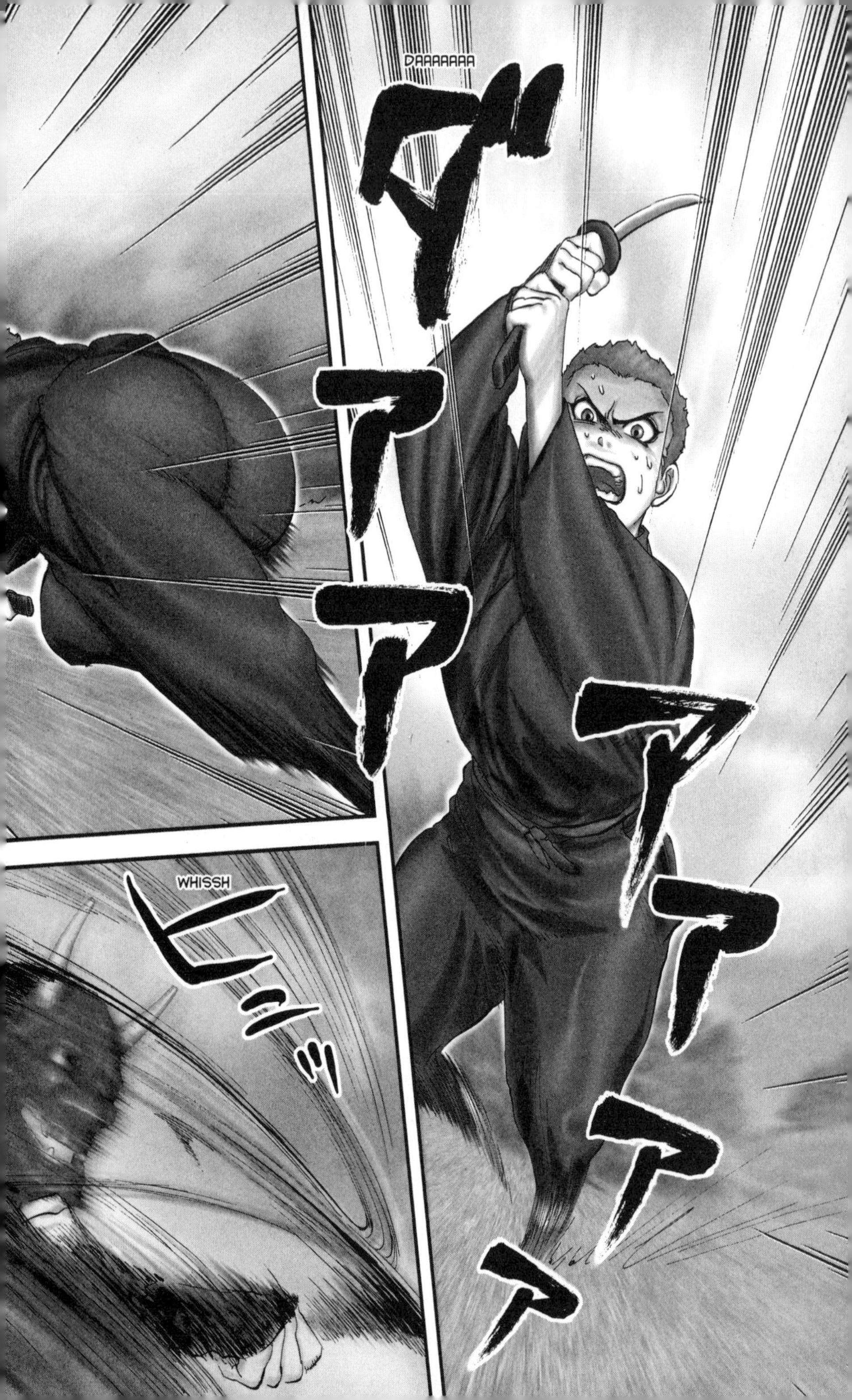
DAAAAAAA
ダアアアアアアア
WHISSH
ヒュッ

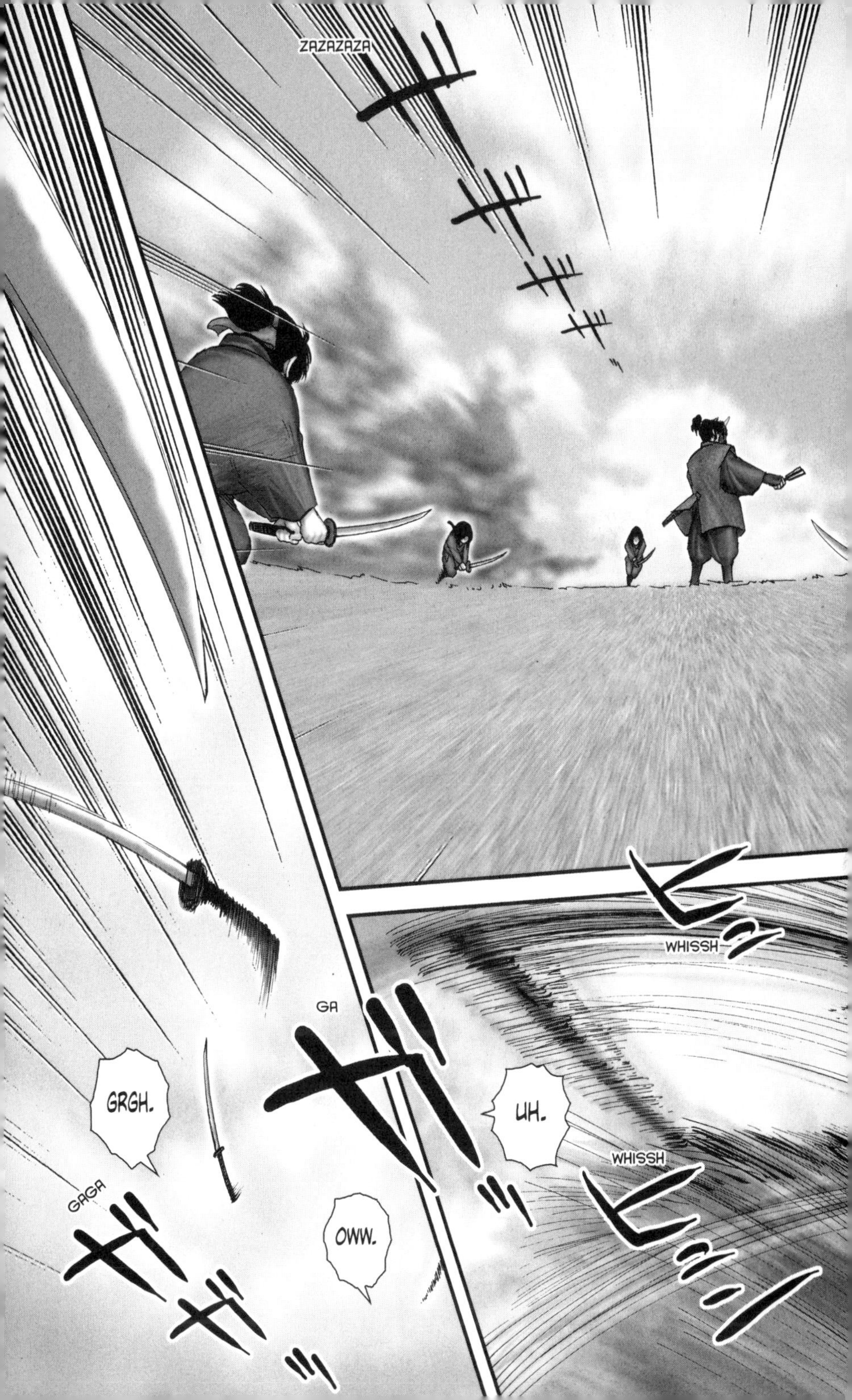
ZAZAZAZA
WHISSH
UH.
WHISSH
GA
GRGH.
GAGA
OWW.

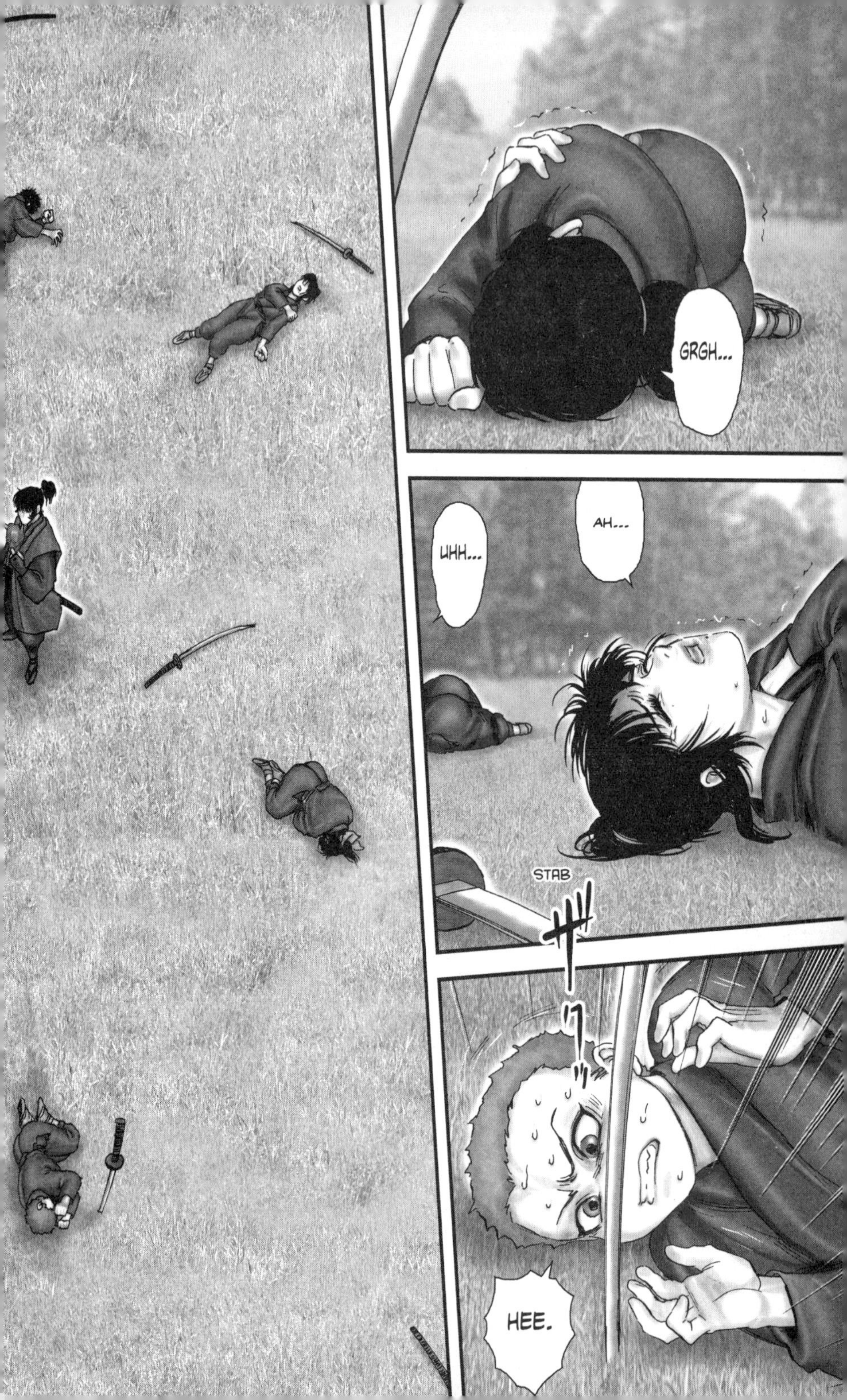
GRGH...
AH...
UHH...
STAB
HEE.

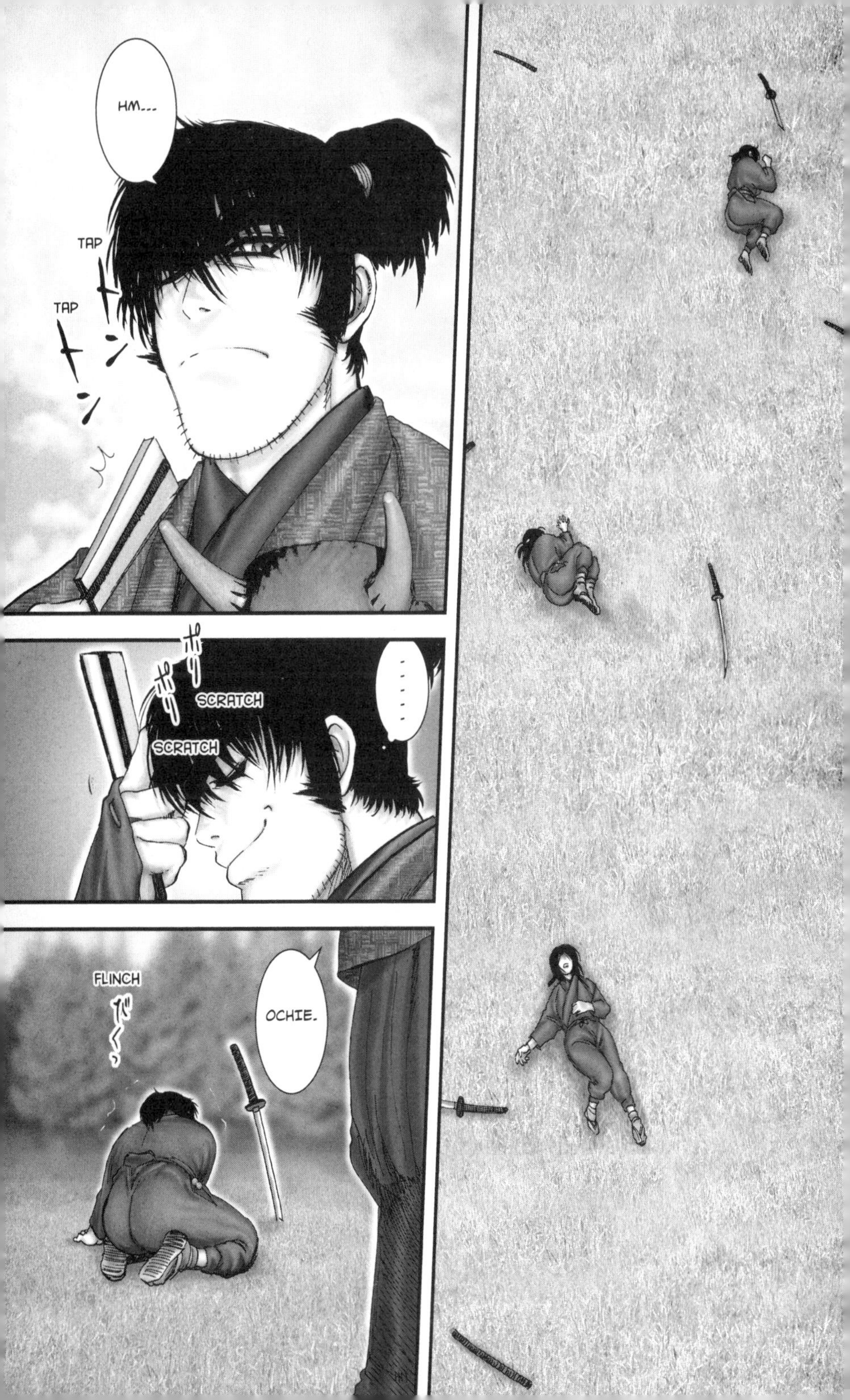
HM...
TAP
TAP
......
SCRATCH
SCRATCH
OCHIE.
FLINCH

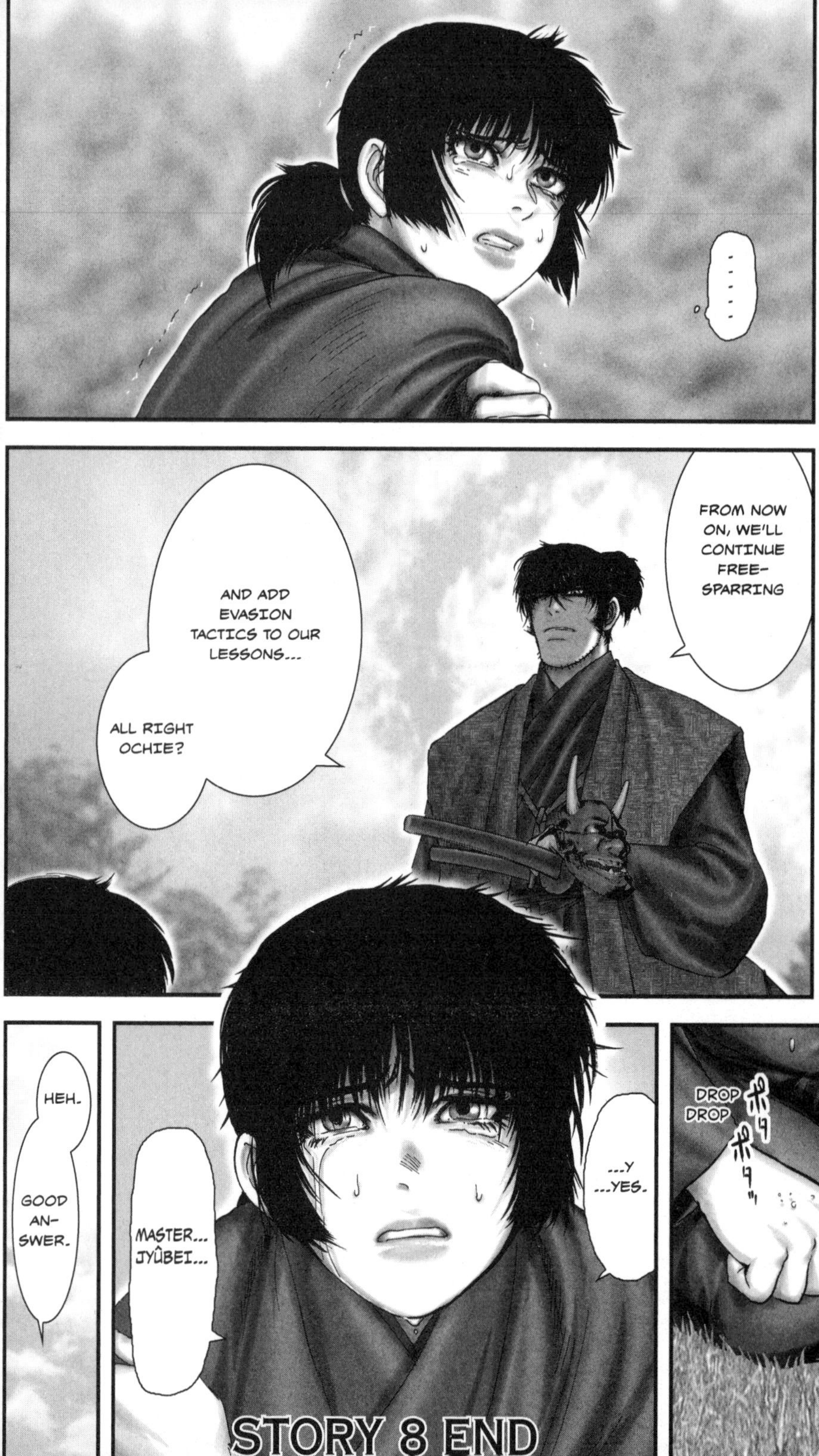
......
FROM NOW ON, WE'LL CONTINUE FREE-SPARRING
AND ADD EVASION TACTICS TO OUR LESSONS...
ALL RIGHT OCHIE?
DROP DROP
...Y ...YES.
MASTER... JYÛBEI...
HEH.
GOOD AN-SWER.
STORY 8 END

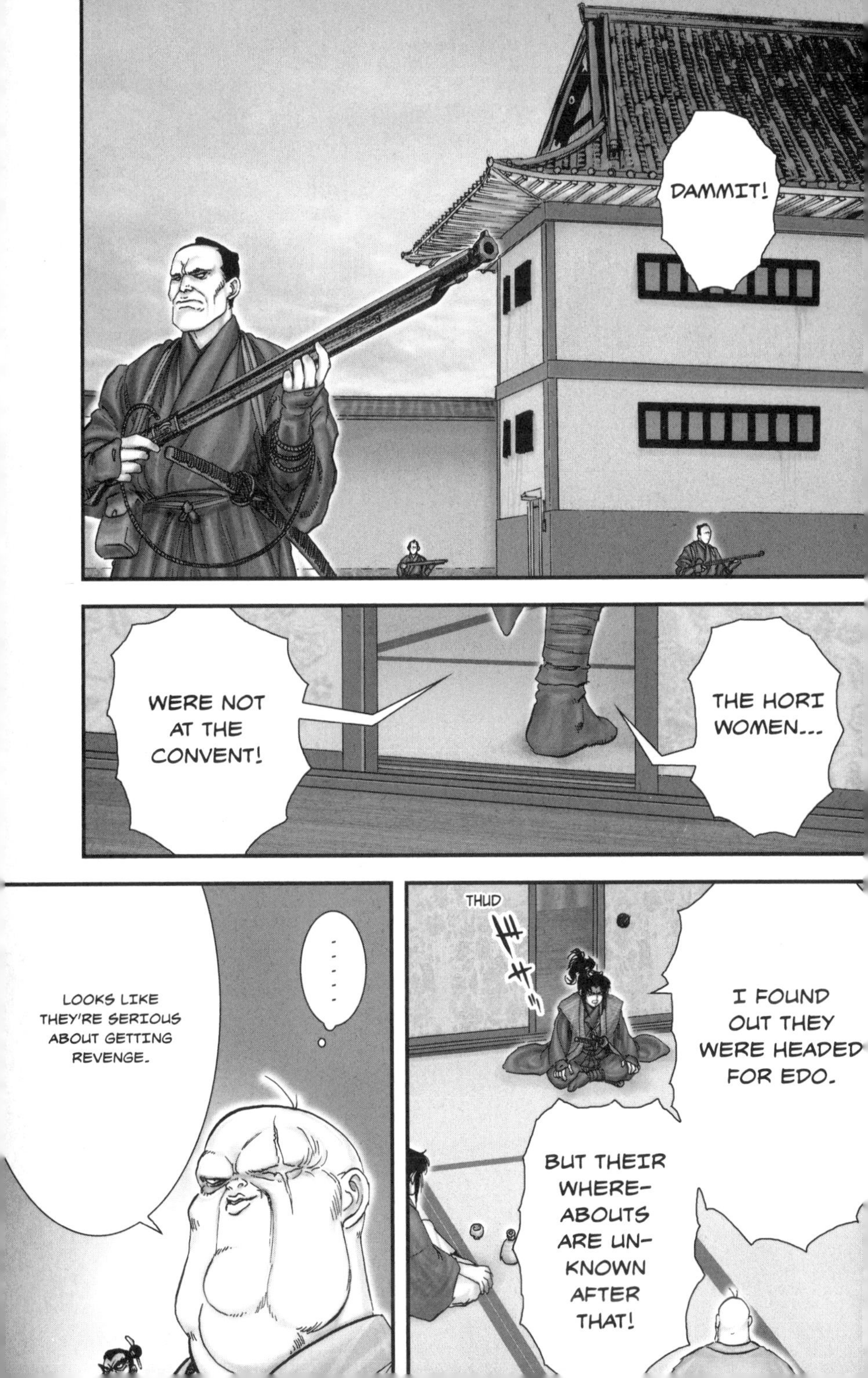
DAMMIT!
THE HORI WOMEN...
WERE NOT AT THE CONVENT!
I FOUND OUT THEY WERE HEADED FOR EDO.
THUD
BUT THEIR WHERE-ABOUTS ARE UN-KNOWN AFTER THAT!
......
LOOKS LIKE THEY'RE SERIOUS ABOUT GETTING REVENGE.

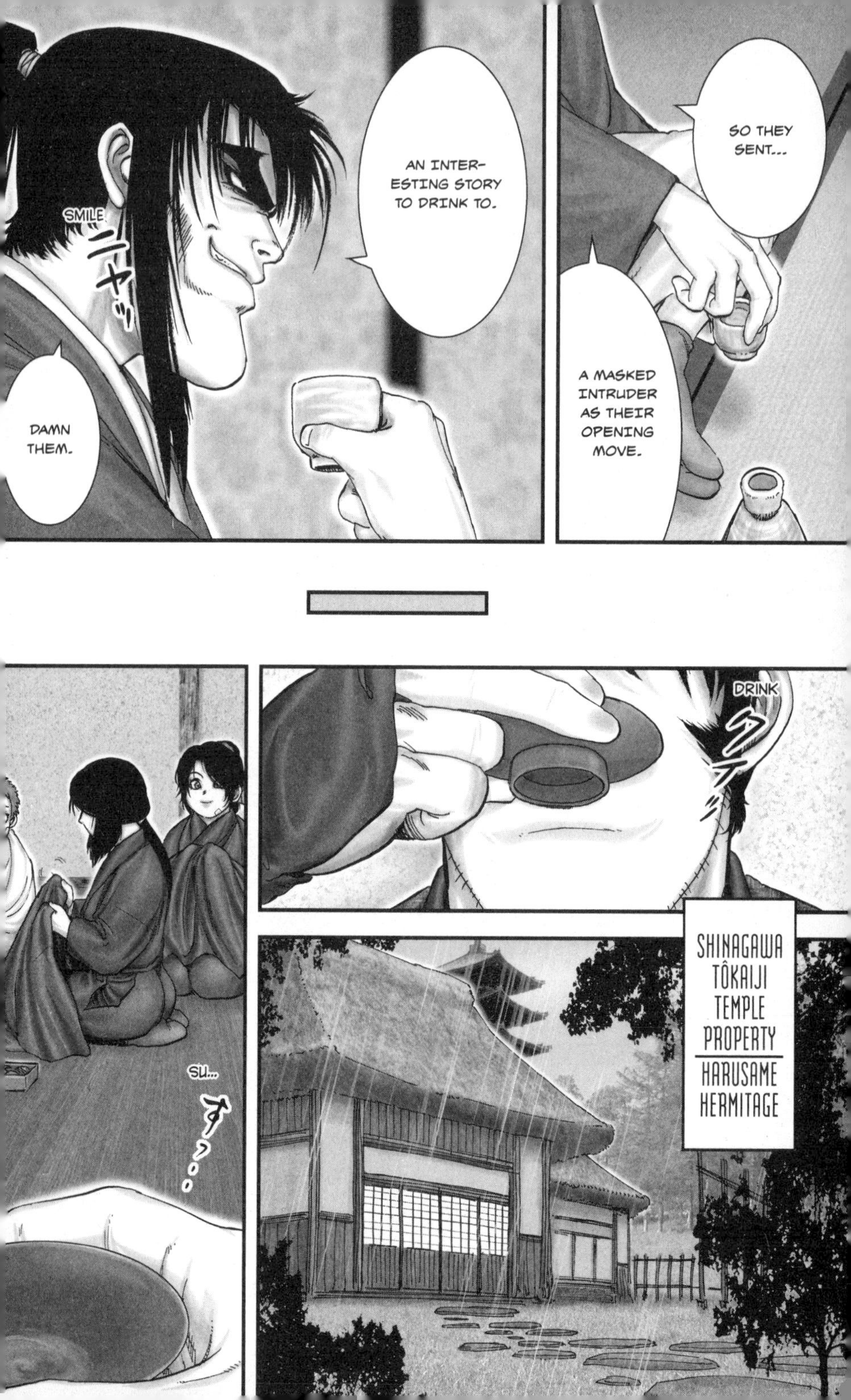
SO THEY SENT...
A MASKED INTRUDER AS THEIR OPENING MOVE.
AN INTER-ESTING STORY TO DRINK TO.
SMILE
DAMN THEM.
DRINK
SHINAGAWA TÔKAIJI TEMPLE PROPERTY
HARUSAME HERMITAGE
SU...

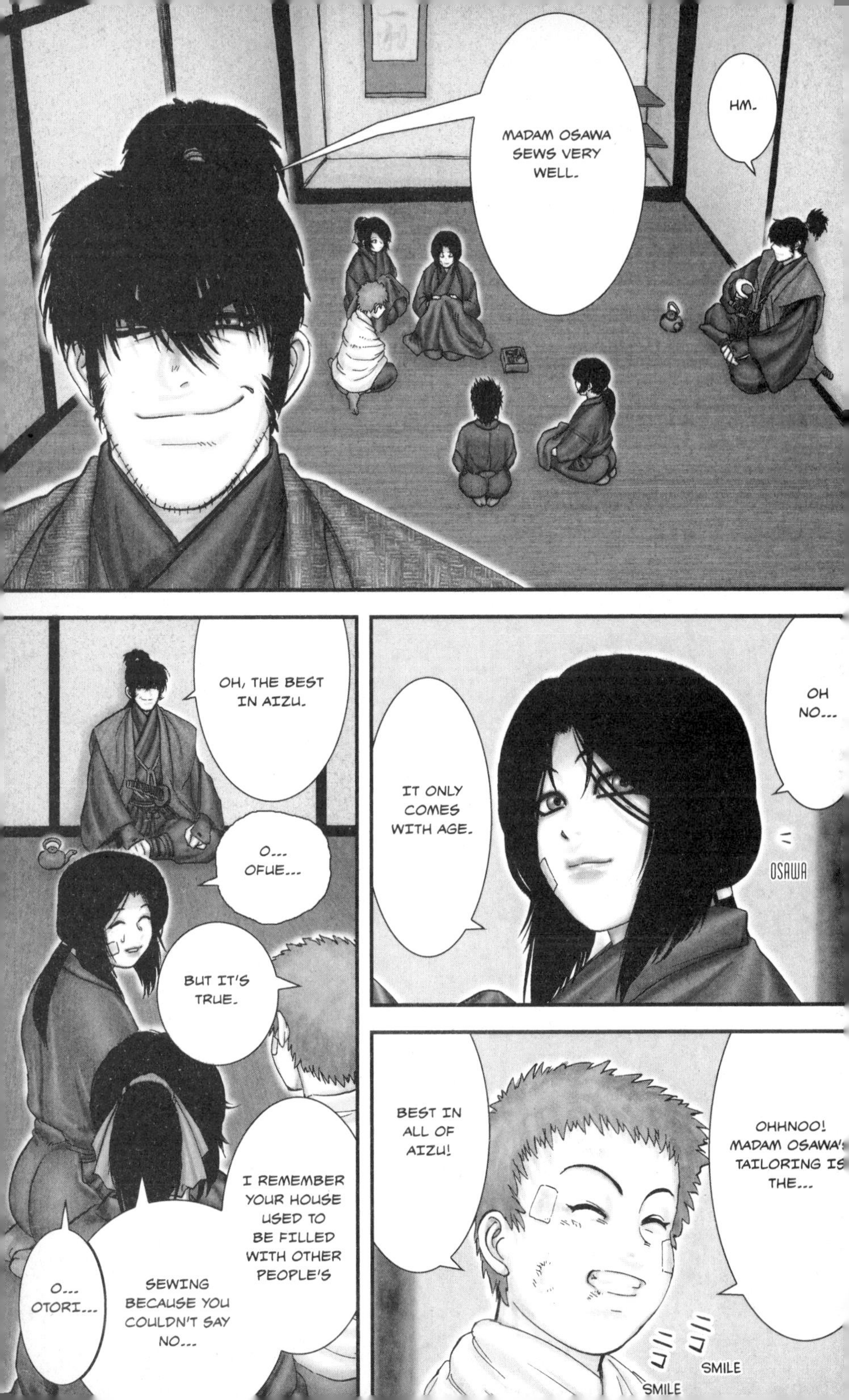
HM.
MADAM OSAWA SEWS VERY WELL.
OH NO...
OSAWA
IT ONLY COMES WITH AGE.
OHHNOO! MADAM OSAWA'S TAILORING IS THE...
BEST IN ALL OF AIZU!
SMILE
SMILE
OH, THE BEST IN AIZU.
O... OFUE...
BUT IT'S TRUE.
I REMEMBER YOUR HOUSE USED TO BE FILLED WITH OTHER PEOPLE'S SEWING BECAUSE YOU COULDN'T SAY NO...
O... OTORI...

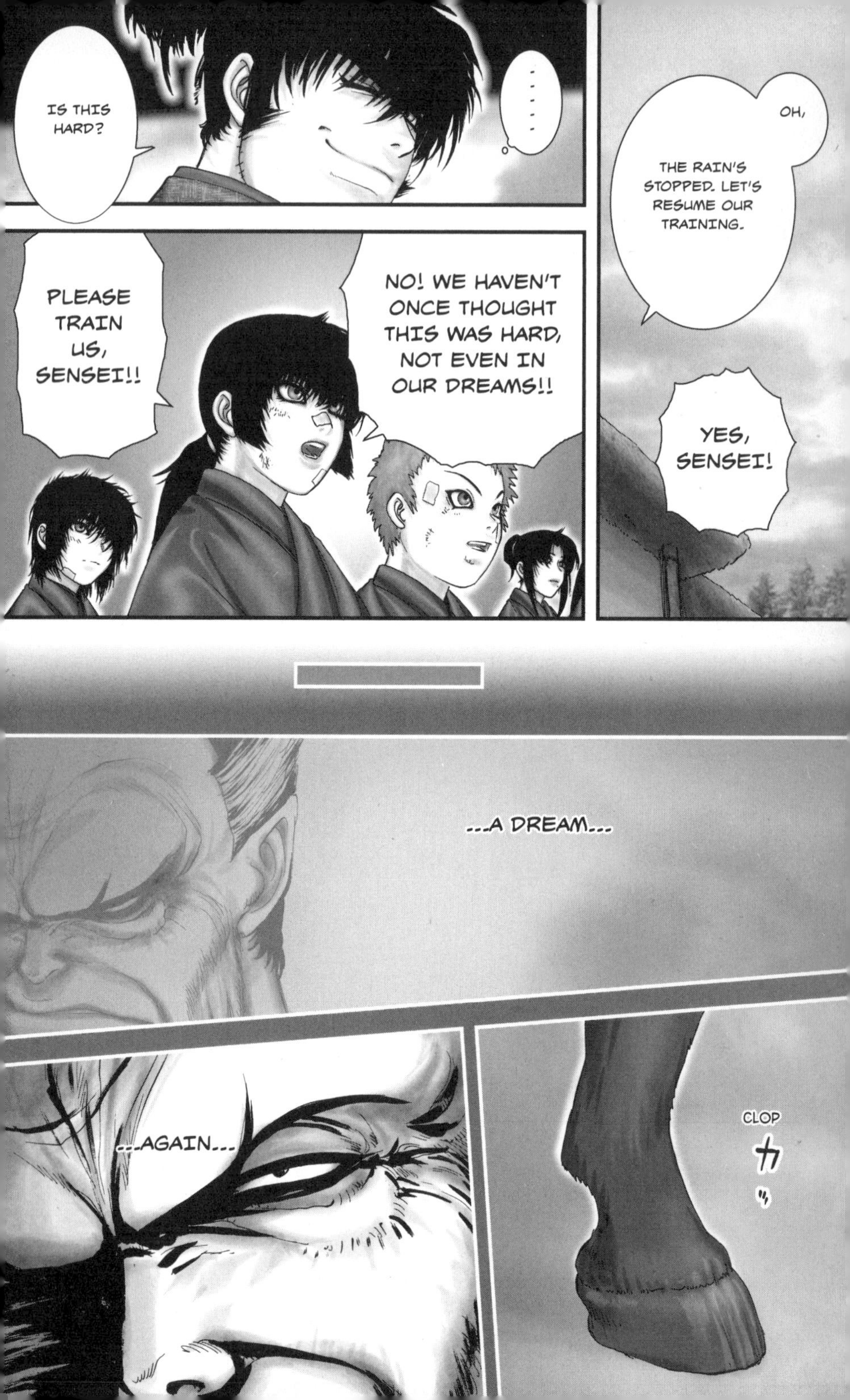
OH,
THE RAIN'S STOPPED. LET'S RESUME OUR TRAINING.
YES, SENSEI!
......
IS THIS HARD?
NO! WE HAVEN'T ONCE THOUGHT THIS WAS HARD, NOT EVEN IN OUR DREAMS!!
PLEASE TRAIN US, SENSEI!!
...A DREAM...
CLOP
カッ
...AGAIN...

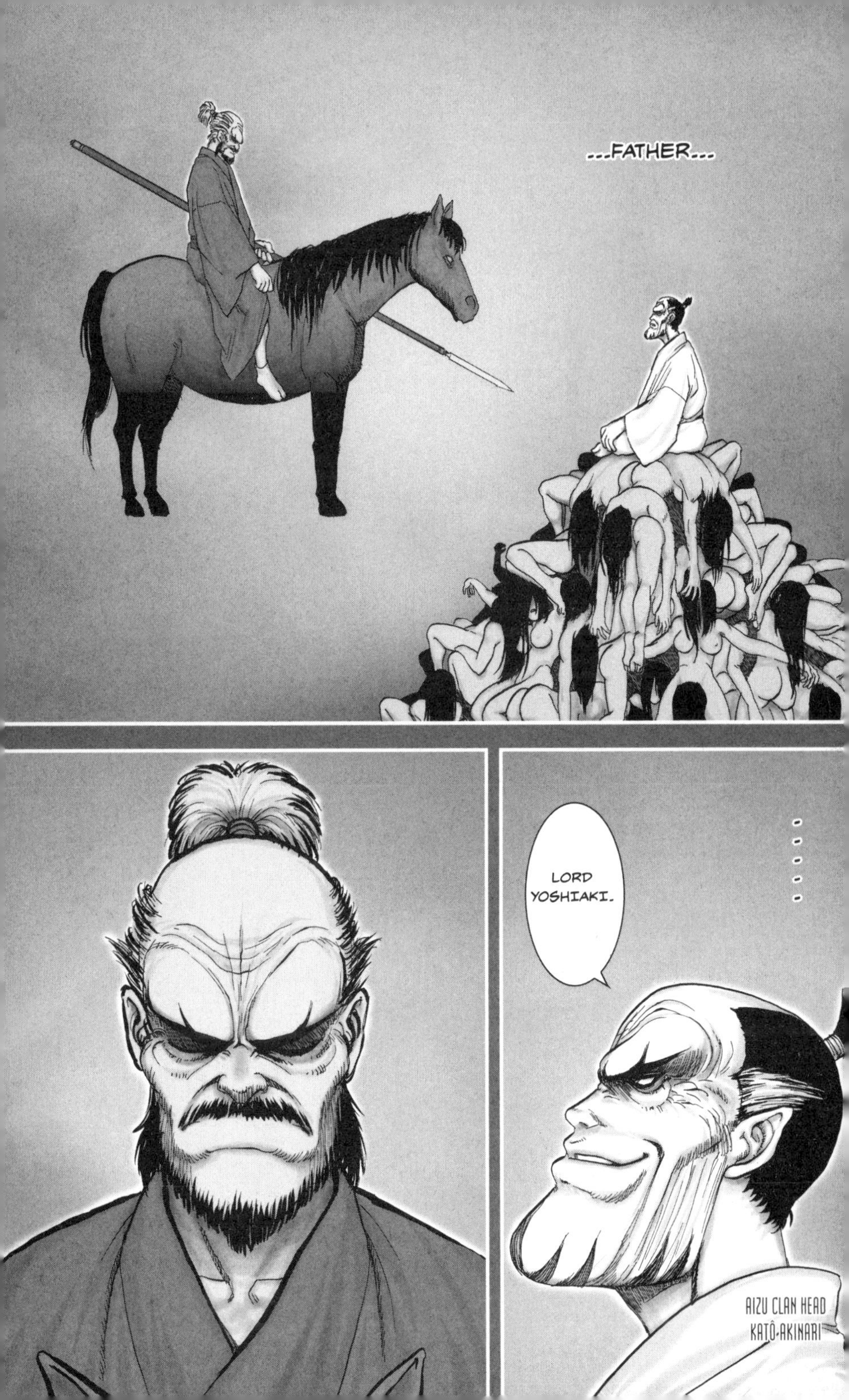
...FATHER...
.....
LORD YOSHIAKI.
AIZU CLAN HEAD
KATÔ AKINARI

STORY 9: JYÛBEI, BASKET BUYER

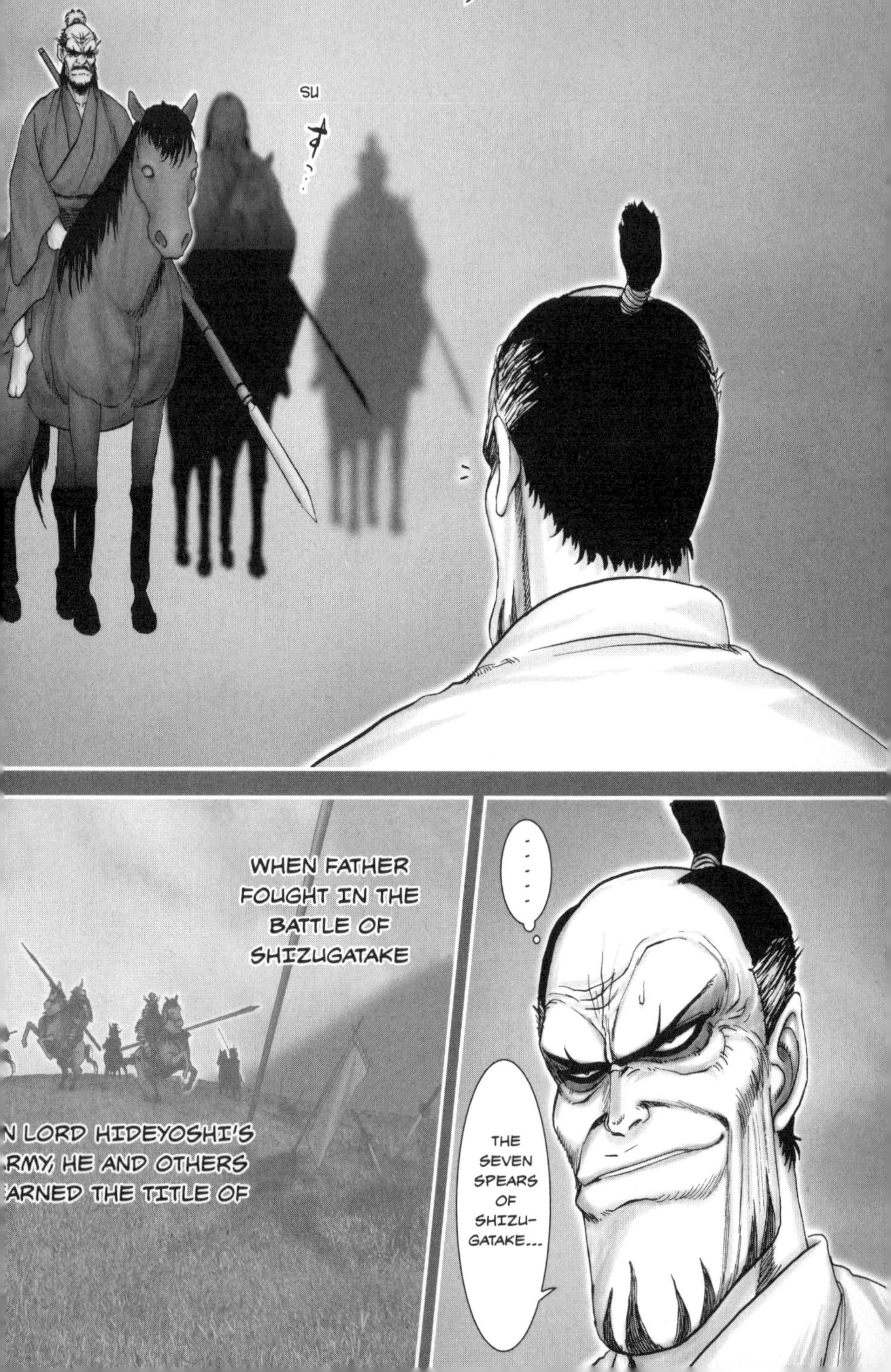
SU
す…
WHEN FATHER FOUGHT IN THE BATTLE OF SHIZUGATAKE
N LORD HIDEYOSHI'S RMY, HE AND OTHERS ARNED THE TITLE OF
......
THE SEVEN SPEARS OF SHIZU-GATAKE...

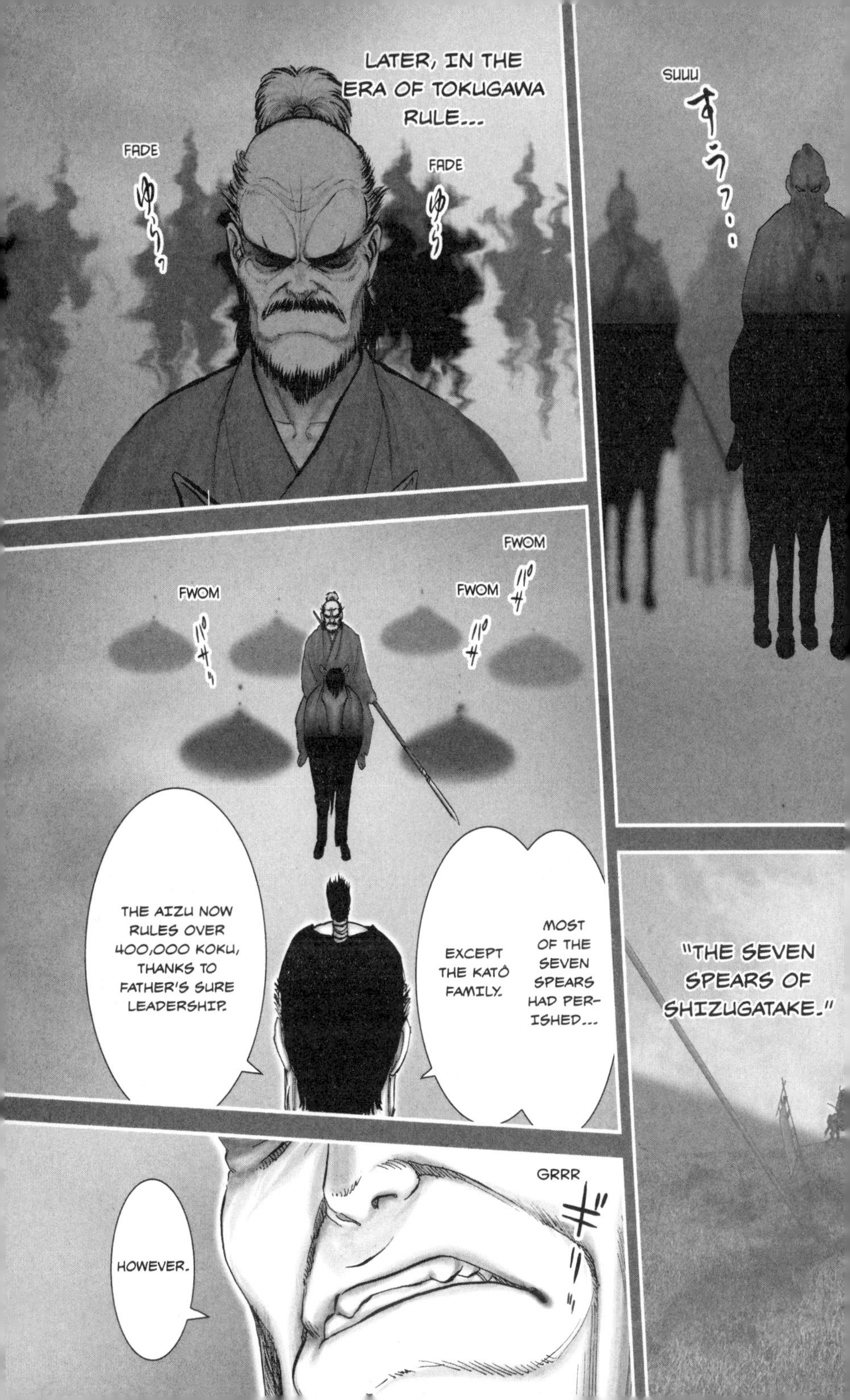
SUUU
LATER, IN THE ERA OF TOKUGAWA RULE...
FADE
FADE
FWOM
FWOM
FWOM
MOST OF THE SEVEN SPEARS HAD PER-ISHED...
EXCEPT THE KATÔ FAMILY.
THE AIZU NOW RULES OVER 400,000 KOKU, THANKS TO FATHER'S SURE LEADERSHIP.
"THE SEVEN SPEARS OF SHIZUGATAKE."
GRRR
HOWEVER.

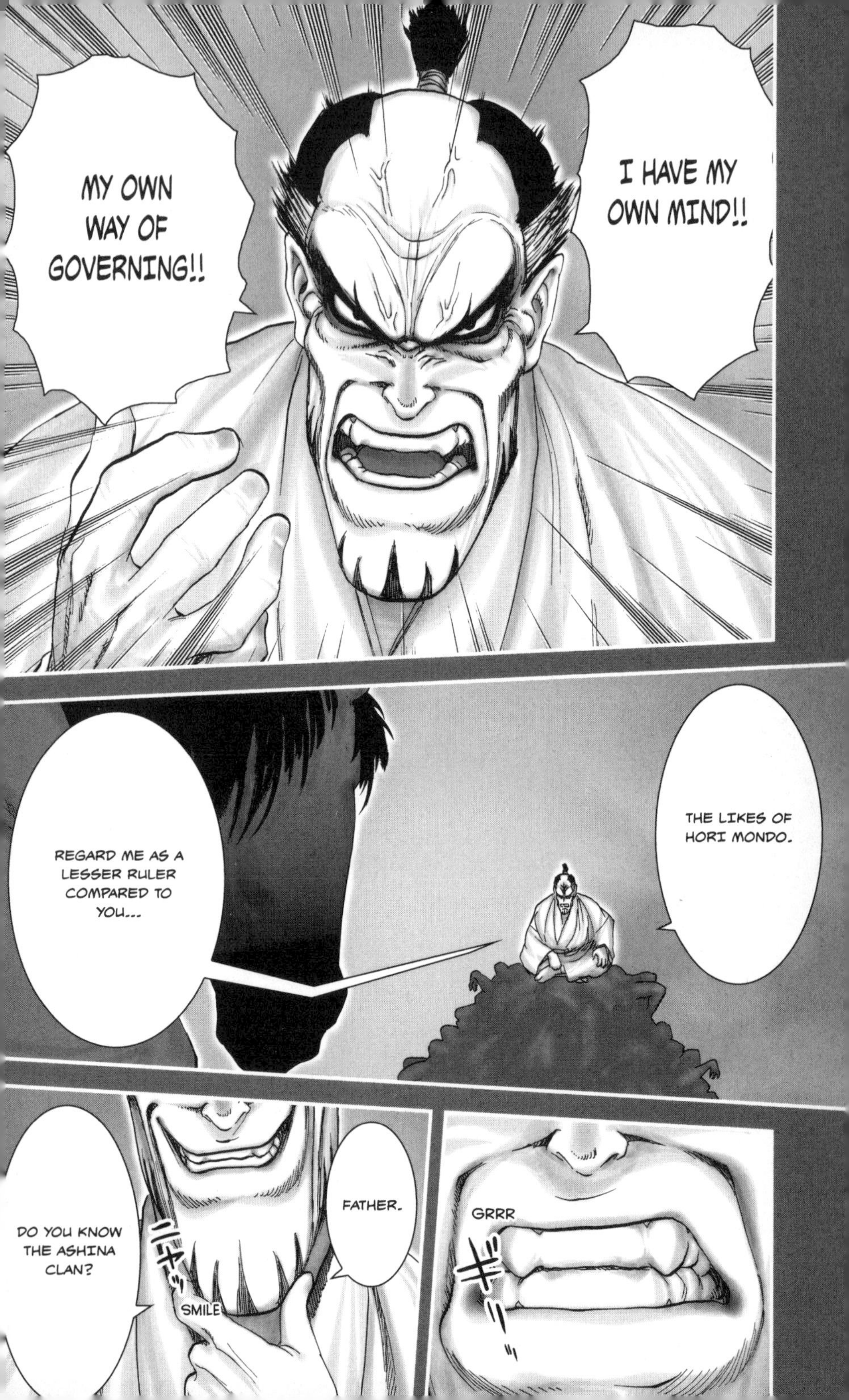
I HAVE MY OWN MIND!!
MY OWN WAY OF GOVERNING!!
THE LIKES OF HORI MONDO.
REGARD ME AS A LESSER RULER COMPARED TO YOU...
GRRR
FATHER.
DO YOU KNOW THE ASHINA CLAN?
SMILE

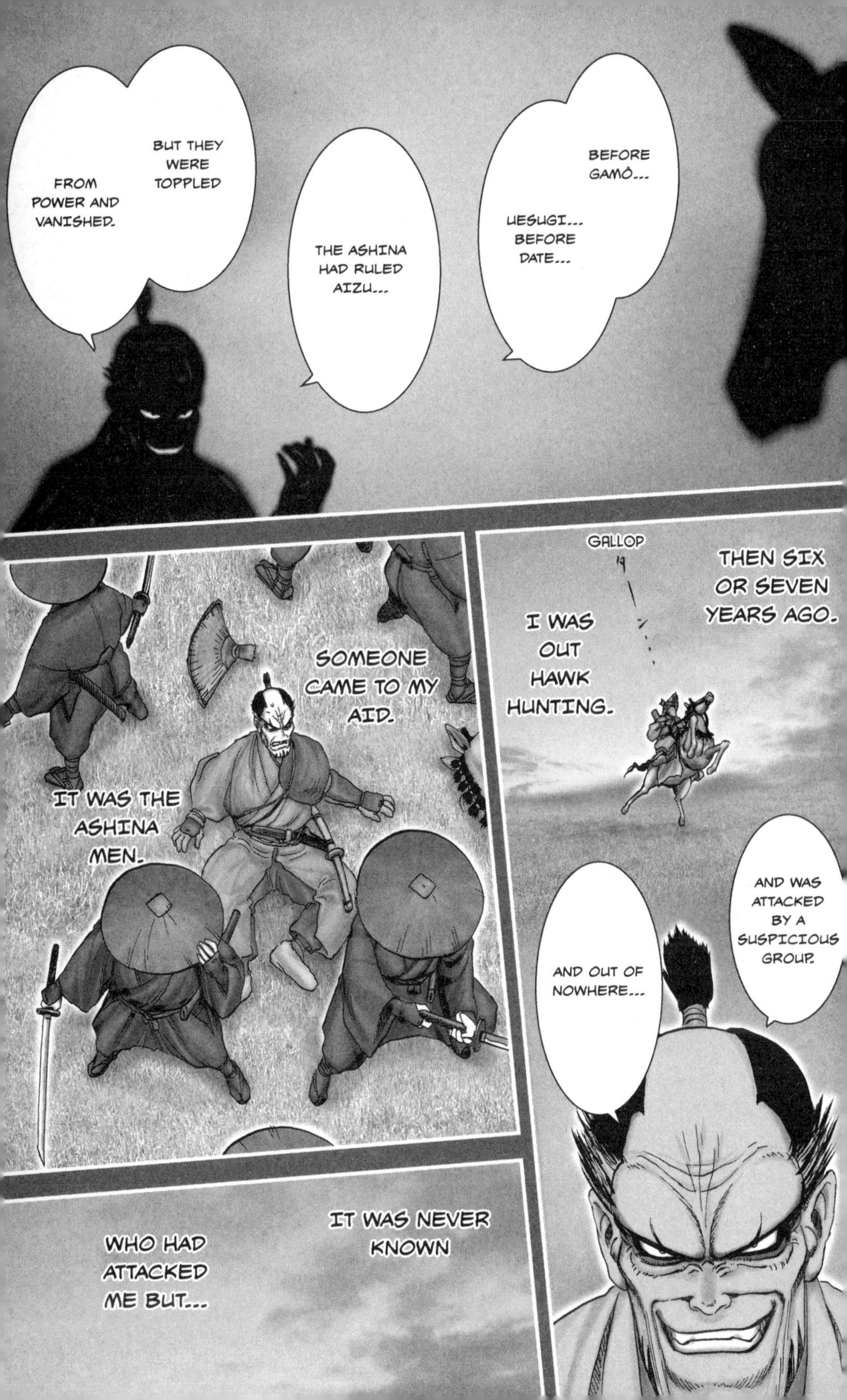

BEFORE GAMÔ...
UESUGI... BEFORE DATE...
THE ASHINA HAD RULED AIZU...
BUT THEY WERE TOPPLED
FROM POWER AND VANISHED.
THEN SIX OR SEVEN YEARS AGO.
GALLOP
I WAS OUT HAWK HUNTING.
AND WAS ATTACKED BY A SUSPICIOUS GROUP.
AND OUT OF NOWHERE...
SOMEONE CAME TO MY AID.
IT WAS THE ASHINA MEN.
IT WAS NEVER KNOWN
WHO HAD ATTACKED ME BUT...

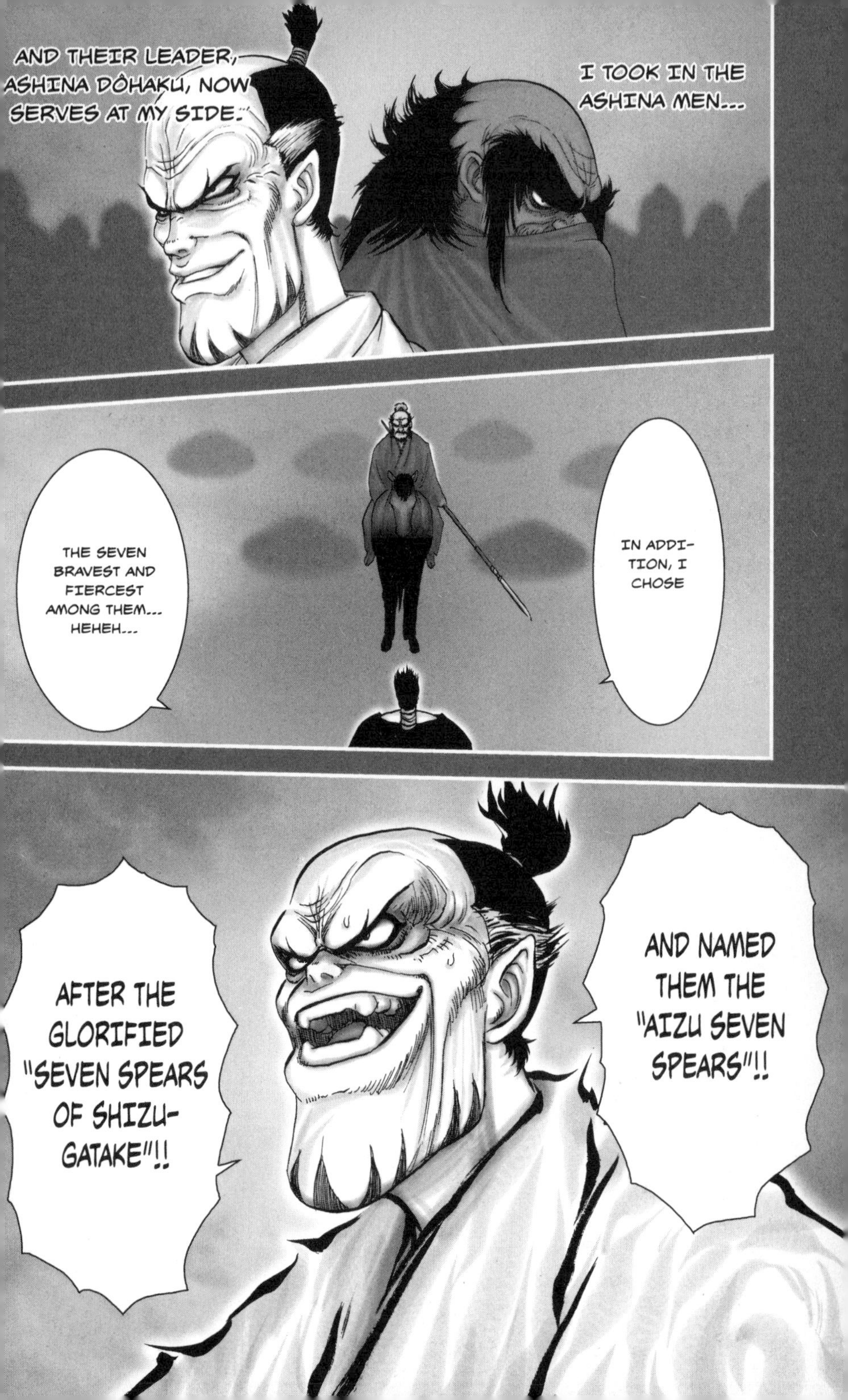
I TOOK IN THE ASHINA MEN...
AND THEIR LEADER, ASHINA DÔHAKU, NOW SERVES AT MY SIDE.
IN ADDITION, I CHOSE
THE SEVEN BRAVEST AND FIERCEST AMONG THEM... HEHEH...
AND NAMED THEM THE "AIZU SEVEN SPEARS"!!
AFTER THE GLORIFIED "SEVEN SPEARS OF SHIZU-GATAKE"!!

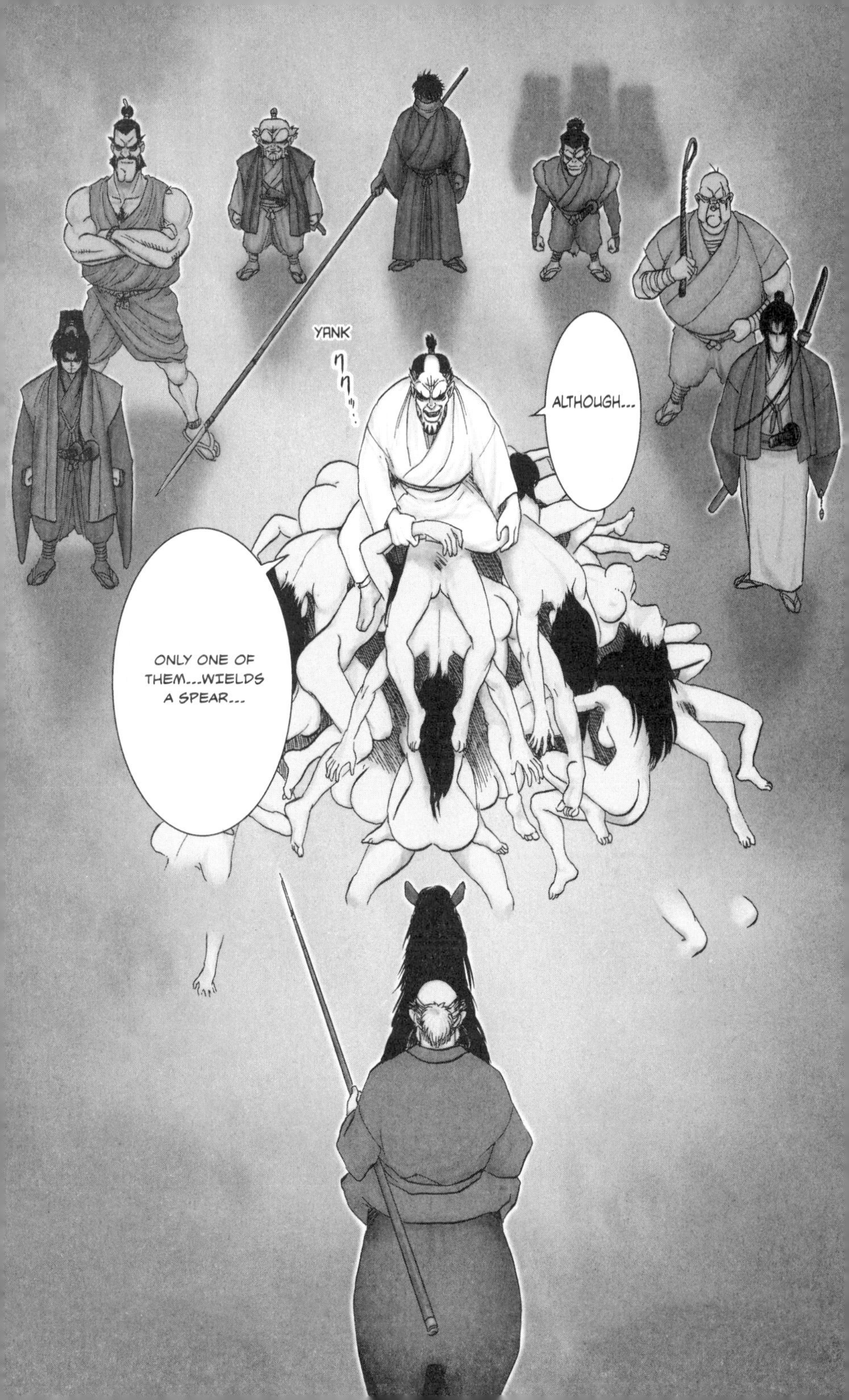
ALTHOUGH...
YANK
ONLY ONE OF THEM...WIELDS A SPEAR...

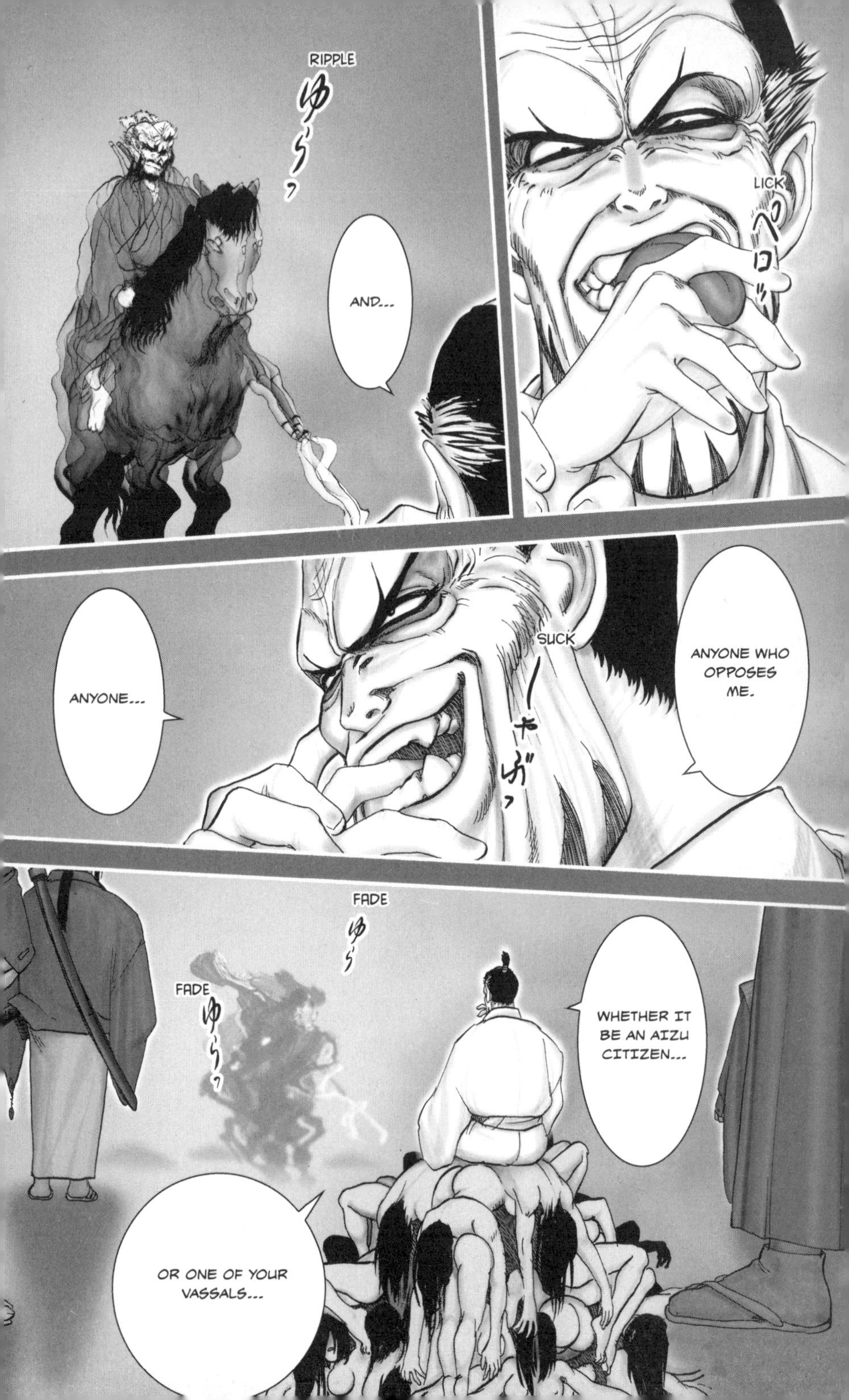
LICK
RIPPLE
AND...
SUCK
ANYONE WHO OPPOSES ME.
ANYONE...
FADE
WHETHER IT BE AN AIZU CITIZEN...
FADE
OR ONE OF YOUR VASSALS...

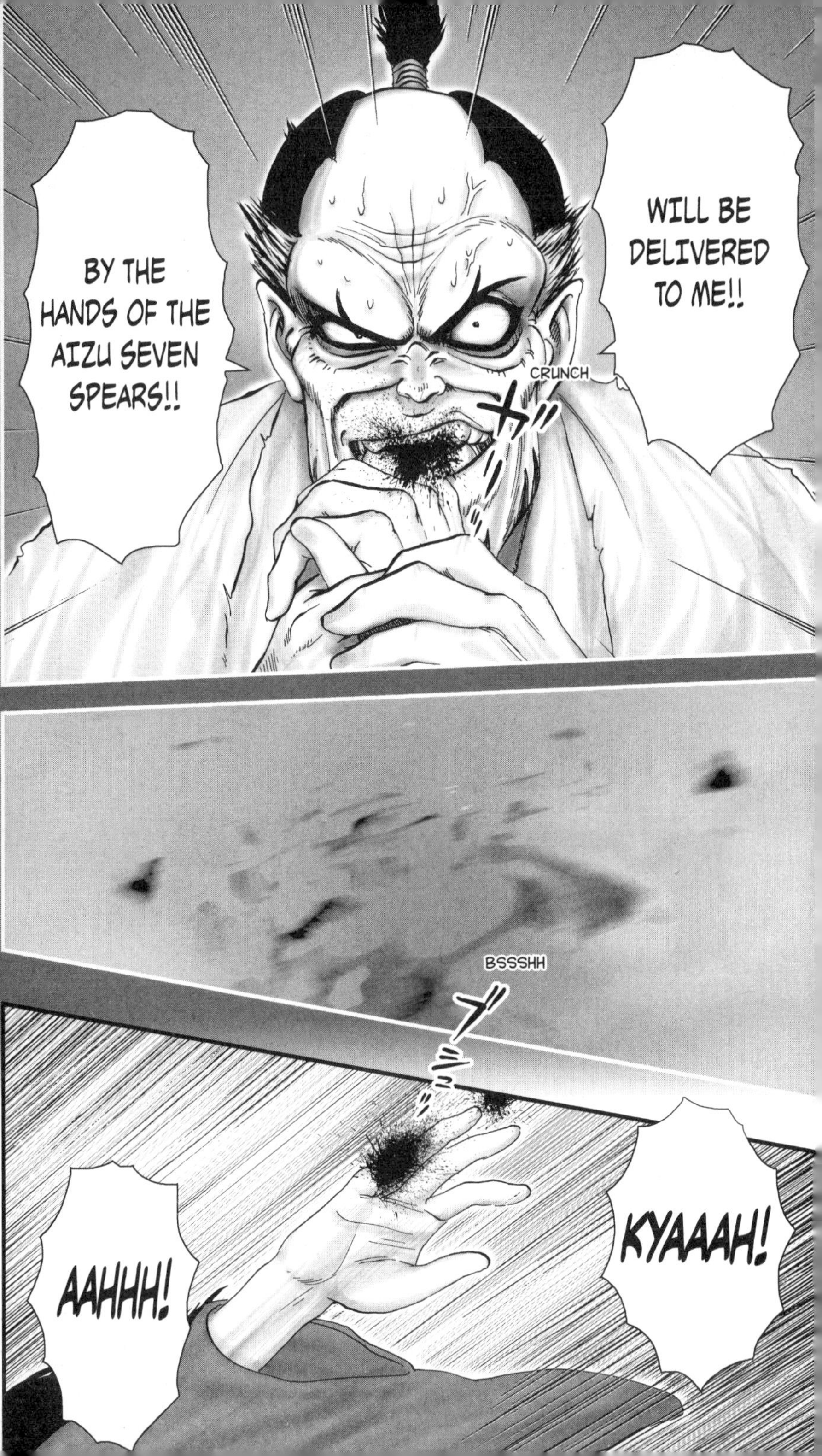
WILL BE DELIVERED TO ME!!
BY THE HANDS OF THE AIZU SEVEN SPEARS!!
CRUNCH
BSSSHH
KYAAAH!
AAHHH!

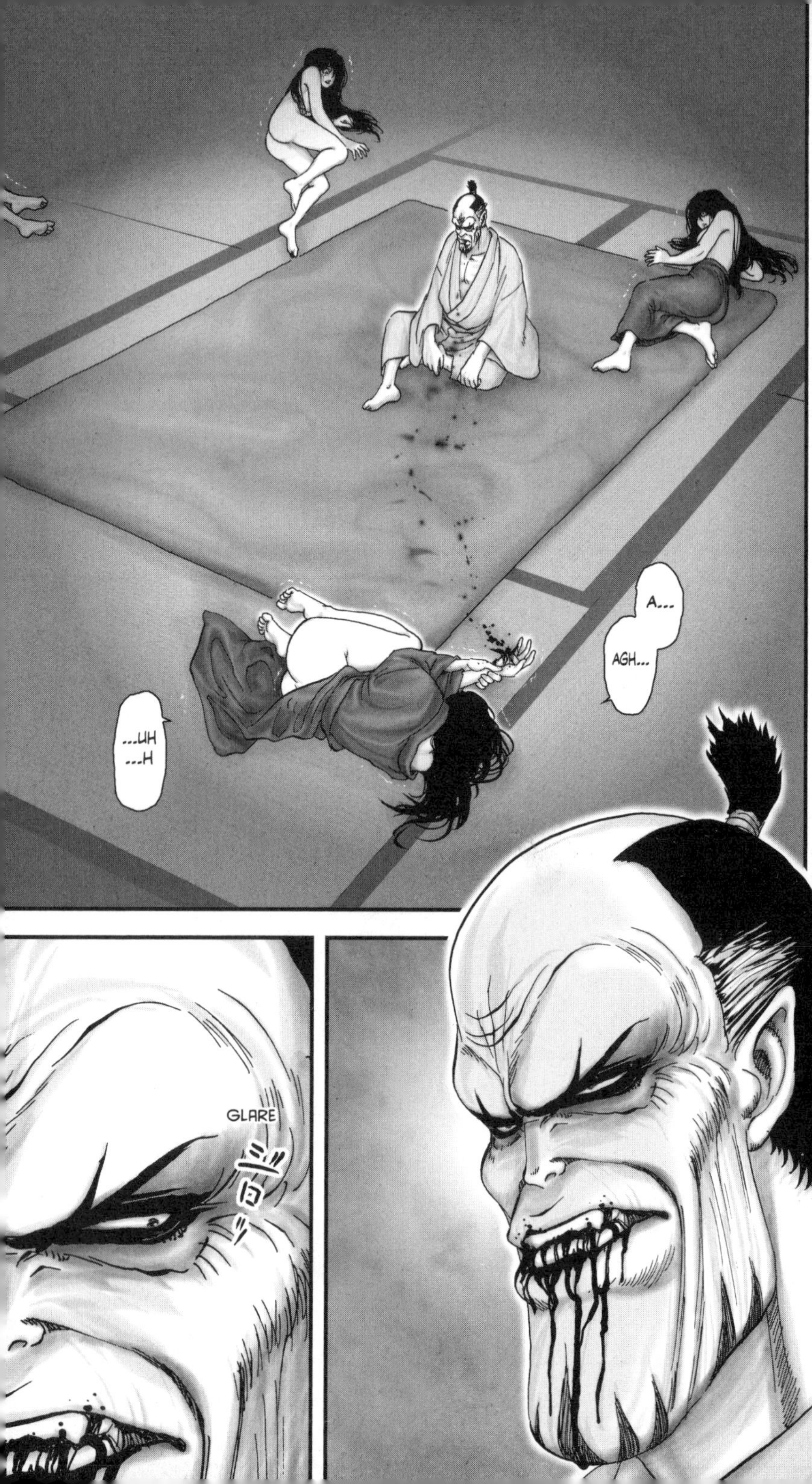

A...
AGH...
...UH ...H
GLARE
ジロッ

HEE.
BRR ぶる
BRR ぶる
BRR ぶる
SPIT べっ
ROLL
ROLL
TAP
SQUIRM ゆらっ
SQUIRM ゆらっ

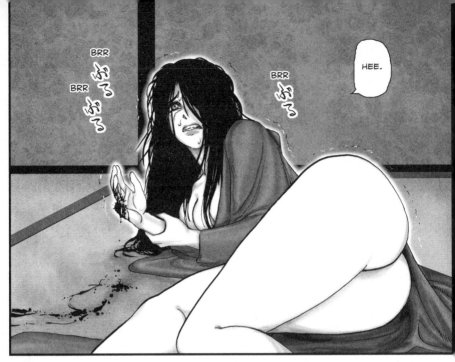

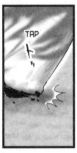

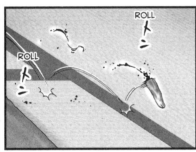

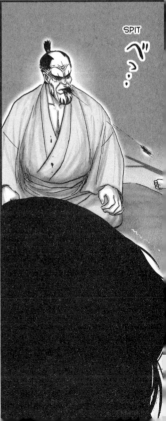

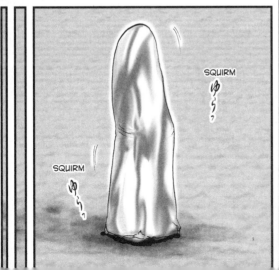

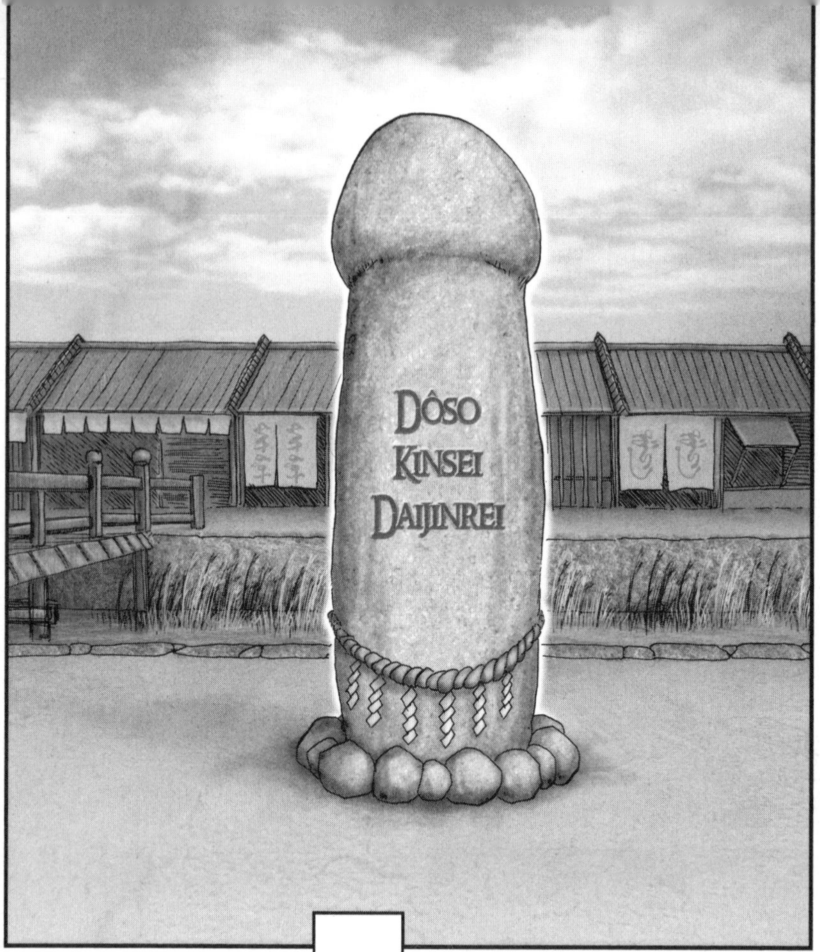
DÔSO
KINSEI
DAIJINREI

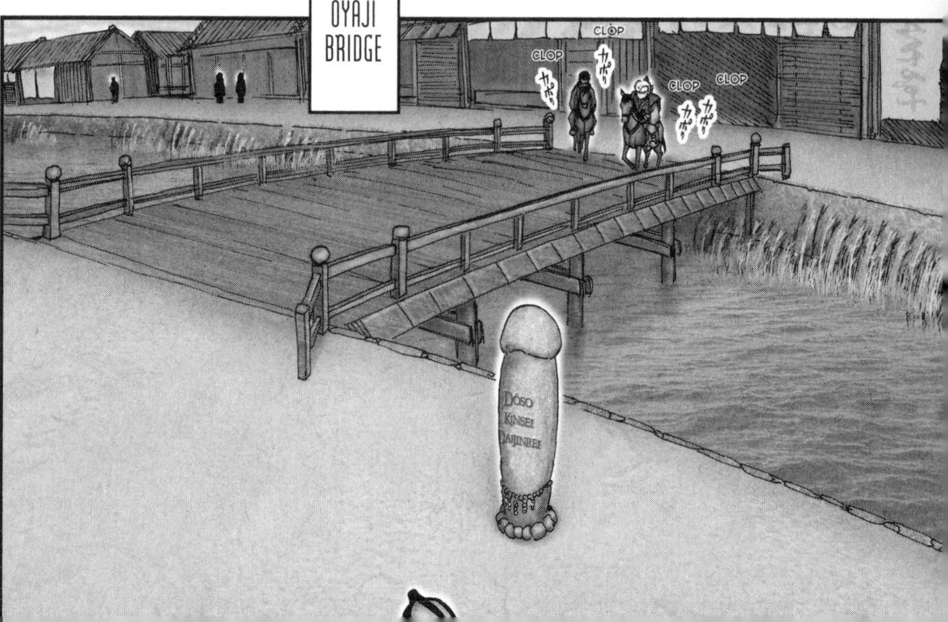
OYAJI
BRIDGE
CLOP
CLOP
CLOP
CLOP
DÔSO
KINSEI
DAIJINREI

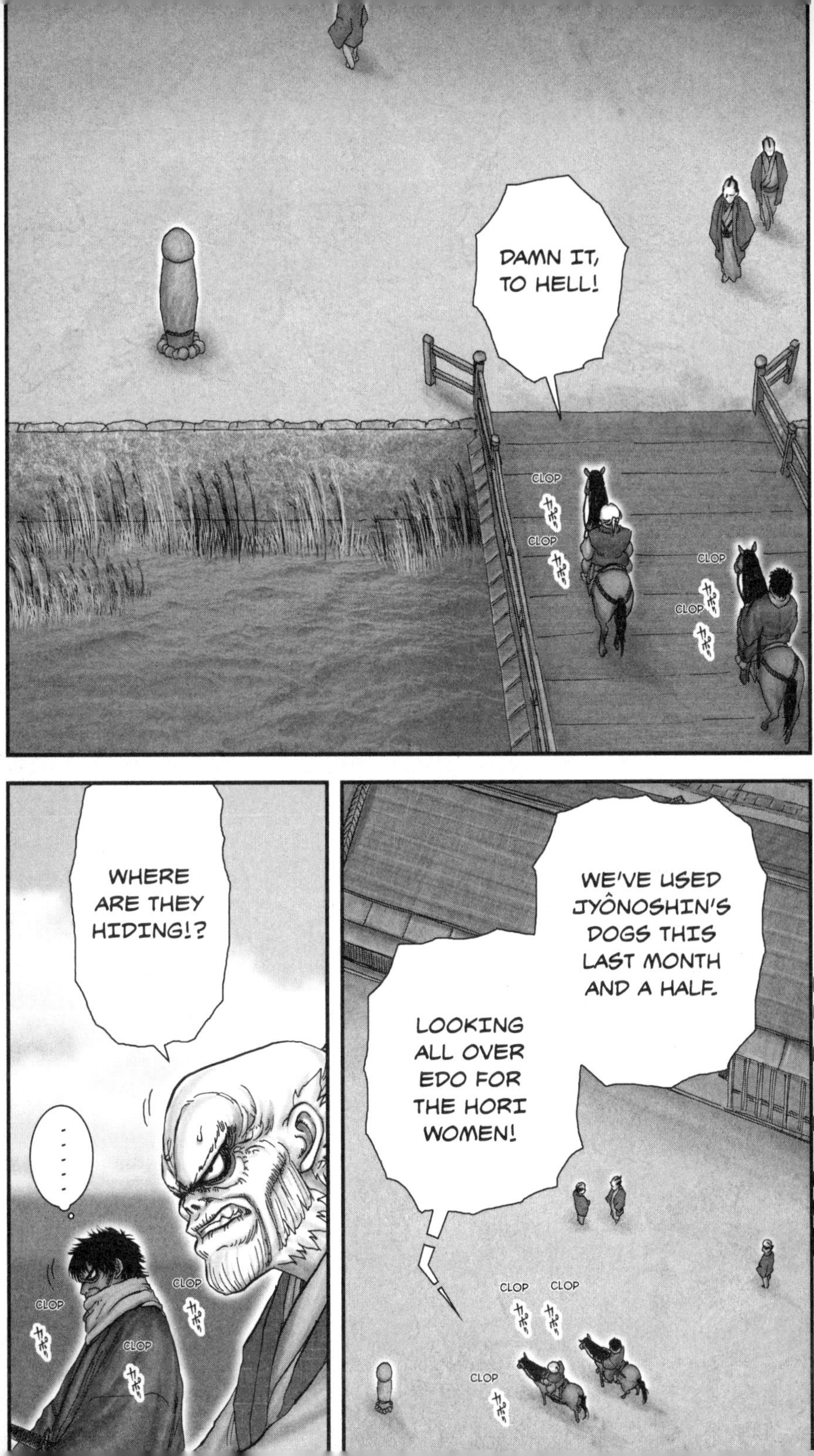
DAMN IT, TO HELL!
CLOP
CLOP
CLOP
CLOP
WE'VE USED JYÔNOSHIN'S DOGS THIS LAST MONTH AND A HALF.
LOOKING ALL OVER EDO FOR THE HORI WOMEN!
CLOP
CLOP
CLOP
WHERE ARE THEY HIDING!?
......
CLOP
CLOP
CLOP

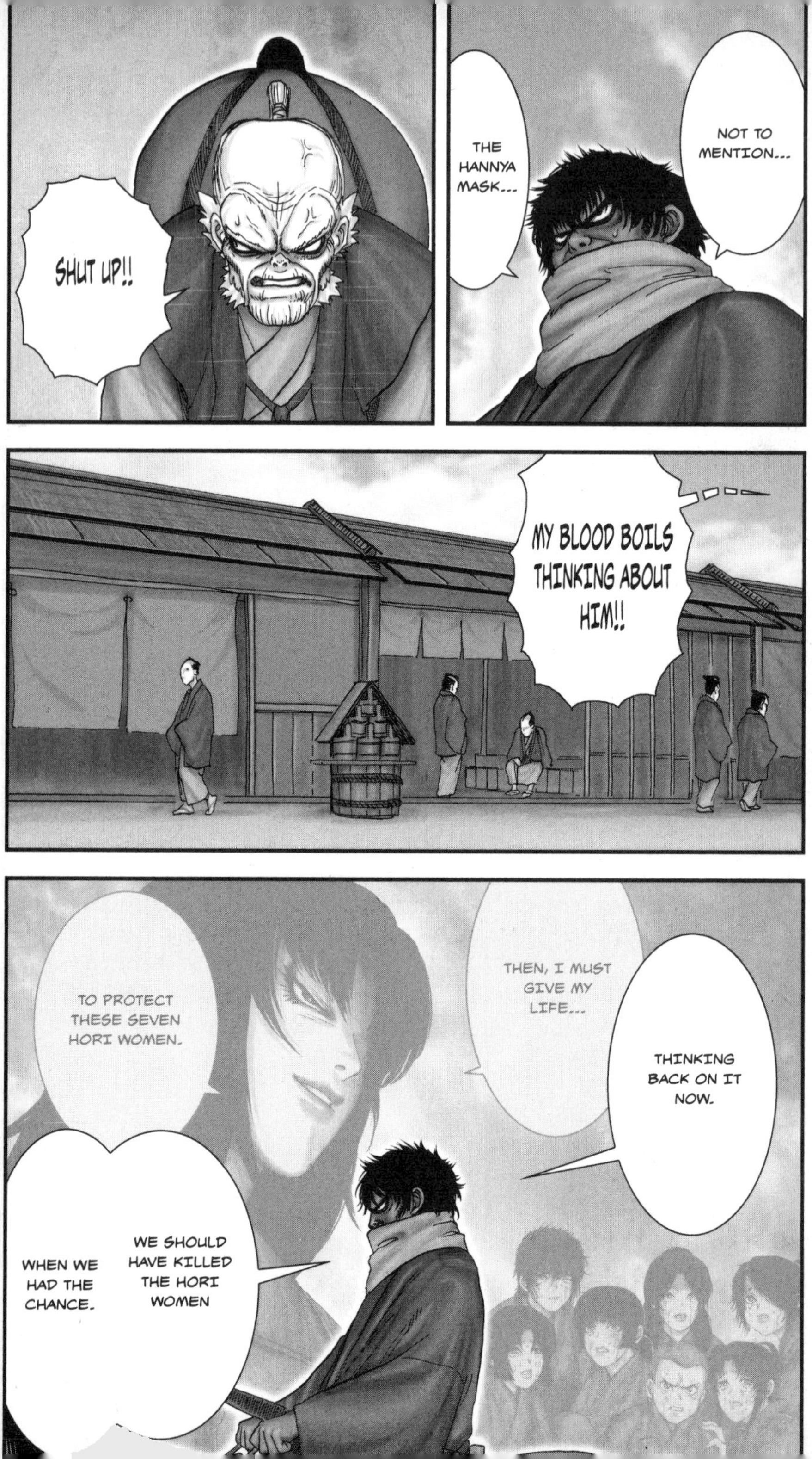
NOT TO MENTION...
THE HANNYA MASK...
SHUT UP!!
MY BLOOD BOILS THINKING ABOUT HIM!!
THEN, I MUST GIVE MY LIFE...
TO PROTECT THESE SEVEN HORI WOMEN.
THINKING BACK ON IT NOW.
WE SHOULD HAVE KILLED THE HORI WOMEN
WHEN WE HAD THE CHANCE.

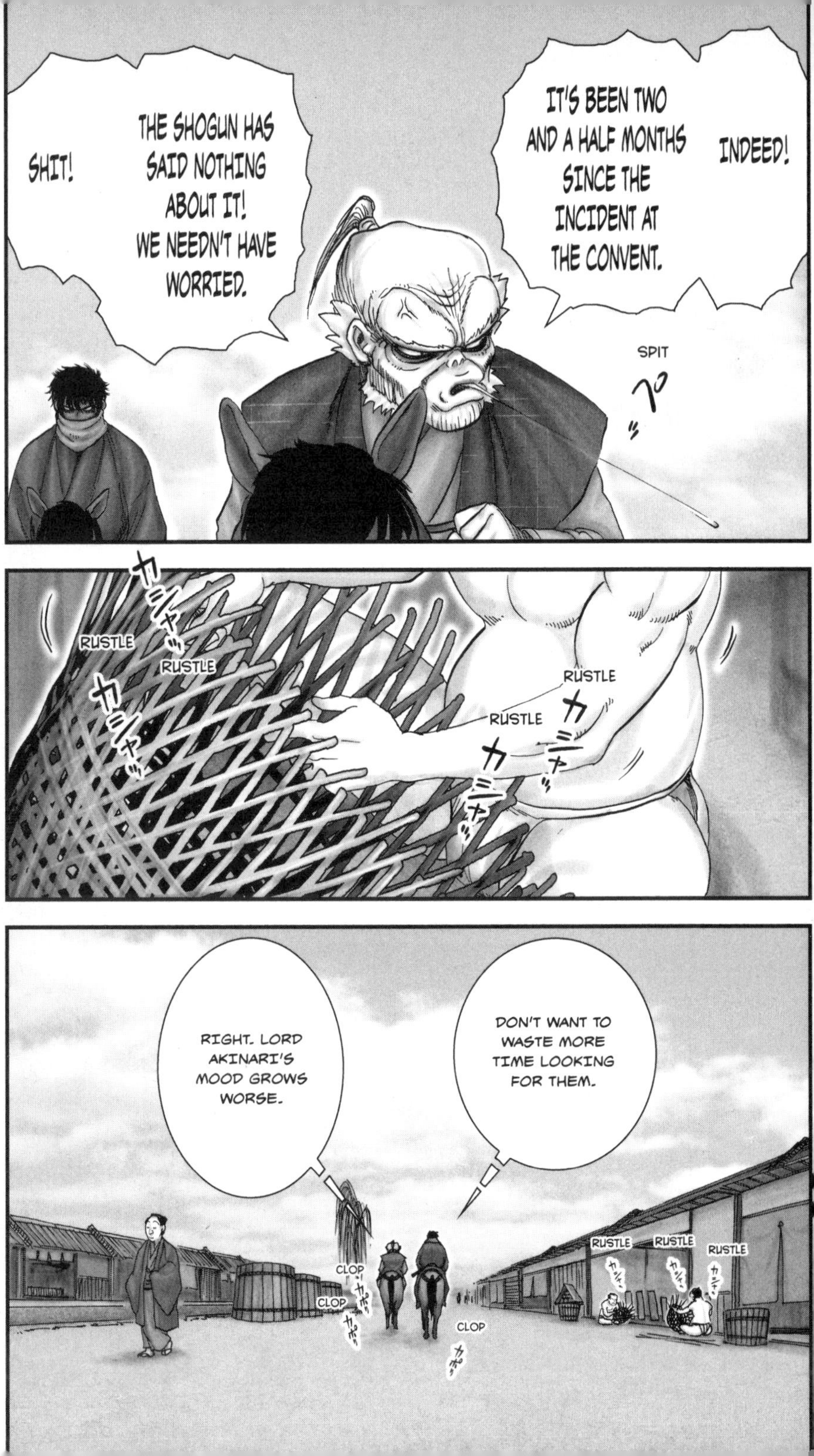
INDEED!
IT'S BEEN TWO AND A HALF MONTHS SINCE THE INCIDENT AT THE CONVENT.
THE SHOGUN HAS SAID NOTHING ABOUT IT! WE NEEDN'T HAVE WORRIED.
SHIT!
SPIT
RUSTLE
RUSTLE
RUSTLE
RUSTLE
DON'T WANT TO WASTE MORE TIME LOOKING FOR THEM.
RIGHT. LORD AKINARI'S MOOD GROWS WORSE.
RUSTLE
RUSTLE
RUSTLE
CLOP
CLOP
CLOP

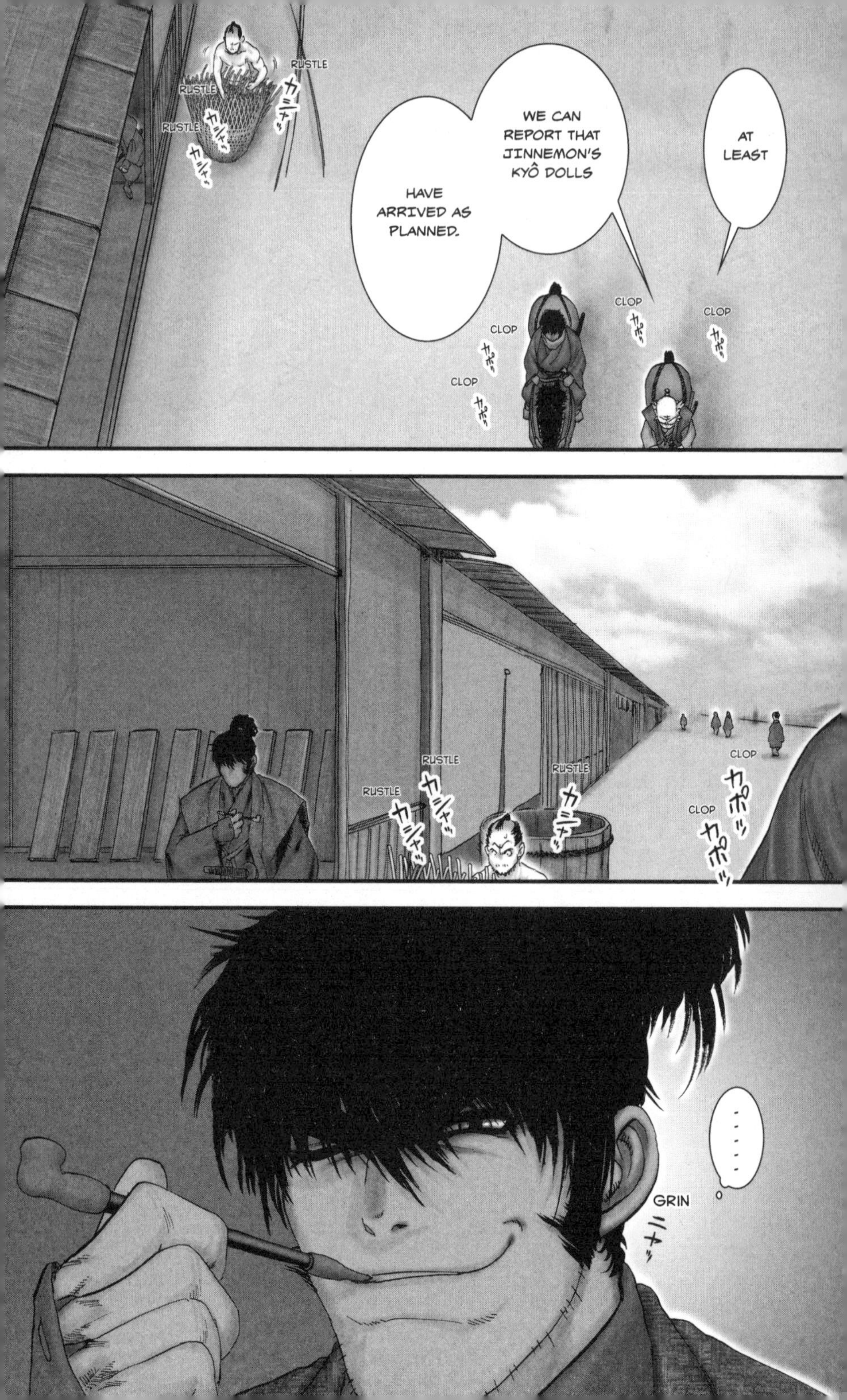
AT LEAST
WE CAN REPORT THAT JINNEMON'S KYÔ DOLLS
HAVE ARRIVED AS PLANNED.
CLOP
CLOP
CLOP
CLOP
RUSTLE
RUSTLE
RUSTLE
CLOP
CLOP
RUSTLE
RUSTLE
......
GRIN

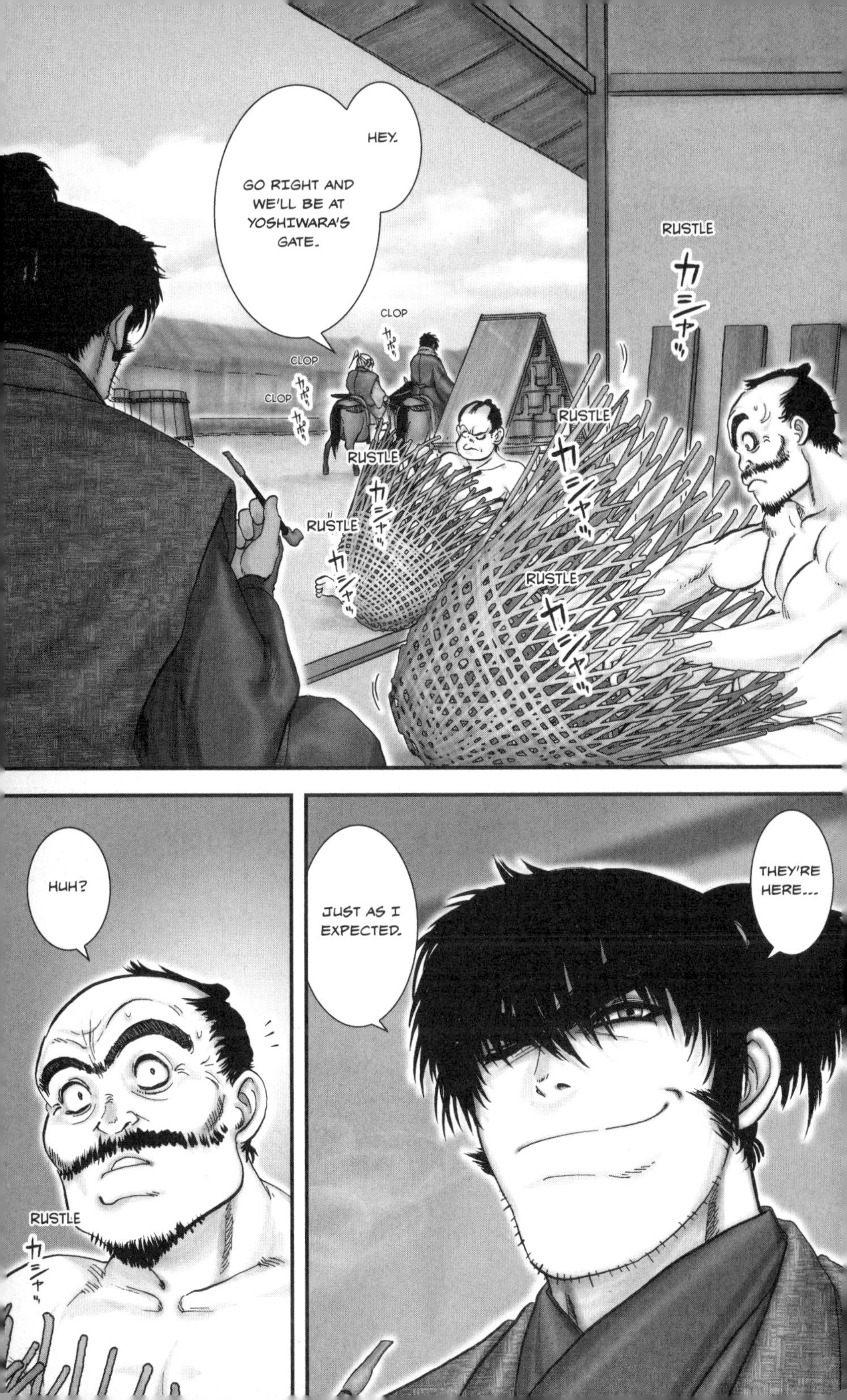
HEY.
GO RIGHT AND WE'LL BE AT YOSHIWARA'S GATE.
RUSTLE
CLOP
CLOP
CLOP
RUSTLE
RUSTLE
RUSTLE
RUSTLE
THEY'RE HERE...
JUST AS I EXPECTED.
HUH?
RUSTLE

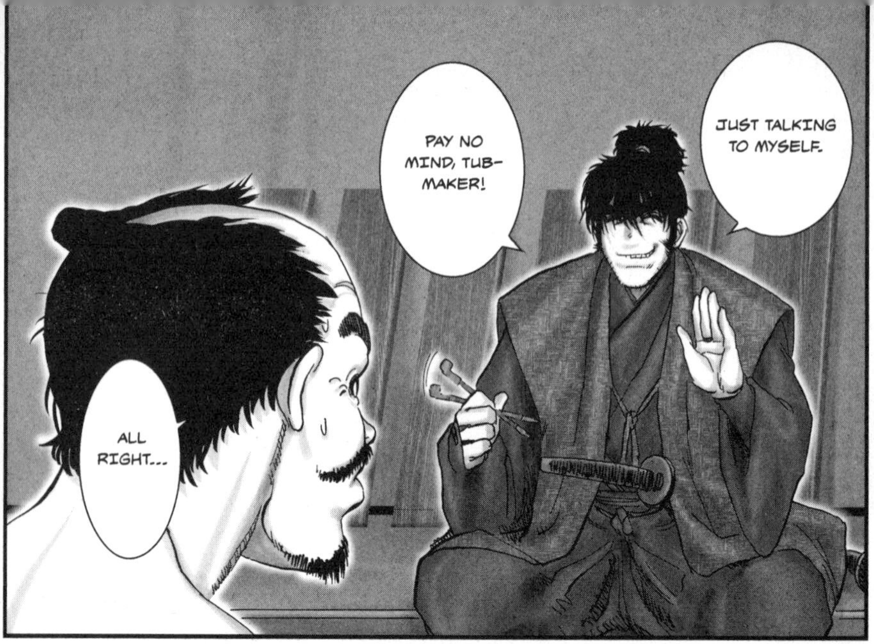
JUST TALKING TO MYSELF.
PAY NO MIND, TUB-MAKER!
ALL RIGHT...

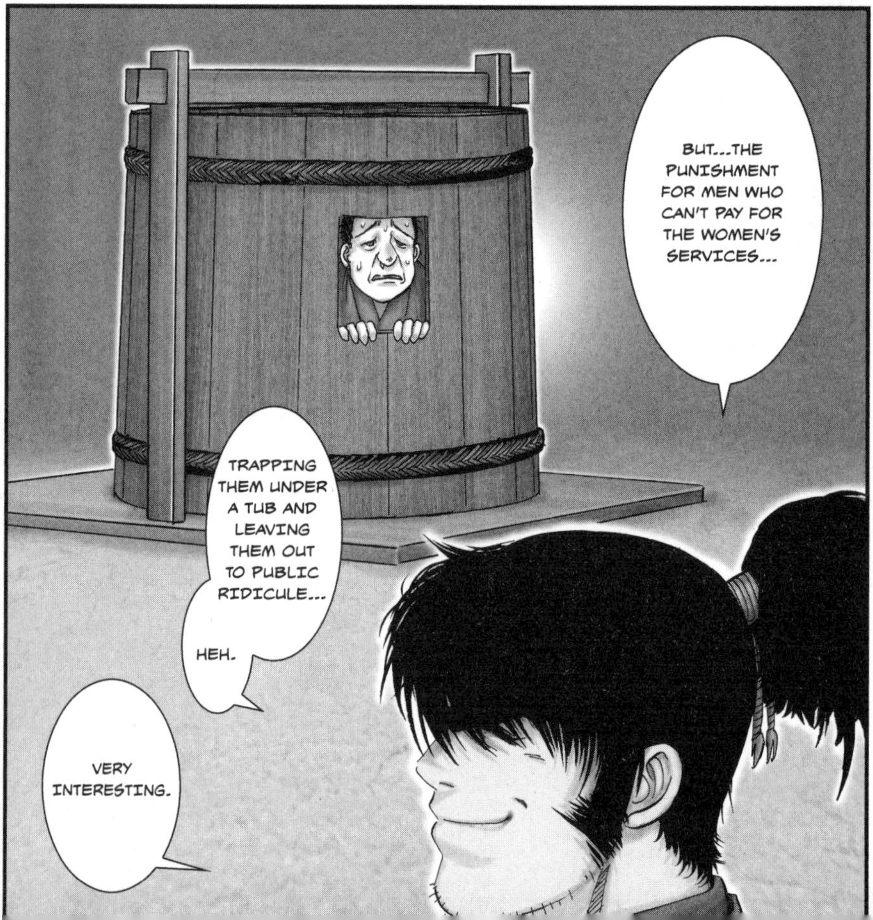
BUT...THE PUNISHMENT FOR MEN WHO CAN'T PAY FOR THE WOMEN'S SERVICES...
TRAPPING THEM UNDER A TUB AND LEAVING THEM OUT TO PUBLIC RIDICULE...
HEH.
VERY INTERESTING.

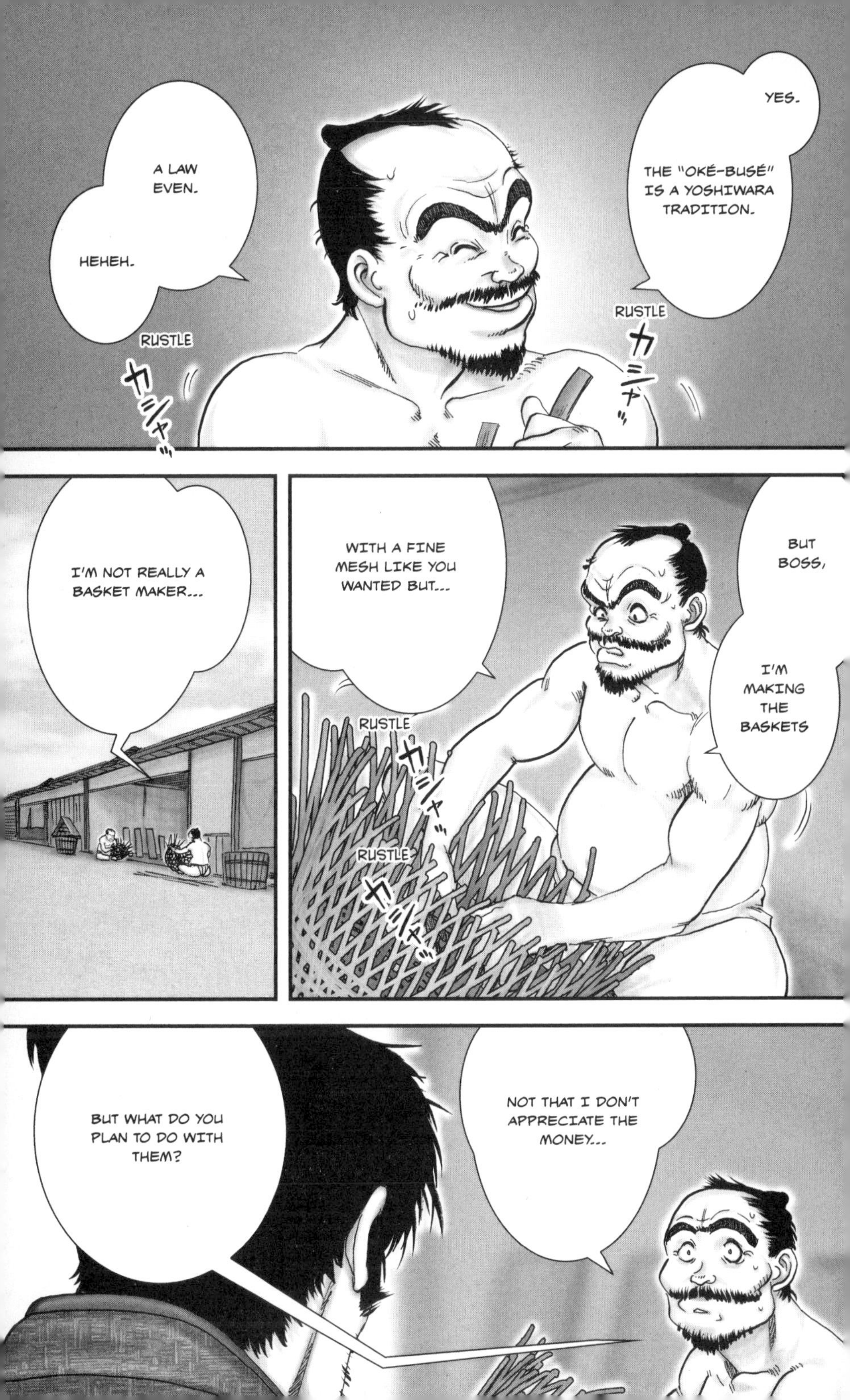
YES.
THE "OKÉ-BUSÉ" IS A YOSHIWARA TRADITION.
RUSTLE
A LAW EVEN.
HEHEH.
RUSTLE
BUT BOSS,
I'M MAKING THE BASKETS
WITH A FINE MESH LIKE YOU WANTED BUT...
RUSTLE
RUSTLE
I'M NOT REALLY A BASKET MAKER...
NOT THAT I DON'T APPRECIATE THE MONEY...
BUT WHAT DO YOU PLAN TO DO WITH THEM?

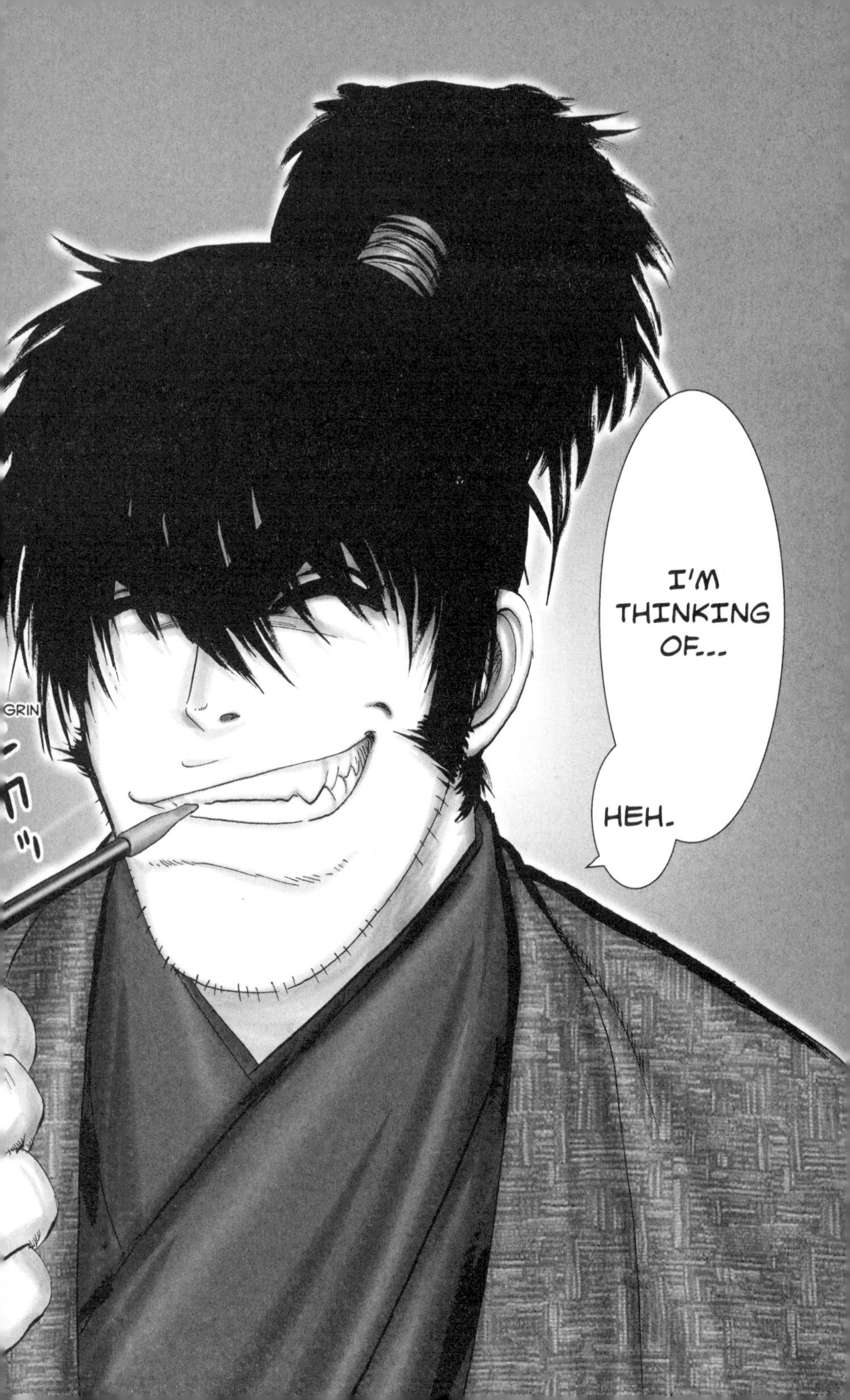
I'M THINKING OF...
HEH.
GRIN

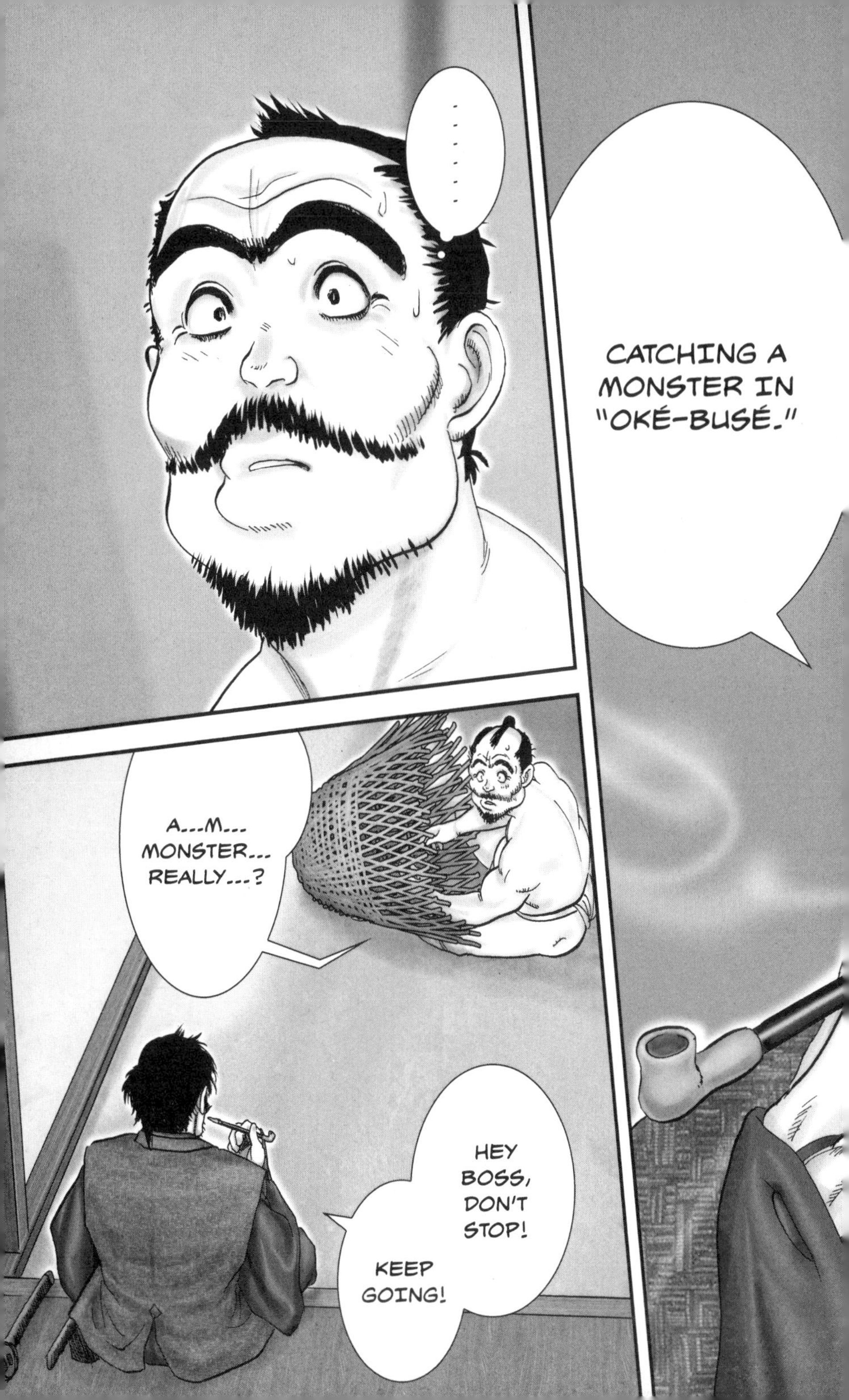
CATCHING A MONSTER IN "OKÉ-BUSÉ."
......
A...M... MONSTER... REALLY...?
HEY BOSS, DON'T STOP!
KEEP GOING!

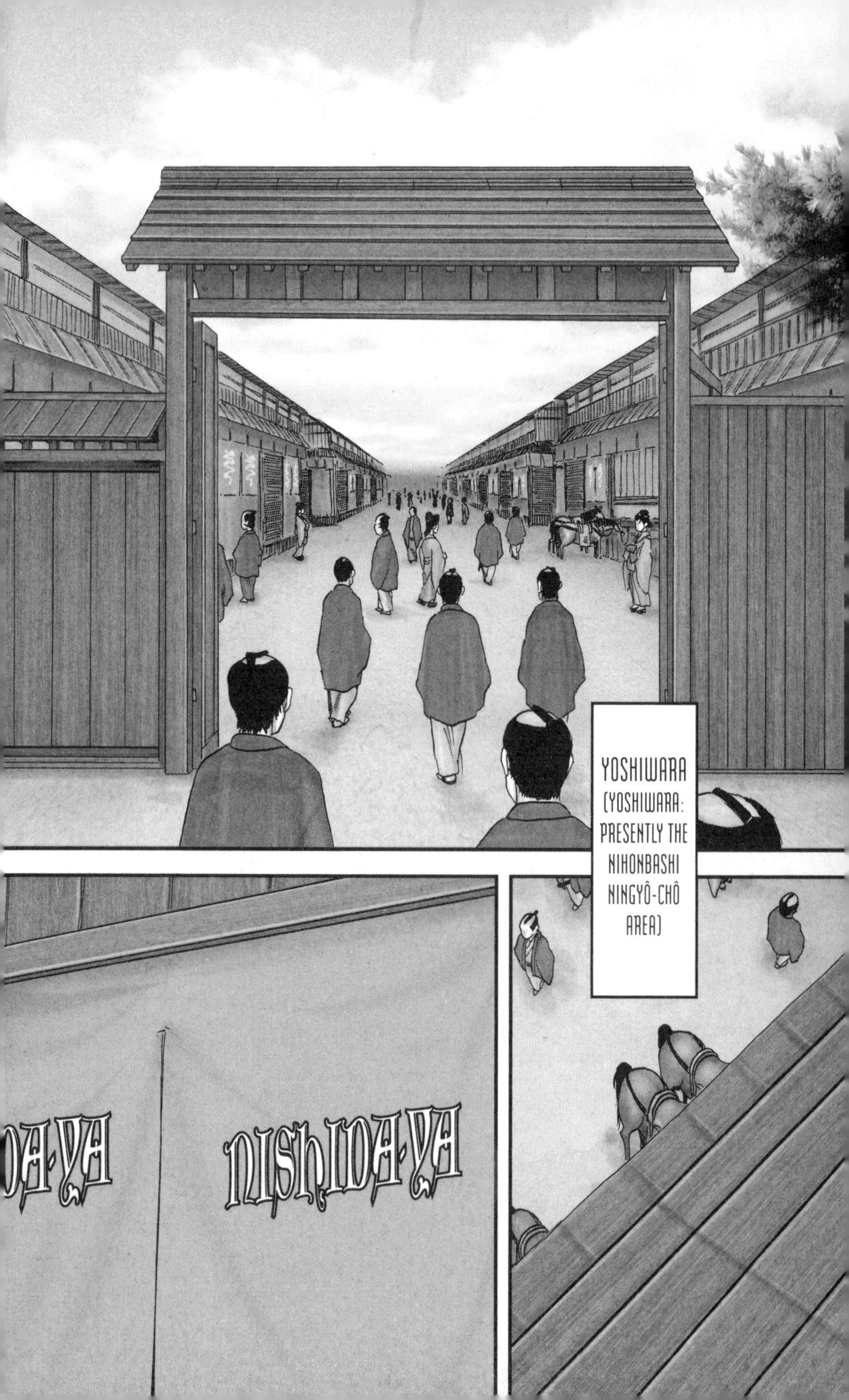
YOSHIWARA
(YOSHIWARA: PRESENTLY THE NIHONBASHI NINGYÔ-CHÔ AREA)
NISHIDA-YA
DA-YA

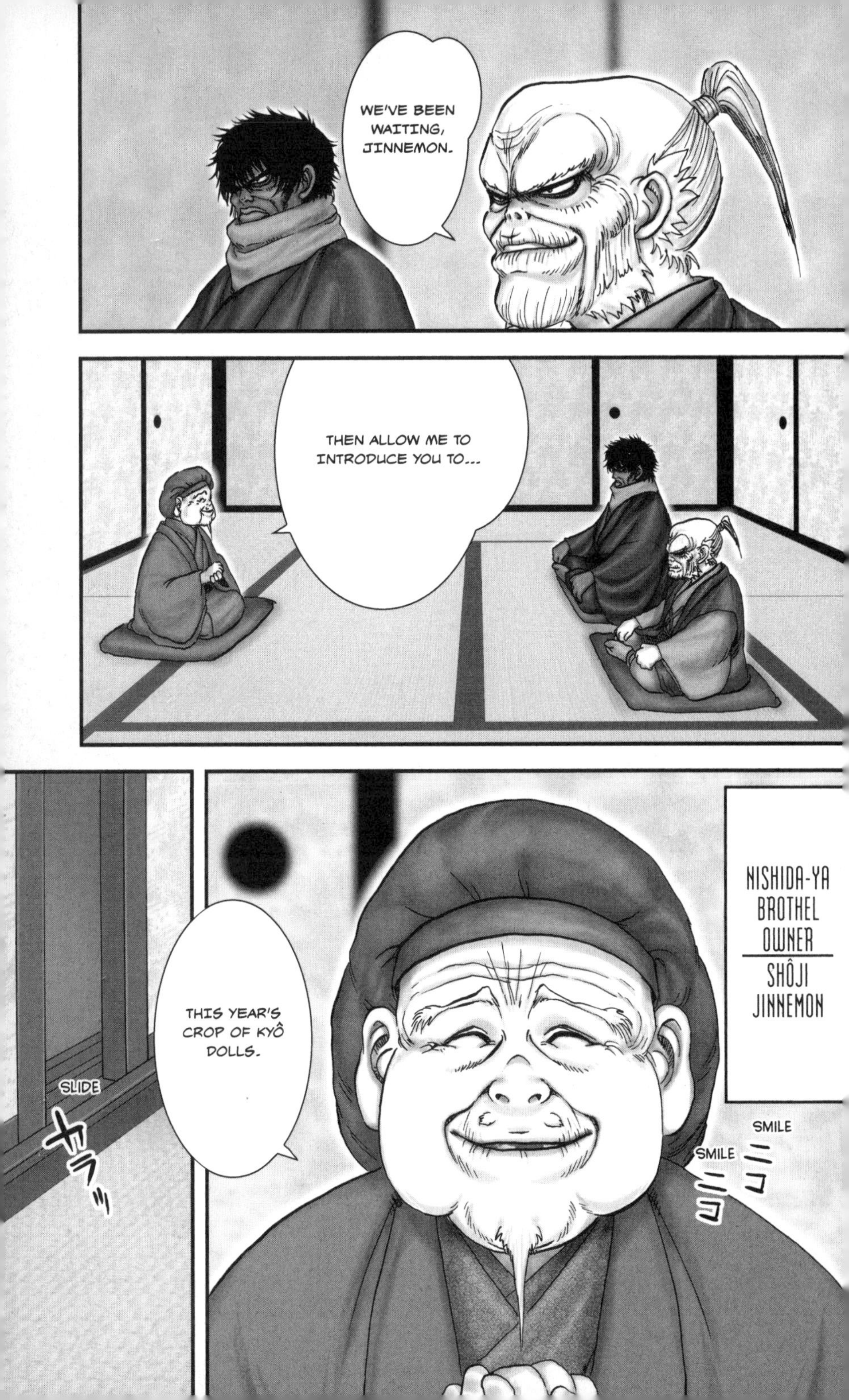
WE'VE BEEN WAITING, JINNEMON.
THEN ALLOW ME TO INTRODUCE YOU TO...
NISHIDA-YA BROTHEL OWNER
SHÔJI JINNEMON
SMILE
SMILE
THIS YEAR'S CROP OF KYÔ DOLLS.
SLIDE

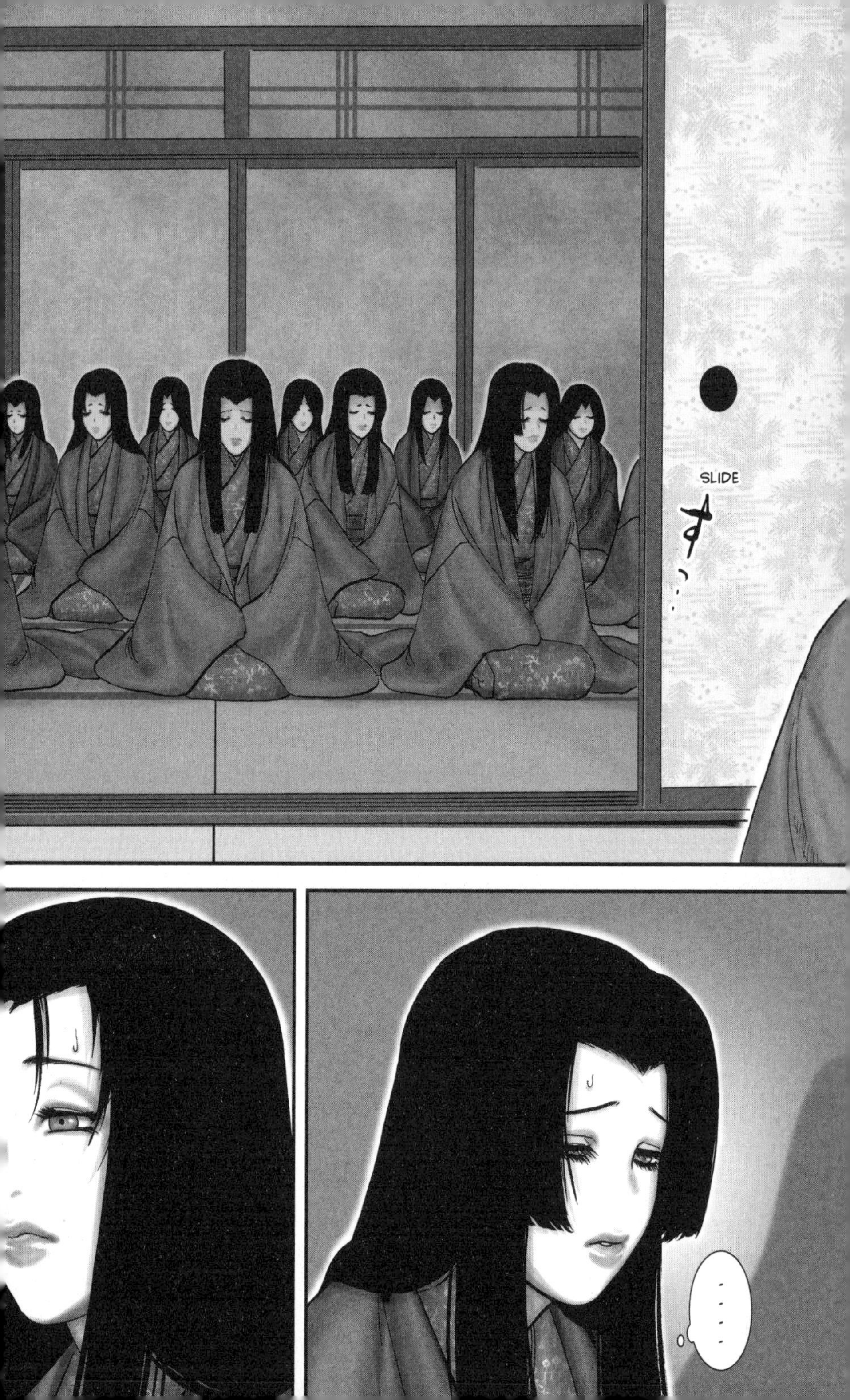
SLIDE
.....

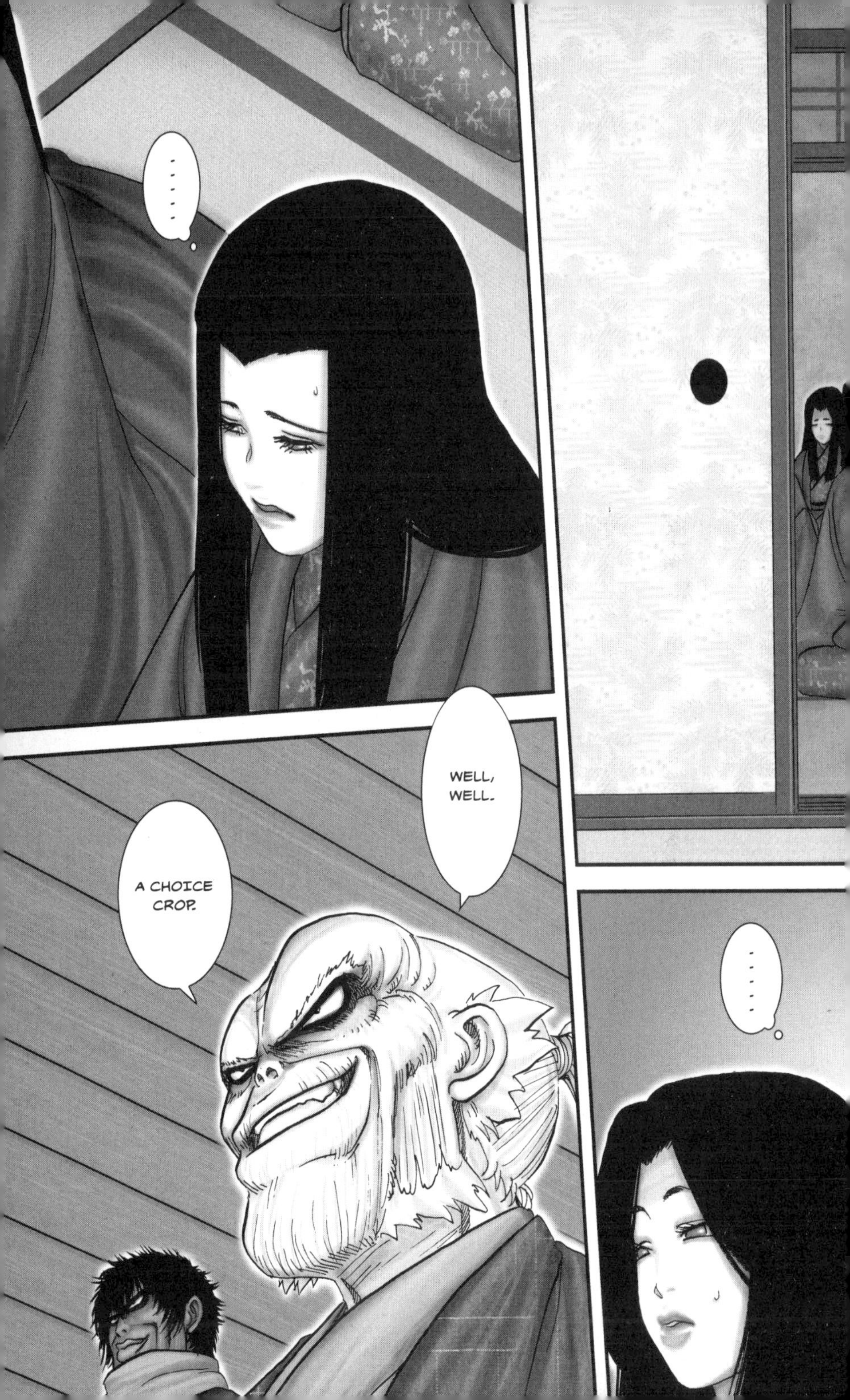
......
WELL, WELL.
A CHOICE CROP.
......

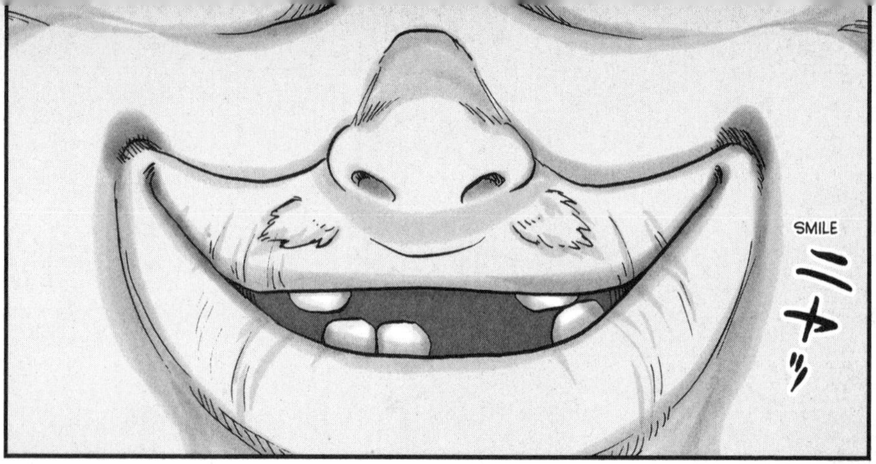
SMILE
ニヤッ

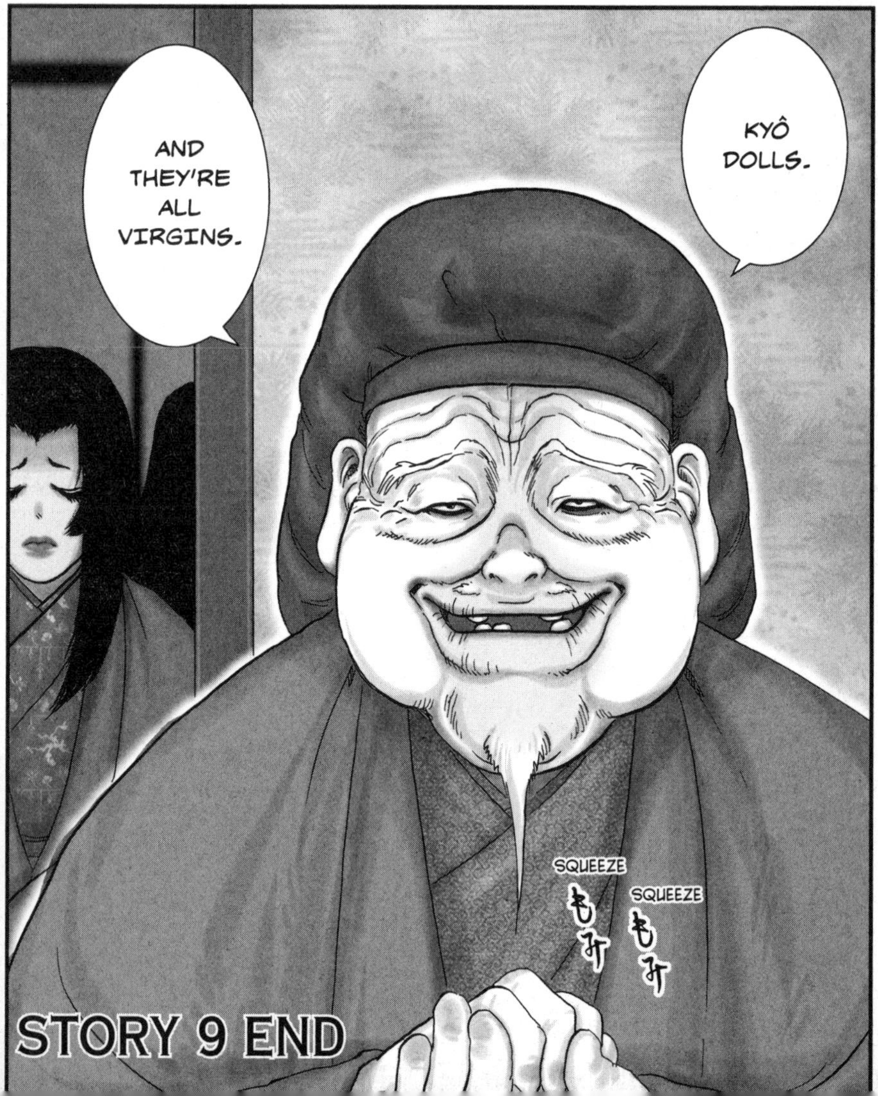
KYÔ DOLLS.
AND THEY'RE ALL VIRGINS.
SQUEEZE
もみ
SQUEEZE
もみ
STORY 9 END

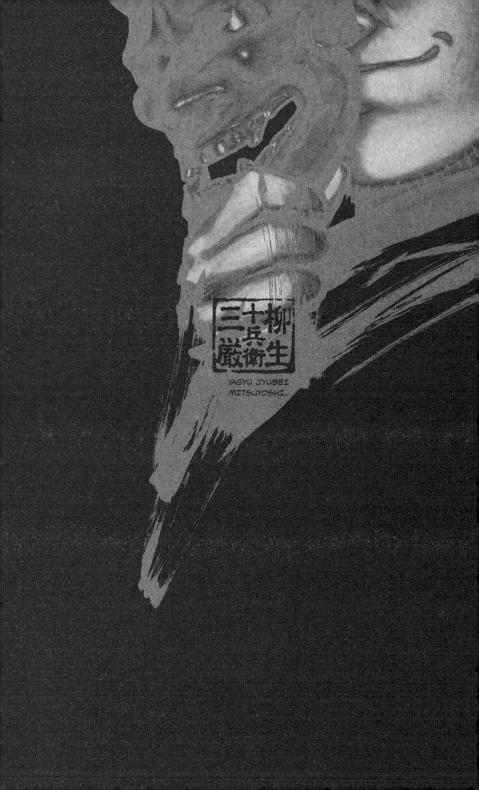

YAGYU JYUBEI
MITSUYOSHI.

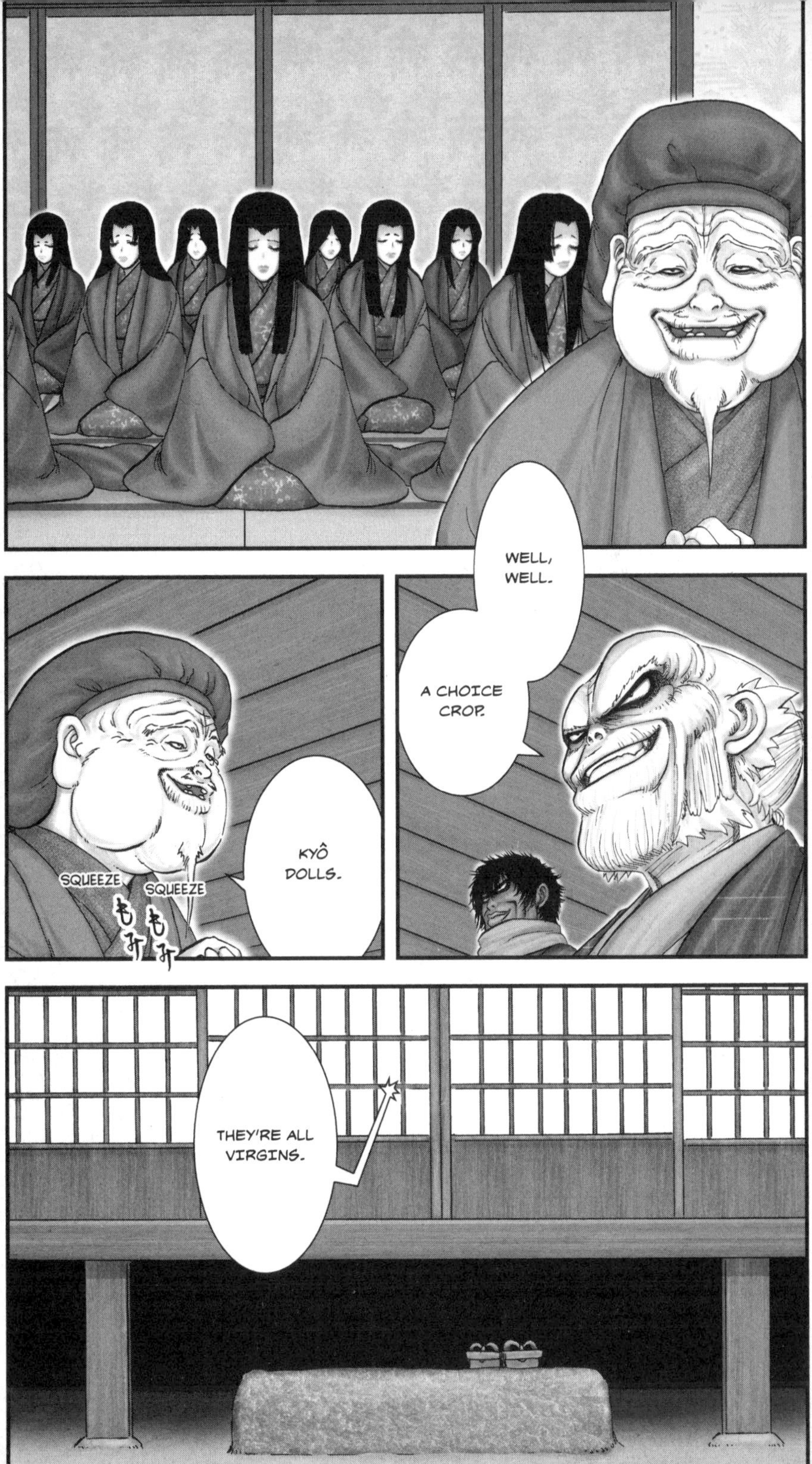

WELL, WELL.
A CHOICE CROP.
KYÔ DOLLS.
SQUEEZE
もみ
SQUEEZE
もみ
THEY'RE ALL VIRGINS.

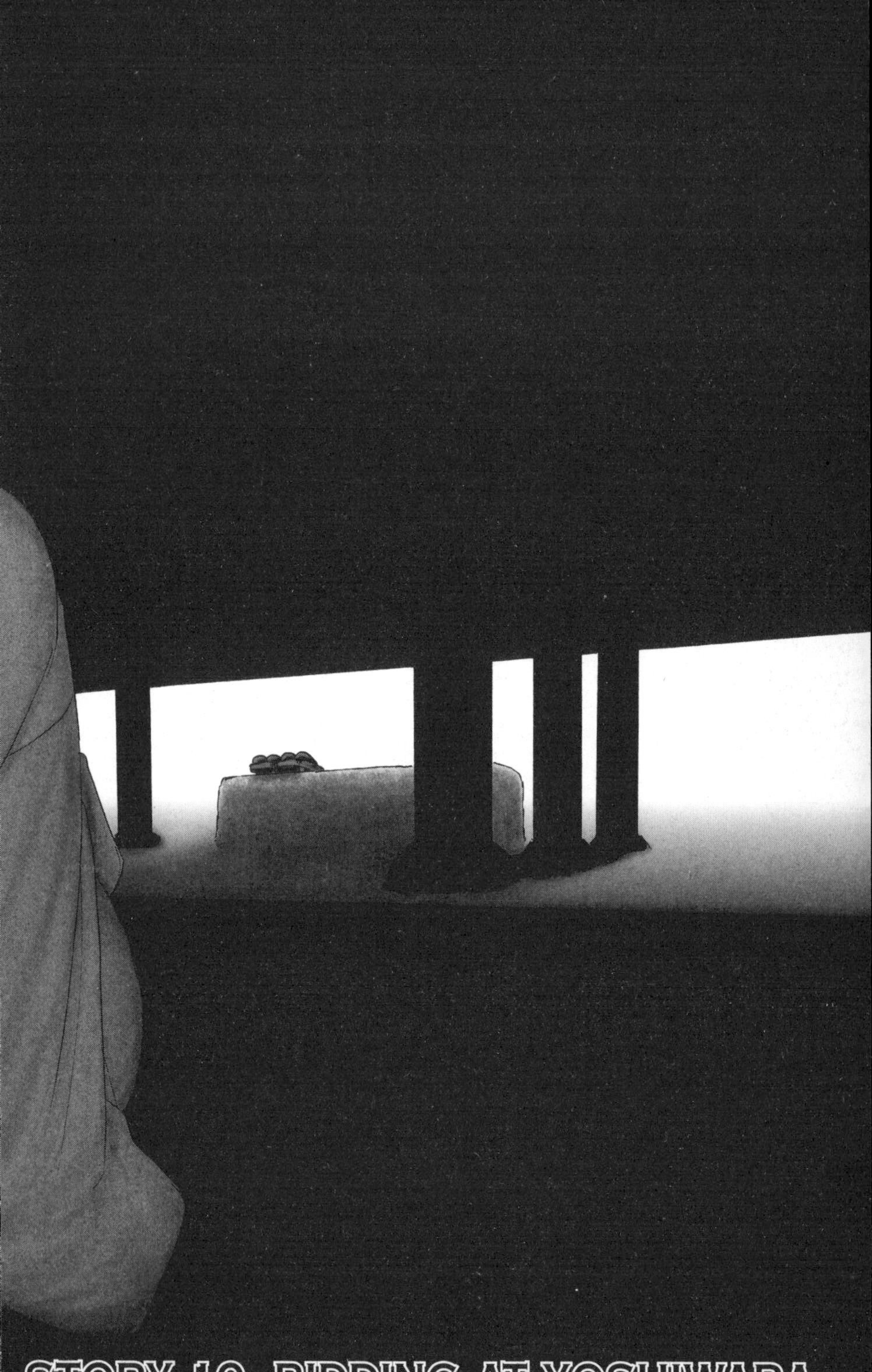

STORY 10: BIDDING AT YOSHIWARA

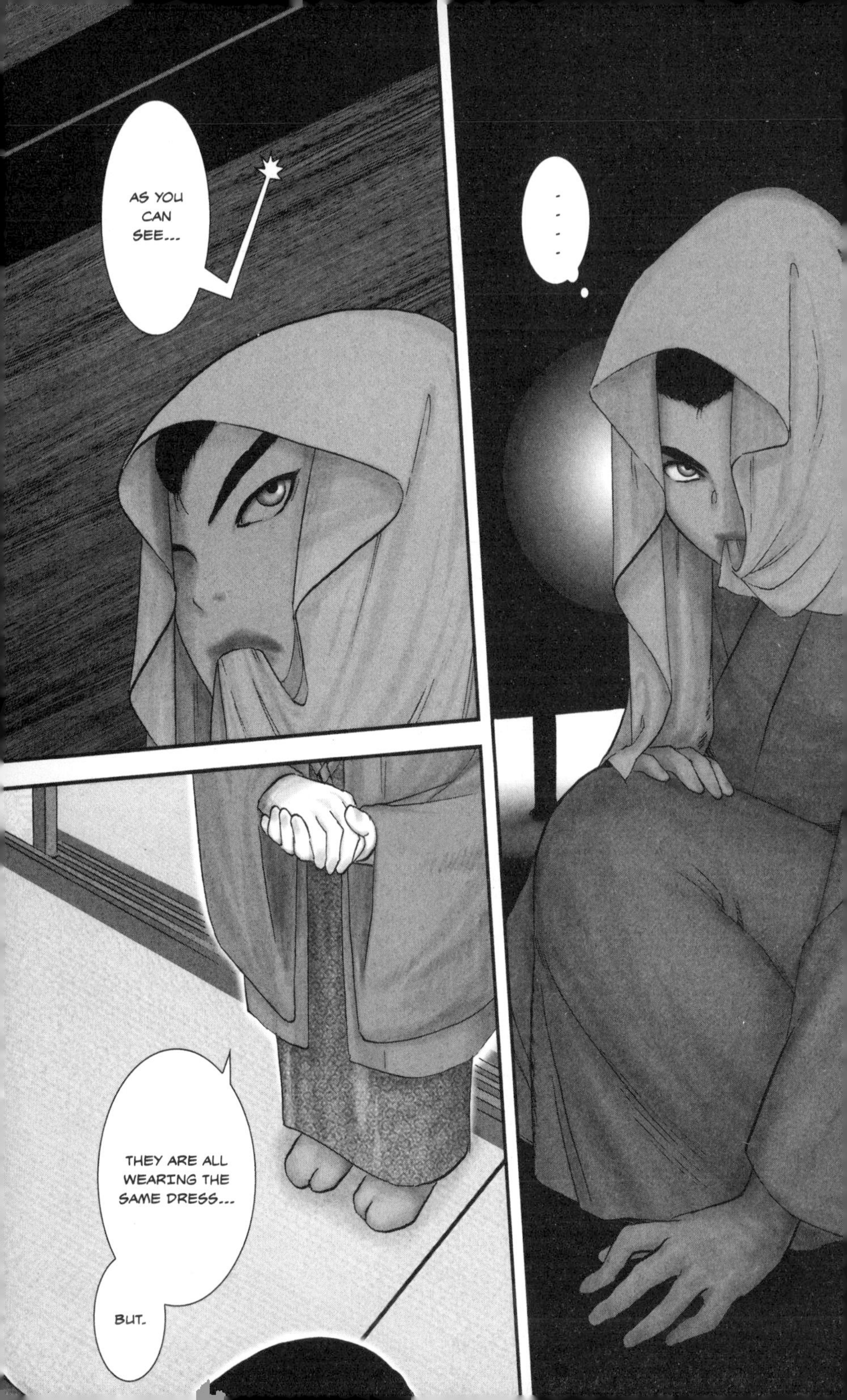
.....
AS YOU CAN SEE...
THEY ARE ALL WEARING THE SAME DRESS...
BUT.

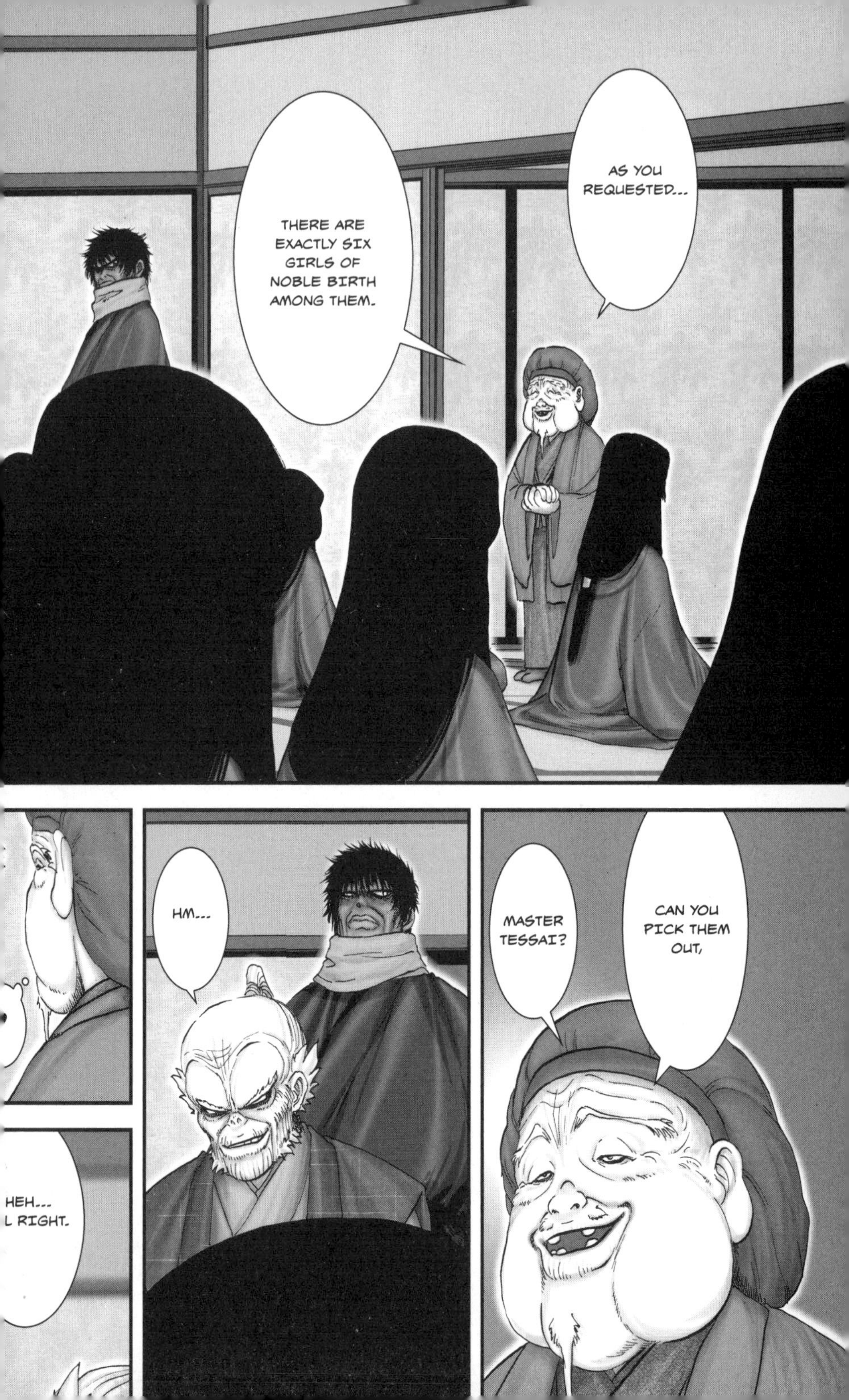
AS YOU REQUESTED...
THERE ARE EXACTLY SIX GIRLS OF NOBLE BIRTH AMONG THEM.
CAN YOU PICK THEM OUT,
MASTER TESSAI?
HM...
HEH...
L RIGHT.

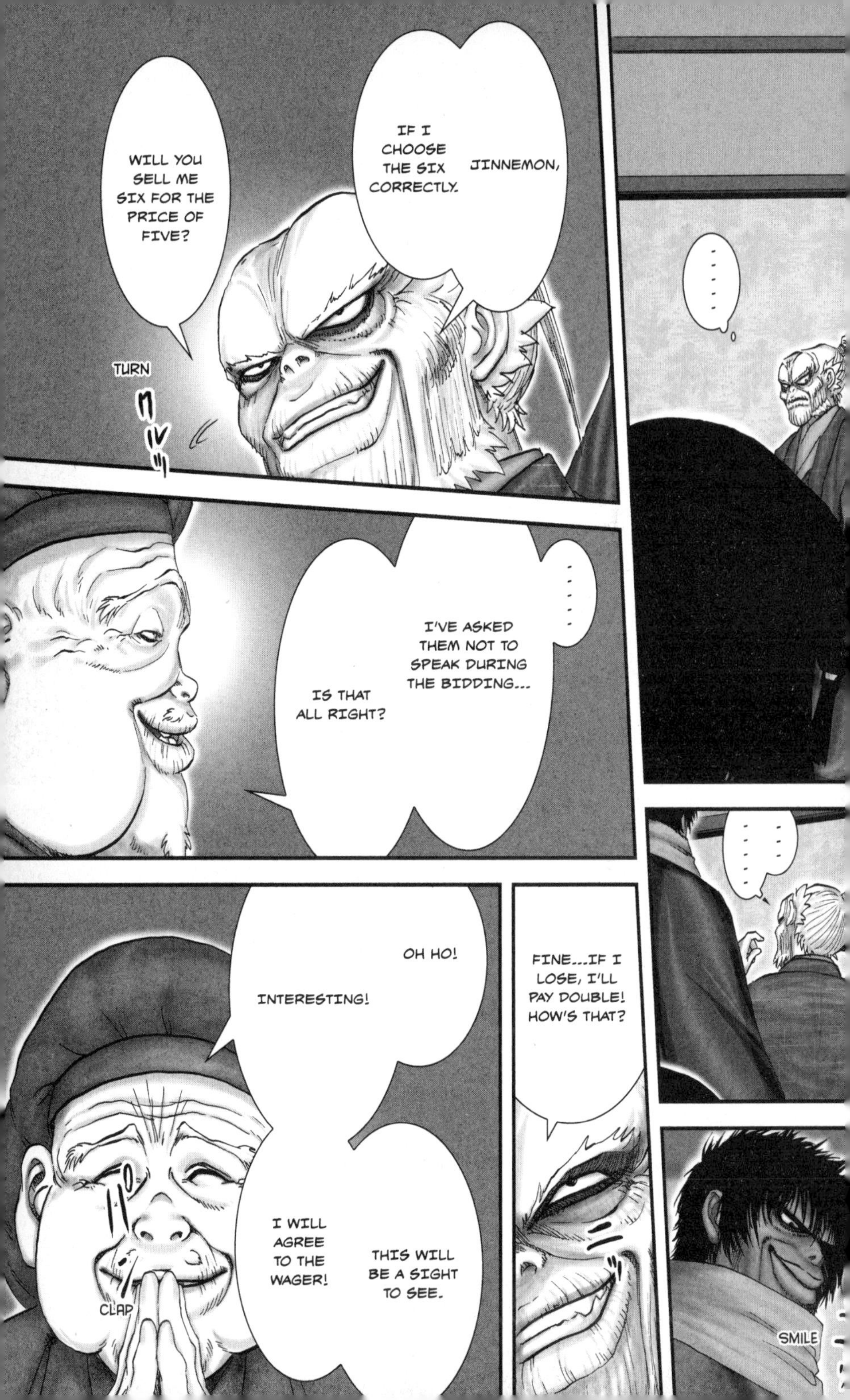
......
JINNEMON,
IF I CHOOSE THE SIX CORRECTLY.
WILL YOU SELL ME SIX FOR THE PRICE OF FIVE?
TURN
......
I'VE ASKED THEM NOT TO SPEAK DURING THE BIDDING...
IS THAT ALL RIGHT?
......
SMILE
FINE...IF I LOSE, I'LL PAY DOUBLE! HOW'S THAT?
OH HO!
INTERESTING!
THIS WILL BE A SIGHT TO SEE.
I WILL AGREE TO THE WAGER!
CLAP

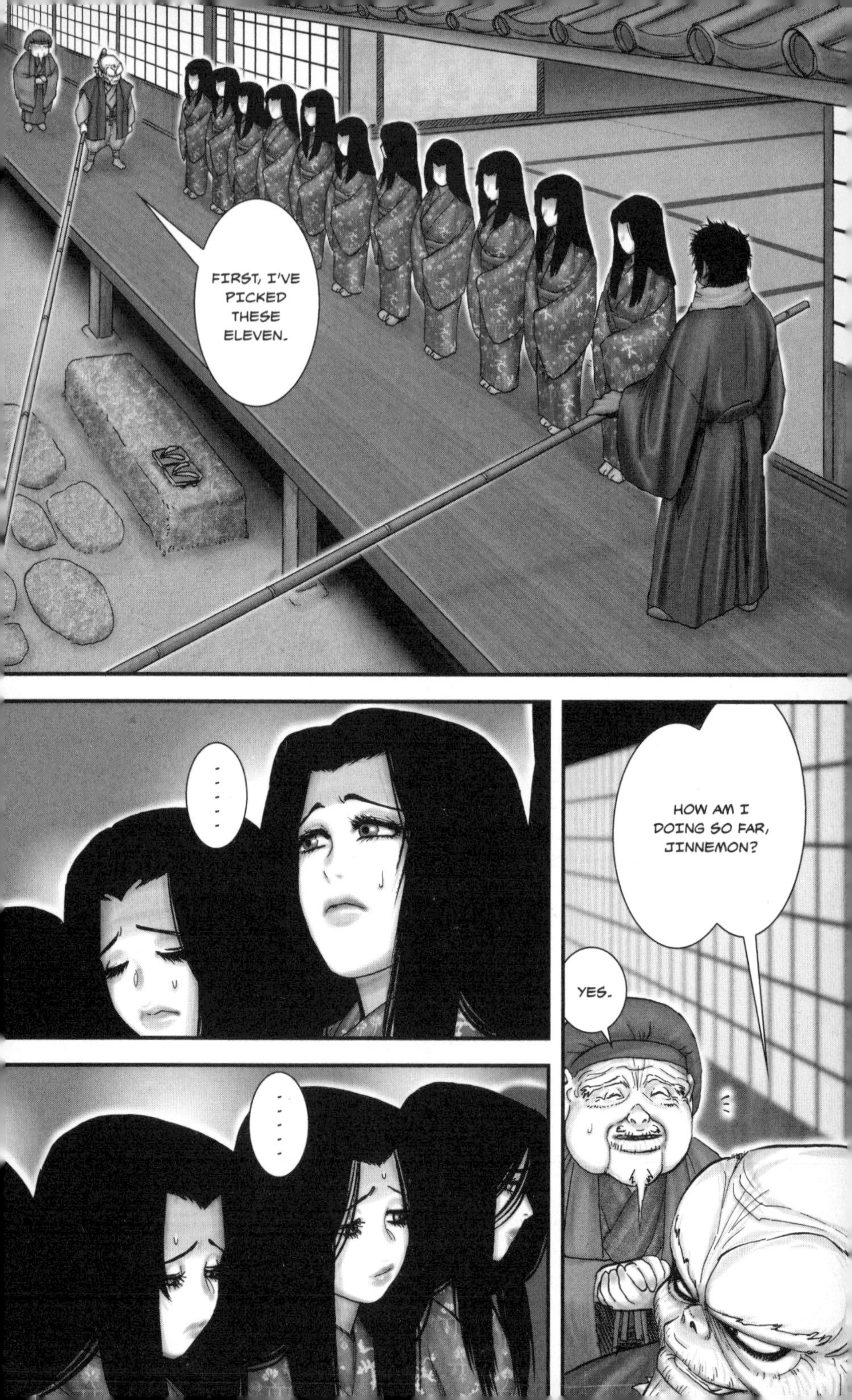
FIRST, I'VE PICKED THESE ELEVEN.
HOW AM I DOING SO FAR, JINNEMON?
YES.
......
......

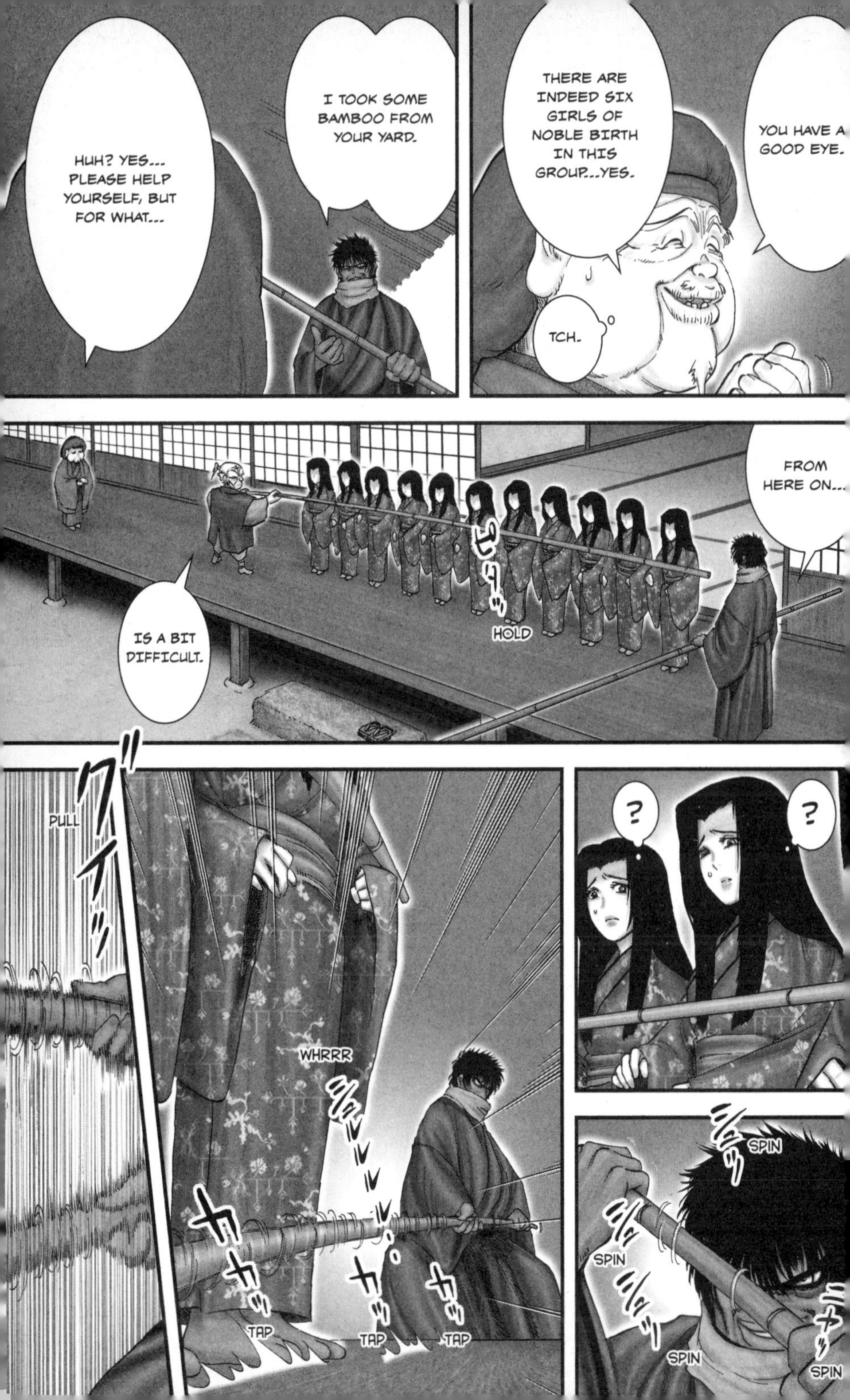
YOU HAVE A GOOD EYE.
THERE ARE INDEED SIX GIRLS OF NOBLE BIRTH IN THIS GROUP...YES.
TCH.
I TOOK SOME BAMBOO FROM YOUR YARD.
HUH? YES... PLEASE HELP YOURSELF, BUT FOR WHAT...
FROM HERE ON...
HOLD
IS A BIT DIFFICULT.
?
?
SPIN
SPIN
SPIN
SPIN
PULL
WHRRR
TAP
TAP
TAP

FLIP

?....

HEE.

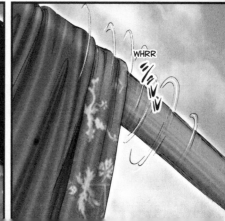

WHRR

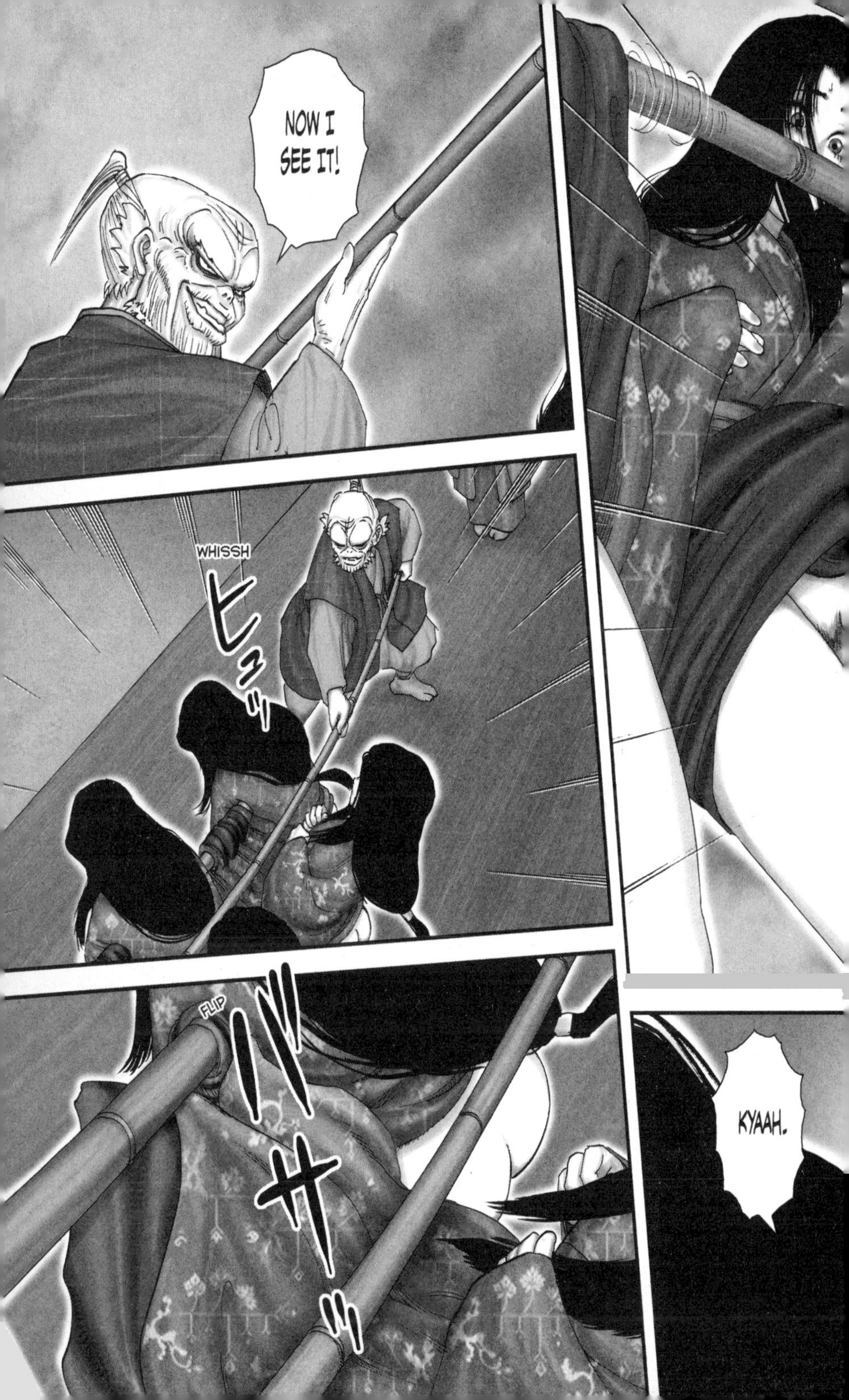
NOW I SEE IT!
WHISSH
ヒュッ
KYAAH.
FLIP
バサッ

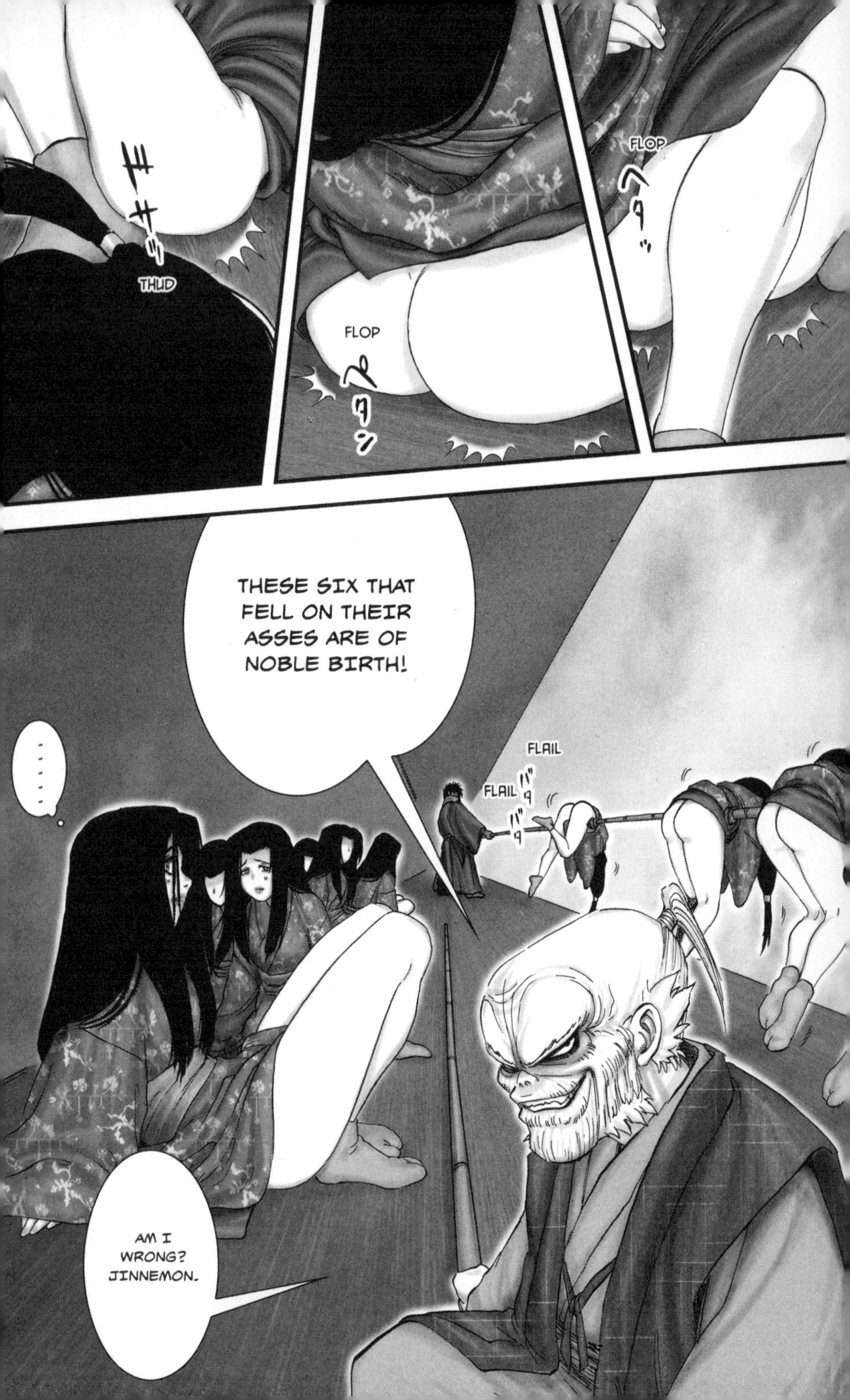
FLOP
FLOP
THUD
THESE SIX THAT FELL ON THEIR ASSES ARE OF NOBLE BIRTH!
FLAIL
FLAIL
......
AM I WRONG? JINNEMON.

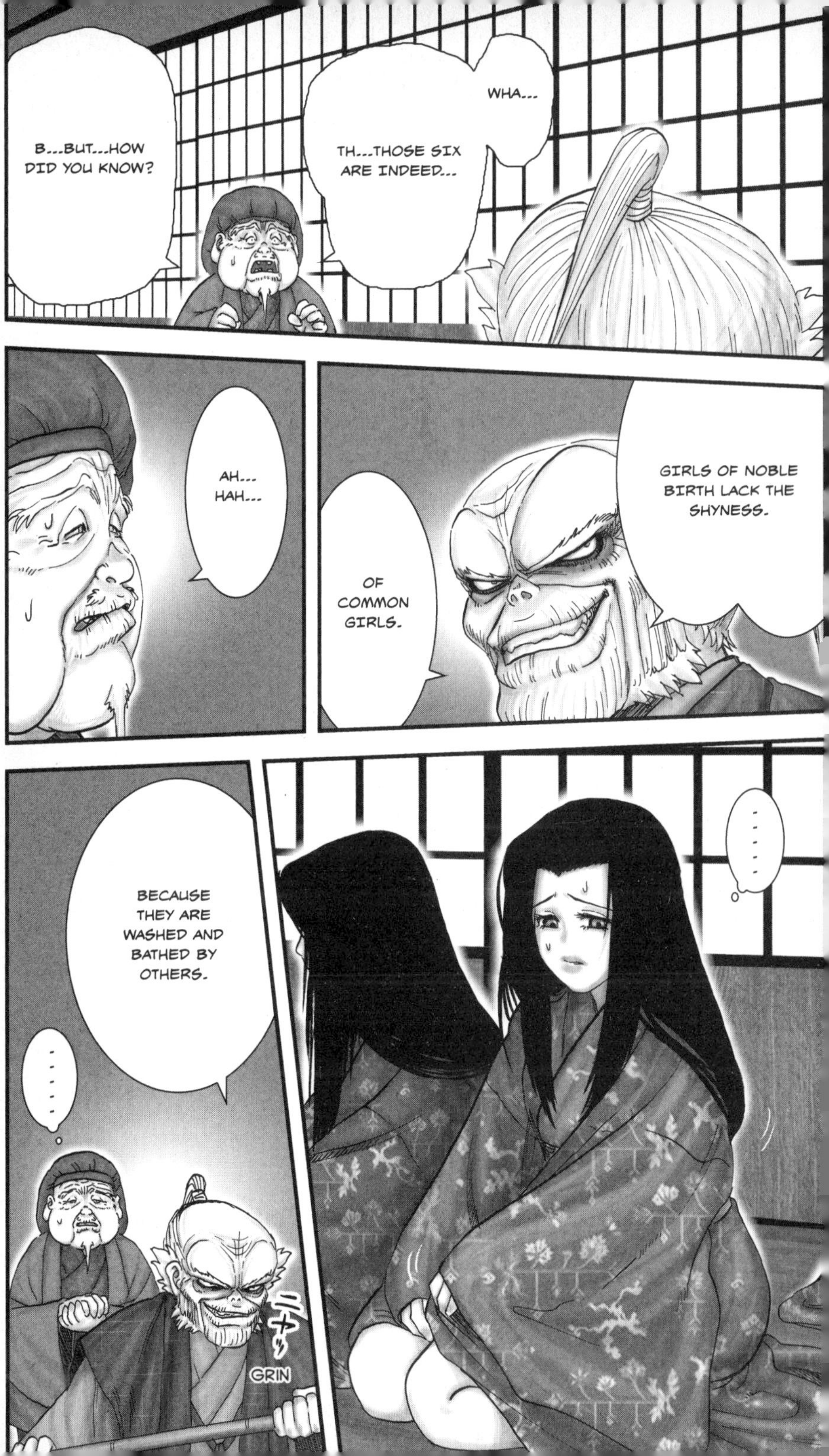
WHA...
TH...THOSE SIX ARE INDEED...
B...BUT...HOW DID YOU KNOW?
GIRLS OF NOBLE BIRTH LACK THE SHYNESS.
OF COMMON GIRLS.
AH... HAH...
......
BECAUSE THEY ARE WASHED AND BATHED BY OTHERS.
......
ニヤッ
GRIN

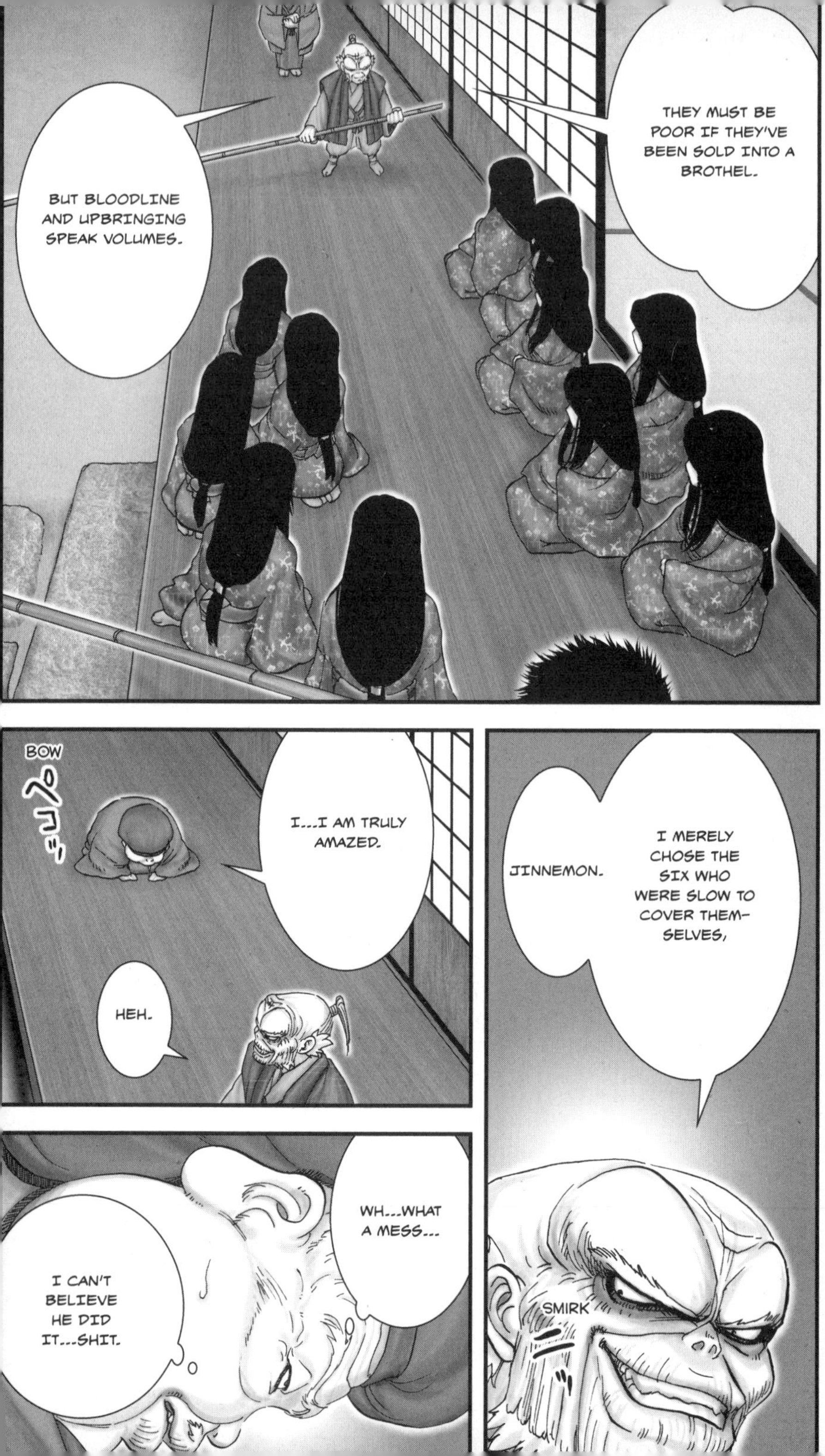
THEY MUST BE POOR IF THEY'VE BEEN SOLD INTO A BROTHEL.
BUT BLOODLINE AND UPBRINGING SPEAK VOLUMES.
I MERELY CHOSE THE SIX WHO WERE SLOW TO COVER THEM-SELVES,
JINNEMON.
SMIRK
BOW
I...I AM TRULY AMAZED.
HEH.
WH...WHAT A MESS...
I CAN'T BELIEVE HE DID IT...SHIT.

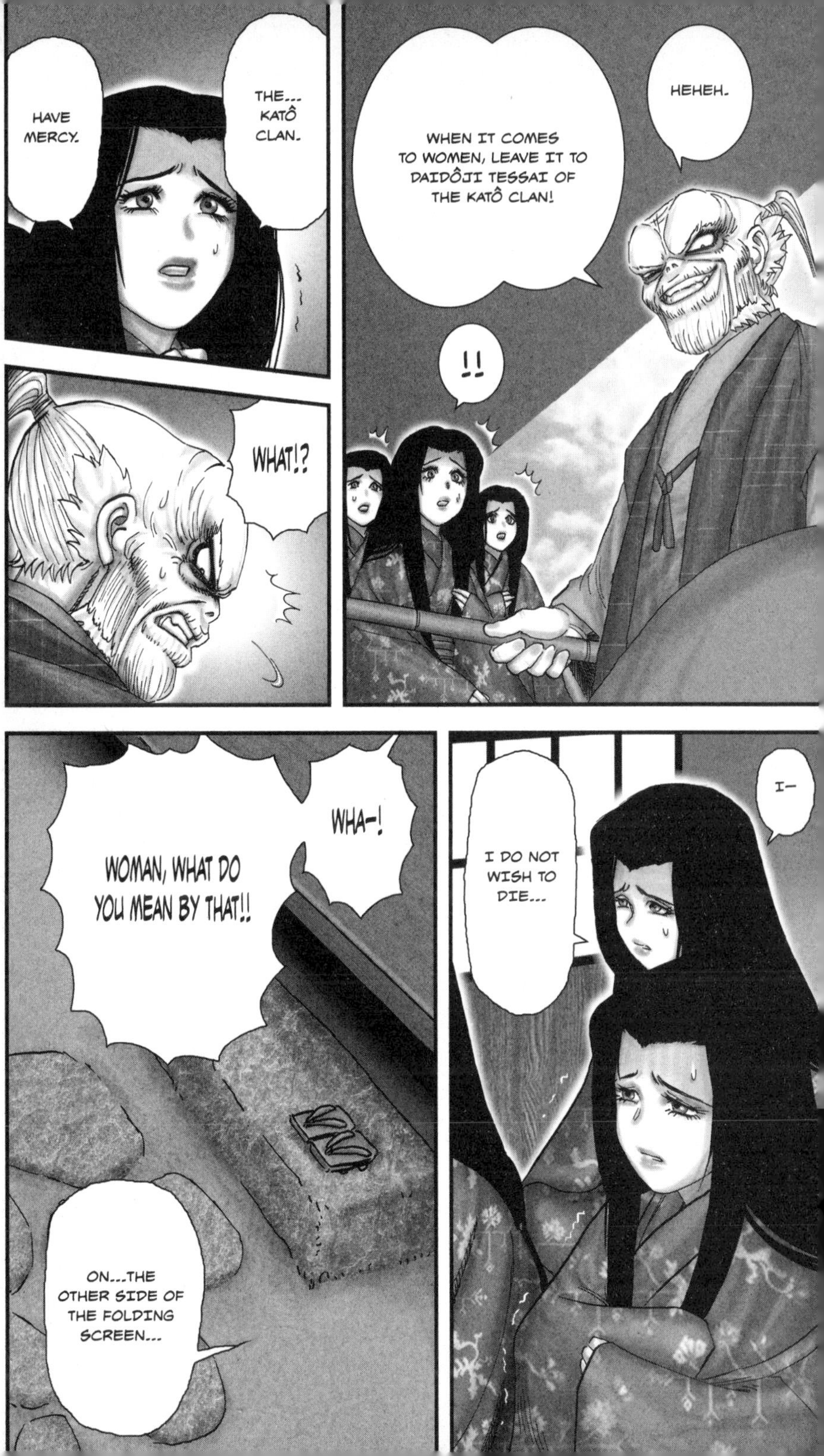
HEHEH.
WHEN IT COMES TO WOMEN, LEAVE IT TO DAIDÔJI TESSAI OF THE KATÔ CLAN!
!!
THE... KATÔ CLAN.
HAVE MERCY.
WHAT!?
I—
I DO NOT WISH TO DIE...
WHA-!
WOMAN, WHAT DO YOU MEAN BY THAT!!
ON...THE OTHER SIDE OF THE FOLDING SCREEN...

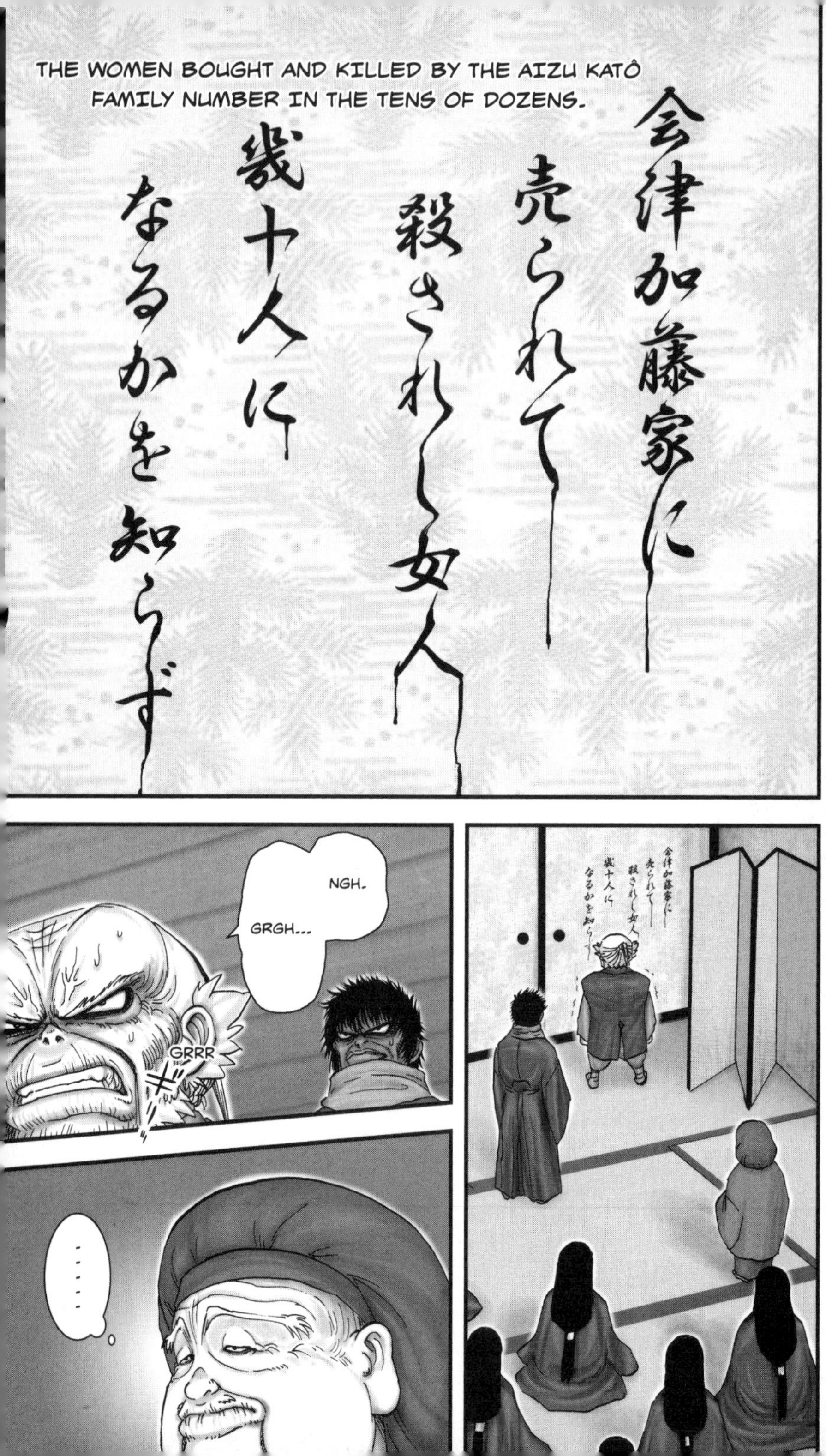

THE WOMEN BOUGHT AND KILLED BY THE AIZU KATÔ FAMILY NUMBER IN THE TENS OF DOZENS.
会津加藤家に
売られて
殺されし女人
幾十人に
なるかを知らず
NGH.
GRGH...
GRRR
......

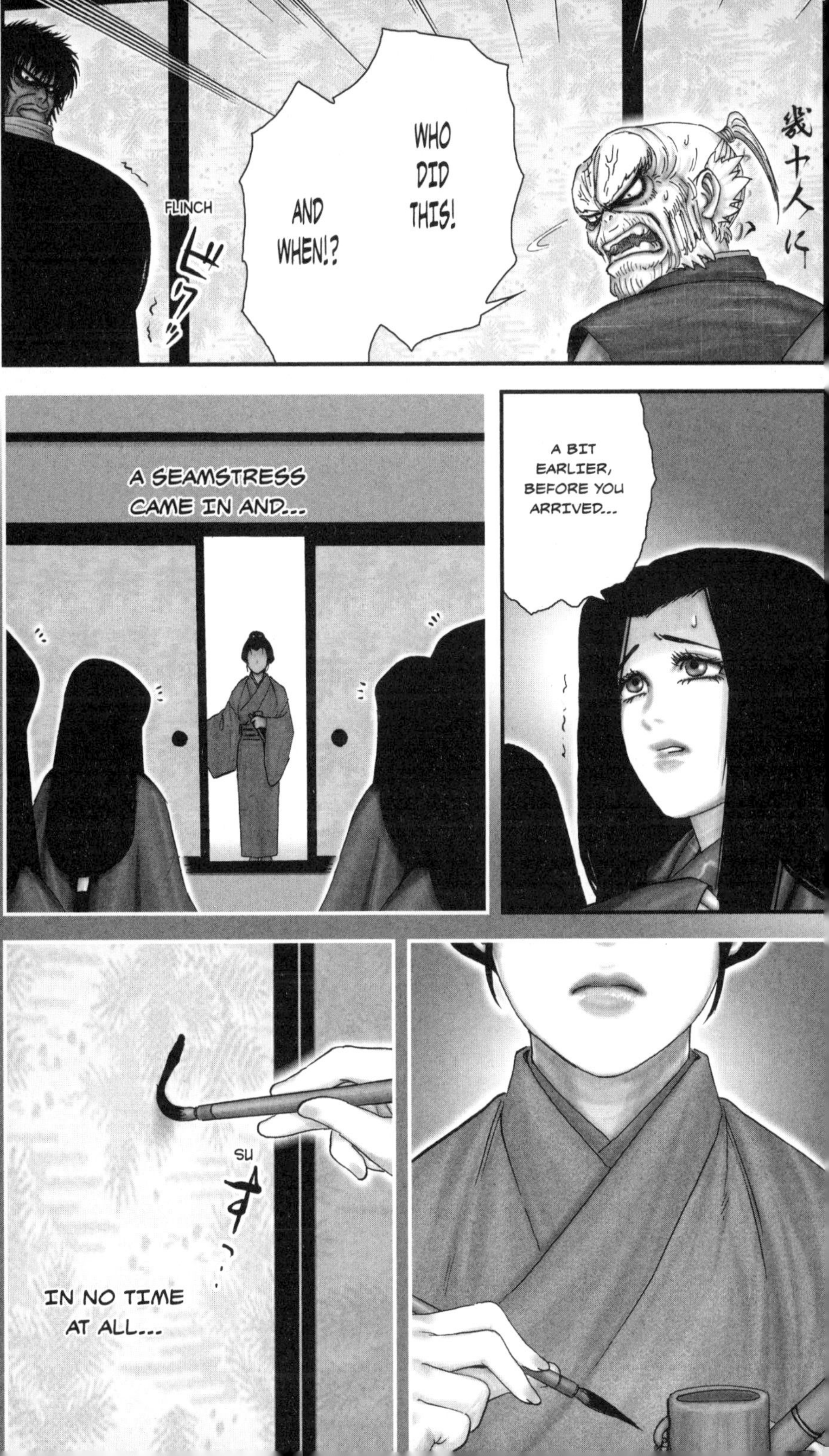
幾十人に
WHO DID THIS!
AND WHEN!?
FLINCH
A BIT EARLIER, BEFORE YOU ARRIVED...
A SEAMSTRESS CAME IN AND...
SU
IN NO TIME AT ALL...

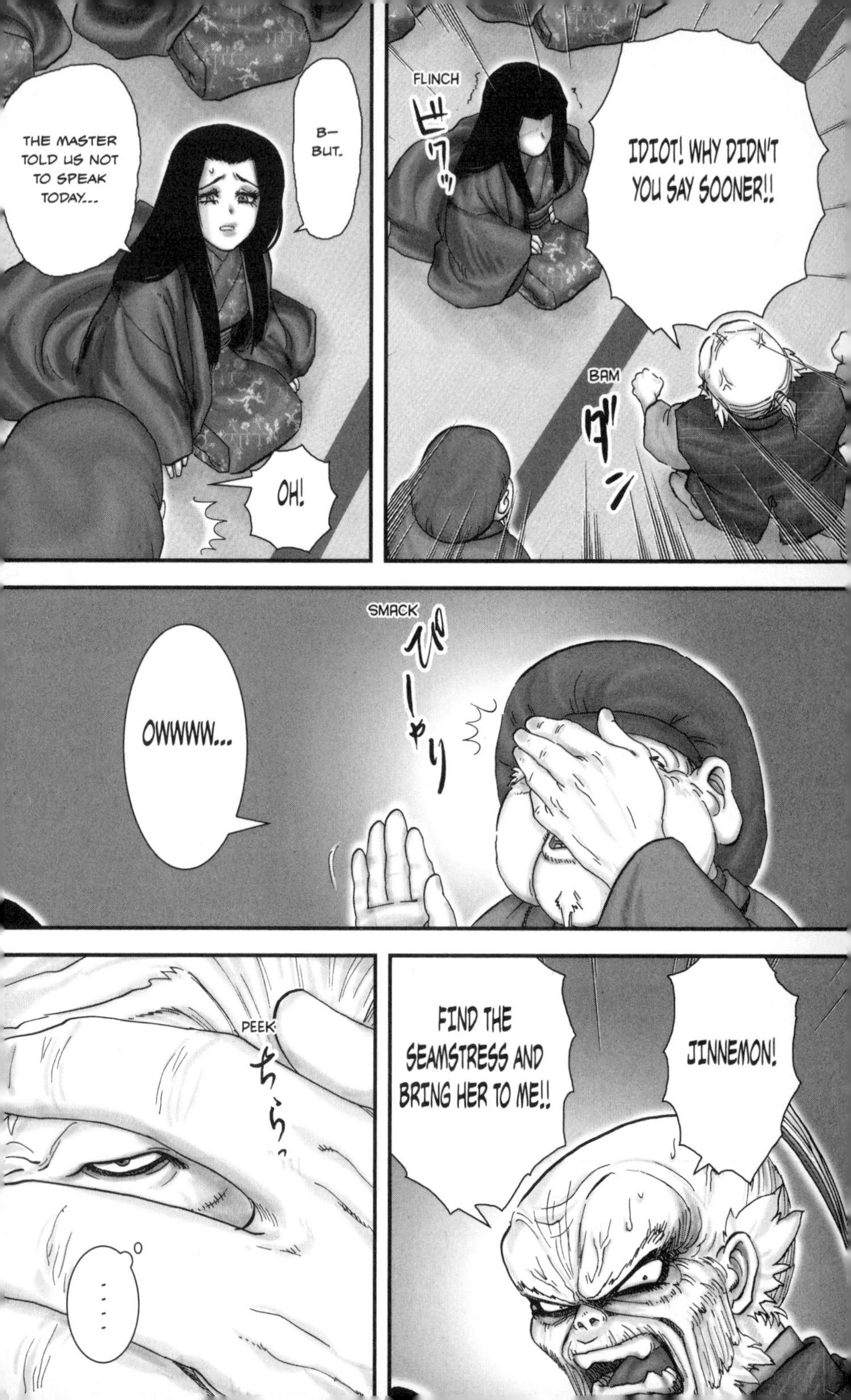
FLINCH
IDIOT! WHY DIDN'T YOU SAY SOONER!!
BAM
B— BUT.
THE MASTER TOLD US NOT TO SPEAK TODAY...
OH!
SMACK
OWWWW...
JINNEMON!
FIND THE SEAMSTRESS AND BRING HER TO ME!!
PEEK
....

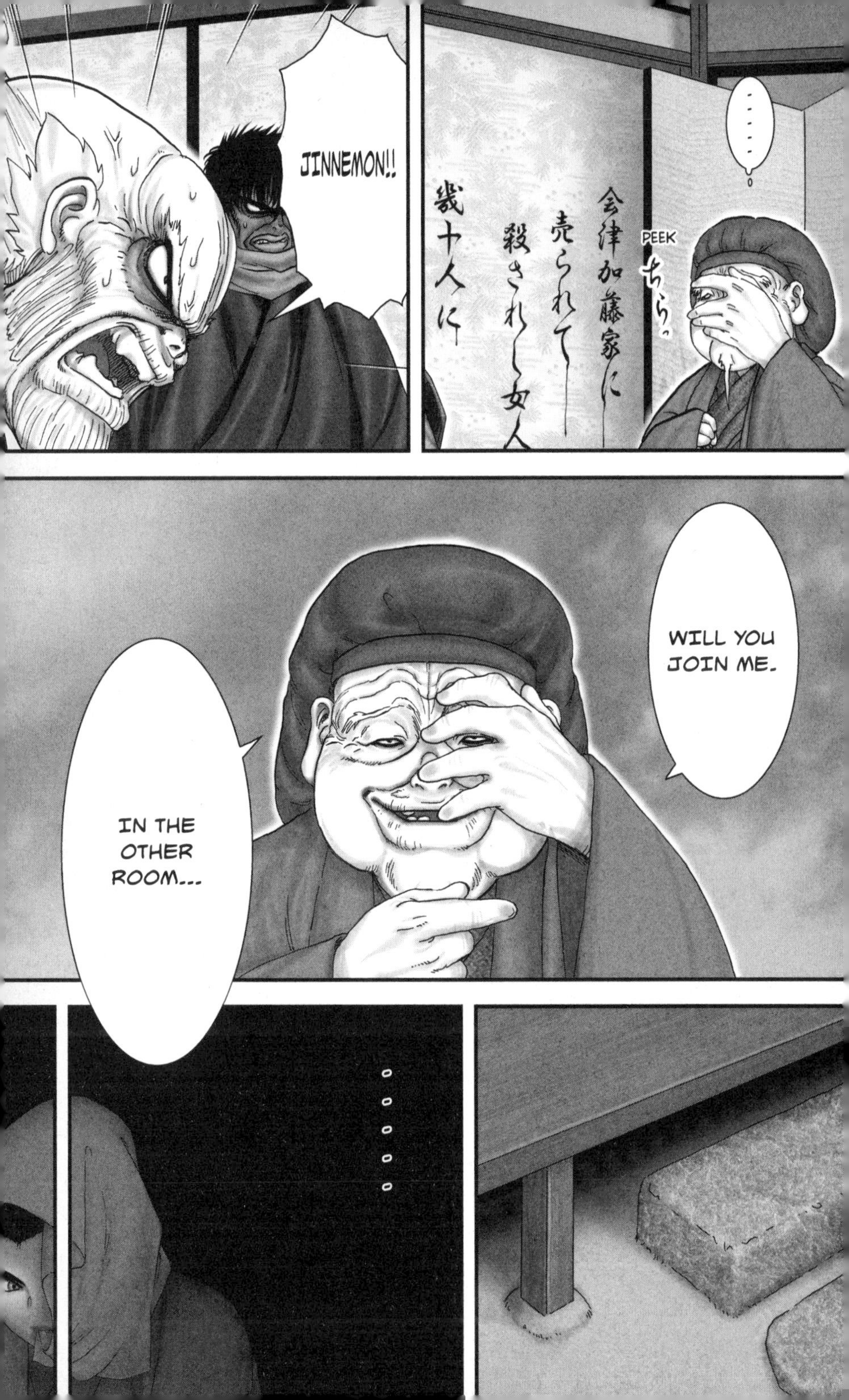
......
PEEK
ちら。
会津加藤家に
売られて
殺されし女人
幾十人に
JINNEMON!!
WILL YOU JOIN ME.
IN THE OTHER ROOM...

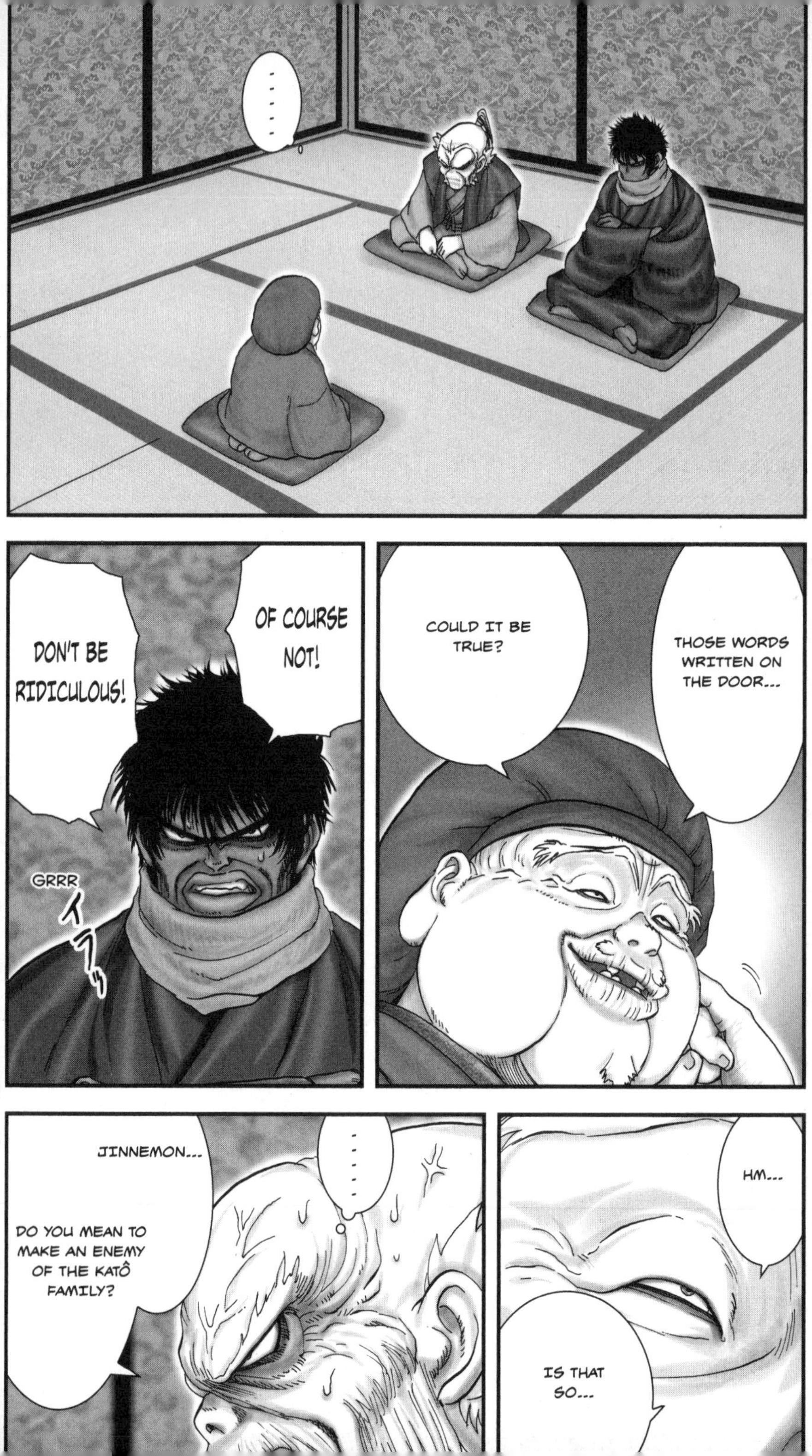
......
THOSE WORDS WRITTEN ON THE DOOR...
COULD IT BE TRUE?
OF COURSE NOT!
DON'T BE RIDICULOUS!
GRRR
イラッ
HM...
IS THAT SO...
......
JINNEMON...
DO YOU MEAN TO MAKE AN ENEMY OF THE KATÔ FAMILY?

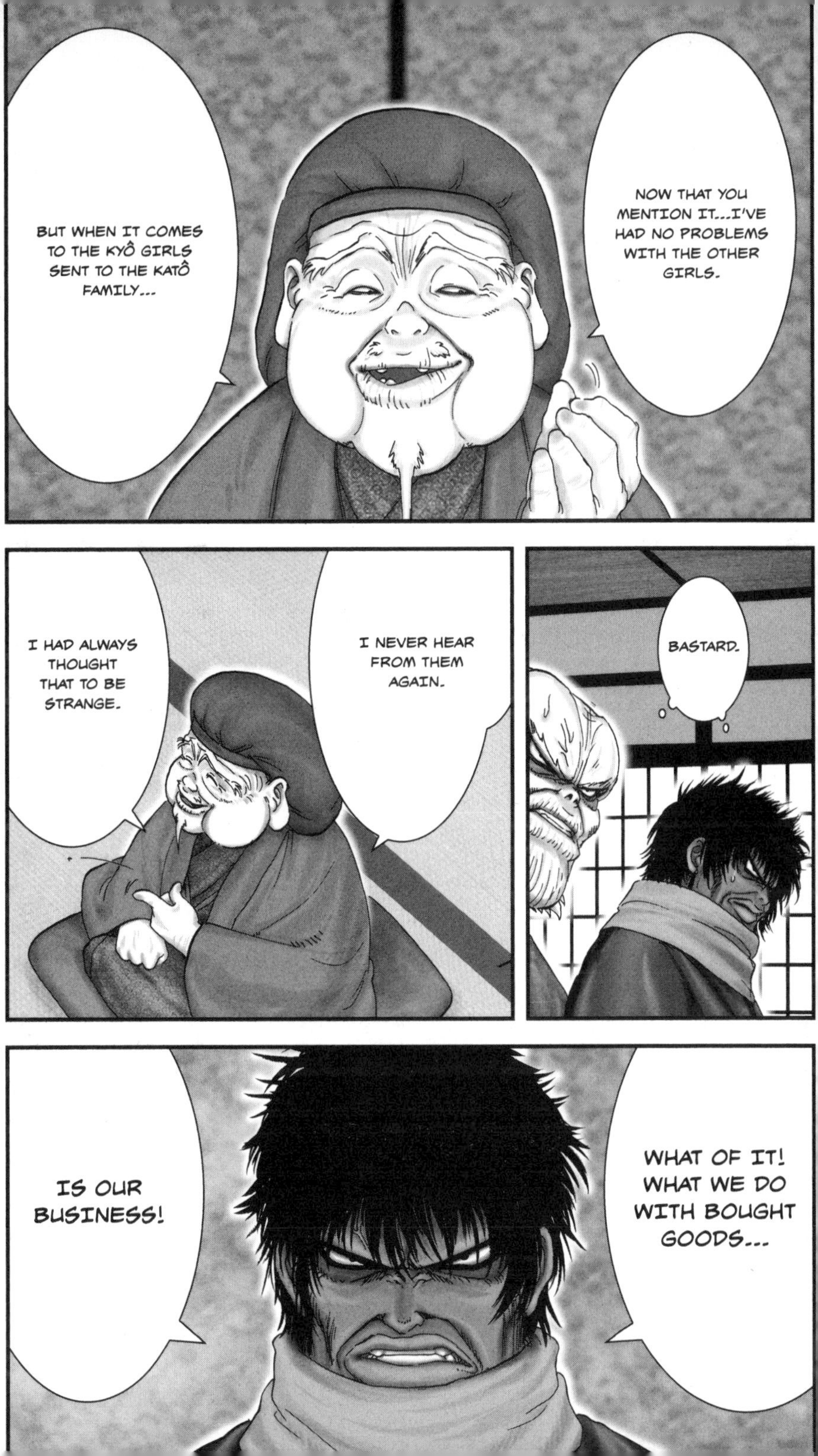
NOW THAT YOU MENTION IT...I'VE HAD NO PROBLEMS WITH THE OTHER GIRLS.
BUT WHEN IT COMES TO THE KYÔ GIRLS SENT TO THE KATÔ FAMILY...
BASTARD.
I NEVER HEAR FROM THEM AGAIN.
I HAD ALWAYS THOUGHT THAT TO BE STRANGE.
WHAT OF IT! WHAT WE DO WITH BOUGHT GOODS...
IS OUR BUSINESS!

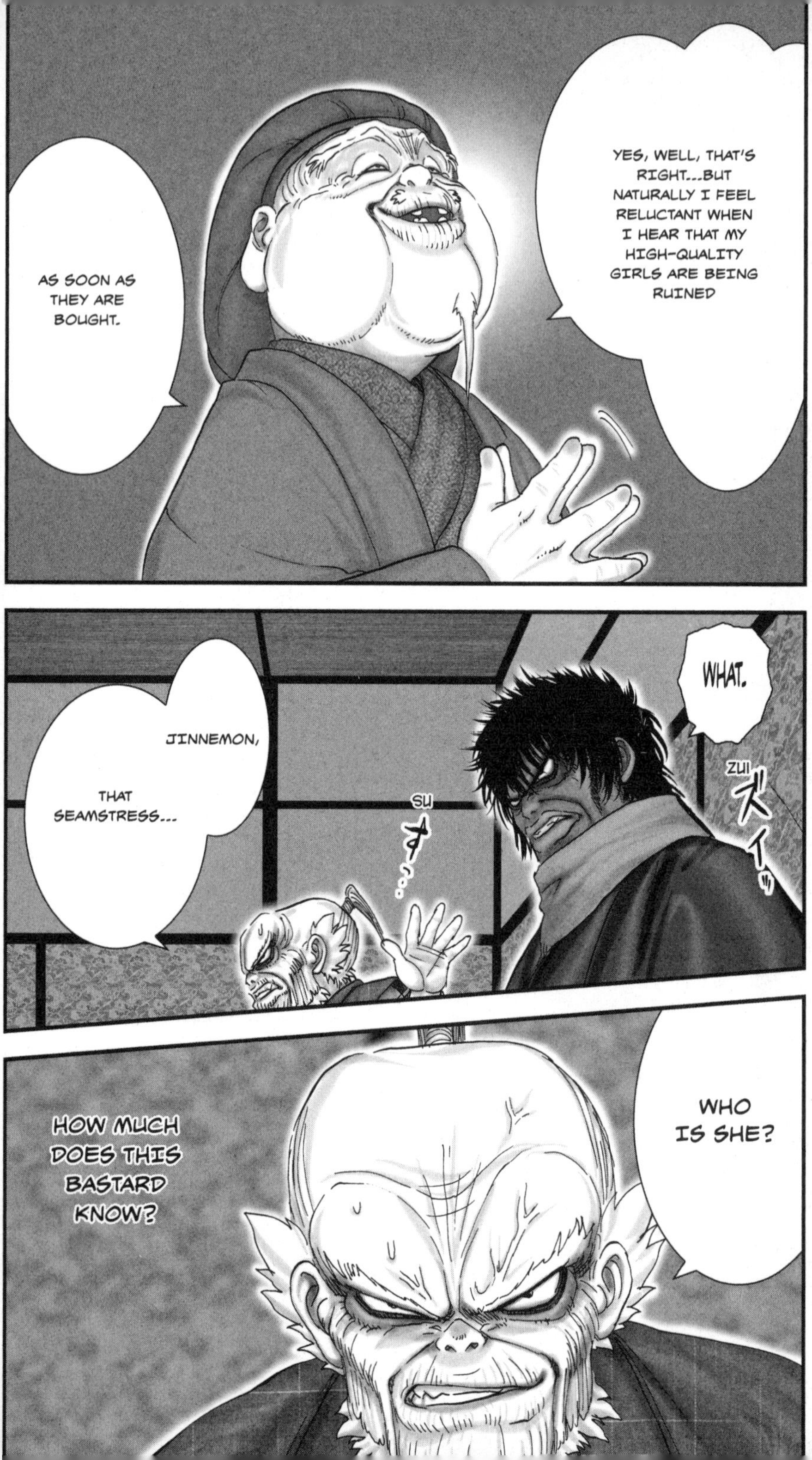
YES, WELL, THAT'S RIGHT...BUT NATURALLY I FEEL RELUCTANT WHEN I HEAR THAT MY HIGH-QUALITY GIRLS ARE BEING RUINED
AS SOON AS THEY ARE BOUGHT.
WHAT.
ZUI
SU
JINNEMON,
THAT SEAMSTRESS...
WHO IS SHE?
HOW MUCH DOES THIS BASTARD KNOW?

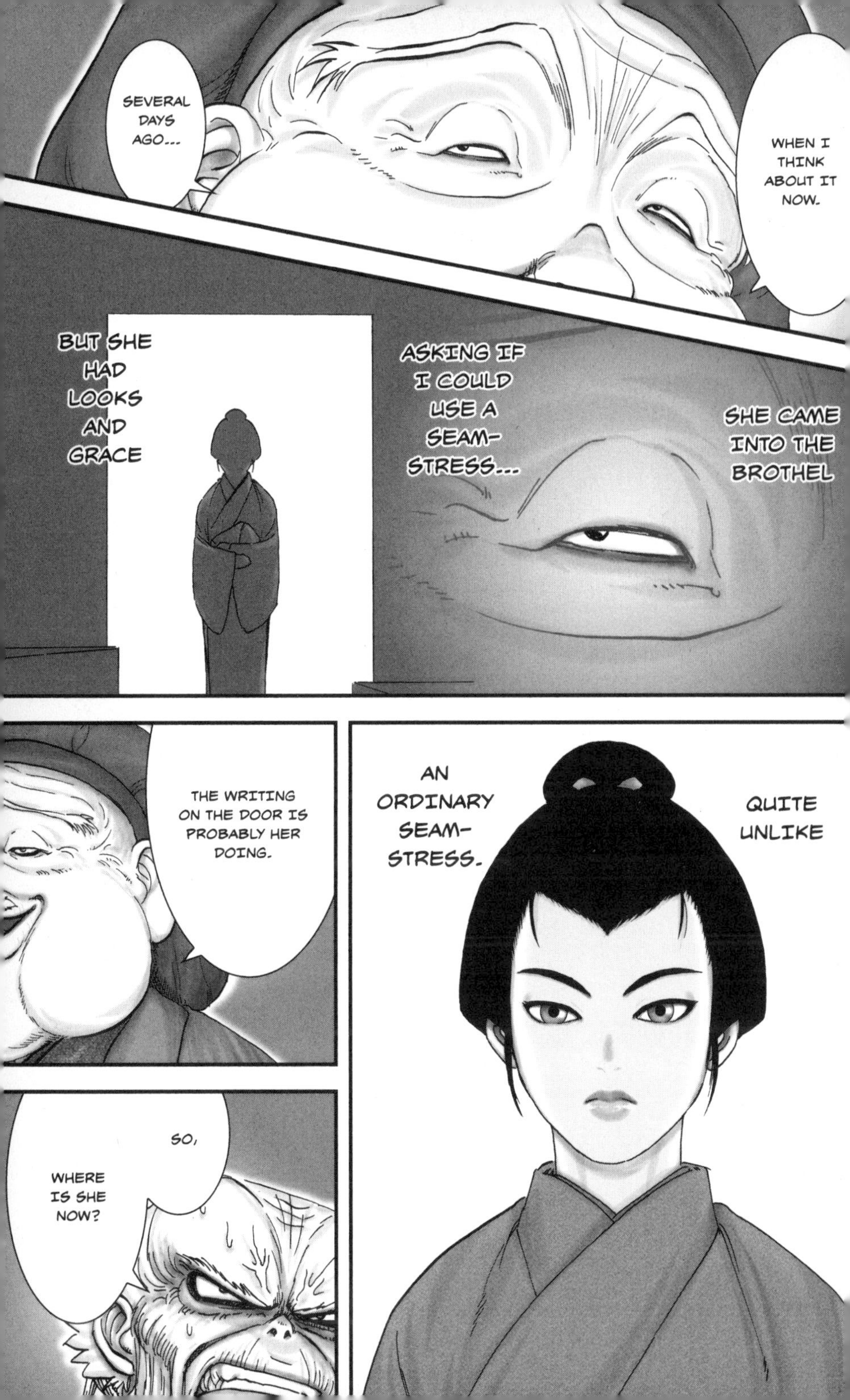

WHEN I THINK ABOUT IT NOW.
SEVERAL DAYS AGO...
SHE CAME INTO THE BROTHEL
ASKING IF I COULD USE A SEAM-STRESS...
BUT SHE HAD LOOKS AND GRACE
QUITE UNLIKE
AN ORDINARY SEAM-STRESS.
THE WRITING ON THE DOOR IS PROBABLY HER DOING.
SO,
WHERE IS SHE NOW?

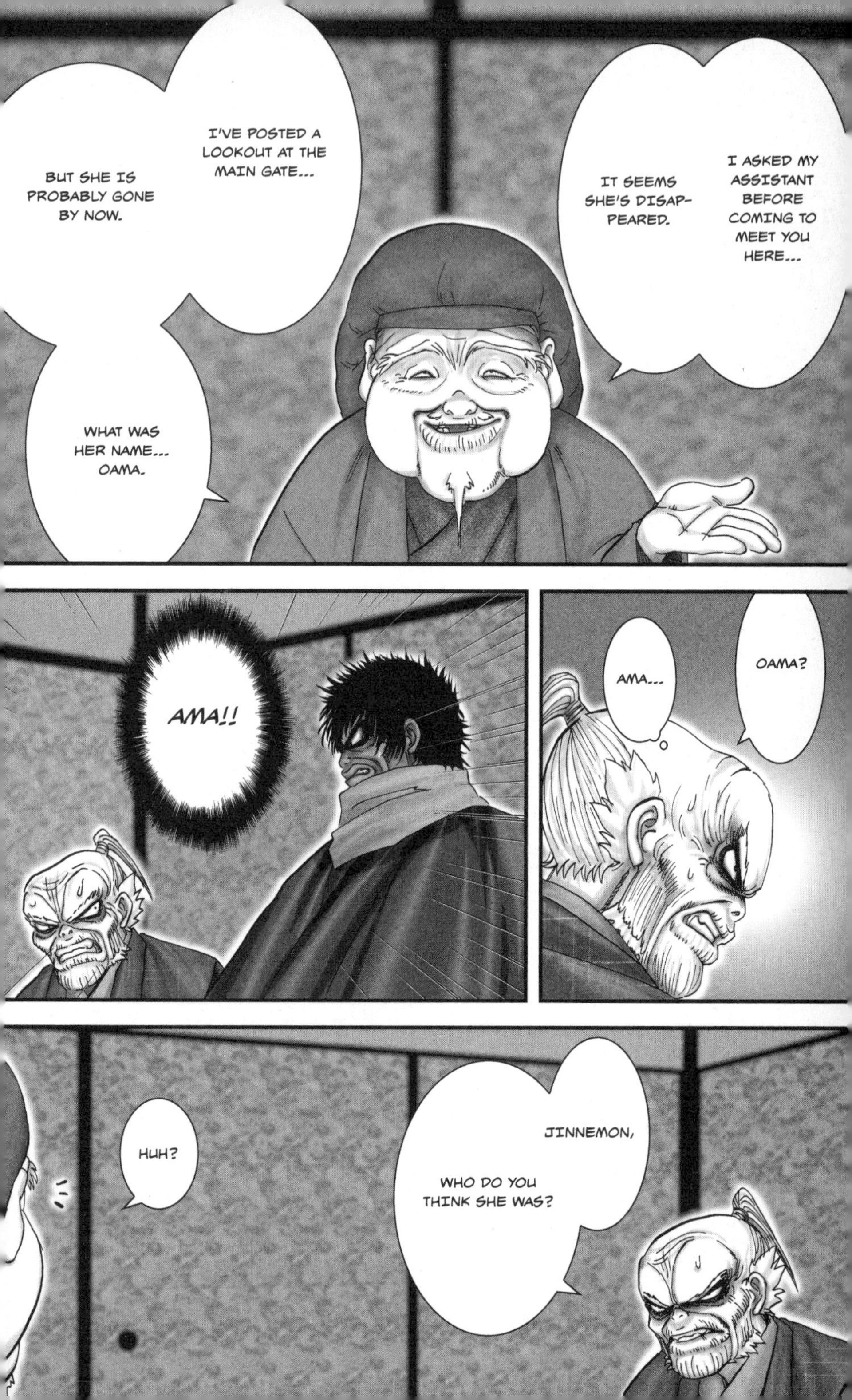
I ASKED MY ASSISTANT BEFORE COMING TO MEET YOU HERE...
IT SEEMS SHE'S DISAP-PEARED.
I'VE POSTED A LOOKOUT AT THE MAIN GATE...
BUT SHE IS PROBABLY GONE BY NOW.
WHAT WAS HER NAME... OAMA.
OAMA?
AMA...
AMA!!
JINNEMON,
WHO DO YOU THINK SHE WAS?
HUH?

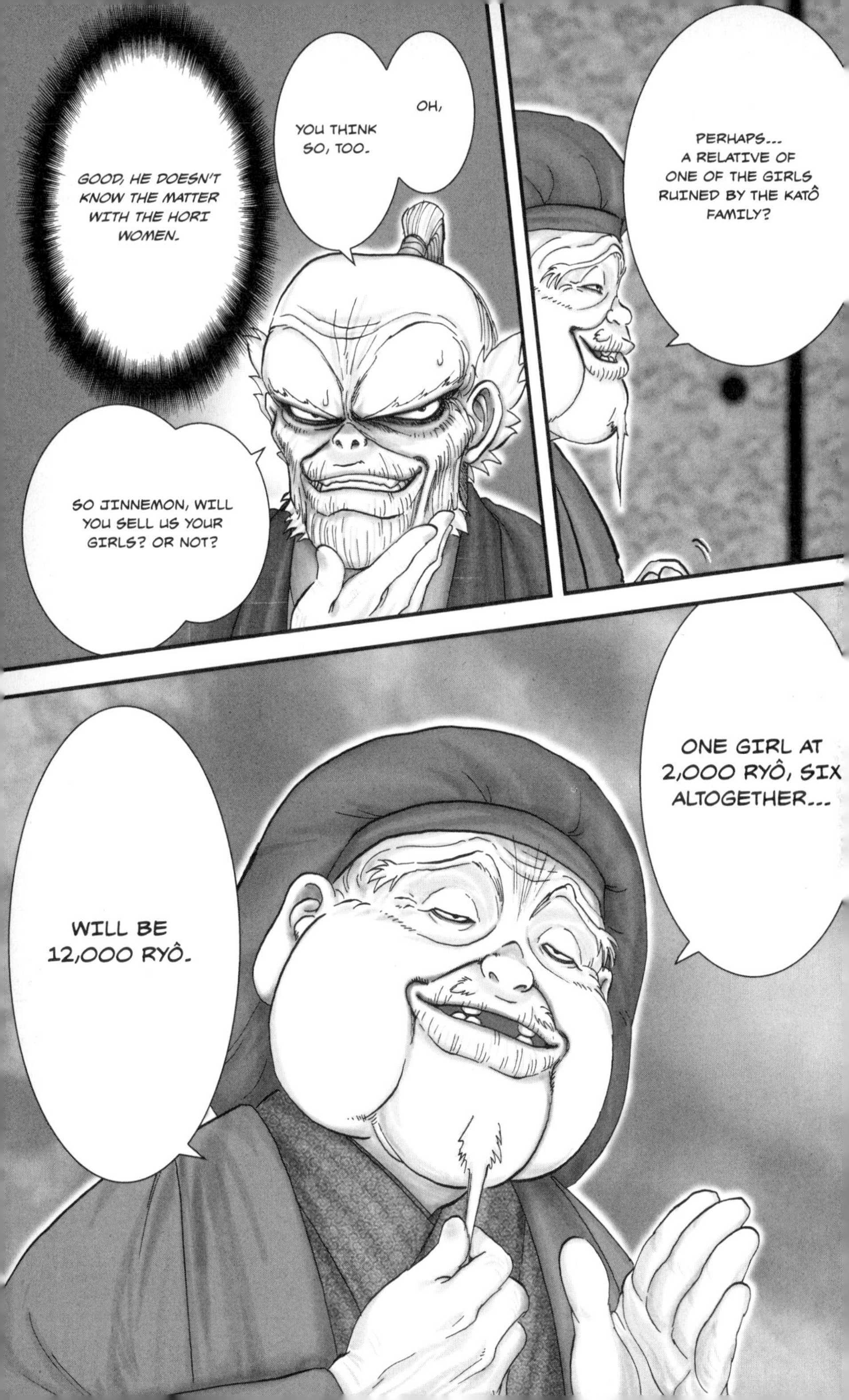
PERHAPS... A RELATIVE OF ONE OF THE GIRLS RUINED BY THE KATÔ FAMILY?
OH, YOU THINK SO, TOO.
GOOD, HE DOESN'T KNOW THE MATTER WITH THE HORI WOMEN.
SO JINNEMON, WILL YOU SELL US YOUR GIRLS? OR NOT?
ONE GIRL AT 2,000 RYÔ, SIX ALTOGETHER...
WILL BE 12,000 RYÔ.

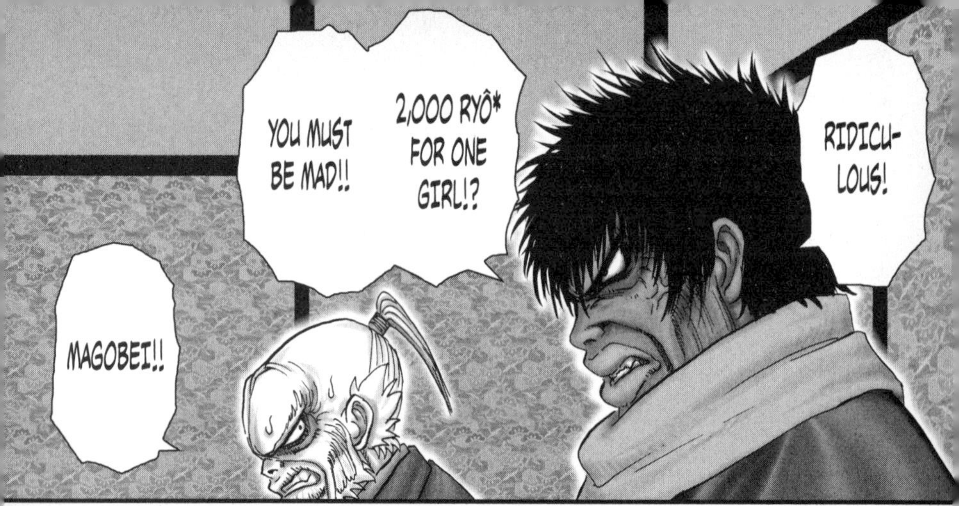
RIDICU-LOUS!
2,000 RYÔ* FOR ONE GIRL!?
YOU MUST BE MAD!!
MAGOBEI!!

2,000 ryô: At the time, the annual salary of a maid or servant was one ryô.

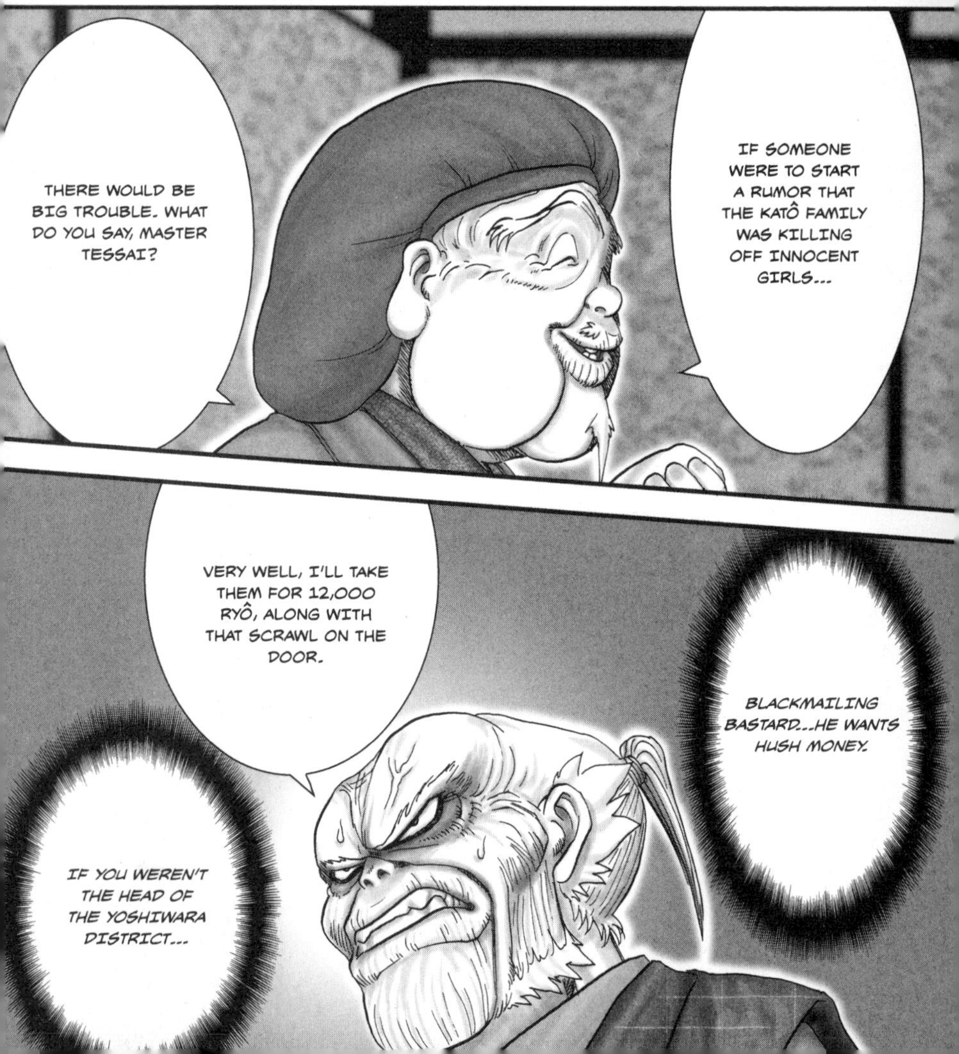
IF SOMEONE WERE TO START A RUMOR THAT THE KATÔ FAMILY WAS KILLING OFF INNOCENT GIRLS...
THERE WOULD BE BIG TROUBLE. WHAT DO YOU SAY, MASTER TESSAI?
VERY WELL, I'LL TAKE THEM FOR 12,000 RYÔ, ALONG WITH THAT SCRAWL ON THE DOOR.
BLACKMAILING BASTARD...HE WANTS HUSH MONEY.
IF YOU WEREN'T THE HEAD OF THE YOSHIWARA DISTRICT...

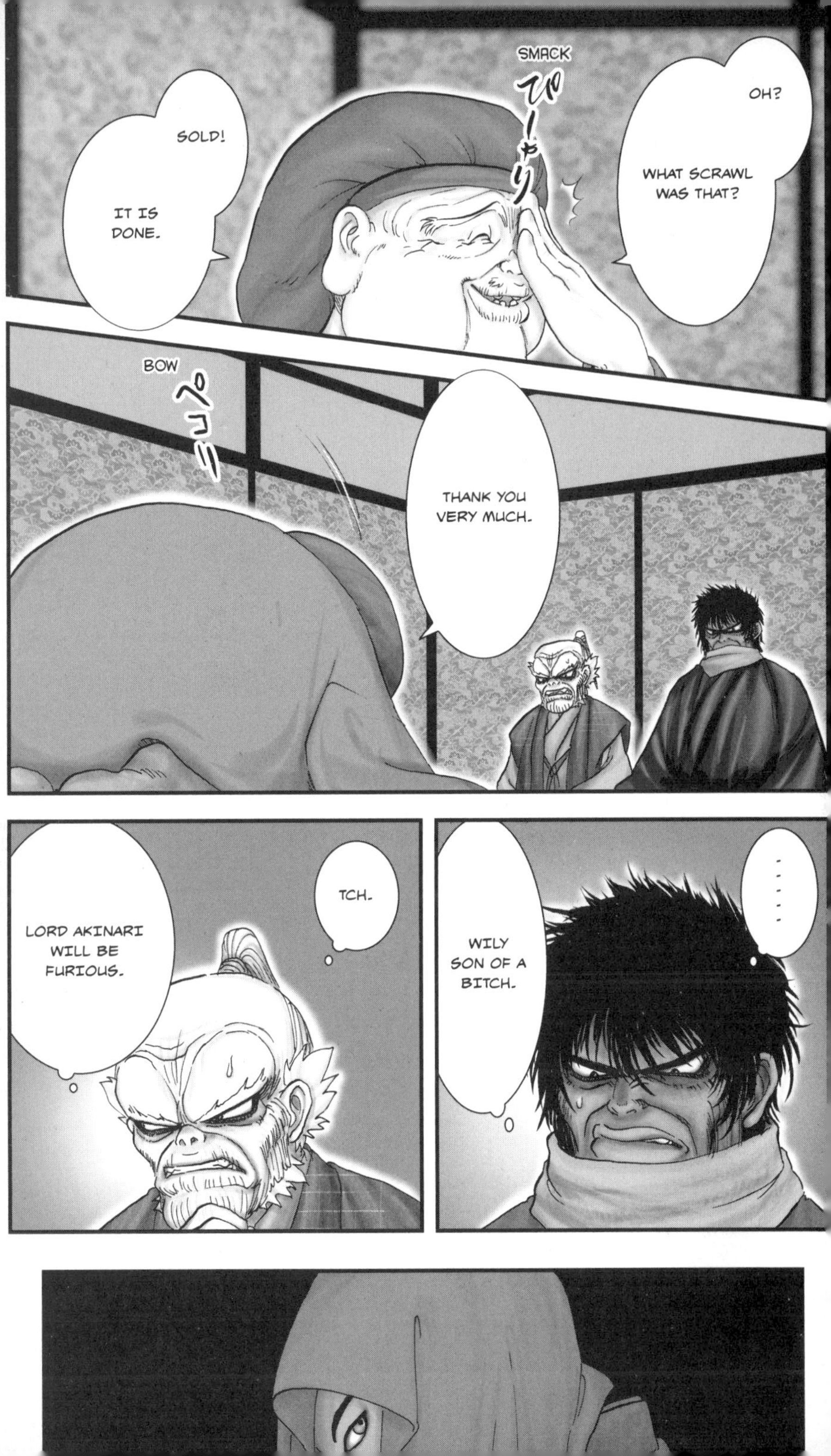
OH?
WHAT SCRAWL WAS THAT?
SMACK
SOLD!
IT IS DONE.
THANK YOU VERY MUCH.
BOW
......
WILY SON OF A BITCH.
TCH.
LORD AKINARI WILL BE FURIOUS.

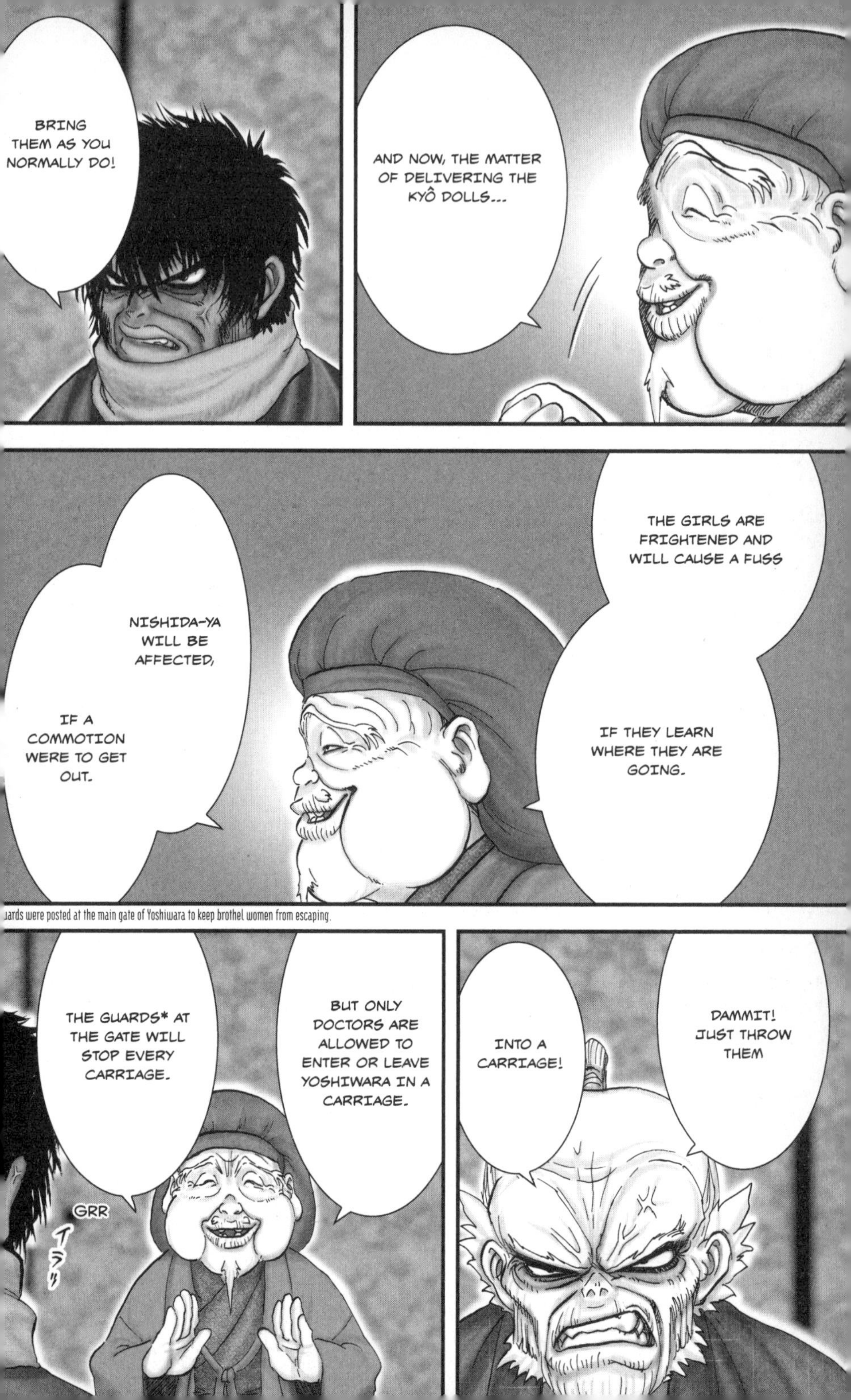
AND NOW, THE MATTER OF DELIVERING THE KYÔ DOLLS...
BRING THEM AS YOU NORMALLY DO!
THE GIRLS ARE FRIGHTENED AND WILL CAUSE A FUSS
IF THEY LEARN WHERE THEY ARE GOING.
NISHIDA-YA WILL BE AFFECTED,
IF A COMMOTION WERE TO GET OUT.
DAMMIT! JUST THROW THEM
INTO A CARRIAGE!
BUT ONLY DOCTORS ARE ALLOWED TO ENTER OR LEAVE YOSHIWARA IN A CARRIAGE.
THE GUARDS* AT THE GATE WILL STOP EVERY CARRIAGE.
GRR
イラッ

uards were posted at the main gate of Yoshiwara to keep brothel women from escaping.

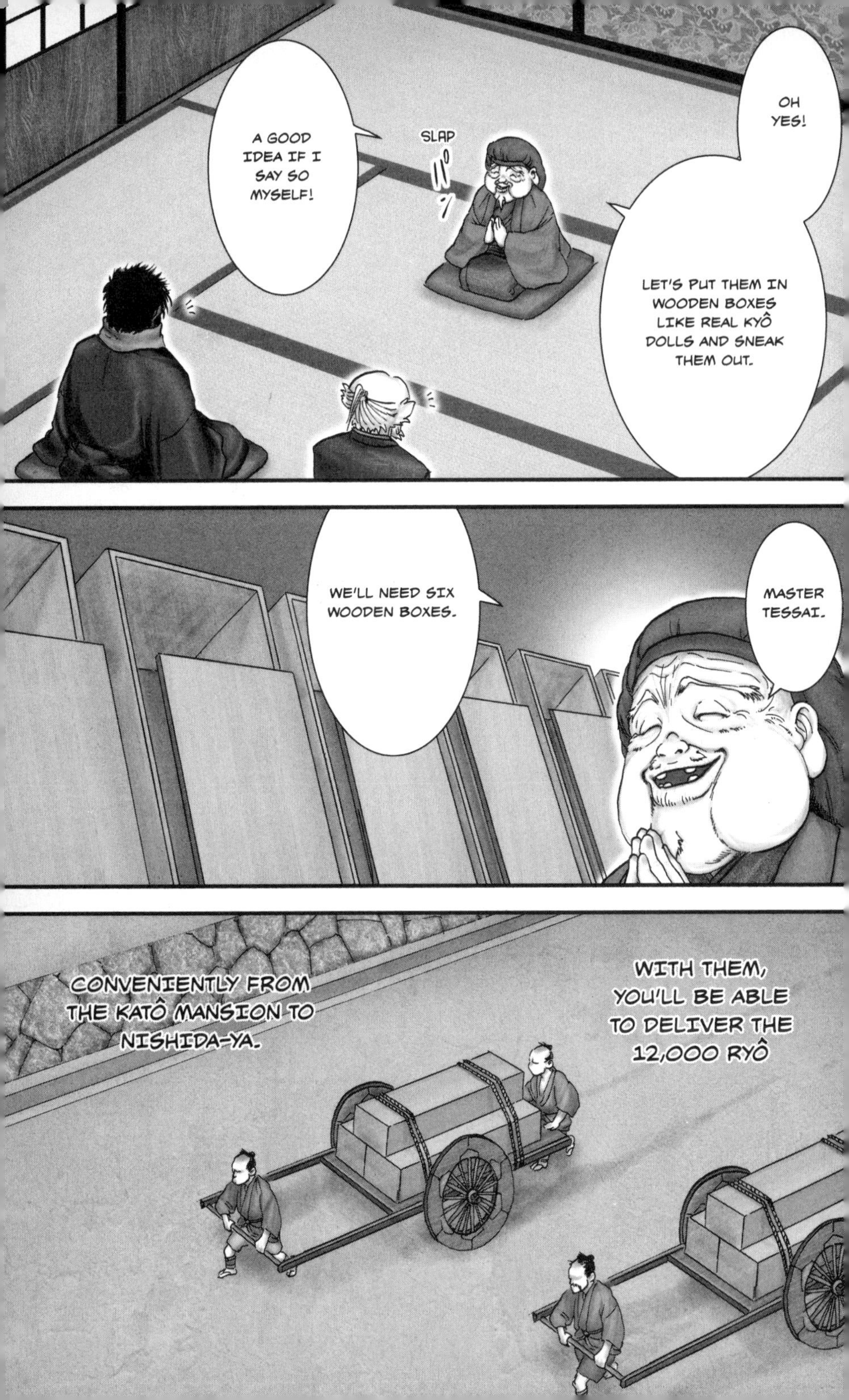
OH YES!
SLAP
LET'S PUT THEM IN WOODEN BOXES LIKE REAL KYÔ DOLLS AND SNEAK THEM OUT.
A GOOD IDEA IF I SAY SO MYSELF!
MASTER TESSAI.
WE'LL NEED SIX WOODEN BOXES.
WITH THEM, YOU'LL BE ABLE TO DELIVER THE 12,000 RYÔ
CONVENIENTLY FROM THE KATÔ MANSION TO NISHIDA-YA.

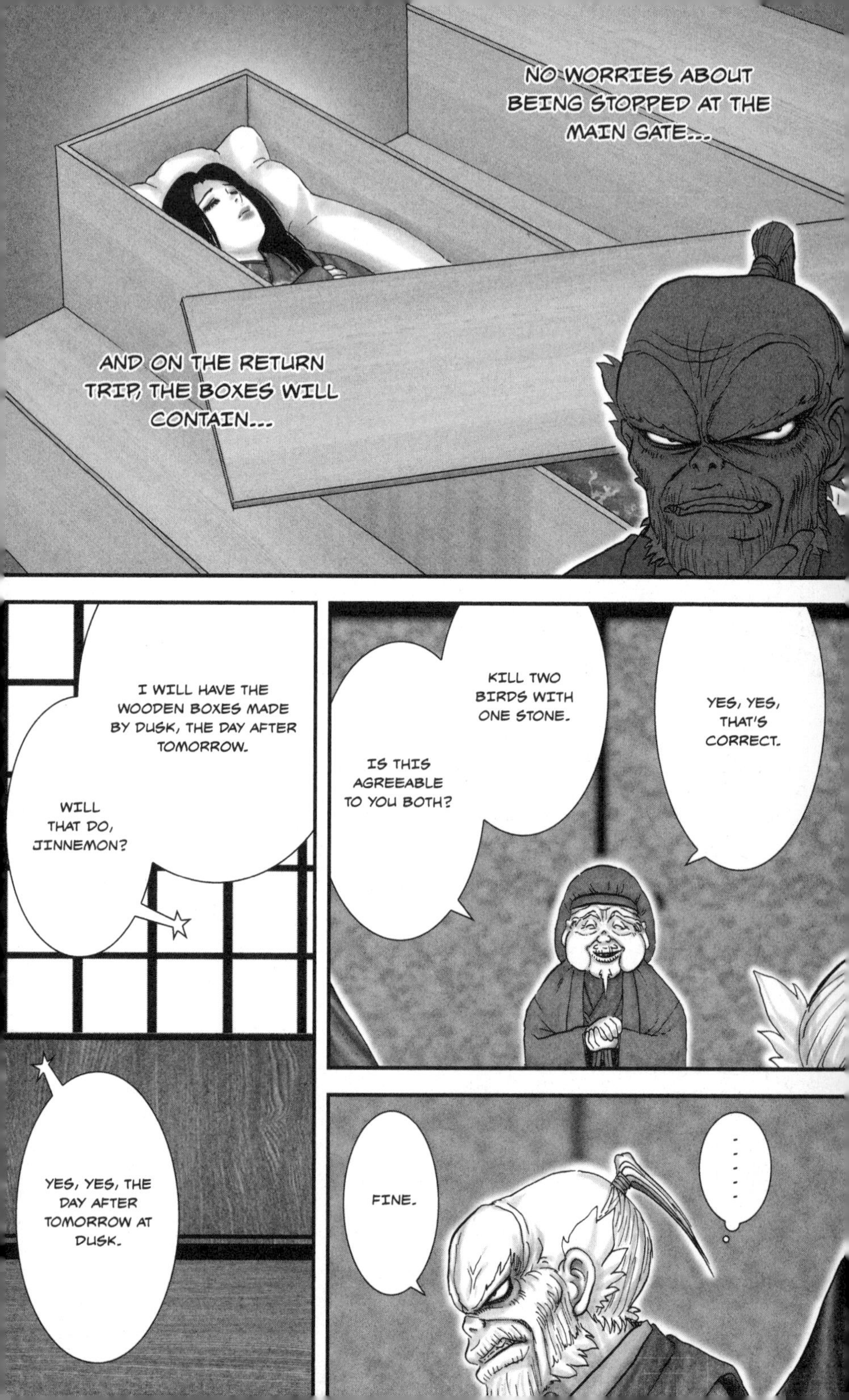
NO WORRIES ABOUT BEING STOPPED AT THE MAIN GATE...
AND ON THE RETURN TRIP, THE BOXES WILL CONTAIN...
YES, YES, THAT'S CORRECT.
KILL TWO BIRDS WITH ONE STONE.
IS THIS AGREEABLE TO YOU BOTH?
......
FINE.
I WILL HAVE THE WOODEN BOXES MADE BY DUSK, THE DAY AFTER TOMORROW.
WILL THAT DO, JINNEMON?
YES, YES, THE DAY AFTER TOMORROW AT DUSK.

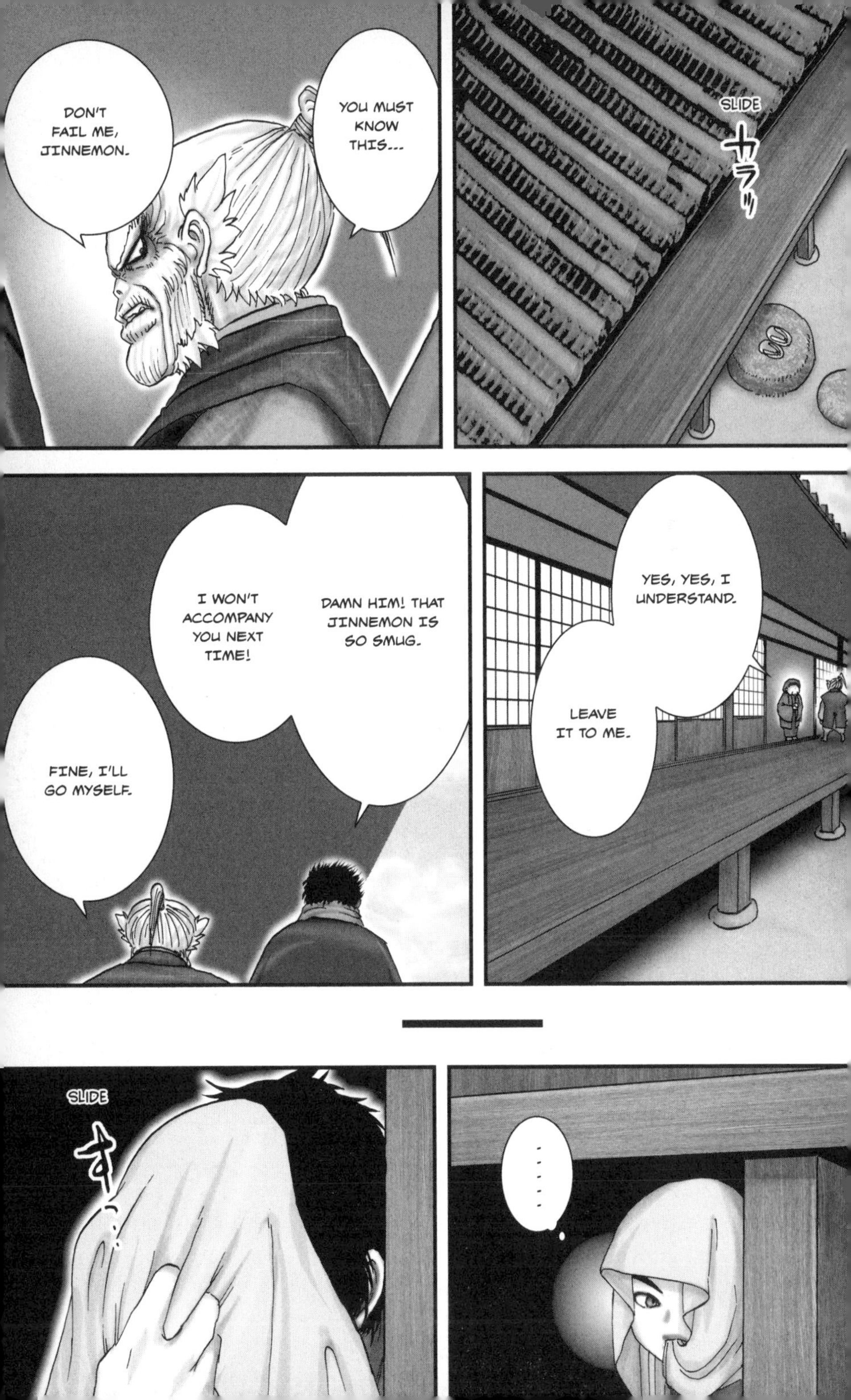
SLIDE
カラッ
YOU MUST KNOW THIS...
DON'T FAIL ME, JINNEMON.
YES, YES, I UNDERSTAND.
LEAVE IT TO ME.
DAMN HIM! THAT JINNEMON IS SO SMUG.
I WON'T ACCOMPANY YOU NEXT TIME!
FINE, I'LL GO MYSELF.
......
SLIDE
すっ

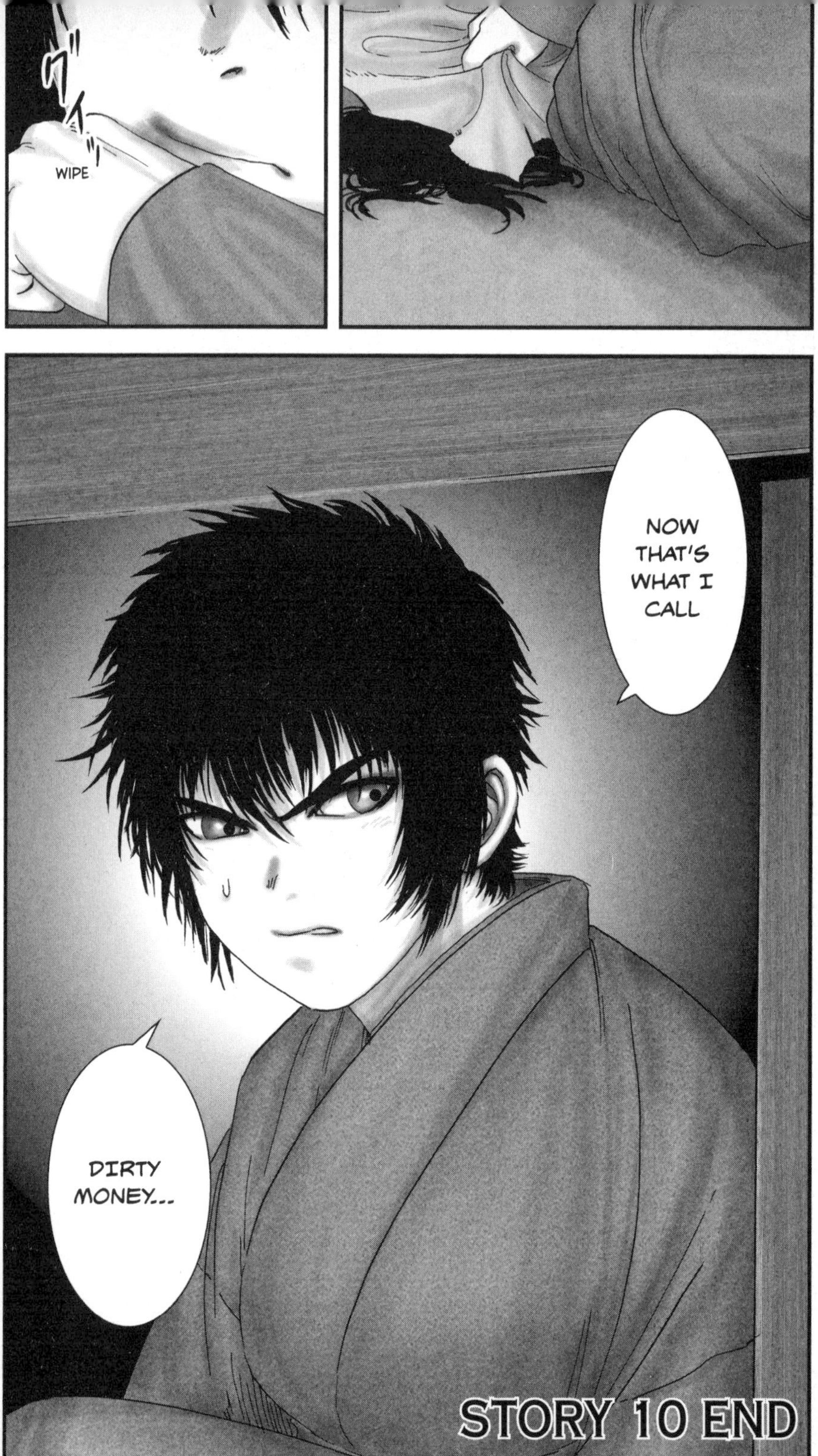
WIPE
NOW THAT'S WHAT I CALL
DIRTY MONEY...
STORY 10 END

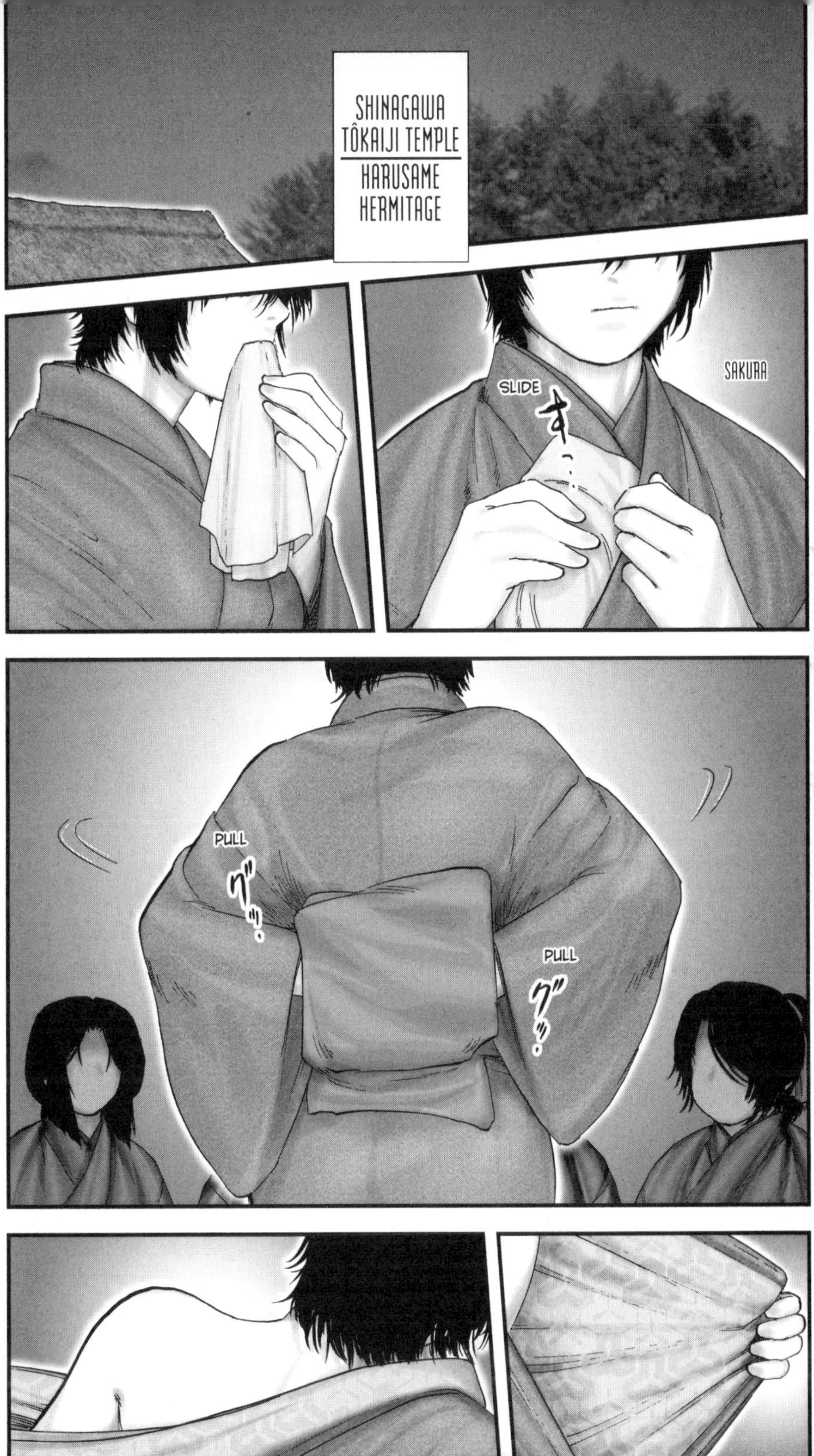
SHINAGAWA
TÔKAIJI TEMPLE
HARUSAME
HERMITAGE
SAKURA
SLIDE
す…
PULL
グッ
PULL
グッ

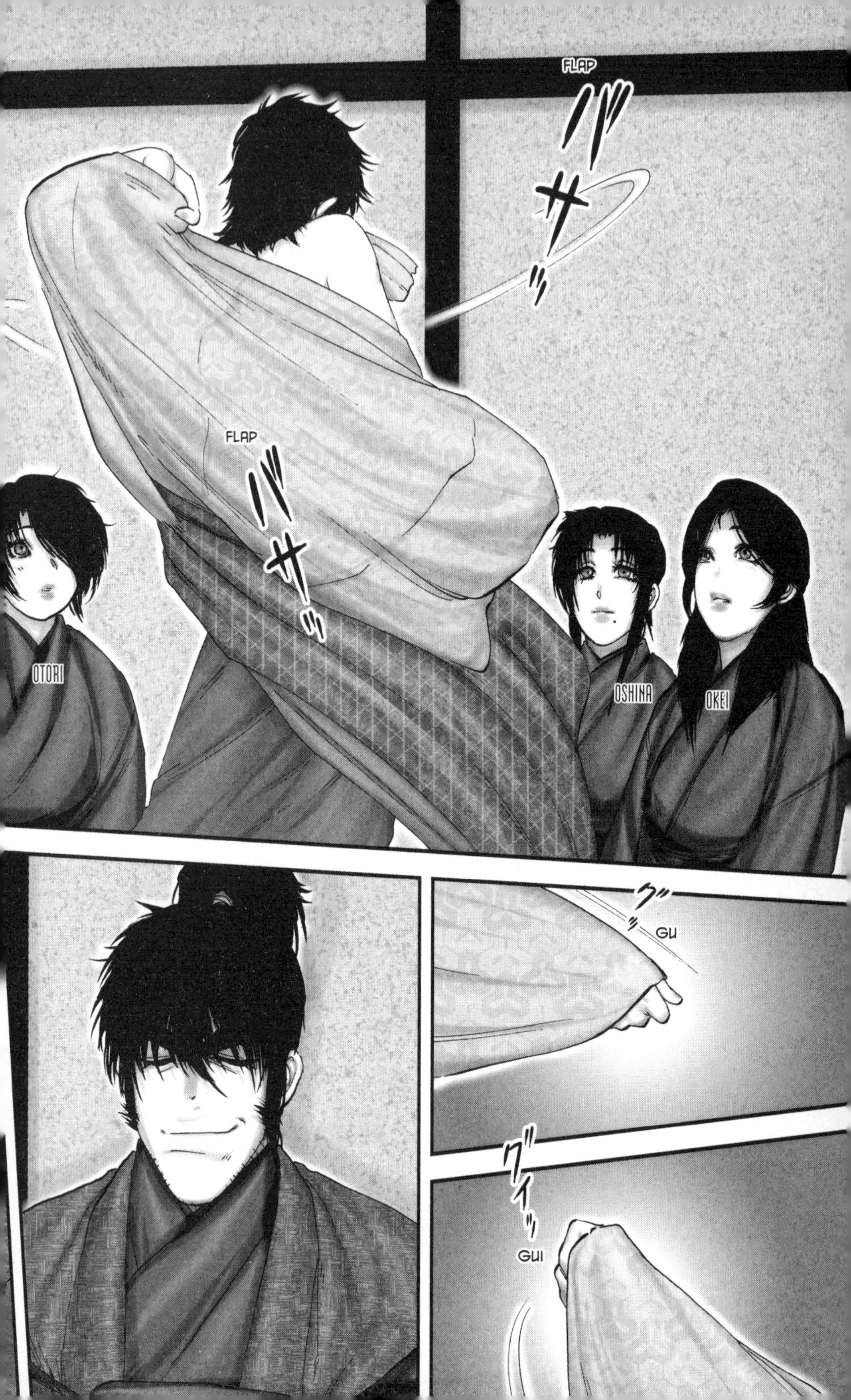
FLAP
バサッ
FLAP
バサッ
OKEI
OSHINA
OTORI
グッ
GU
グイッ
GUI

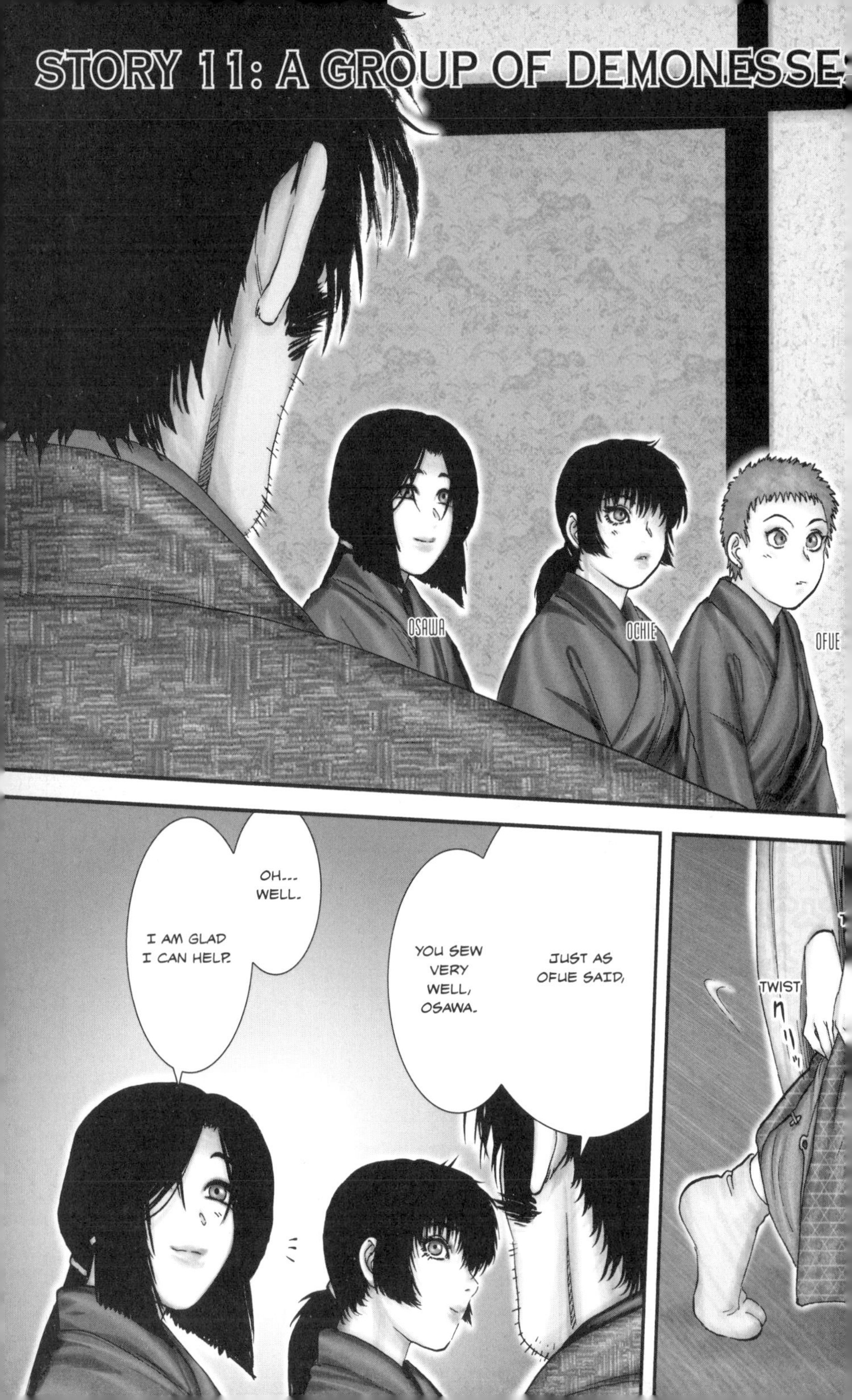
STORY 11: A GROUP OF DEMONESSES
OFUE
OCHIE
OSAWA
TWIST
JUST AS OFUE SAID,
YOU SEW VERY WELL, OSAWA.
OH... WELL.
I AM GLAD I CAN HELP.

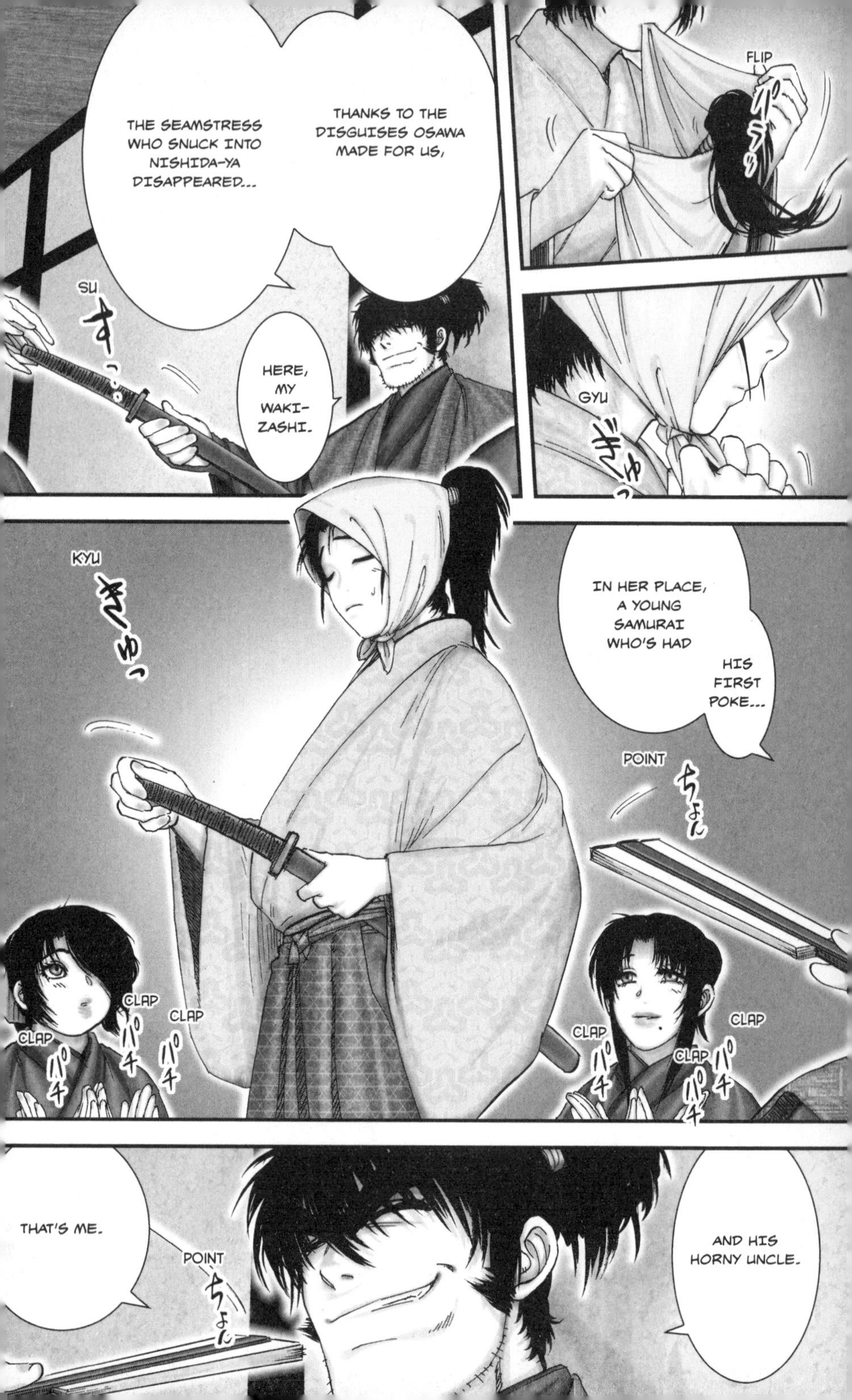
FLIP
パラッ
GYU
ぎゅっ
THANKS TO THE DISGUISES OSAWA MADE FOR US,
THE SEAMSTRESS WHO SNUCK INTO NISHIDA-YA DISAPPEARED...
HERE, MY WAKI-ZASHI.
SU
すっ
IN HER PLACE, A YOUNG SAMURAI WHO'S HAD
HIS FIRST POKE...
POINT
ちょん
KYU
きゅっ
CLAP
パチ
CLAP
パチ
CLAP
パチ
CLAP
パチ
CLAP
パチ
AND HIS HORNY UNCLE.
POINT
ちょん
THAT'S ME.

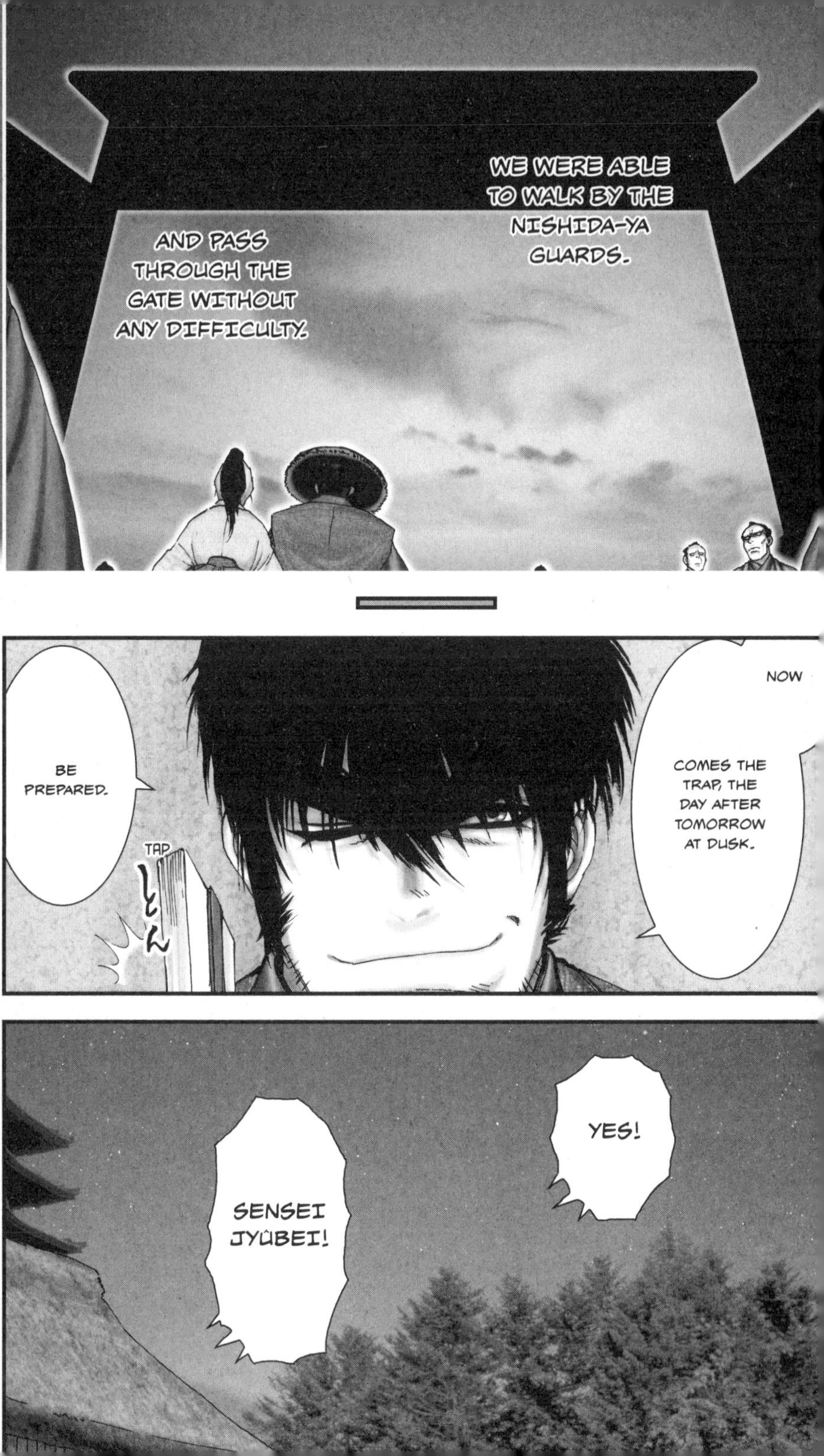
WE WERE ABLE TO WALK BY THE NISHIDA-YA GUARDS.
AND PASS THROUGH THE GATE WITHOUT ANY DIFFICULTY.
NOW
COMES THE TRAP, THE DAY AFTER TOMORROW AT DUSK.
TAP
とん
BE PREPARED.
YES!
SENSEI JYÛBEI!

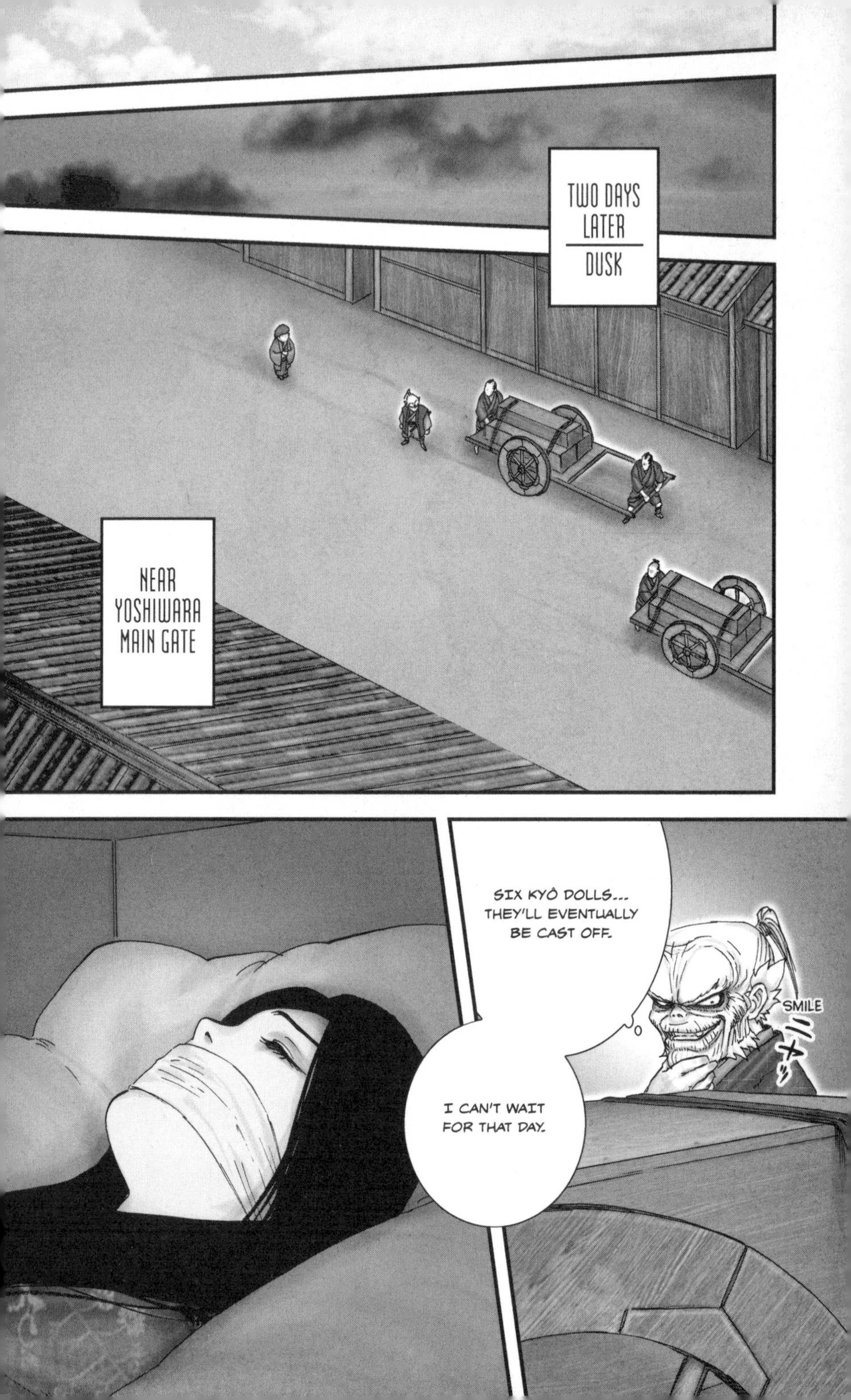

TWO DAYS LATER
DUSK
NEAR YOSHIWARA MAIN GATE
SIX KYÔ DOLLS... THEY'LL EVENTUALLY BE CAST OFF.
SMILE
I CAN'T WAIT FOR THAT DAY.

HMPH.

WELL NOW, MASTER TESSAI

I WILL SEE YOU OFF FROM HERE.

SQUEEZE

SQUEEZE

MASTER TESSAI, YOU'RE SO SEVERE...

YOU WANT TO GO BACK AND COUNT YOUR MONEY.

DON'T YOU, JINNEMON.

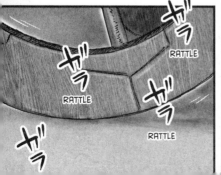

ガラ

ガラ

RATTLE

ガラ

RATTLE

ガラ

RATTLE

Y— YES!

LET'S GO, MEN!

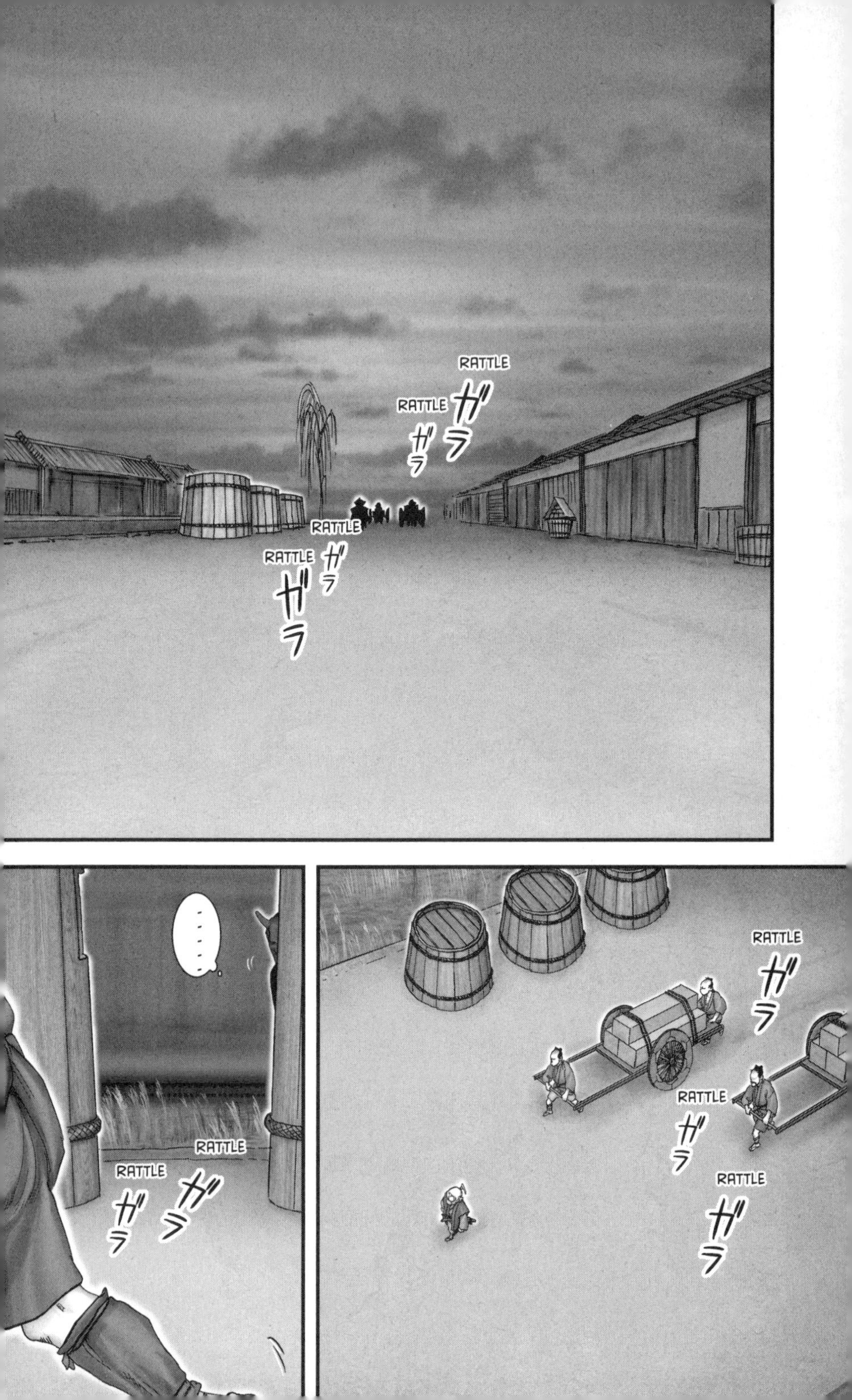
RATTLE ガラ
RATTLE ガラ
RATTLE ガラ
RATTLE ガラ
RATTLE ガラ
RATTLE ガラ
RATTLE ガラ
......
RATTLE ガラ
RATTLE ガラ

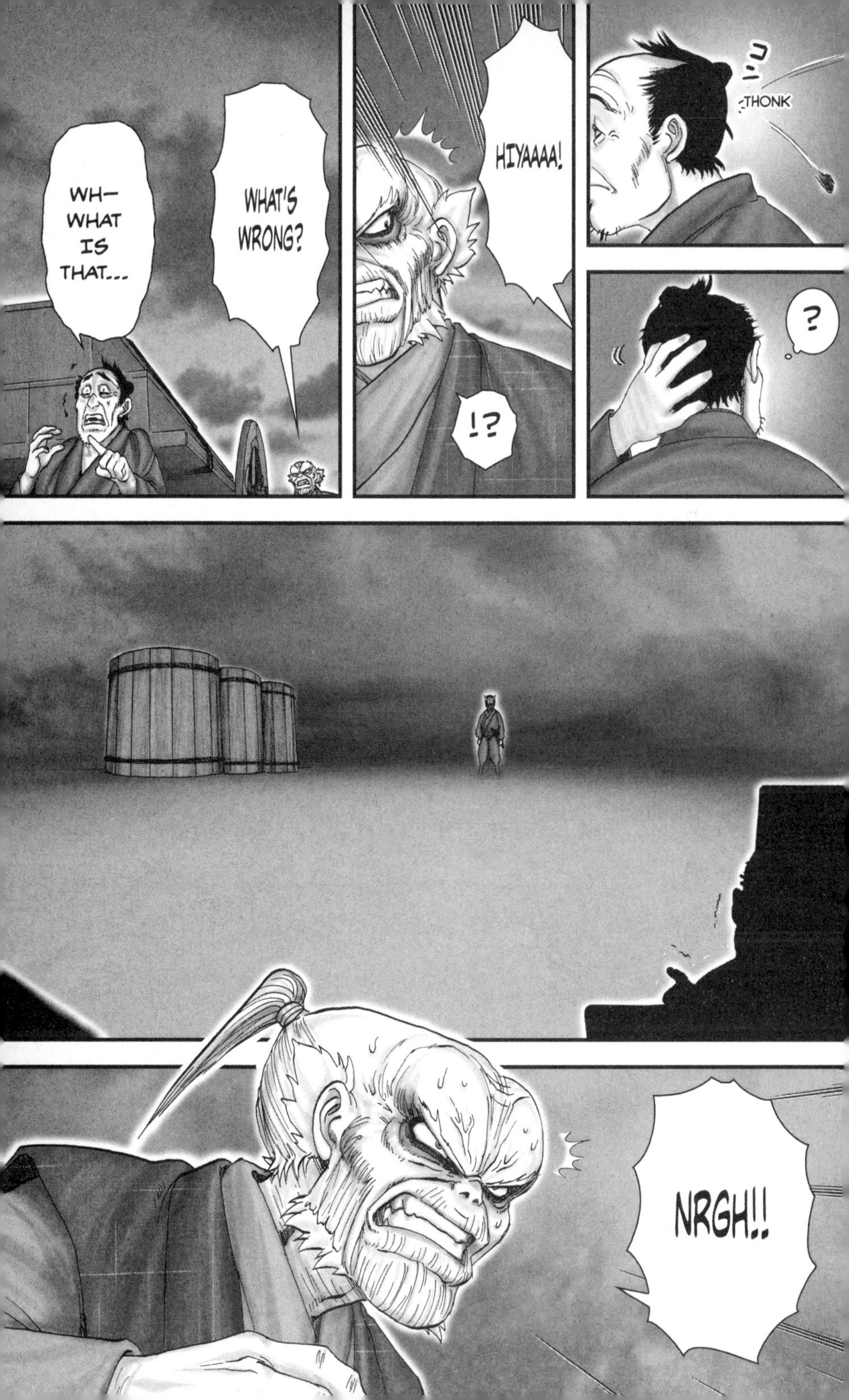
THONK
?
HIYAAAA!
!?
WHAT'S WRONG?
WH— WHAT IS THAT...
NRGH!!

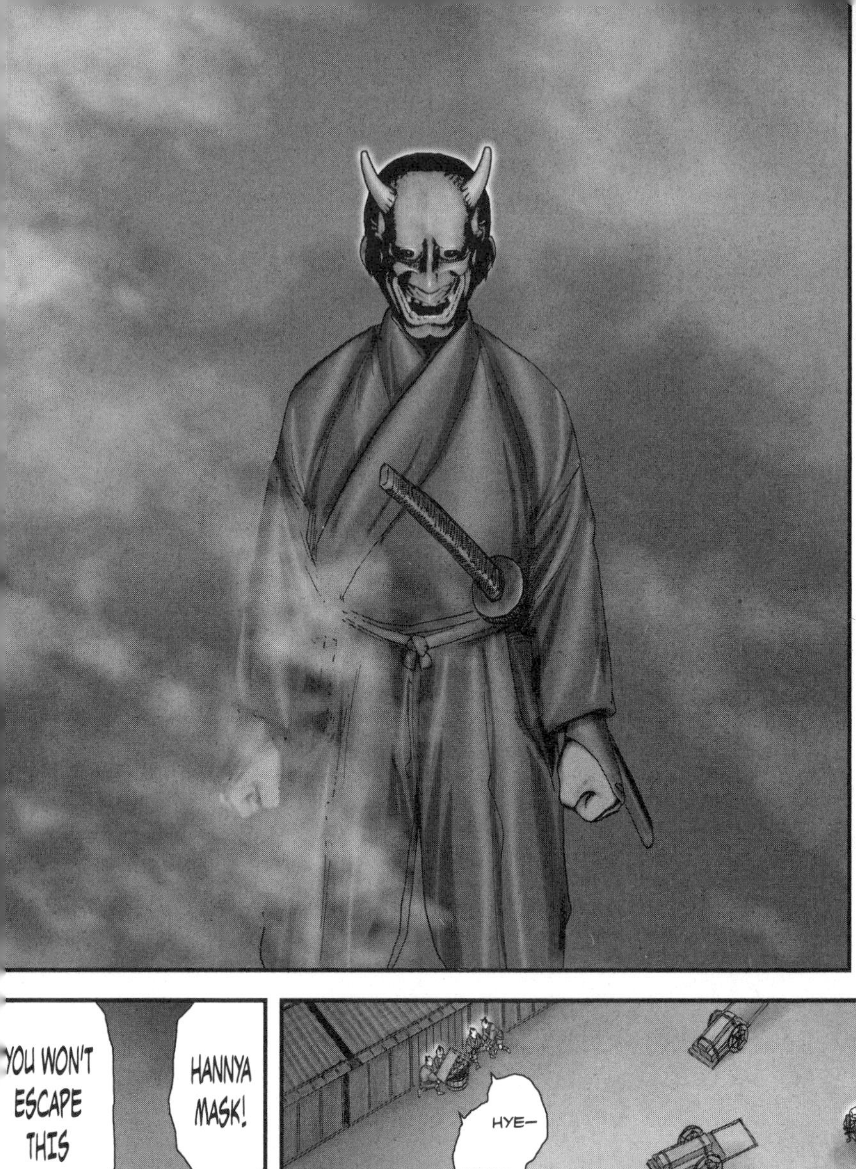

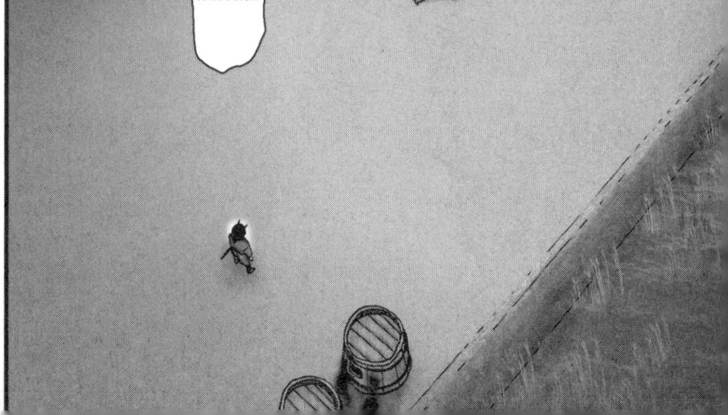
HYE—
HYEEEEH...

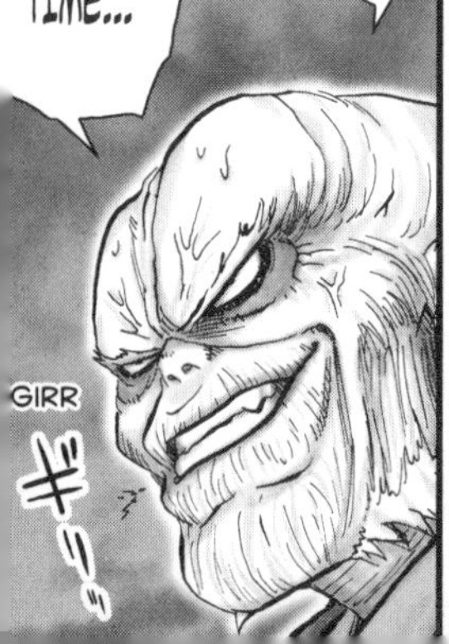
HANNYA MASK!
YOU WON'T ESCAPE THIS TIME...
GIRR

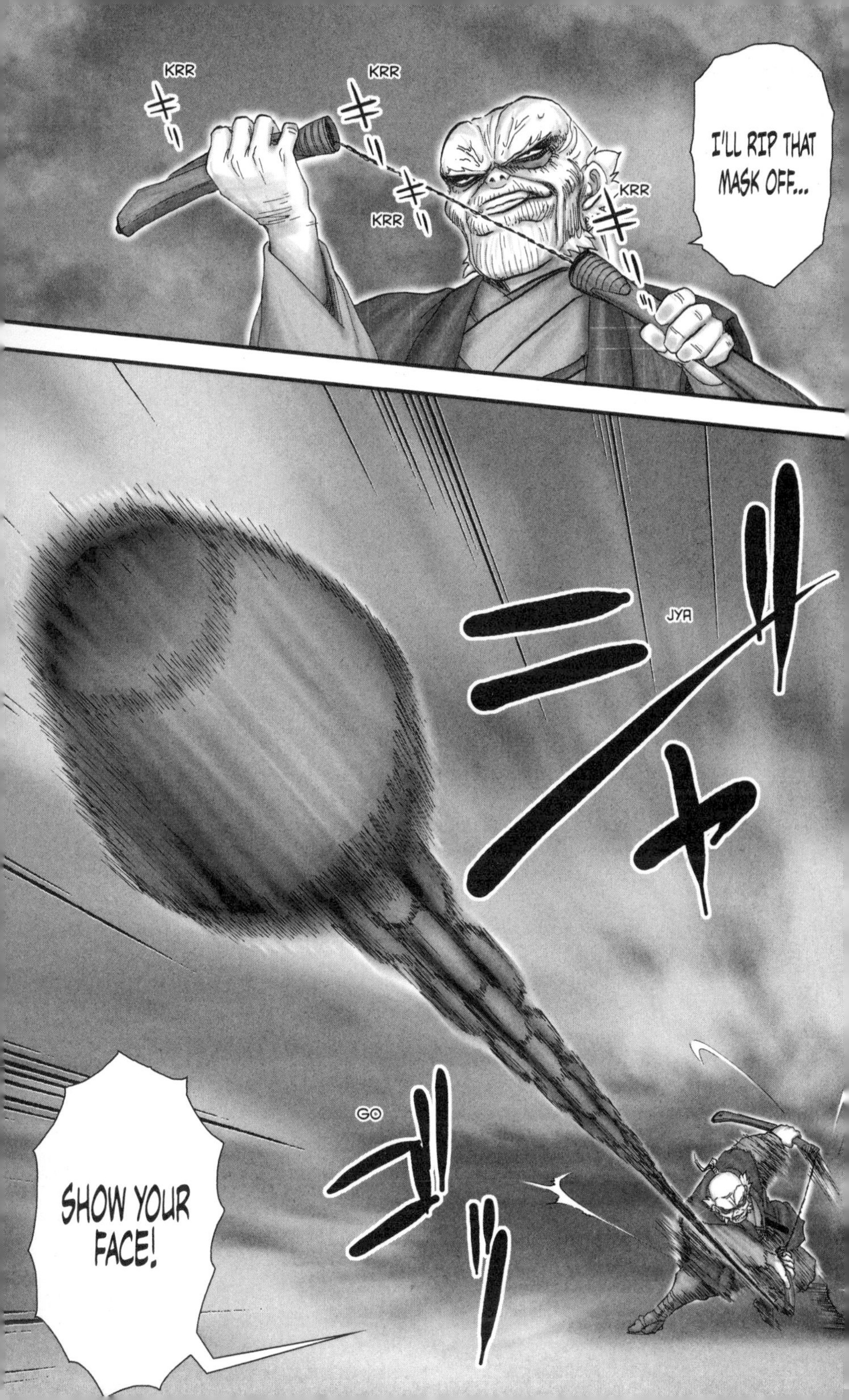
I'LL RIP THAT MASK OFF...
KRR
KRR
KRR
KRR
JYA
GO
SHOW YOUR FACE!

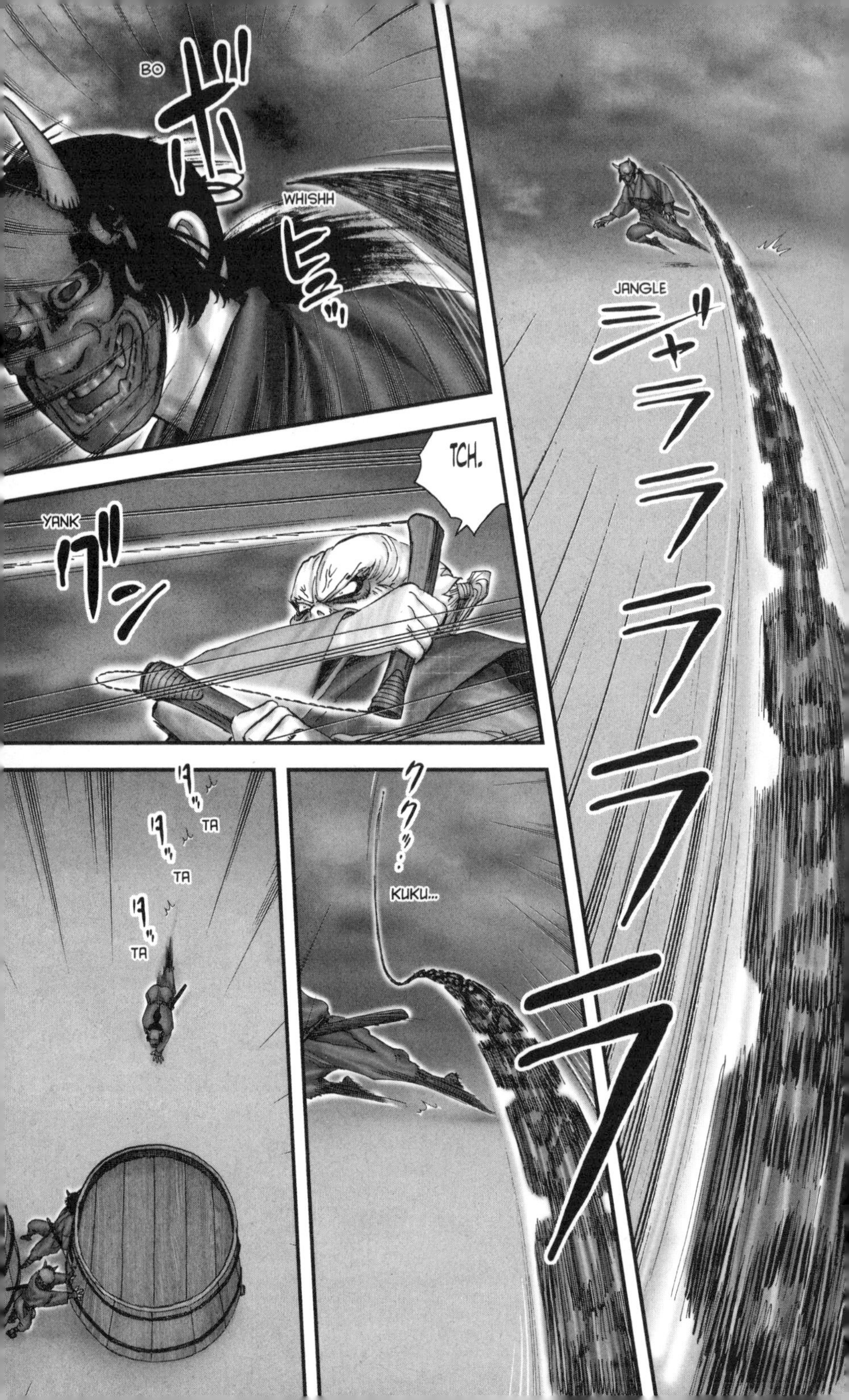
JANGLE
BO
WHISHH
TCH.
YANK
KUKU...
TA
TA
TA

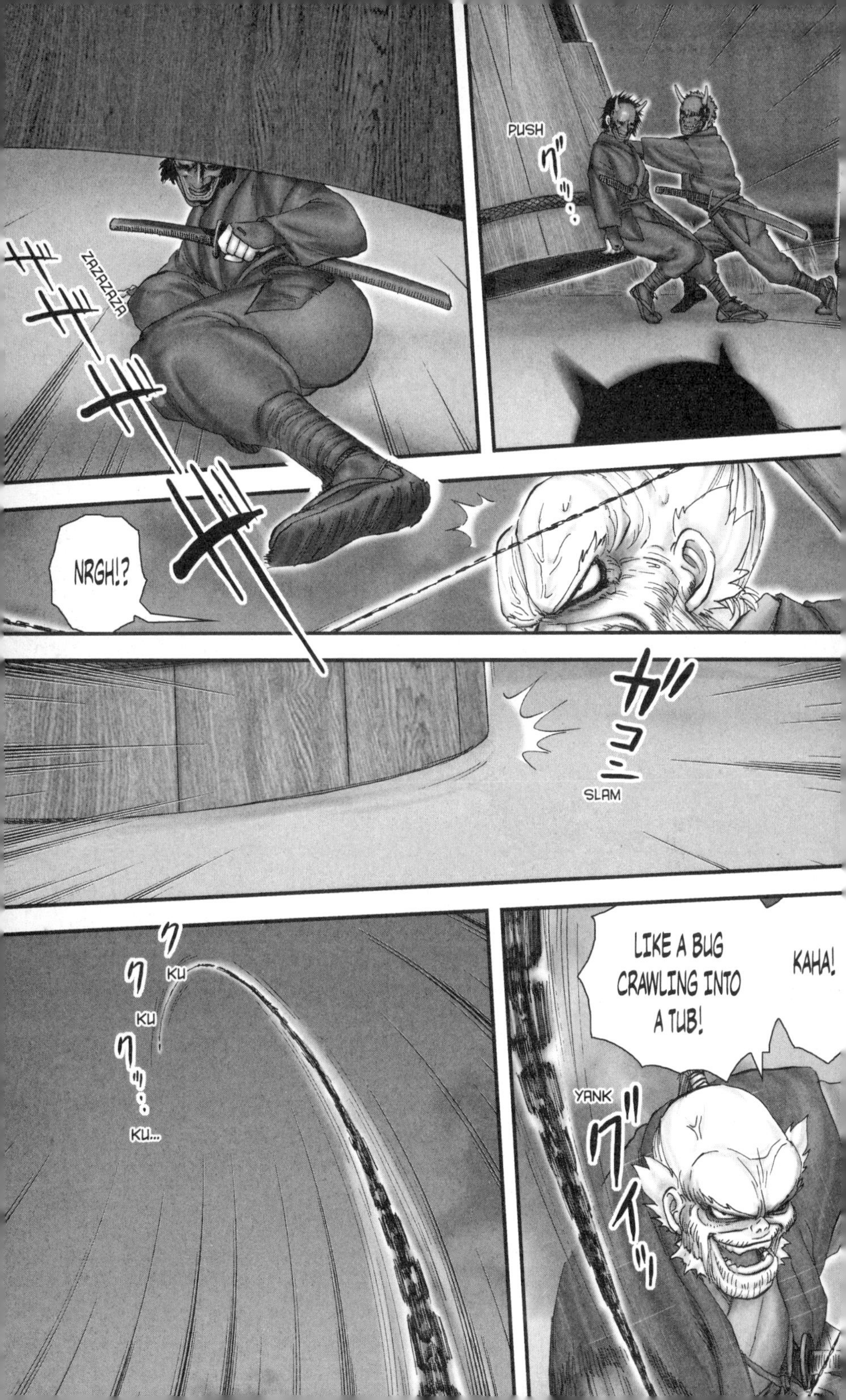
PUSH
ZAZAZAZA
NRGH!?
SLAM
LIKE A BUG CRAWLING INTO A TUB!
KAHA!
YANK
KU
KU
KU...

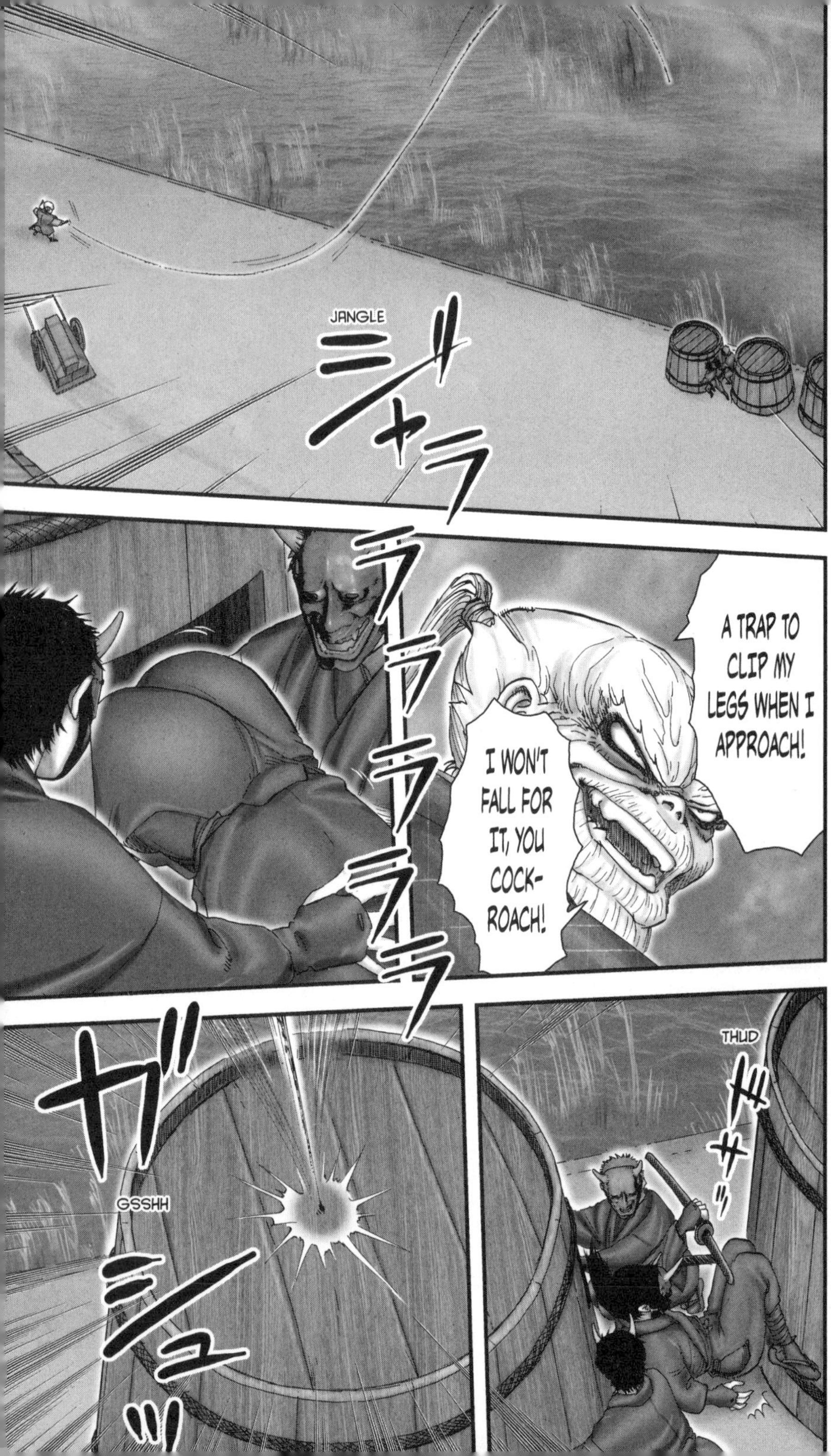
JANGLE
A TRAP TO CLIP MY LEGS WHEN I APPROACH!
I WON'T FALL FOR IT, YOU COCK-ROACH!
THUD
GSSHH

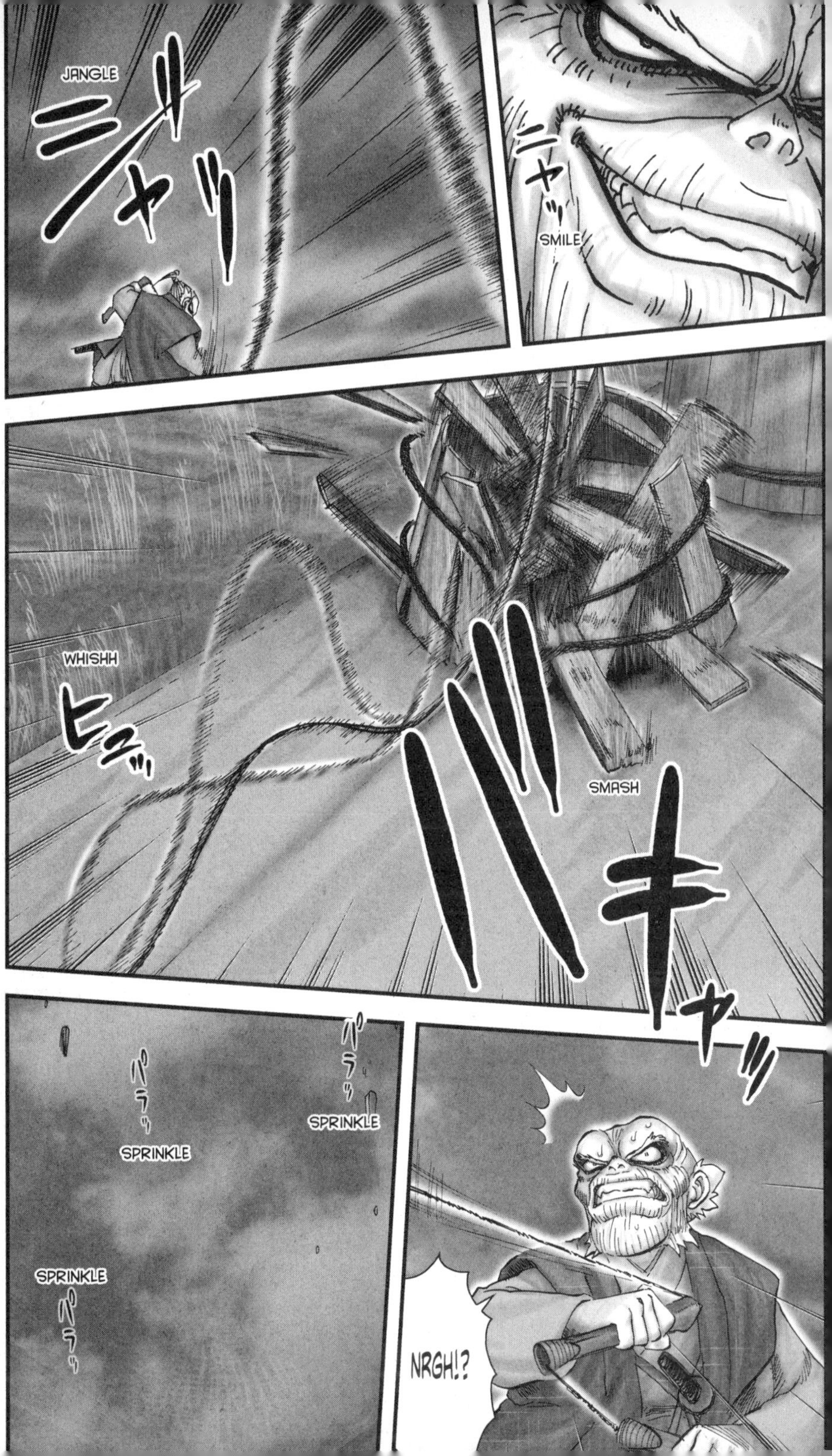
ニヤッ
SMILE
ジャッ
JANGLE
バキャッ
SMASH
ヒュッ
WHISHH
NRGH!?
パラッ
SPRINKLE
パラッ
SPRINKLE
SPRINKLE
パラッ

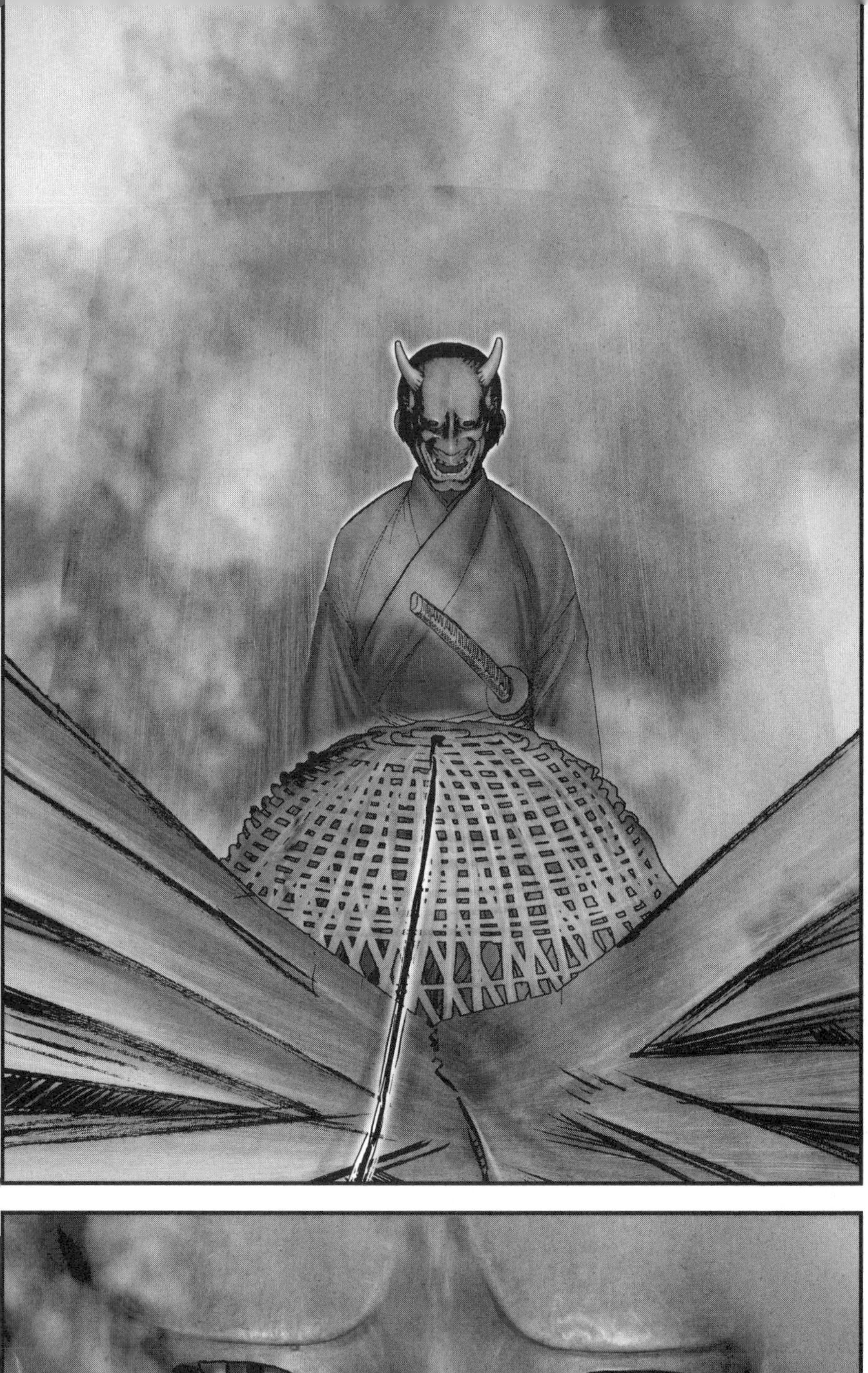
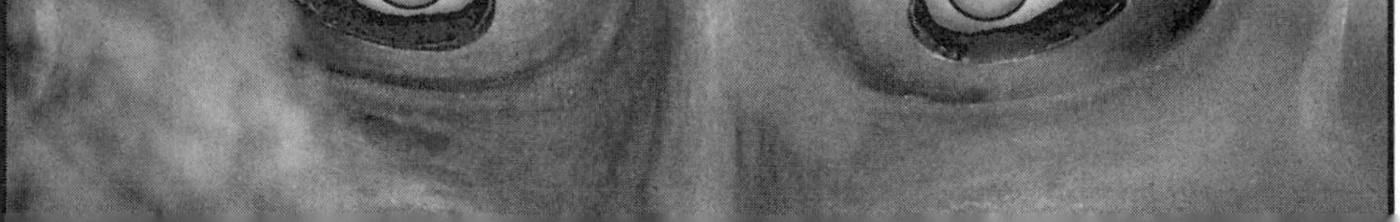

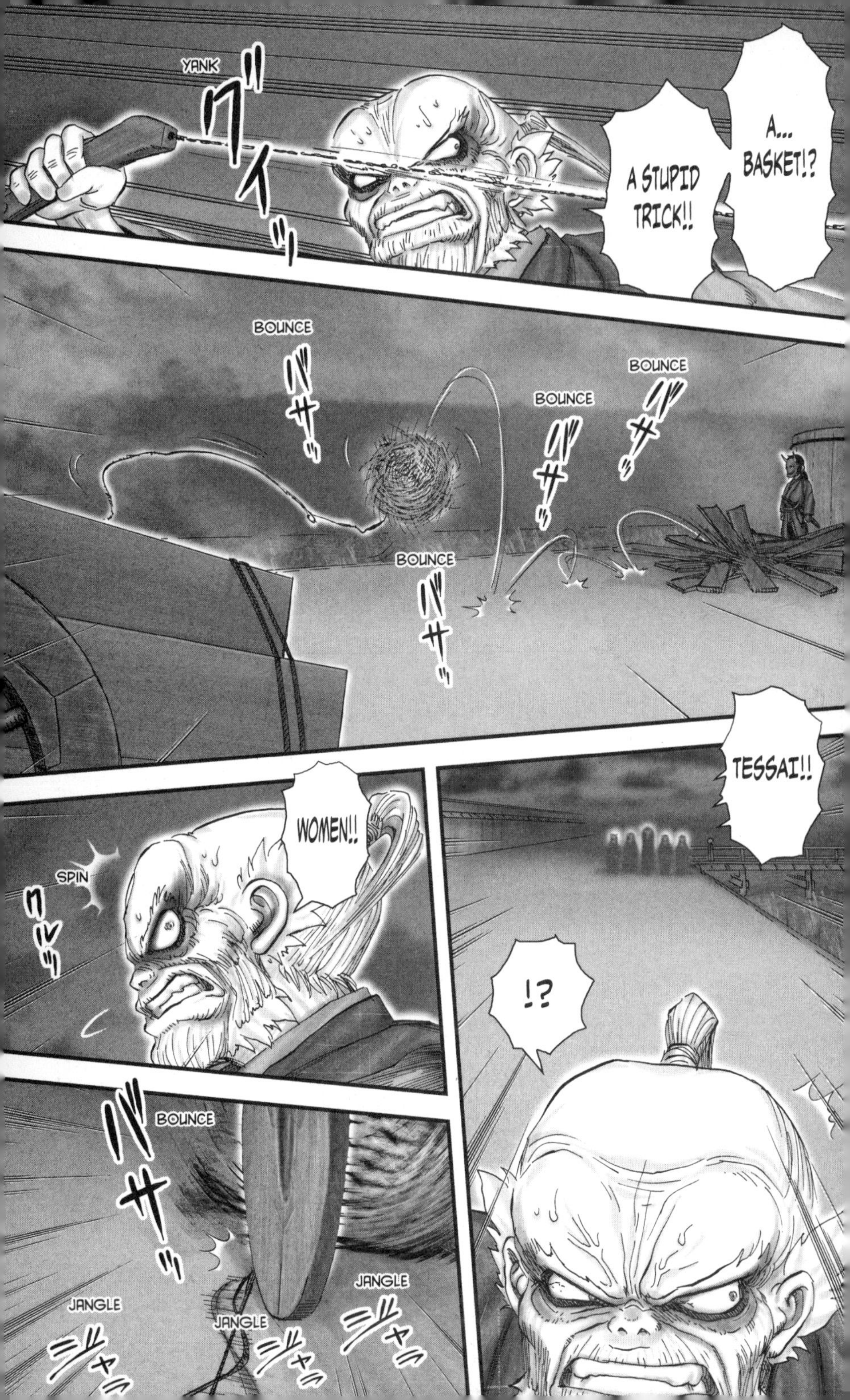
A... BASKET!?
A STUPID TRICK!!
YANK
BOUNCE
BOUNCE
BOUNCE
BOUNCE
TESSAI!!
!?
WOMEN!!
SPIN
BOUNCE
JANGLE
JANGLE
JANGLE

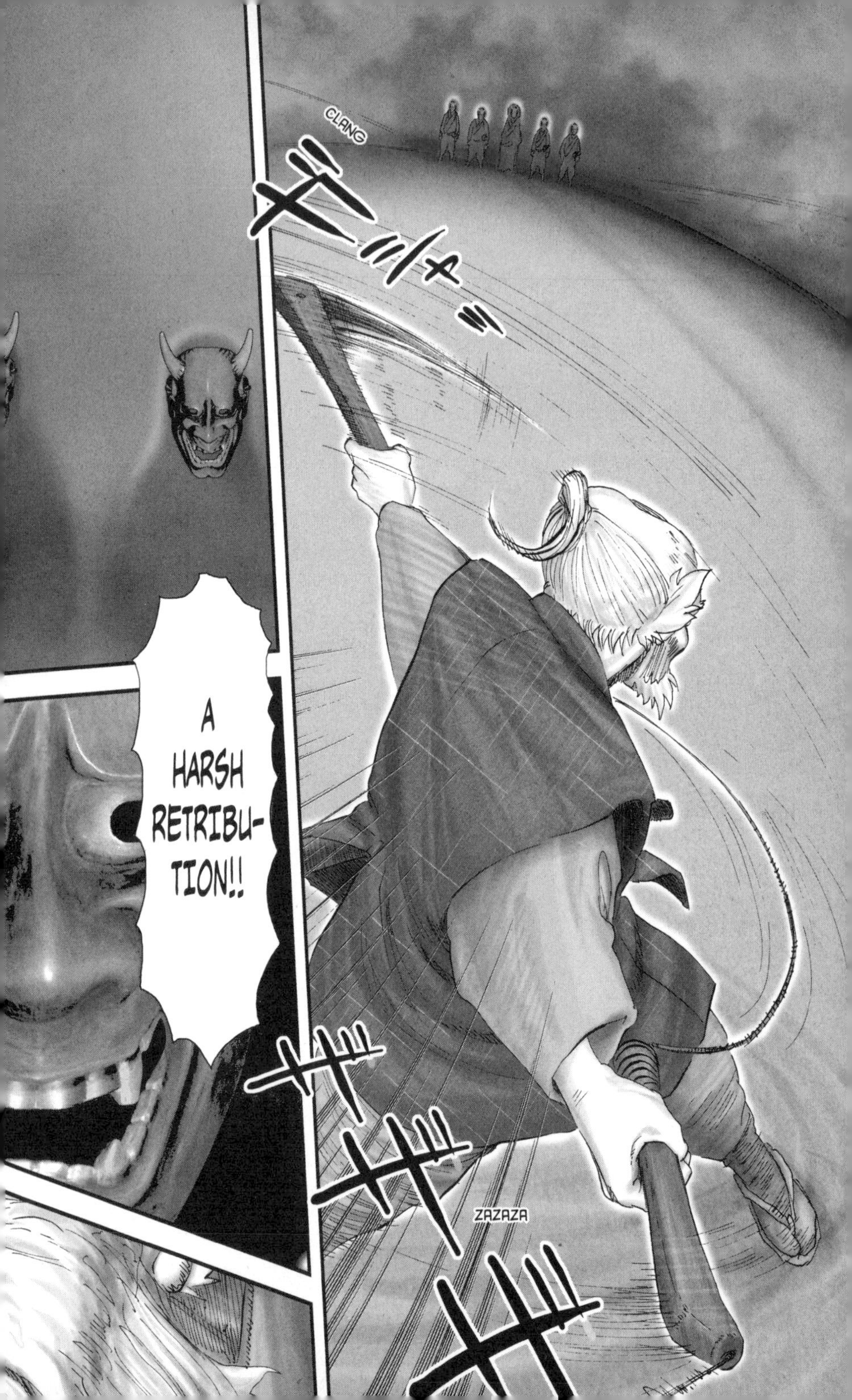
CLANG
A HARSH RETRIBUTION!!
ZAZAZA

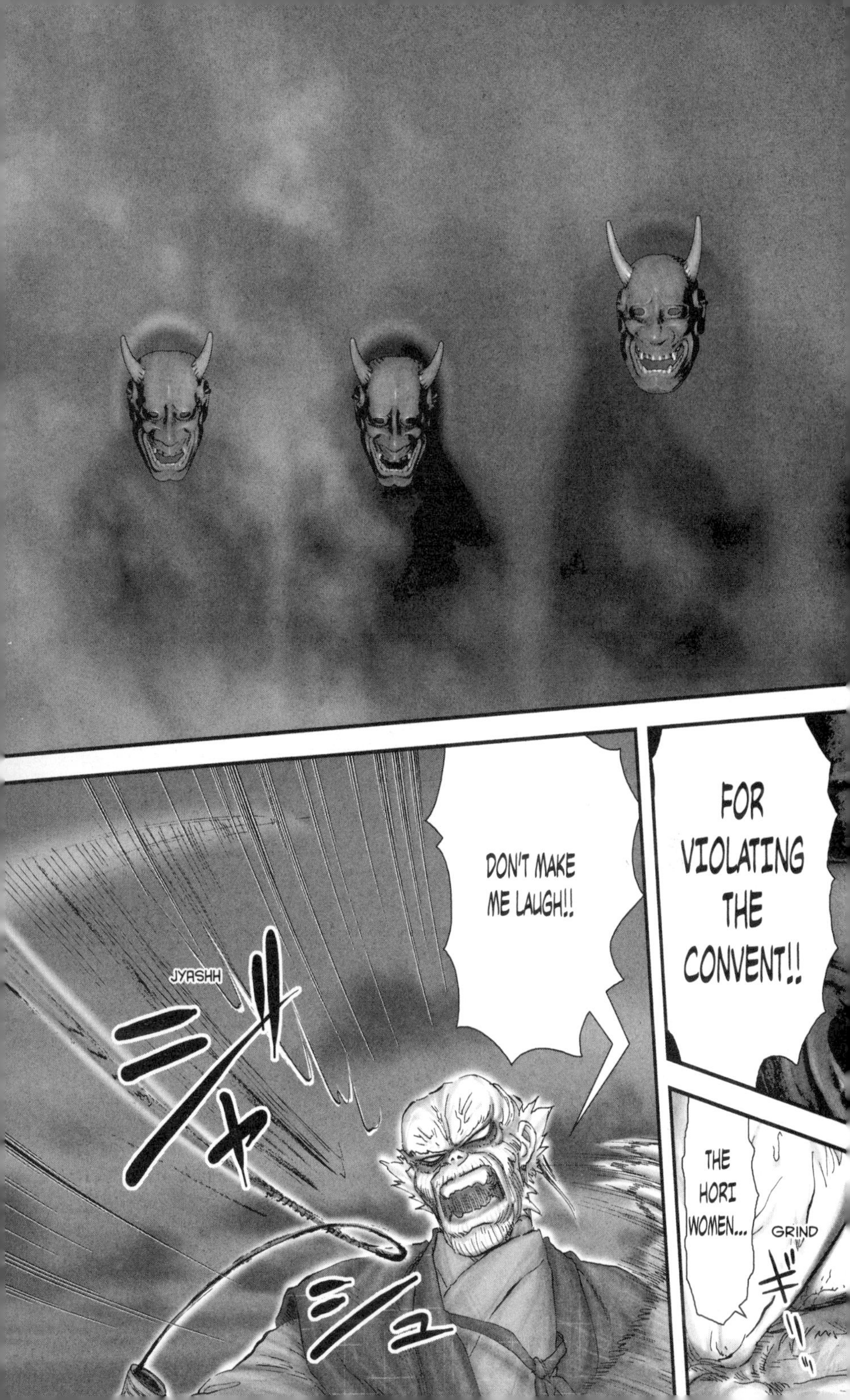
FOR VIOLATING THE CONVENT!!
THE HORI WOMEN...
GRIND
DON'T MAKE ME LAUGH!!
JYASHH

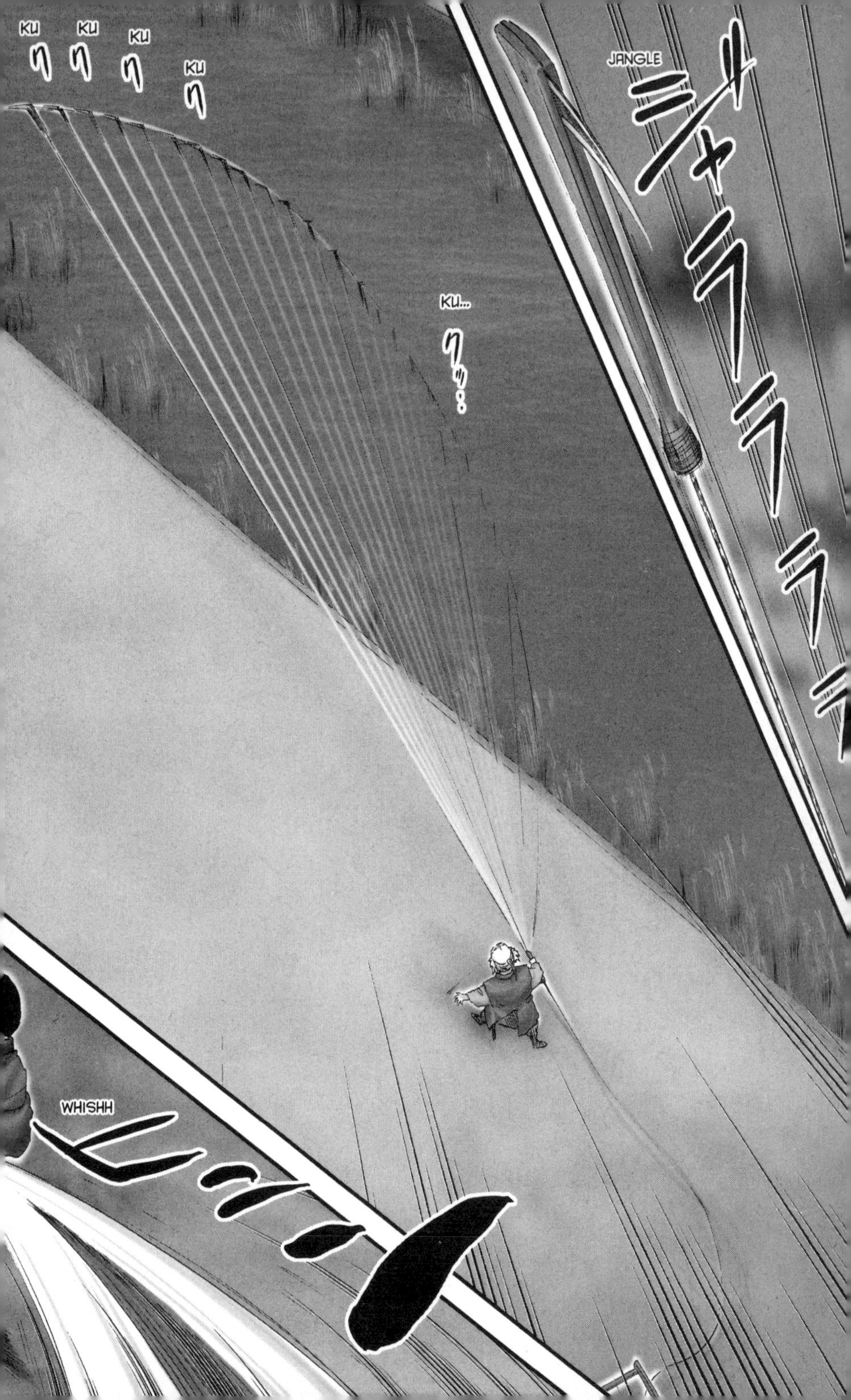
JANGLE
KU...
KU
KU
KU
KU
WHISHH

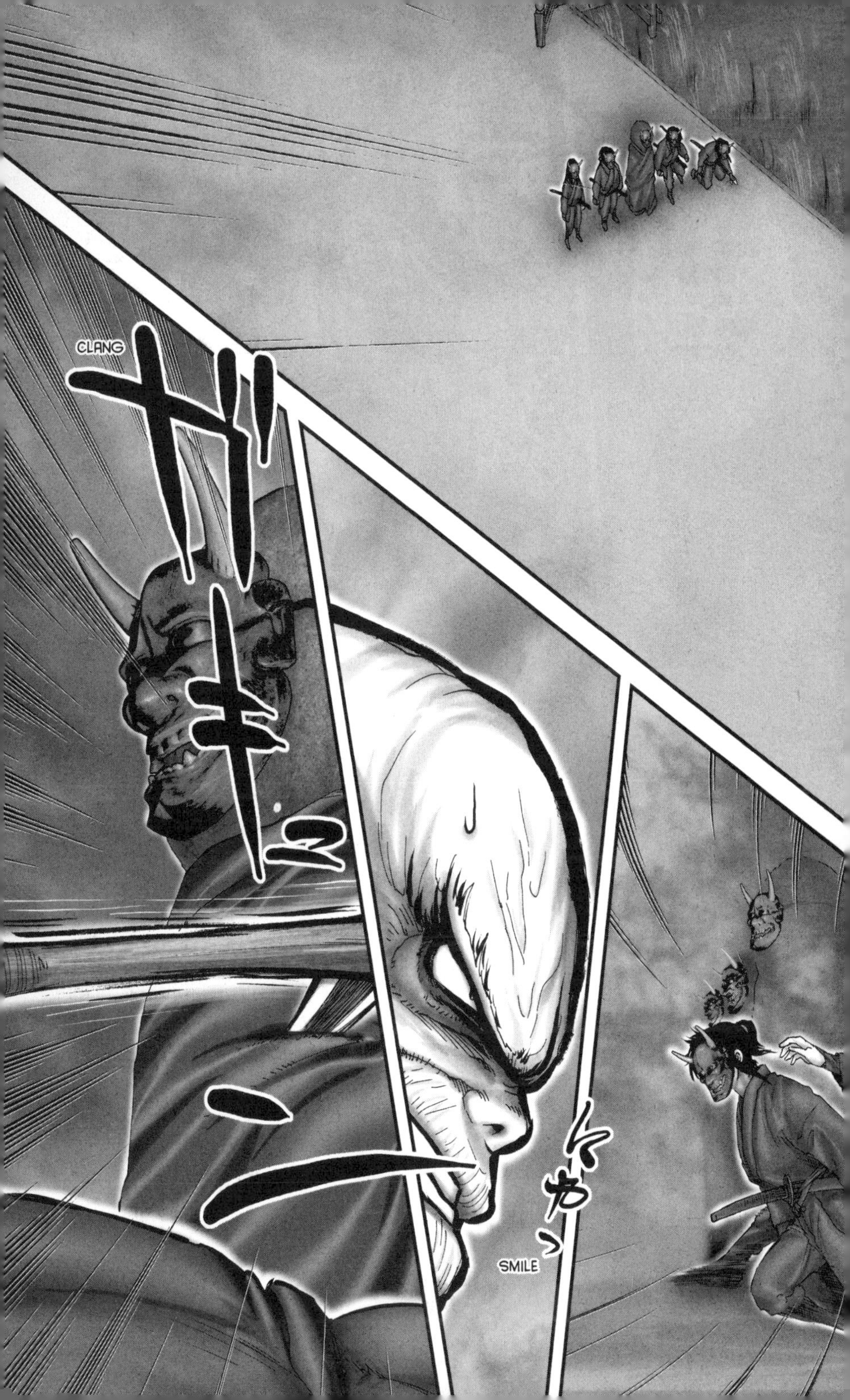
CLANG
ガギッ
ニカッ
SMILE

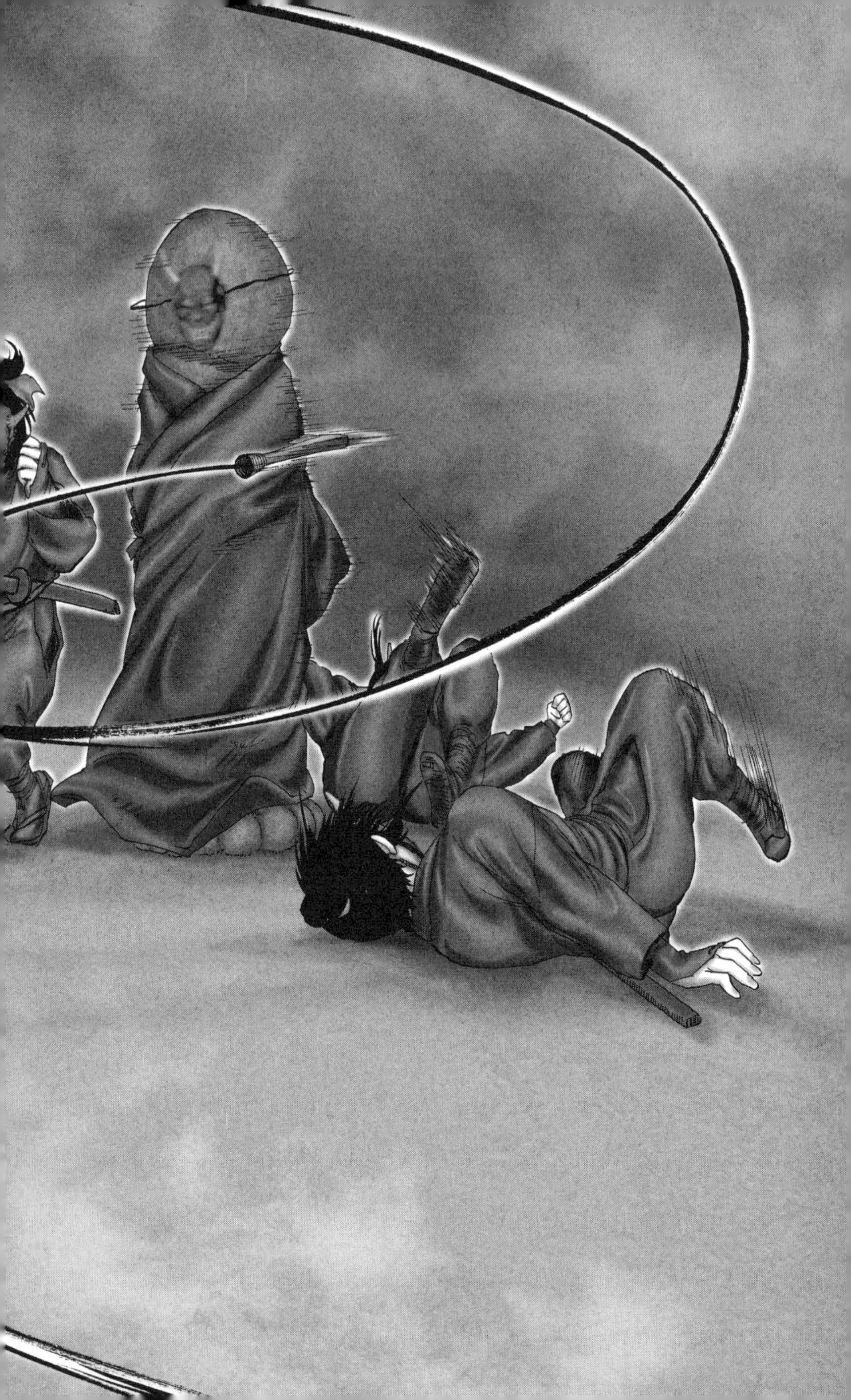

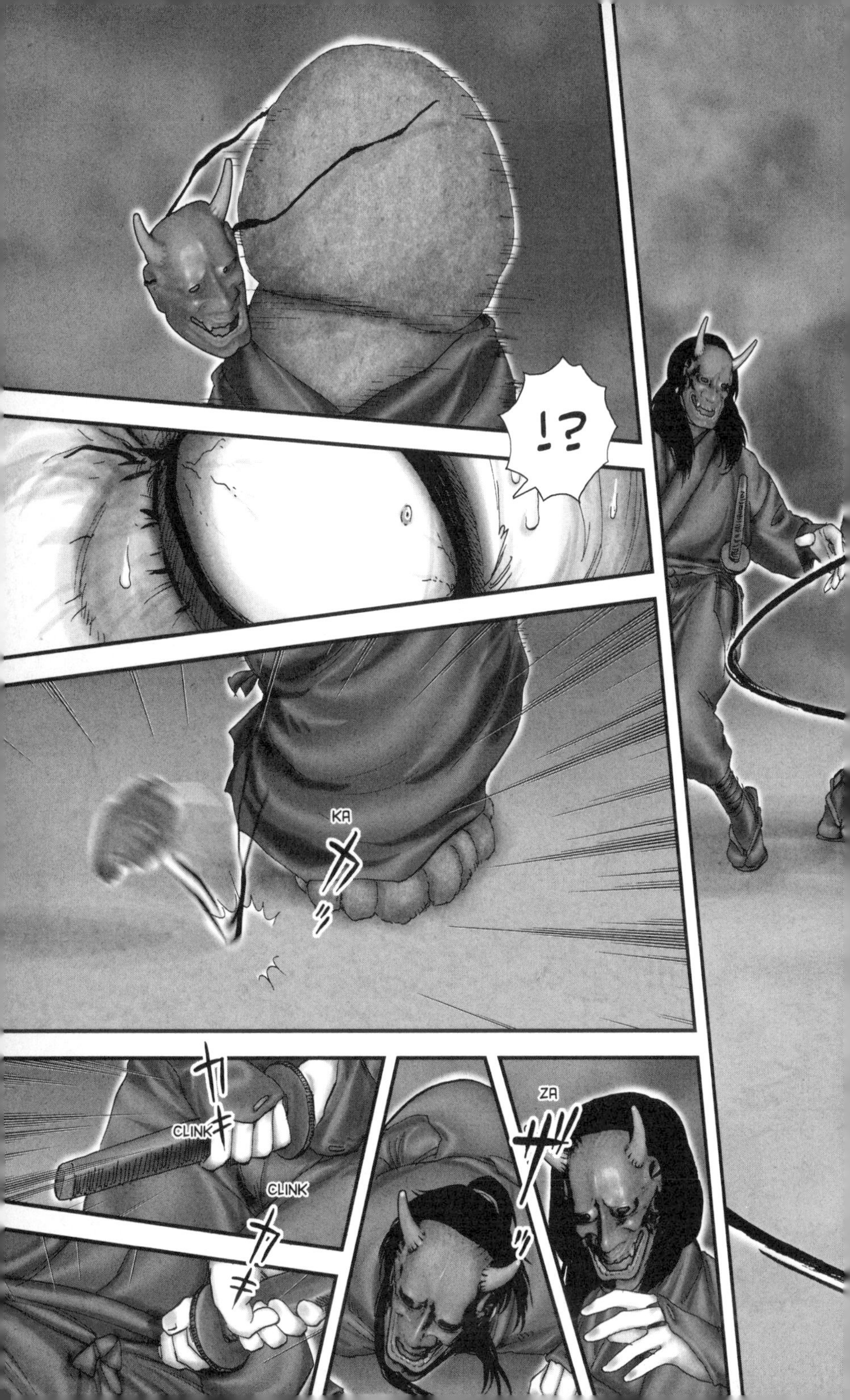
!?
KA
ZA
CLINK
CLINK

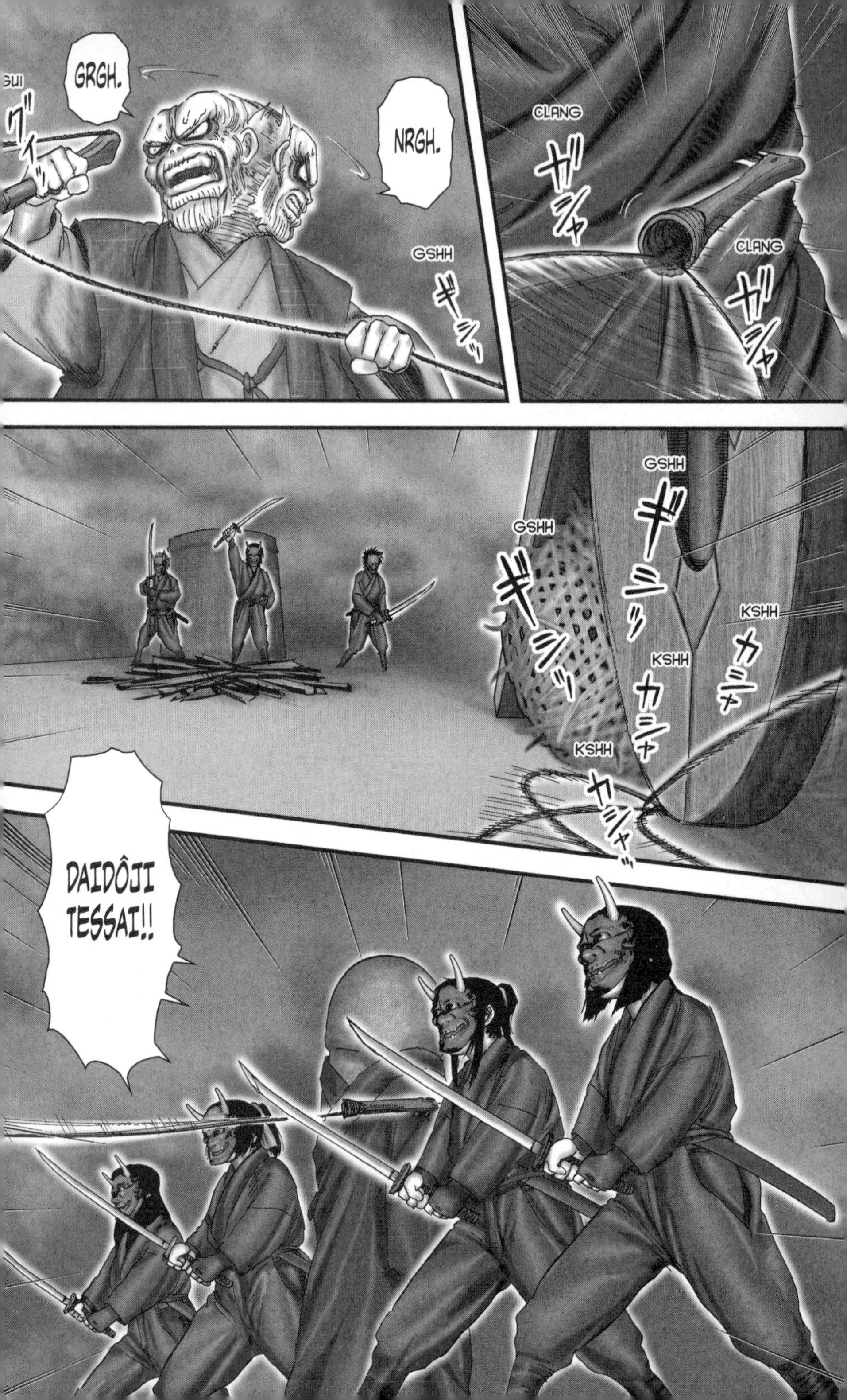
CLANG
ガシャ
CLANG
ガシャ
NRGH.
GRGH.
GUI
グイッ
GSHH
ギシッ
GSHH
ギシッ
GSHH
ギシッ
KSHH
カシャ
KSHH
カシャ
KSHH
カシャッ
DAIDÔJI TESSAI!!

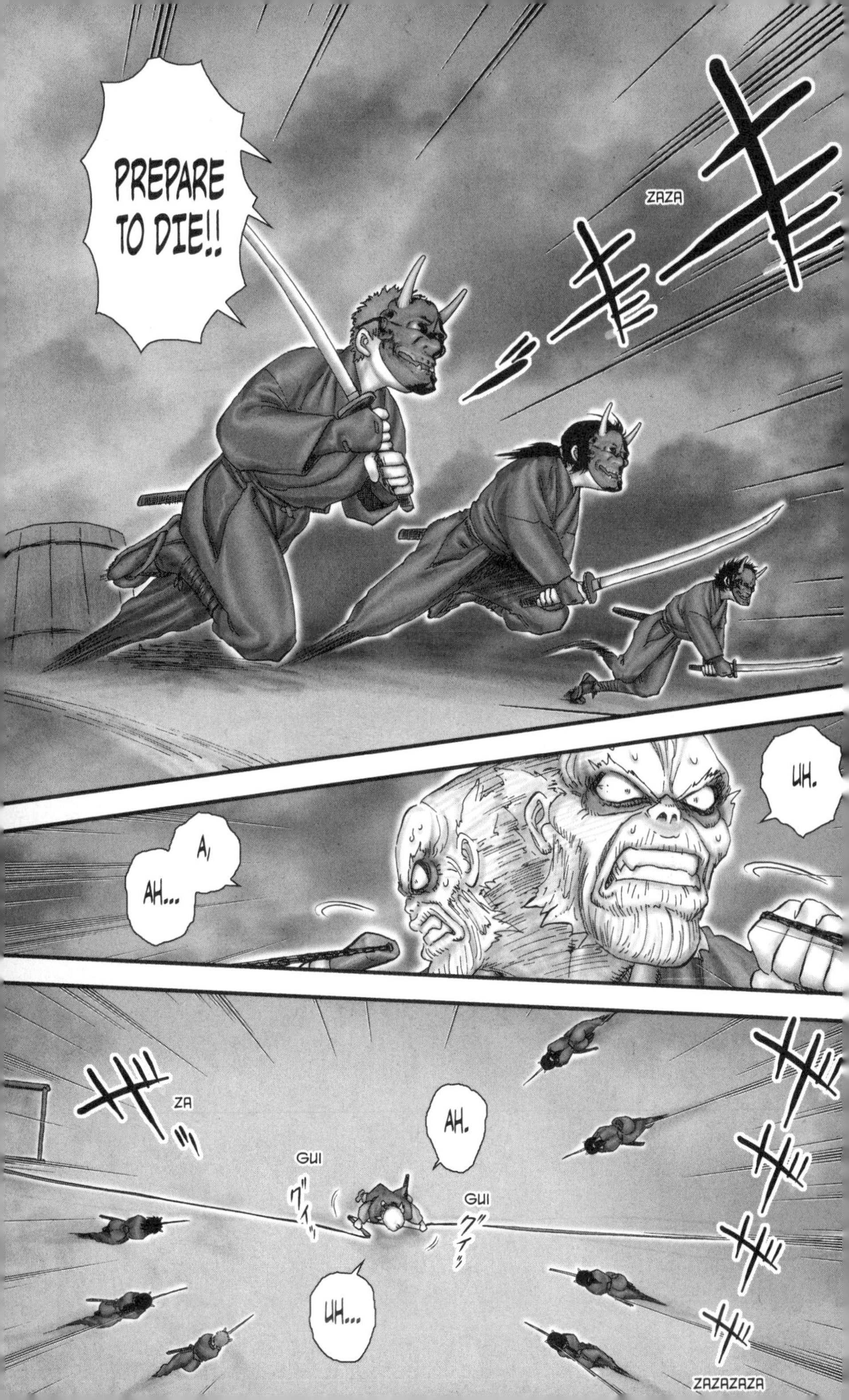
ZAZA
PREPARE TO DIE!!
UH.
A, AH...
ZAZAZAZA
AH.
GUI
GUI
UH...
ZA

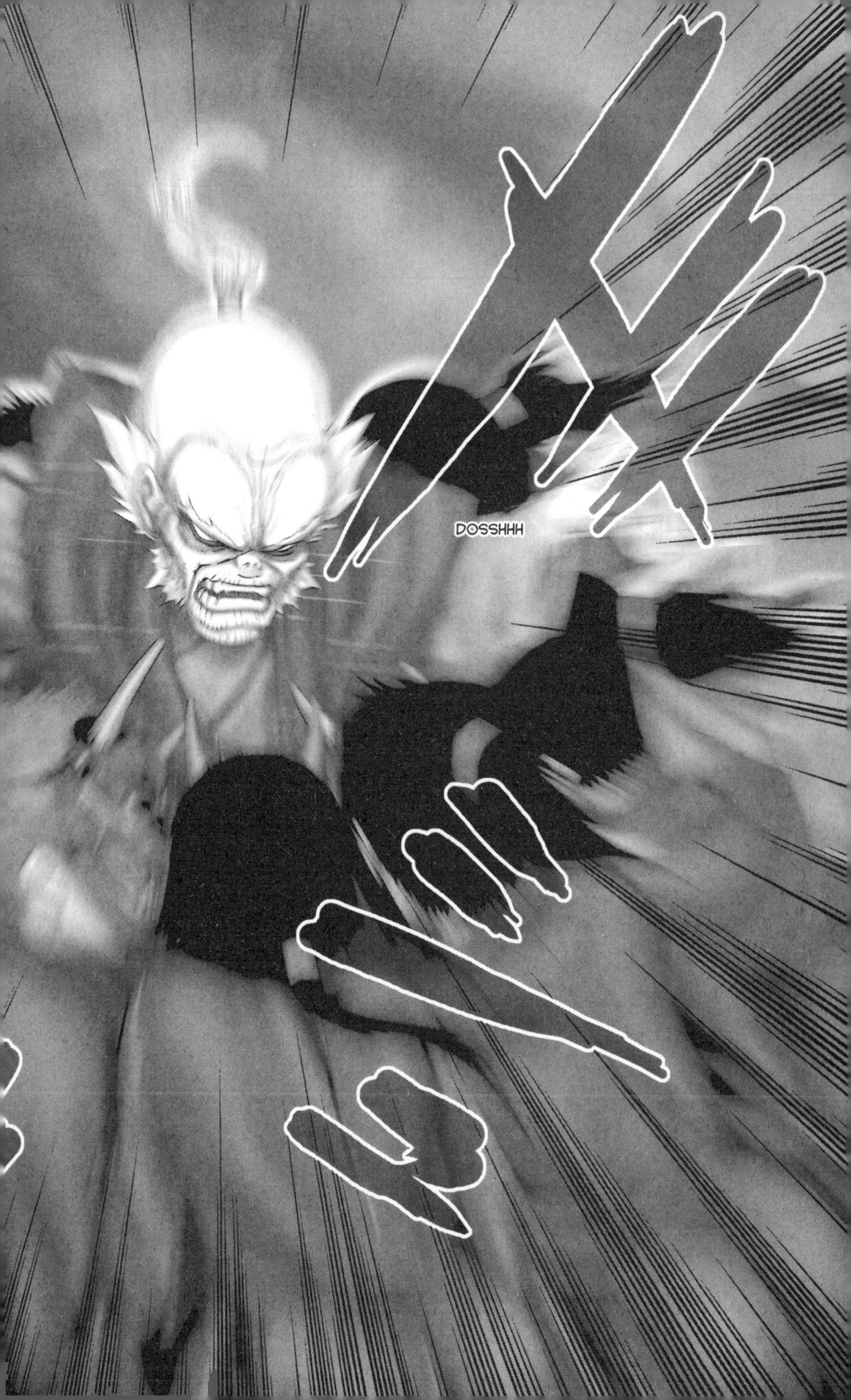
DOSSHHH

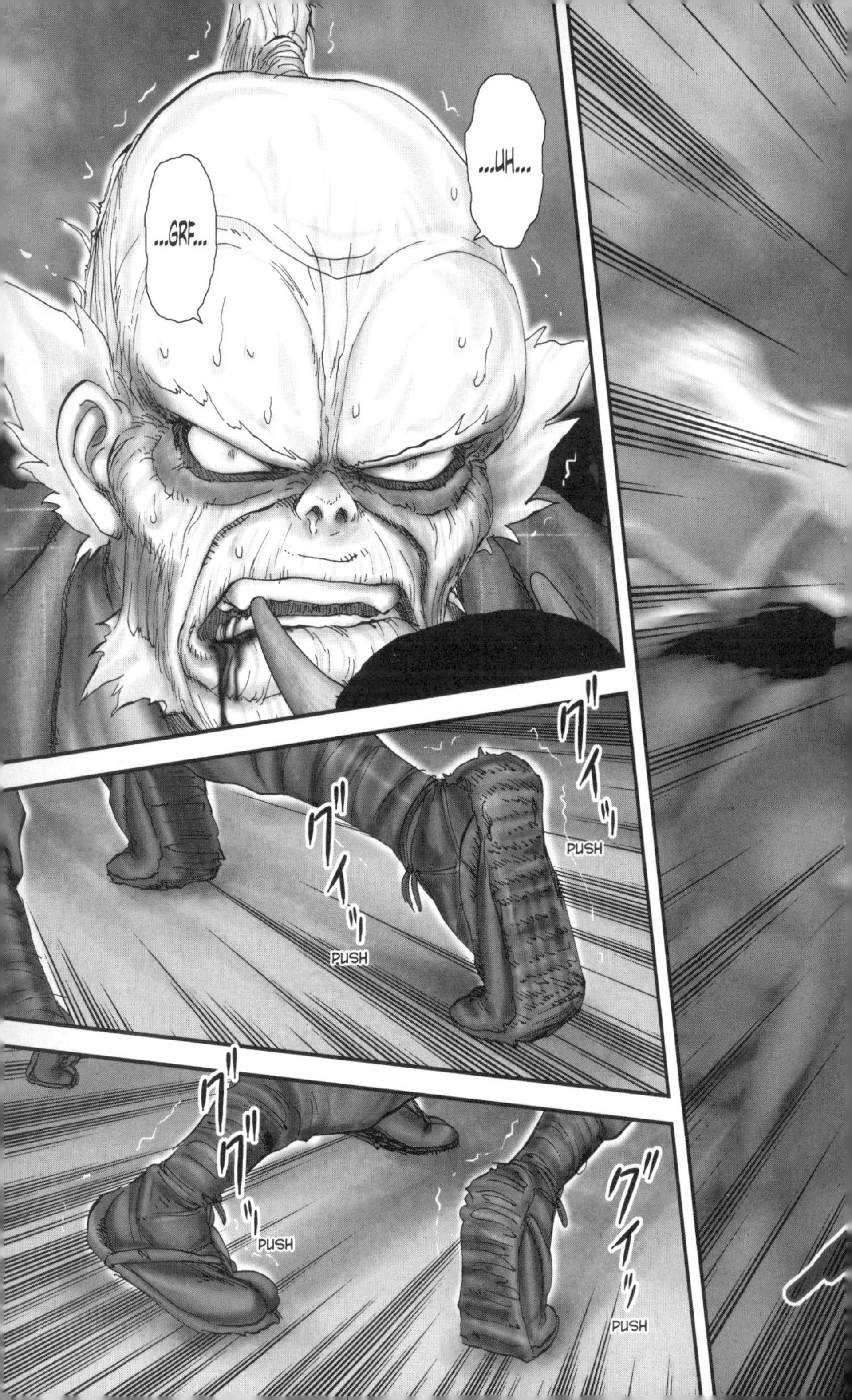
...UH...
...GRF...
グイッ
PUSH
グイッ
PUSH
グイッ
PUSH
ググッ
PUSH

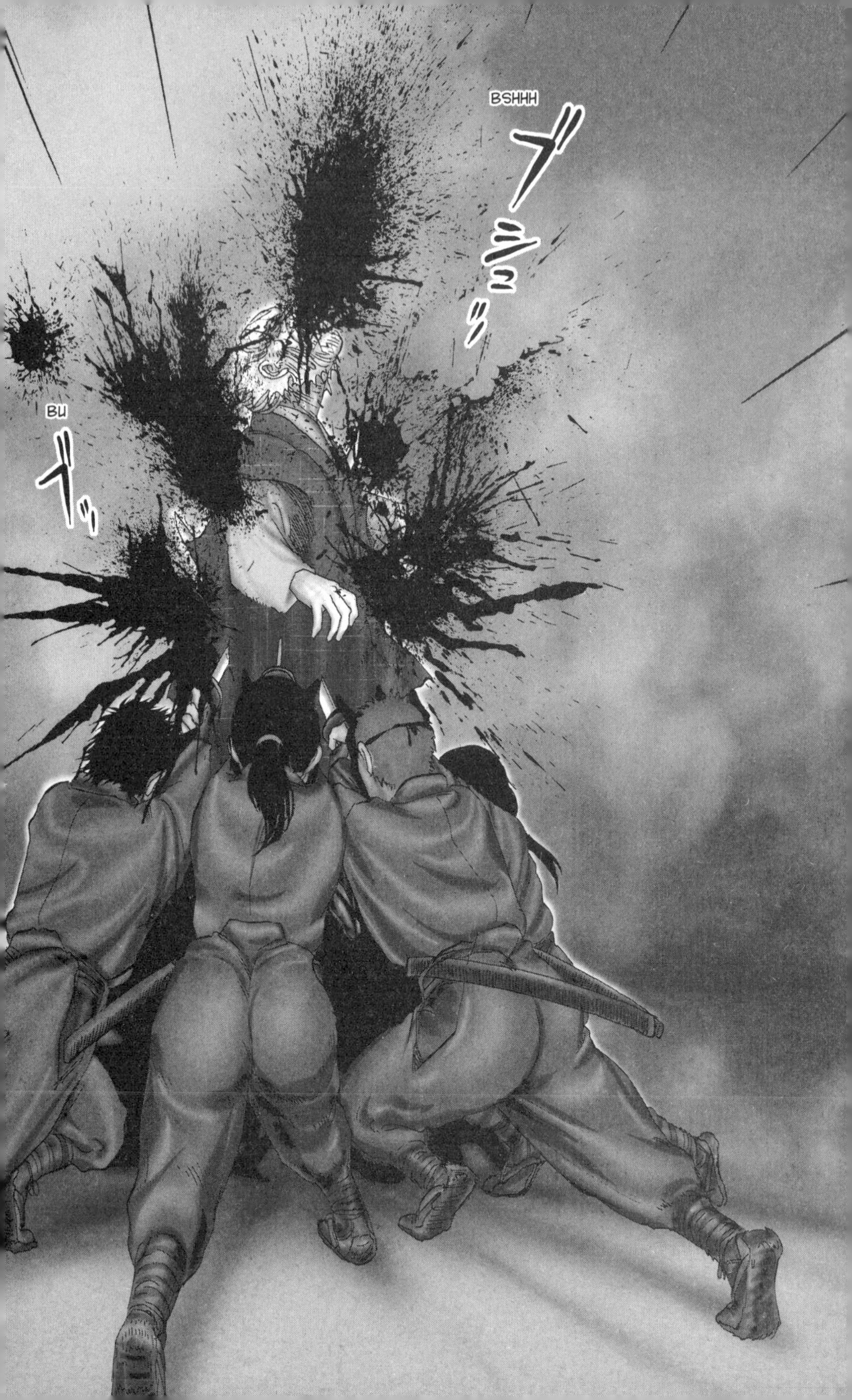
BSHHH
ブシュッ
BU
ブッ

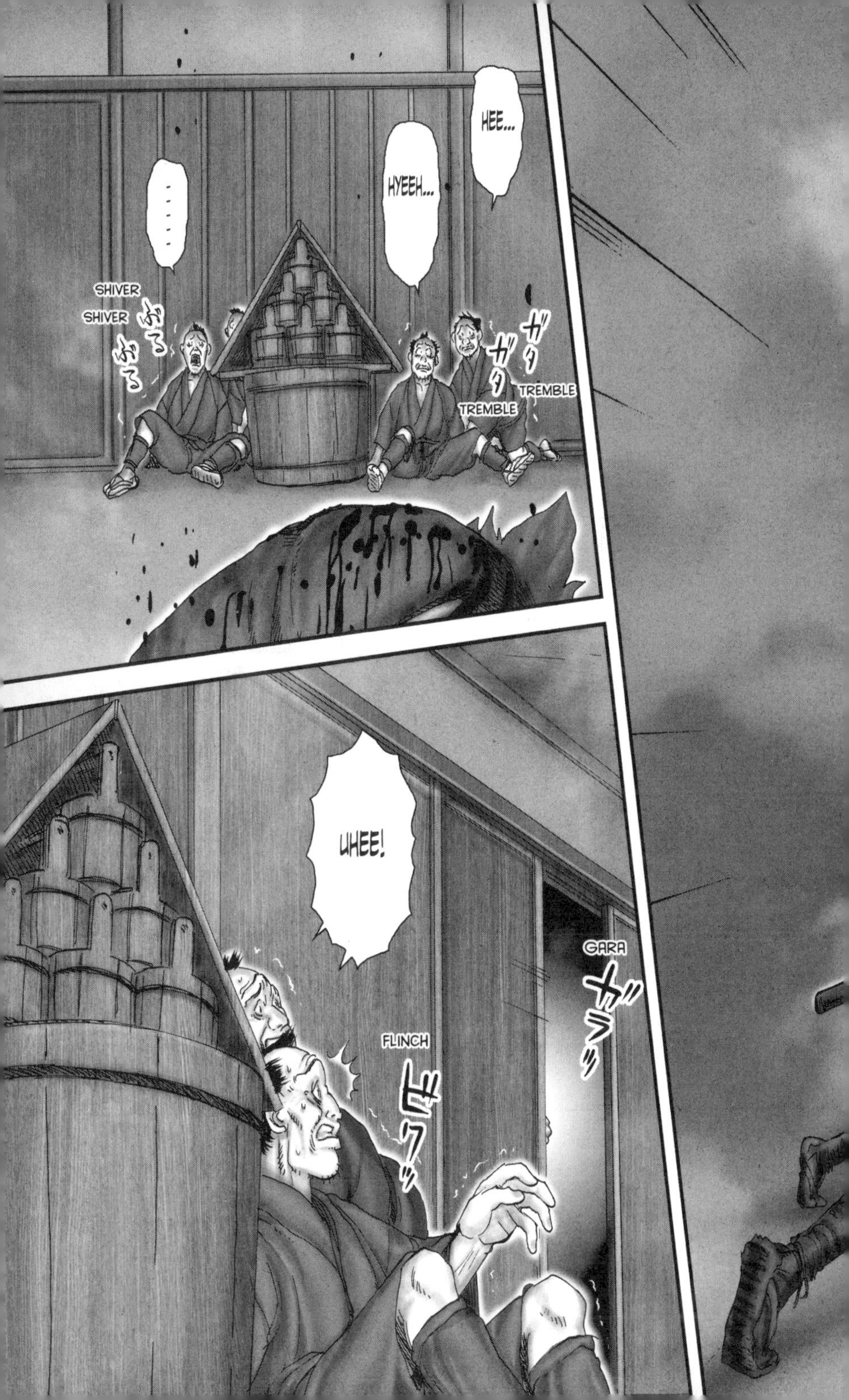
HEE...
HYEEH...
TREMBLE
TREMBLE
ガタ ガタ
......
SHIVER
SHIVER
ぶる ぶる
GARA
ガラッ
UHEE!
FLINCH
ビクッ

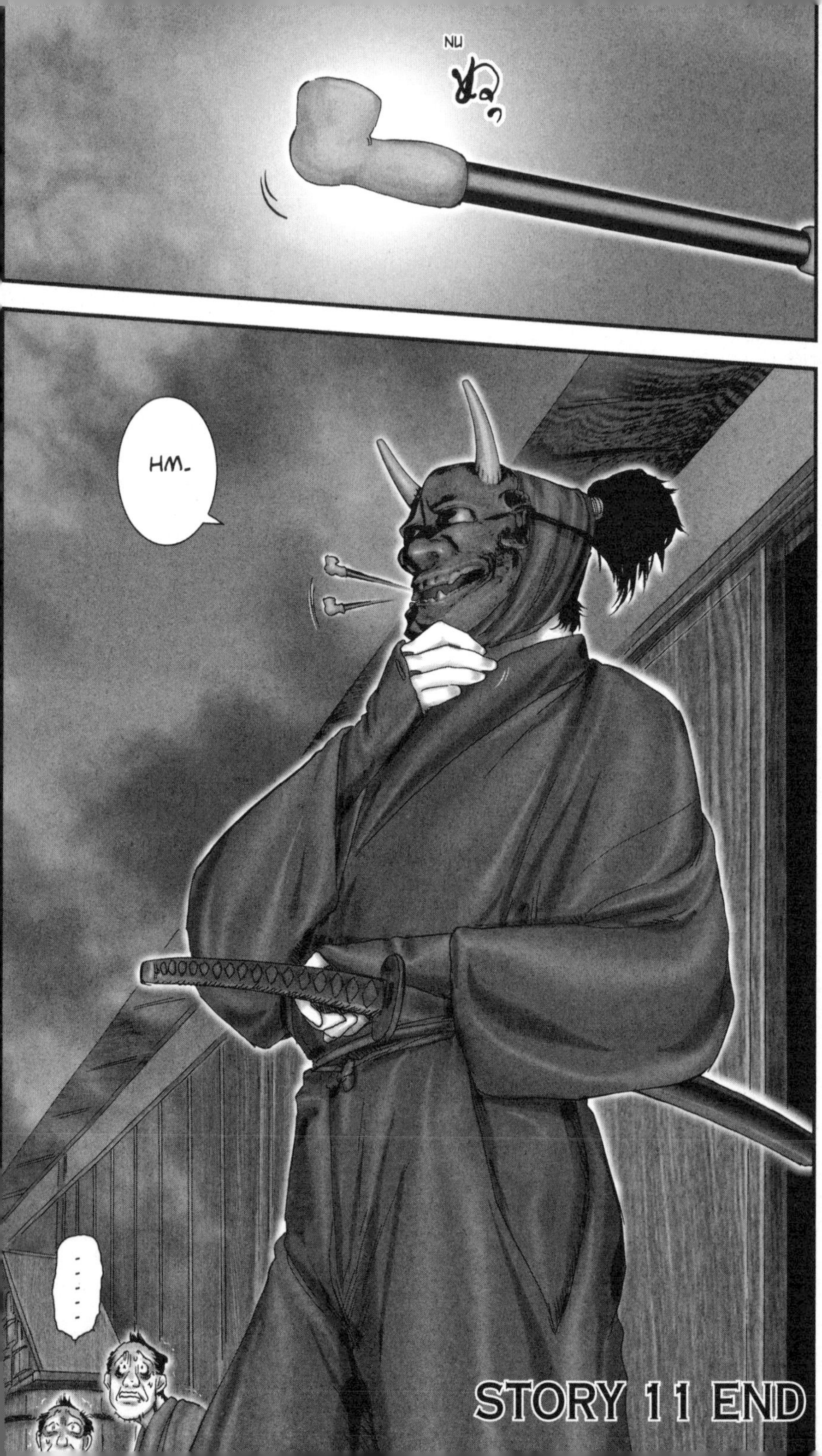
NU
ぬっ
HM.
......
STORY 11 END

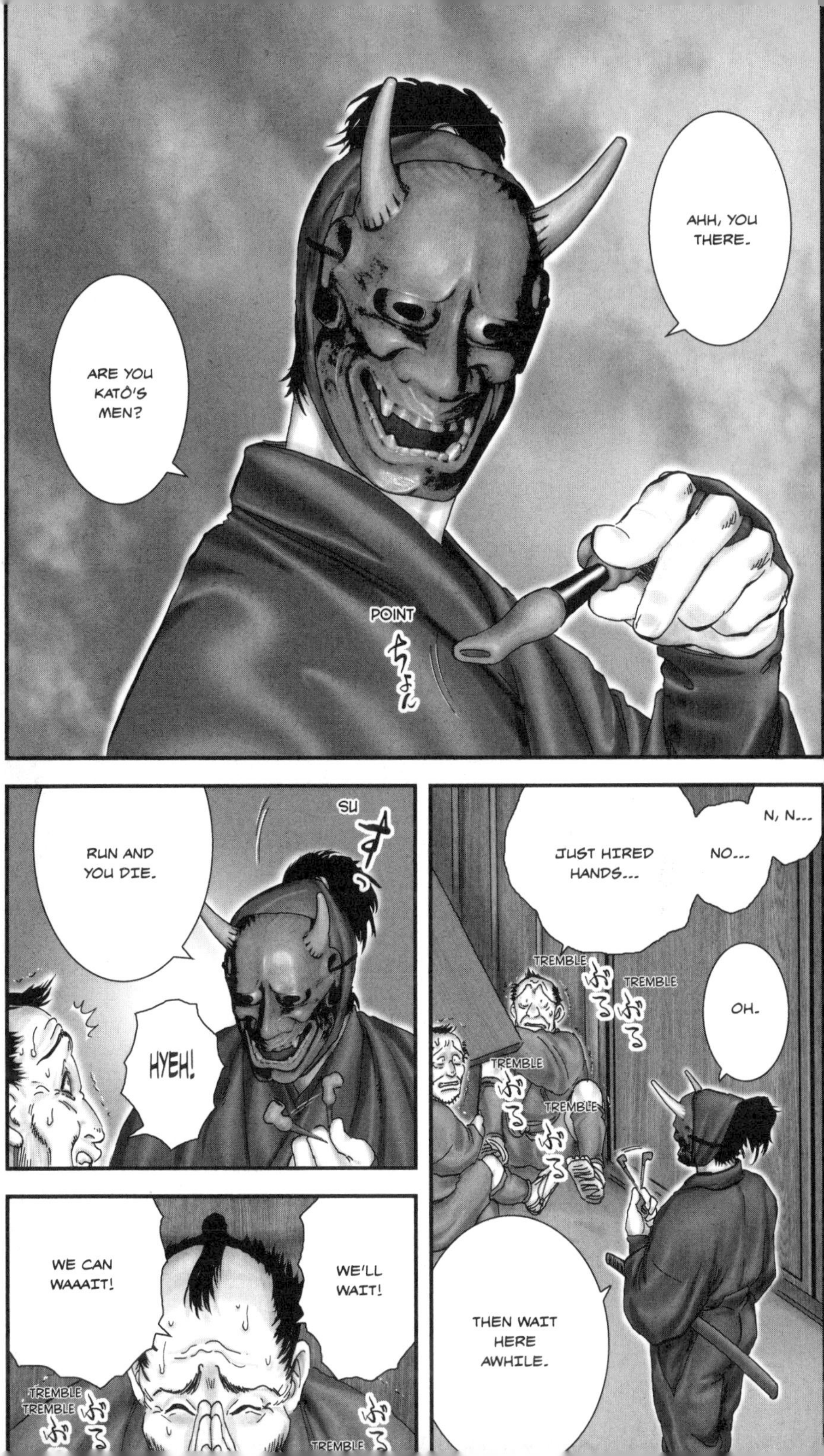
AHH, YOU THERE.
ARE YOU KATÔ'S MEN?
POINT
ちょん
N, N...
NO...
JUST HIRED HANDS...
TREMBLE
ぶる
TREMBLE
ぶる
TREMBLE
ぶる
TREMBLE
ぶる
OH.
THEN WAIT HERE AWHILE.
SU
すっ
RUN AND YOU DIE.
HYEH!
WE'LL WAIT!
WE CAN WAAAIT!
TREMBLE
TREMBLE
ぶる
TREMBLE

STORY 12: A GROUP OF DEMONESSES (2)

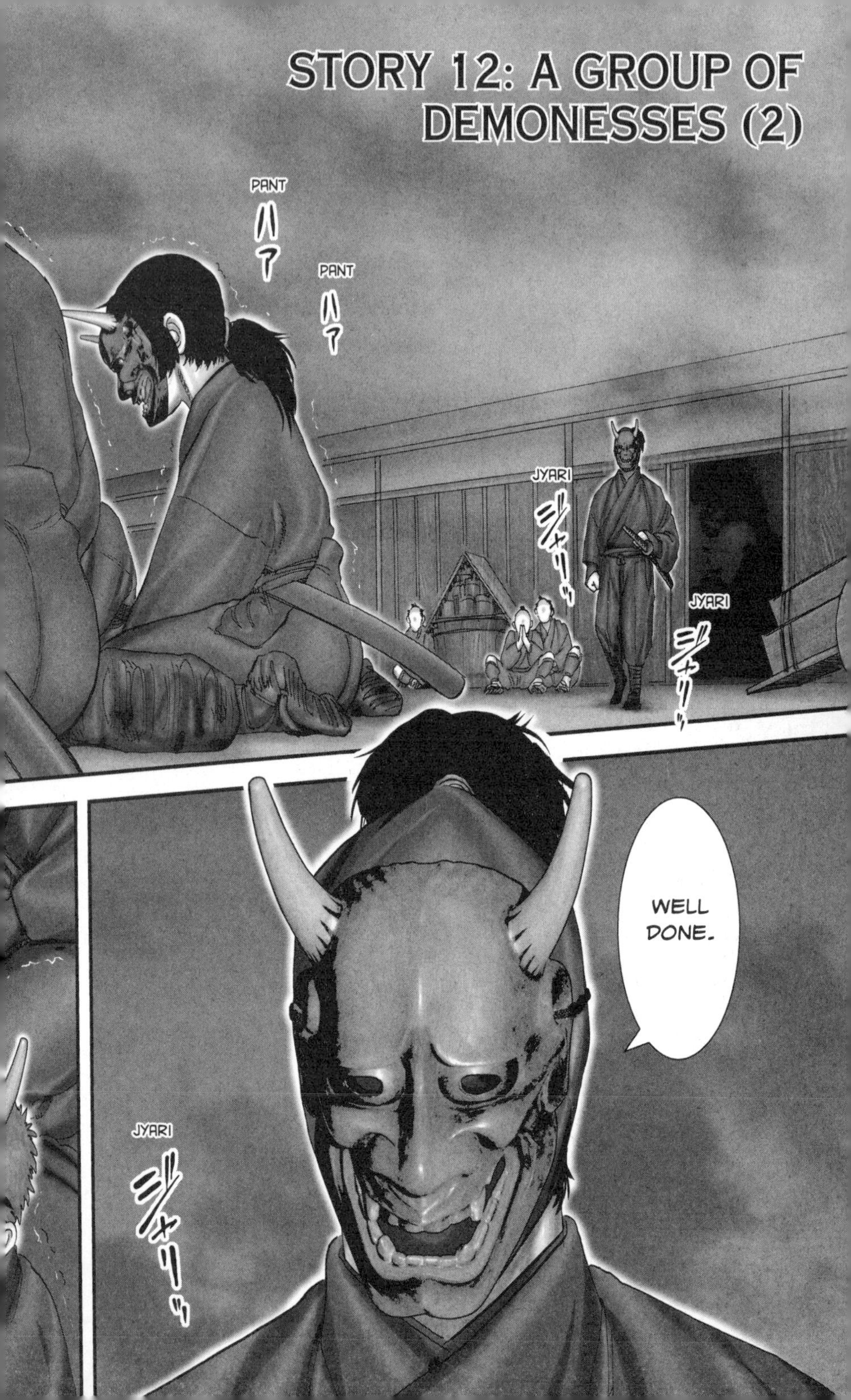
JYARI
ジャリッ
JYARI
ジャリッ
PANT
ハア
PANT
ハア
WELL DONE.
JYARI
ジャリッ

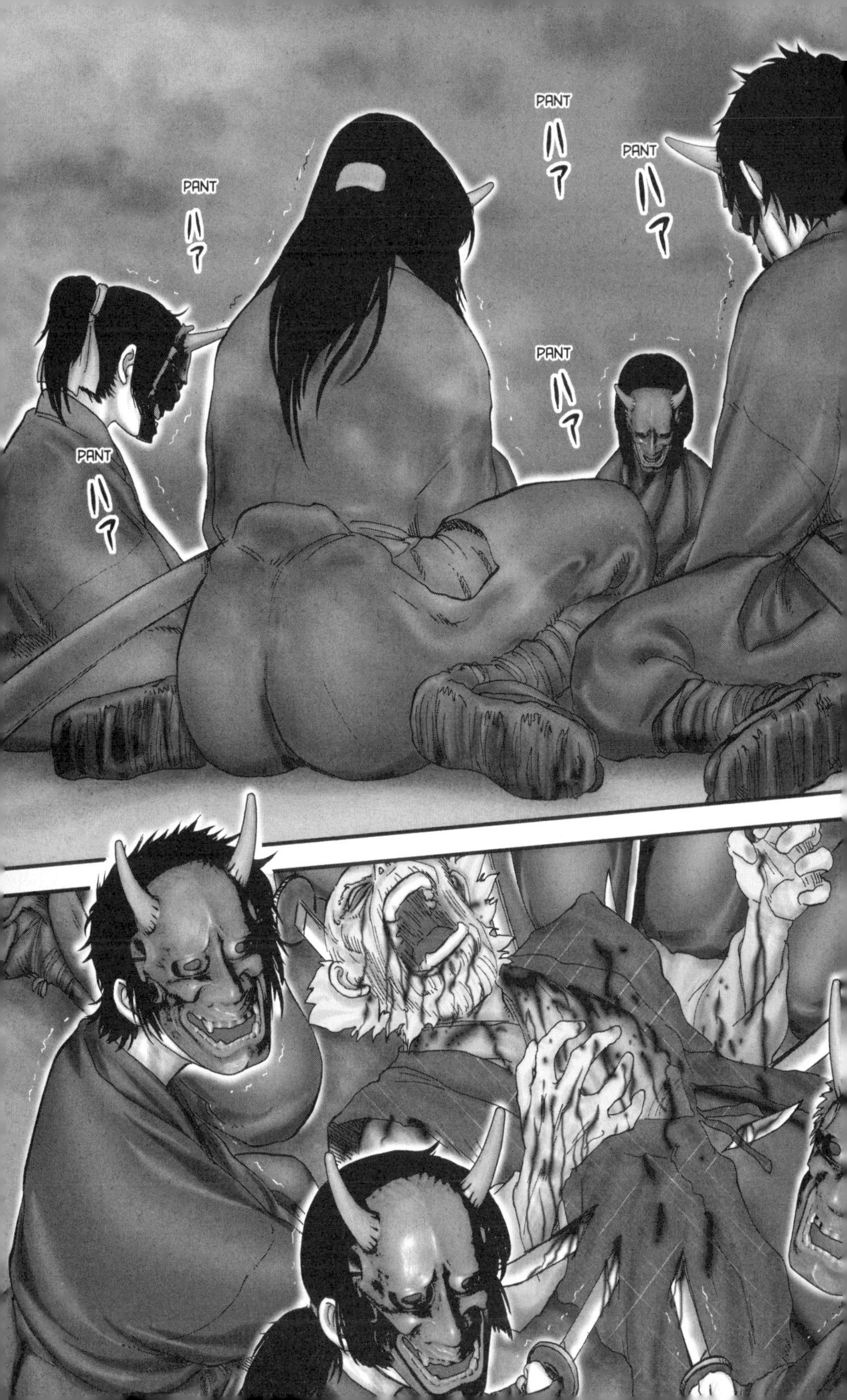
PANT ハア
PANT ハア
PANT ハア
PANT ハア
PANT ハア

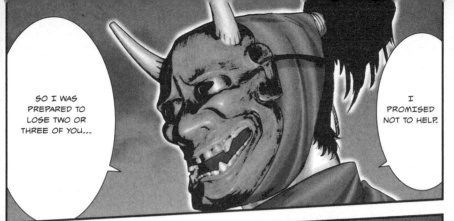

I PROMISED NOT TO HELP.
SO I WAS PREPARED TO LOSE TWO OR THREE OF YOU...
REALLY.
WELL DONE.
SENSEI JYŪBEI...

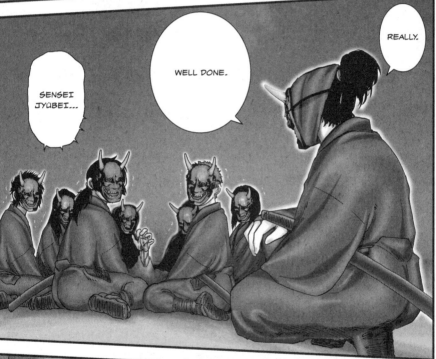

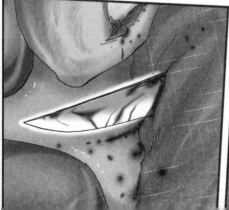

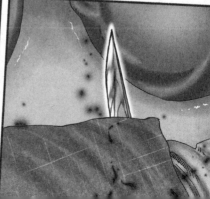

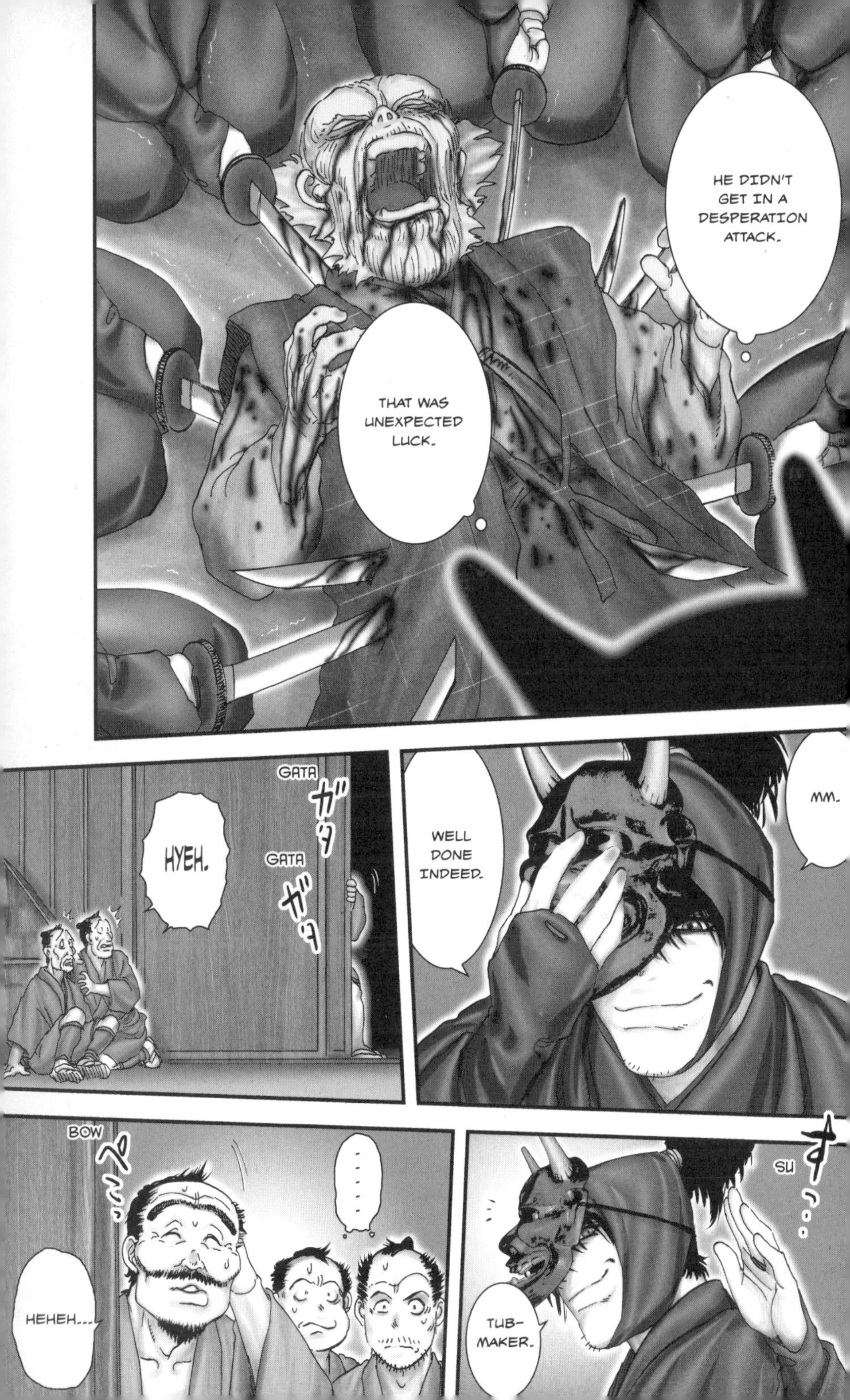
HE DIDN'T GET IN A DESPERATION ATTACK.
THAT WAS UNEXPECTED LUCK.
MM.
WELL DONE INDEED.
GATA
ガタ
GATA
ガタ
HYEH.
SU
すっ...
TUB-MAKER.
......
BOW
ぺこっ
HEHEH...

AH...

YOU SHOULD GO. LEAVE THE REST TO ME.

NOW, OCHIE.

HM.

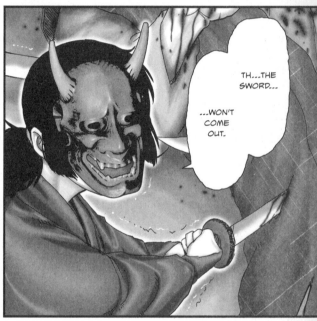

TH...THE SWORD...

...WON'T COME OUT.

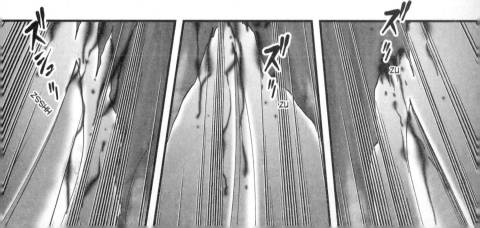

ZSSHH

ZU

ZU

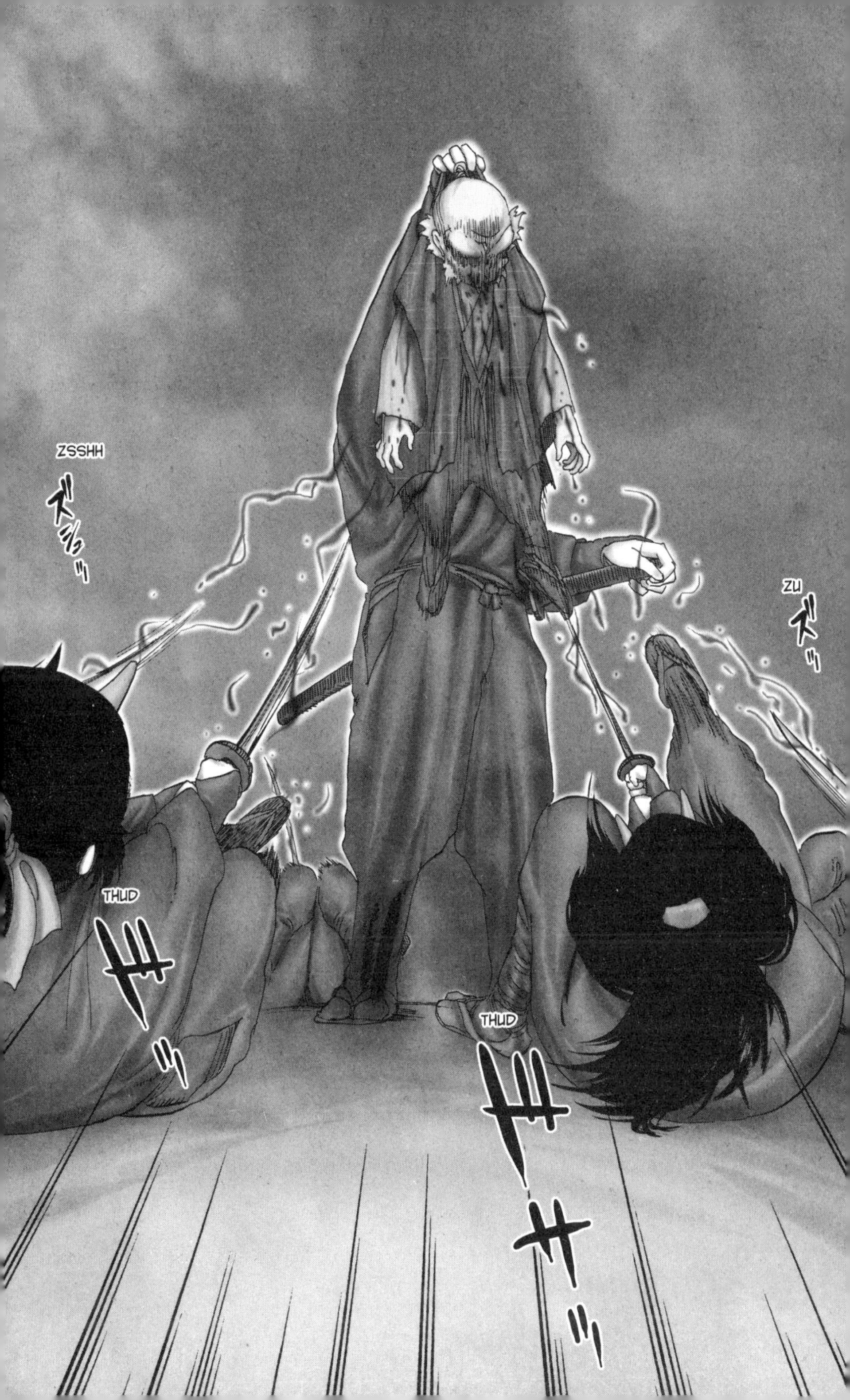
ZSSHH
ZU
THUD
THUD

YE—YES!

NOW GO.

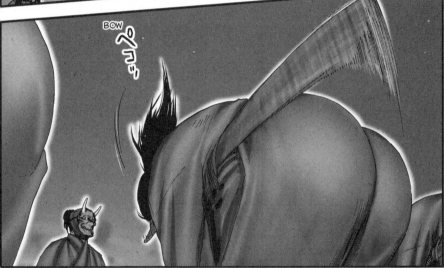

BOW

BOSS...

WHAT THE...

RUNNING

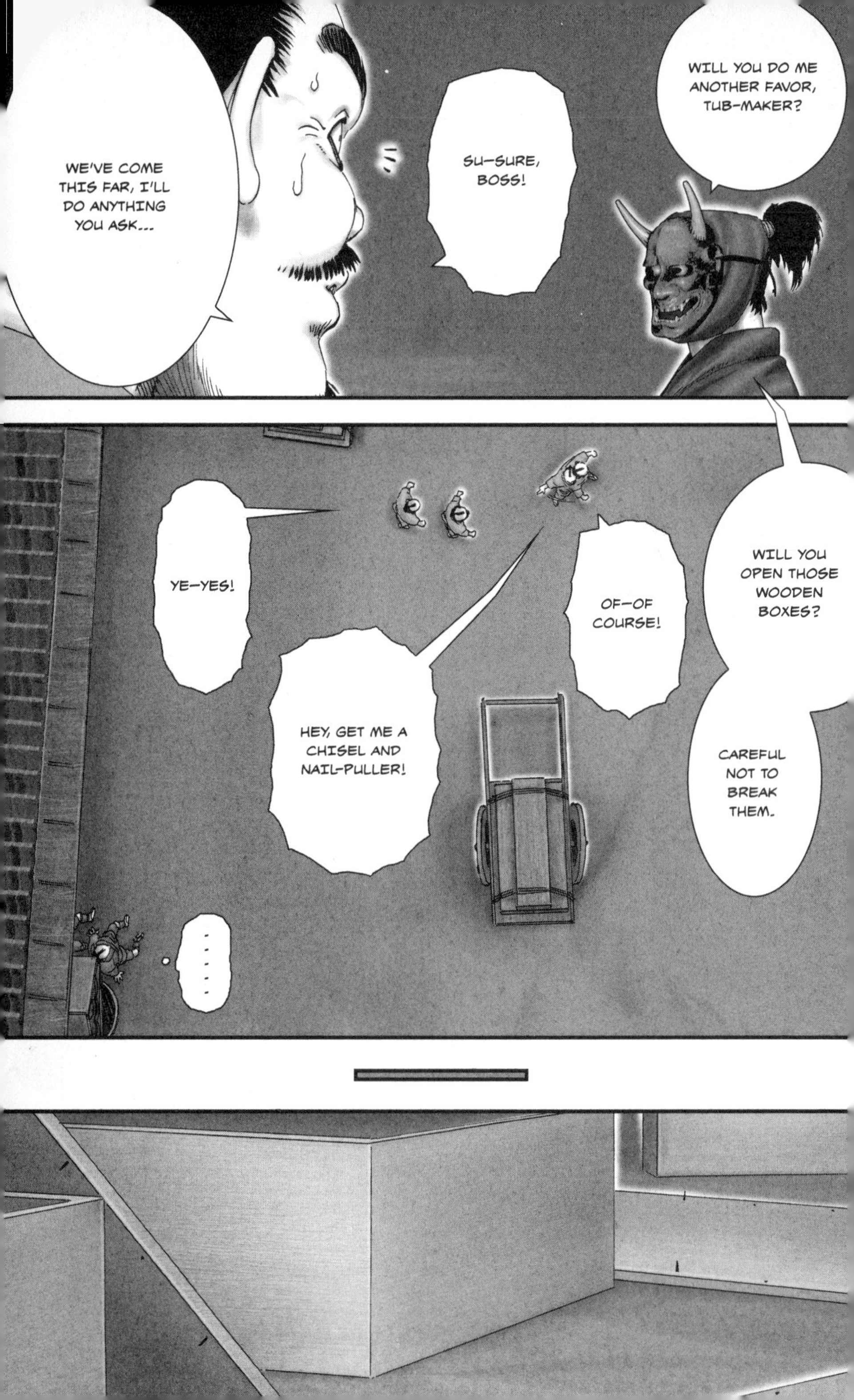
WILL YOU DO ME ANOTHER FAVOR, TUB-MAKER?
SU-SURE, BOSS!
WE'VE COME THIS FAR, I'LL DO ANYTHING YOU ASK...
WILL YOU OPEN THOSE WOODEN BOXES?
CAREFUL NOT TO BREAK THEM.
OF—OF COURSE!
HEY, GET ME A CHISEL AND NAIL-PULLER!
YE—YES!
......

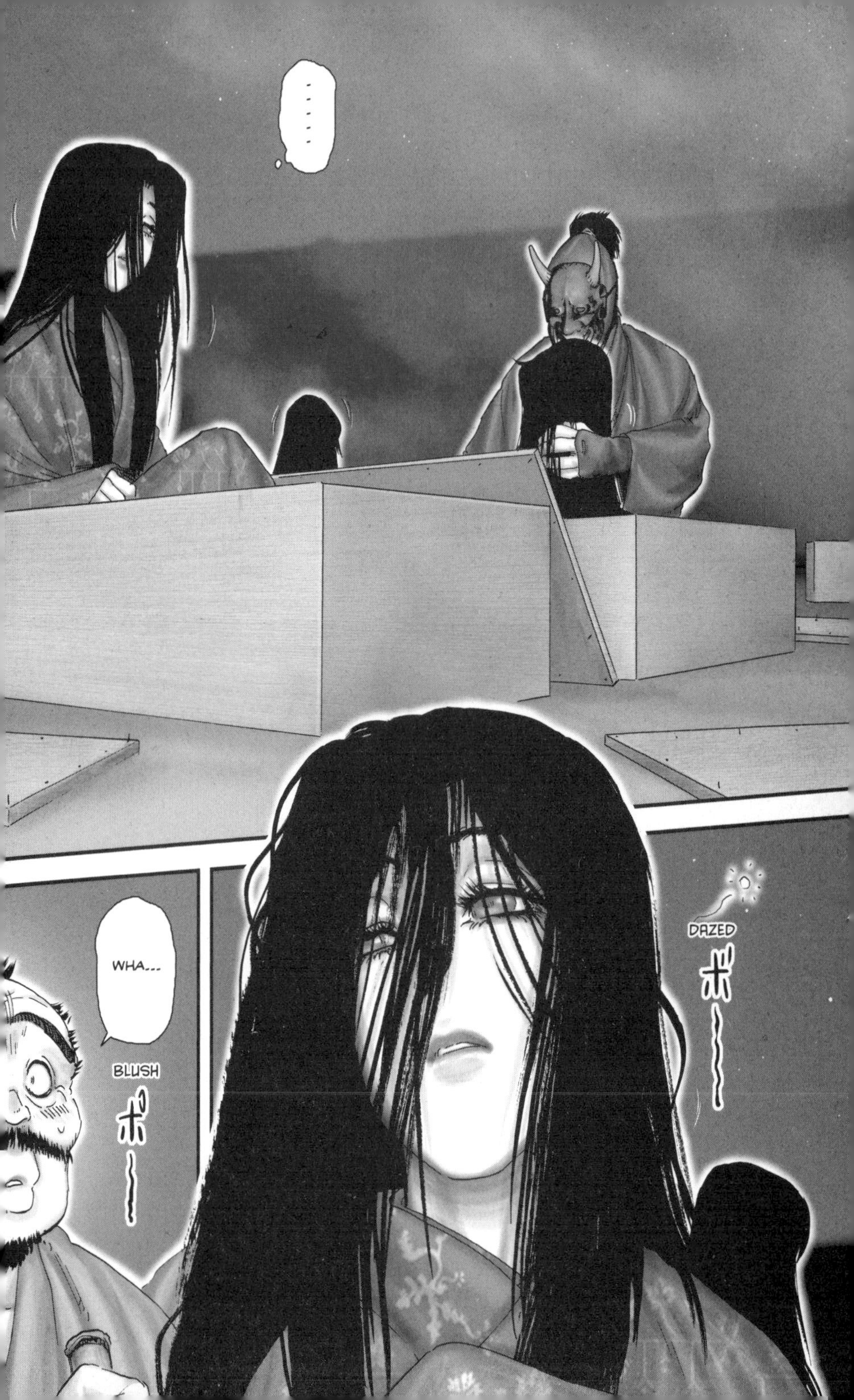
......
DAZED
ボ〜〜〜
WHA...
BLUSH
ポ〜〜

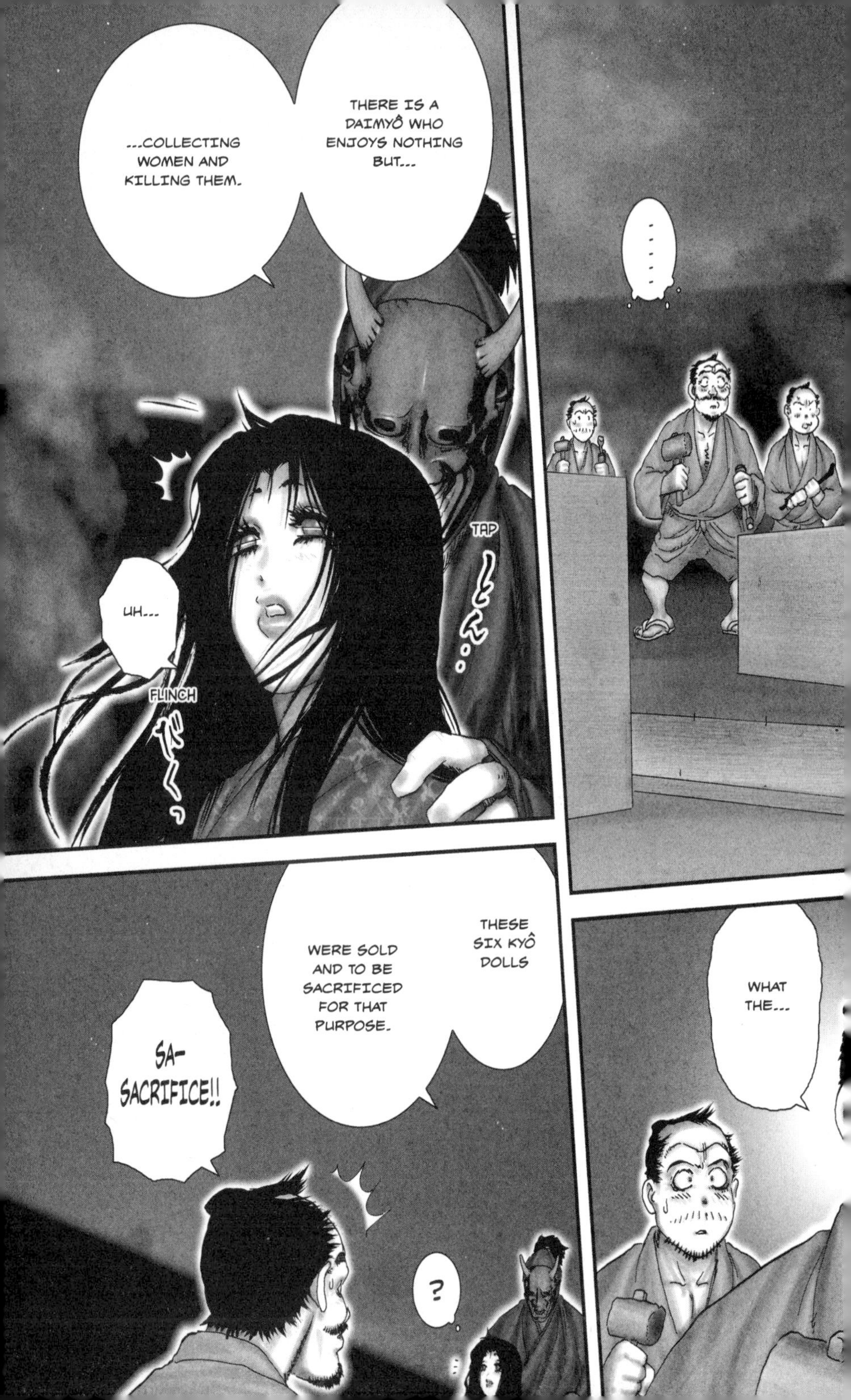
......
THERE IS A DAIMYÔ WHO ENJOYS NOTHING BUT...
...COLLECTING WOMEN AND KILLING THEM.
TAP
UH...
FLINCH
WHAT THE...
THESE SIX KYÔ DOLLS
WERE SOLD AND TO BE SACRIFICED FOR THAT PURPOSE.
SA-SACRIFICE!!
?

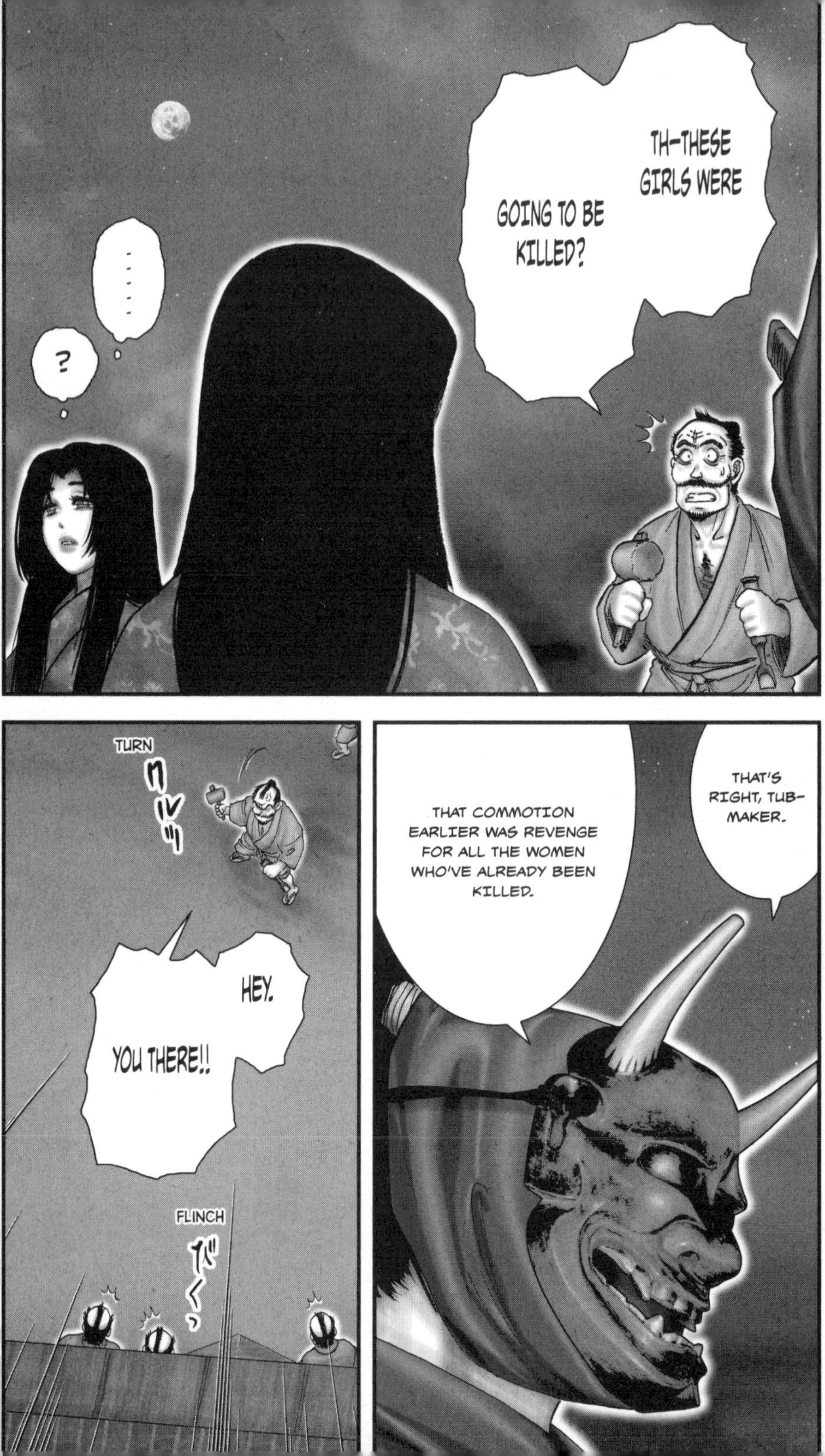
TH-THESE GIRLS WERE GOING TO BE KILLED?
......
?
THAT'S RIGHT, TUB-MAKER.
THAT COMMOTION EARLIER WAS REVENGE FOR ALL THE WOMEN WHO'VE ALREADY BEEN KILLED.
TURN
HEY.
YOU THERE!!
FLINCH

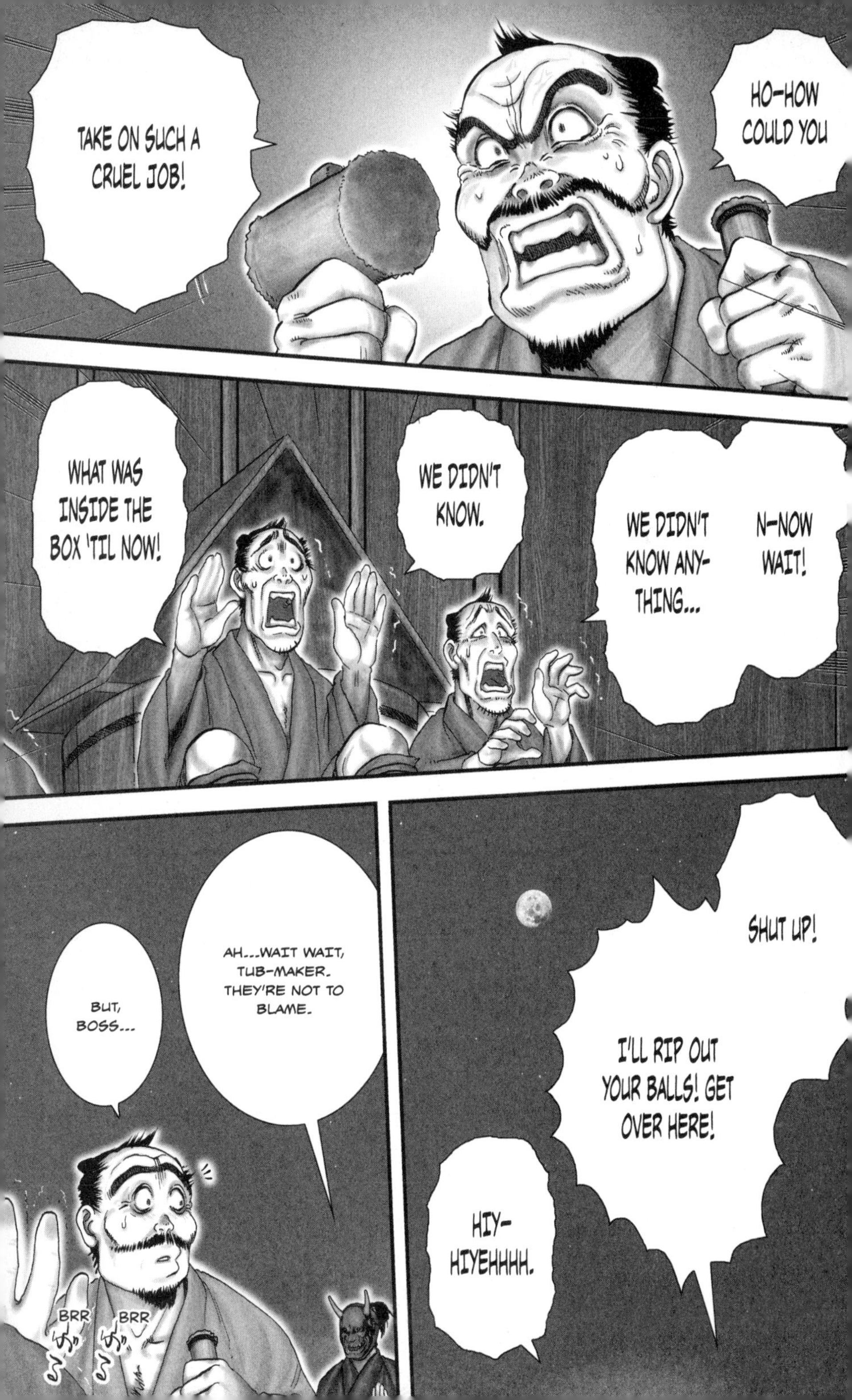
HO-HOW COULD YOU
TAKE ON SUCH A CRUEL JOB!
N-NOW WAIT!
WE DIDN'T KNOW ANY-THING...
WE DIDN'T KNOW.
WHAT WAS INSIDE THE BOX 'TIL NOW!
SHUT UP!
I'LL RIP OUT YOUR BALLS! GET OVER HERE!
HIY-HIYEHHHH.
AH...WAIT WAIT, TUB-MAKER. THEY'RE NOT TO BLAME.
BUT, BOSS...
BRR
BRR

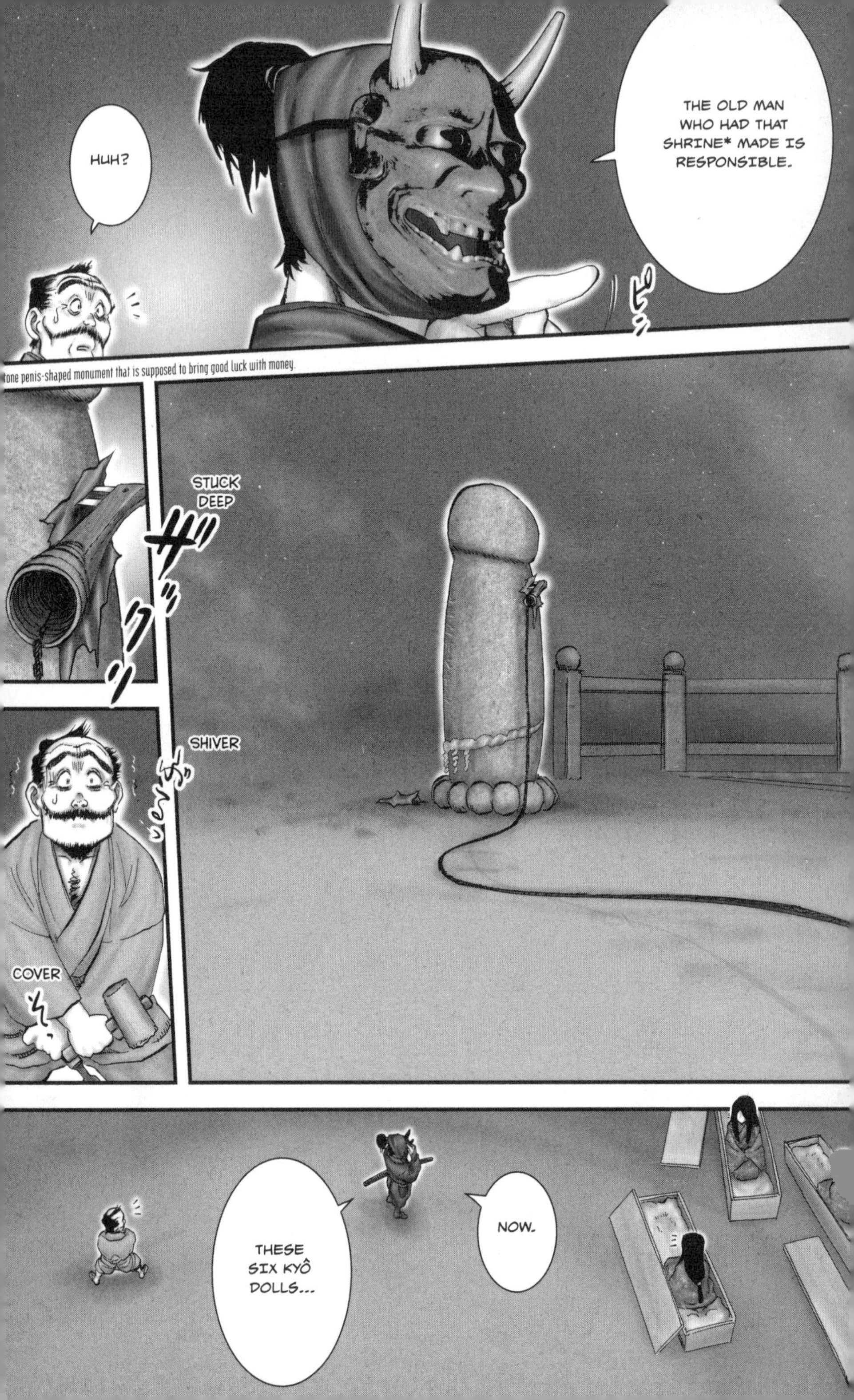
THE OLD MAN WHO HAD THAT SHRINE* MADE IS RESPONSIBLE.
HUH?
STUCK DEEP
SHIVER
COVER
NOW.
THESE SIX KYÔ DOLLS...

tone penis-shaped monument that is supposed to bring good luck with money.

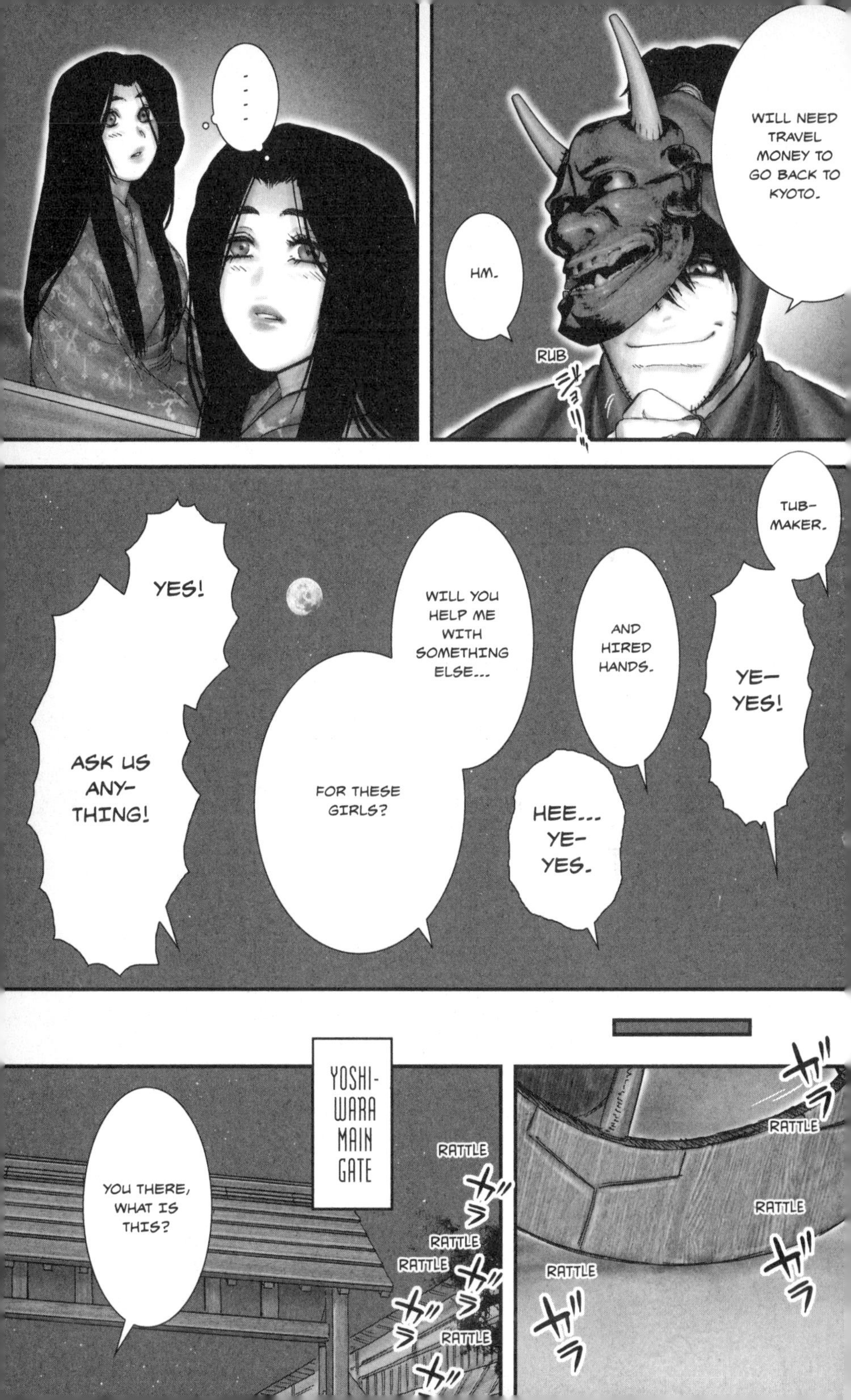
WILL NEED TRAVEL MONEY TO GO BACK TO KYOTO.
HM.
RUB
.....
TUB-MAKER.
YE-YES!
AND HIRED HANDS.
HEE... YE-YES.
WILL YOU HELP ME WITH SOMETHING ELSE...
FOR THESE GIRLS?
YES!
ASK US ANYTHING!
RATTLE
RATTLE
RATTLE
RATTLE
YOSHIWARA MAIN GATE
RATTLE
RATTLE
RATTLE
RATTLE
YOU THERE, WHAT IS THIS?

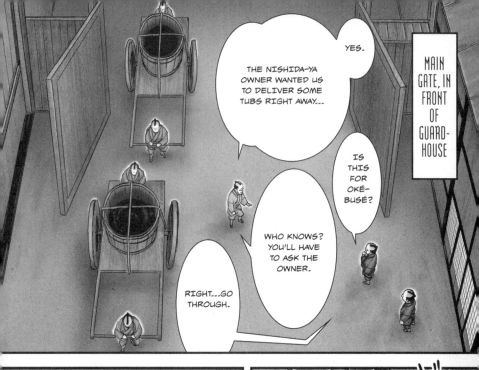

MAIN GATE, IN FRONT OF GUARDHOUSE
YES.
THE NISHIDA-YA OWNER WANTED US TO DELIVER SOME TUBS RIGHT AWAY...
IS THIS FOR OKÉ-BUSÉ?
WHO KNOWS? YOU'LL HAVE TO ASK THE OWNER.
RIGHT...GO THROUGH.
RATTLE
ガラ
RATTLE
ガラ
RATTLE
ガラ
RATTLE
ガラ
HEH.
RATTLE
ガラ
RATTLE
ガラ
RATTLE
ガラ
RATTLE
ガラ
INSIDE YOSHIWARA EDO 1-CHÔME
RATTLE
ガラ
RATTLE
ガラ
RATTLE
ガラ
RATTLE
ガラ
NISHIDA-YA

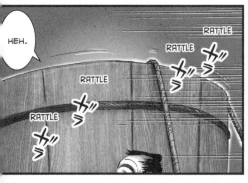

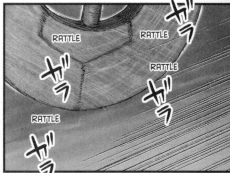

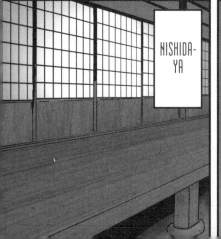

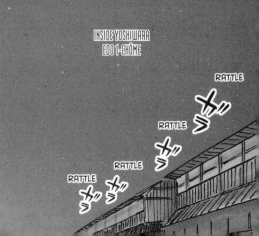

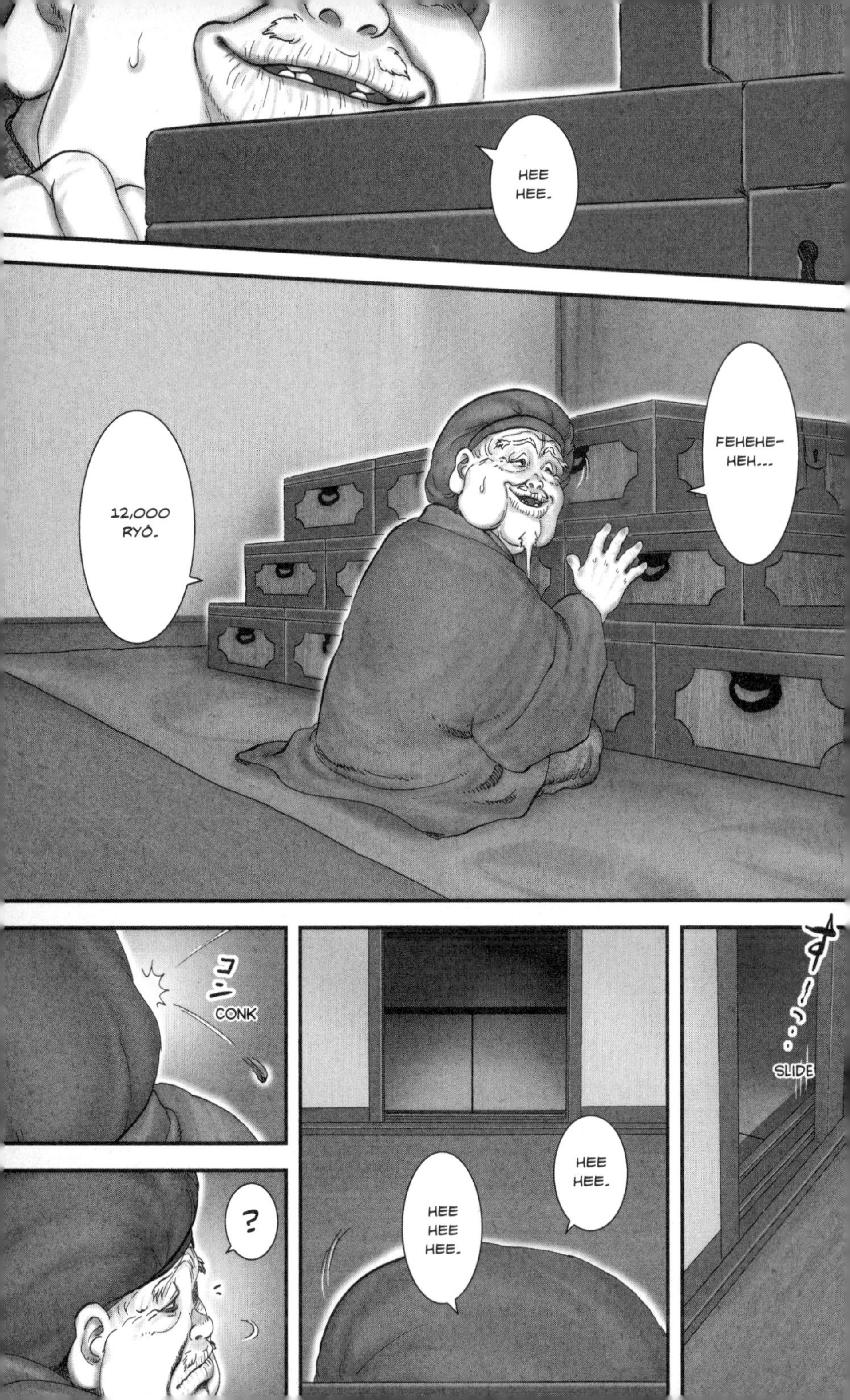
HEE HEE.
FEHEHE-HEH...
12,000 RYŌ.
SLIDE
HEE HEE.
HEE HEE HEE.
CONK
?

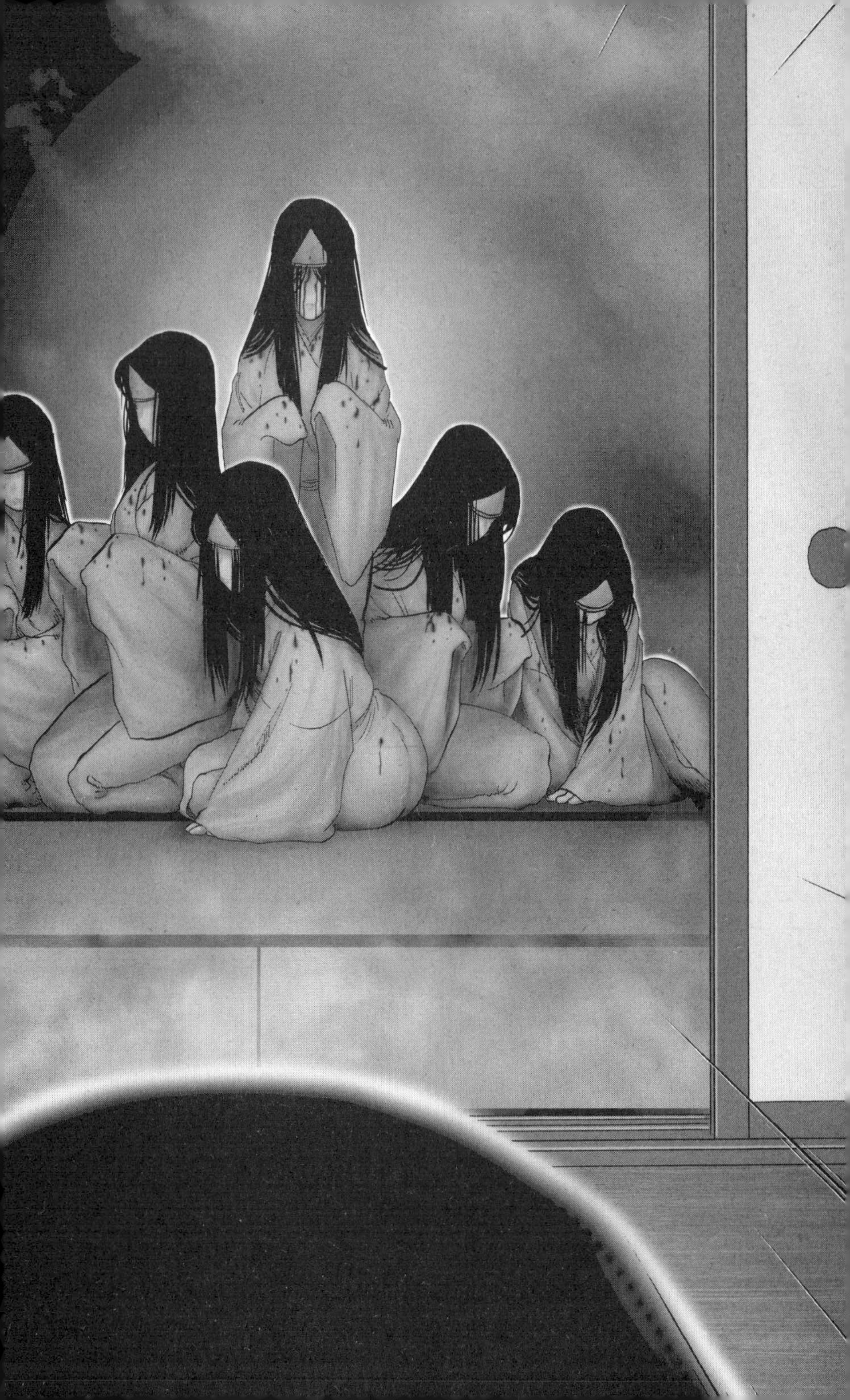

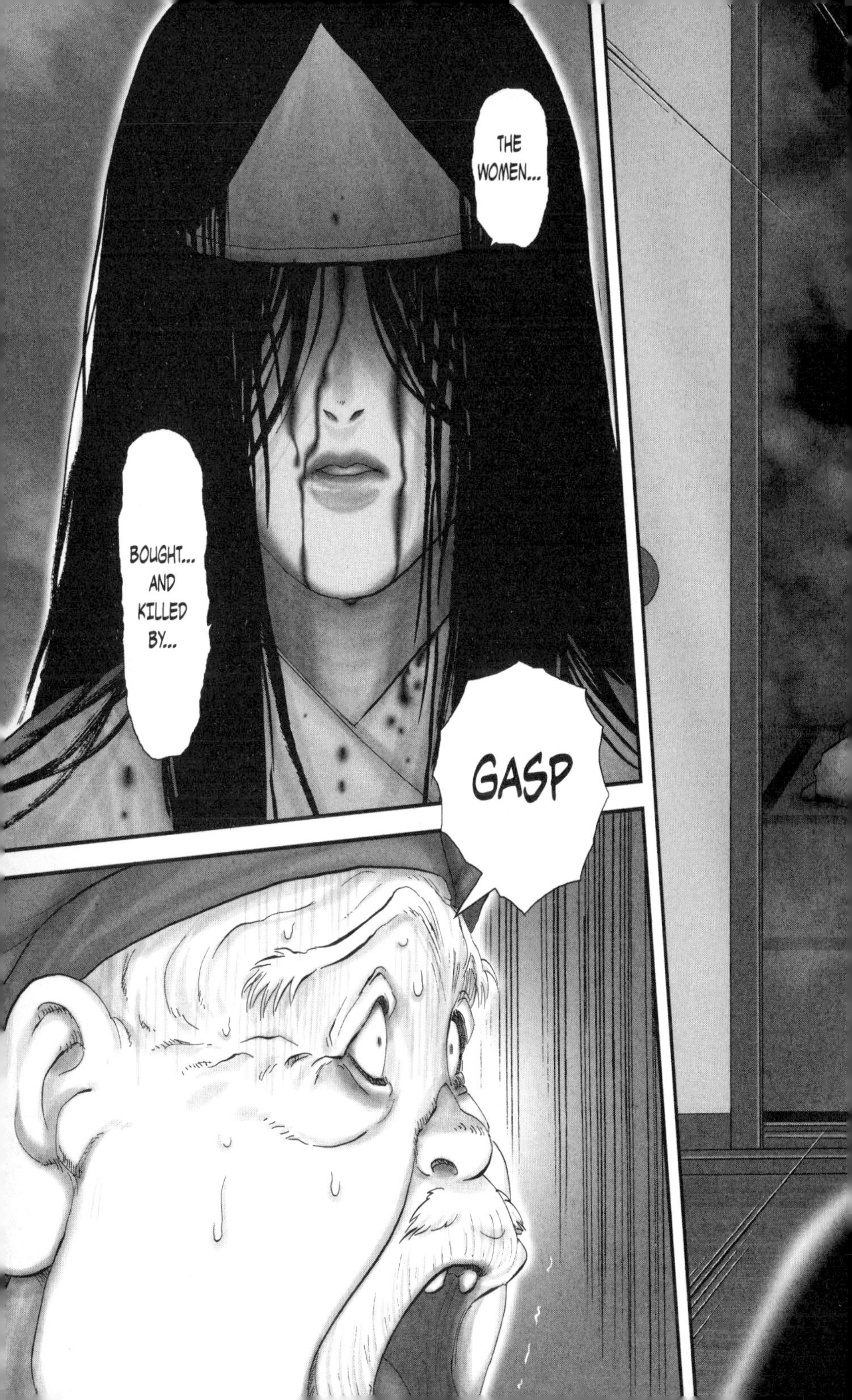
THE WOMEN...
BOUGHT... AND KILLED BY...
GASP

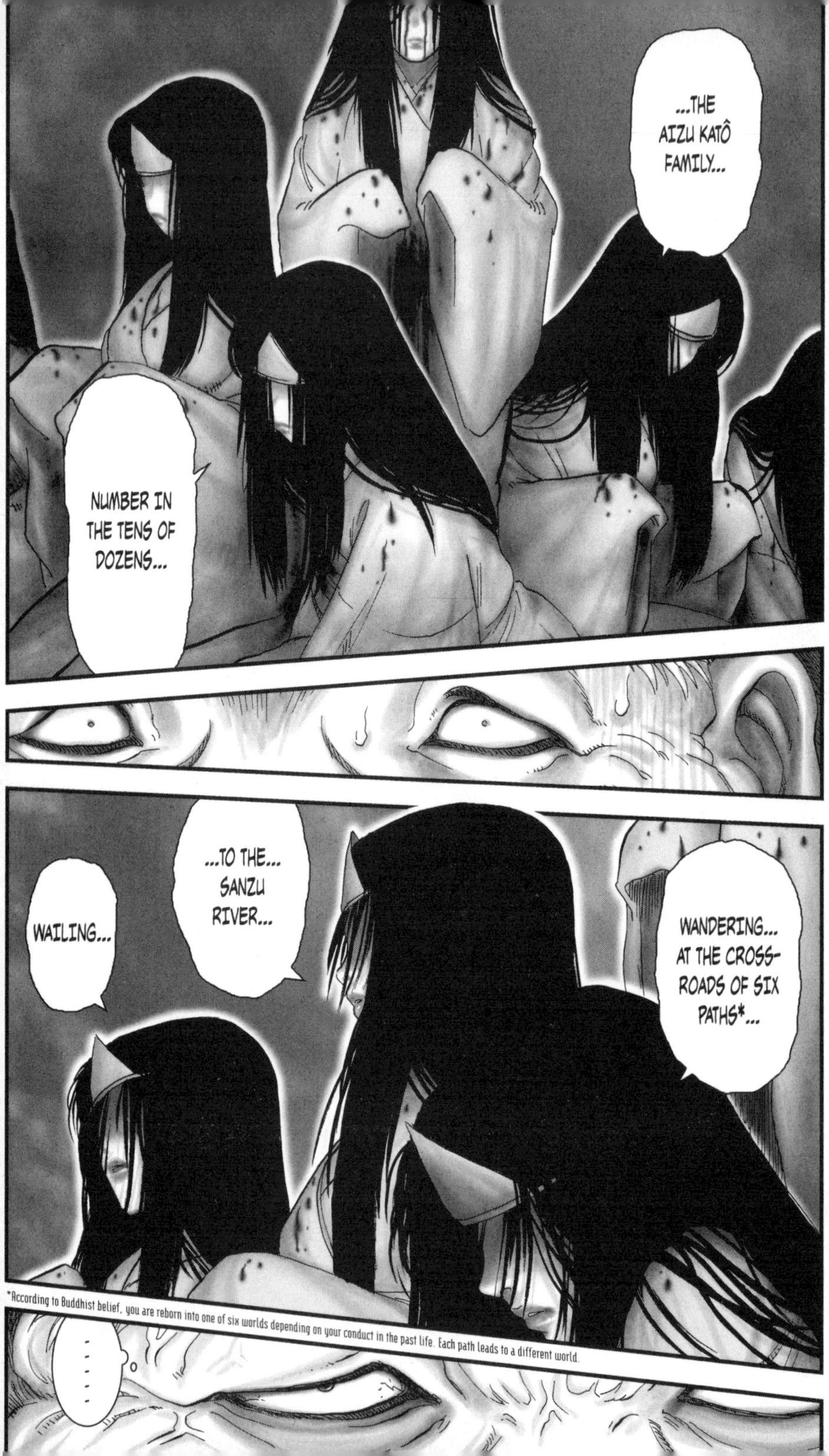
...THE AIZU KATÔ FAMILY...
NUMBER IN THE TENS OF DOZENS...
WANDERING... AT THE CROSS-ROADS OF SIX PATHS*...
...TO THE... SANZU RIVER...
WAILING...
......

*According to Buddhist belief, you are reborn into one of six worlds depending on your conduct in the past life. Each path leads to a different world.

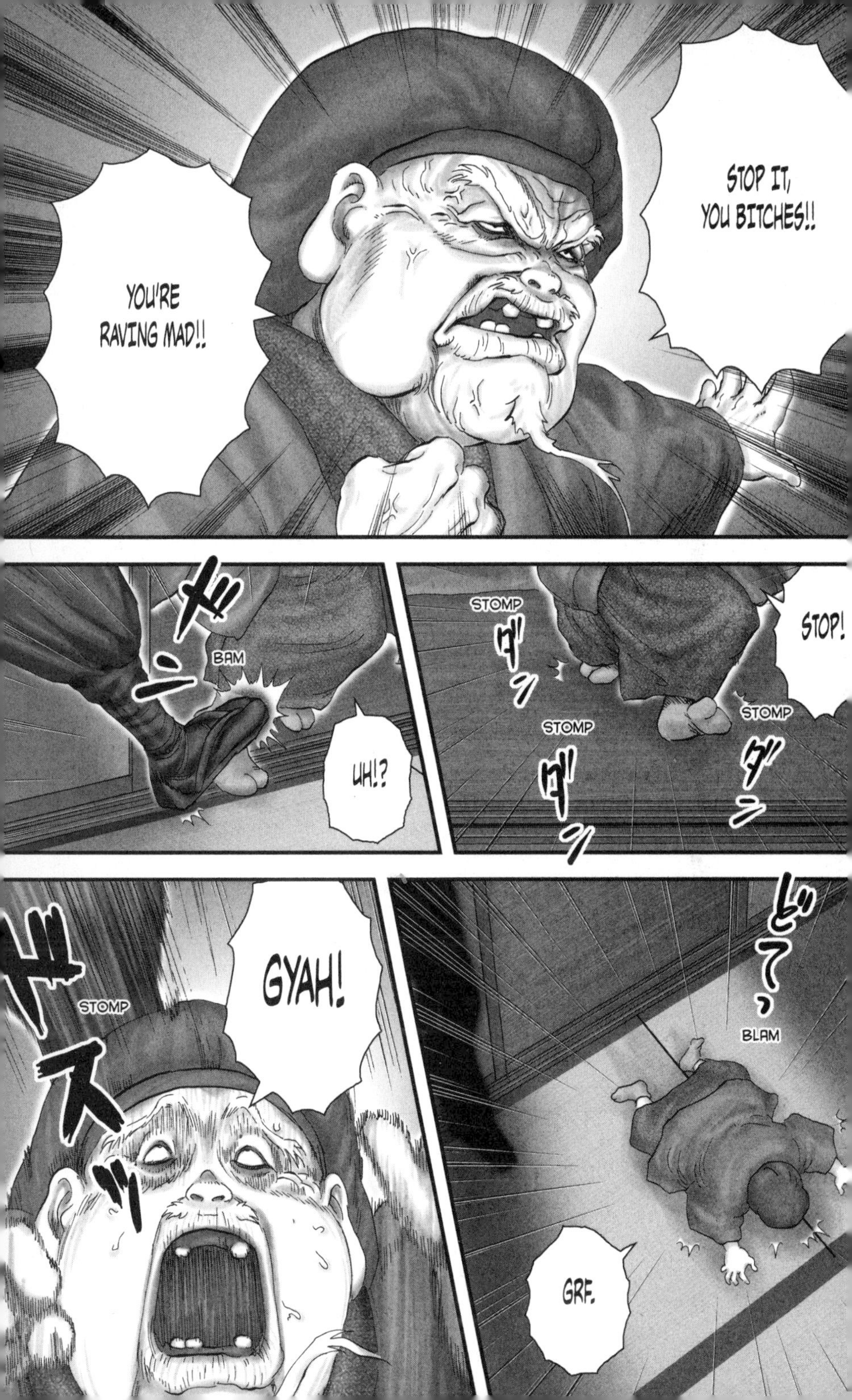
STOP IT, YOU BITCHES!!
YOU'RE RAVING MAD!!
STOP!
STOMP
STOMP
STOMP
BAM
UH!?
BLAM
GRF.
GYAH!
STOMP

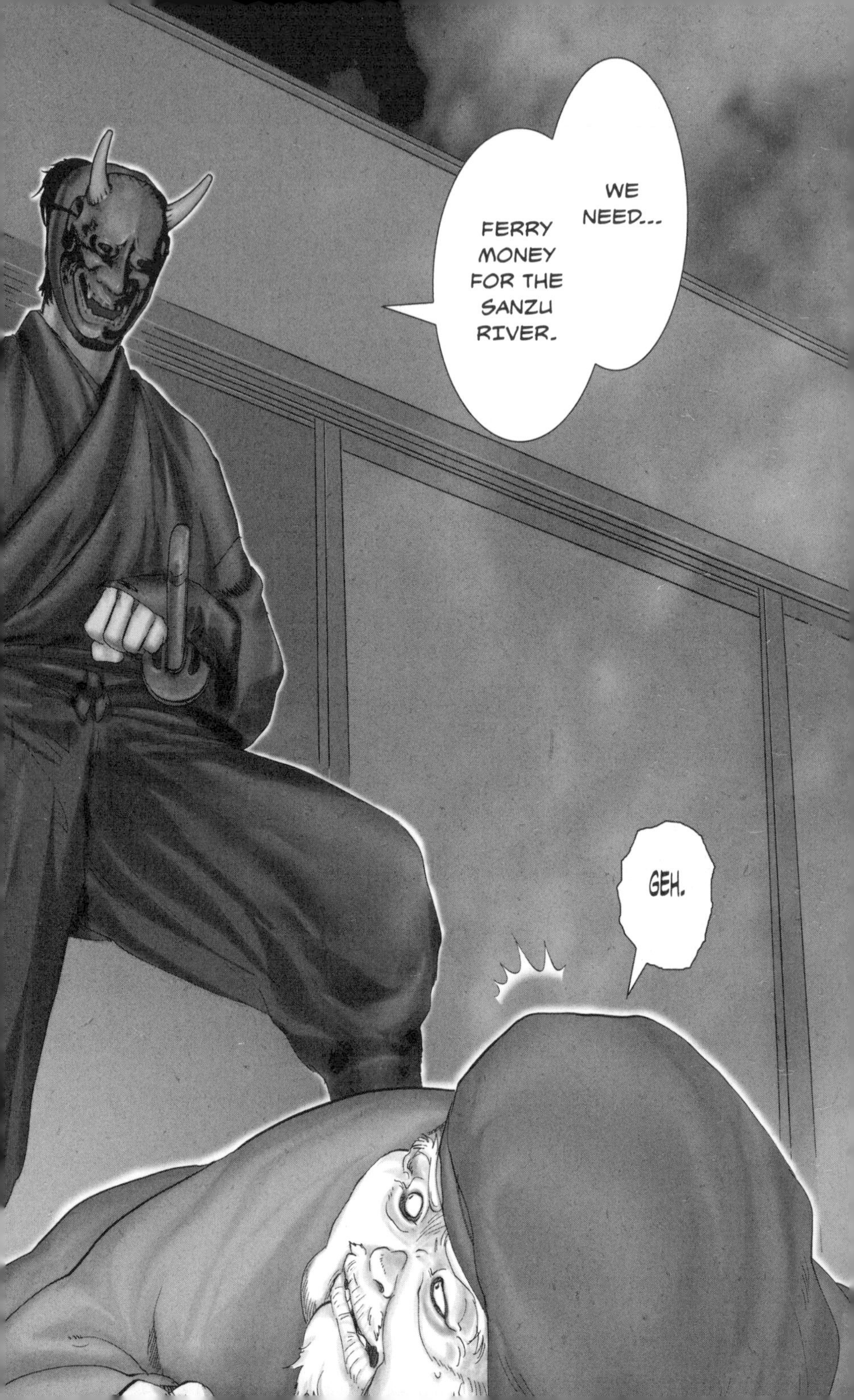
WE NEED...
FERRY MONEY FOR THE SANZU RIVER.
GEH.

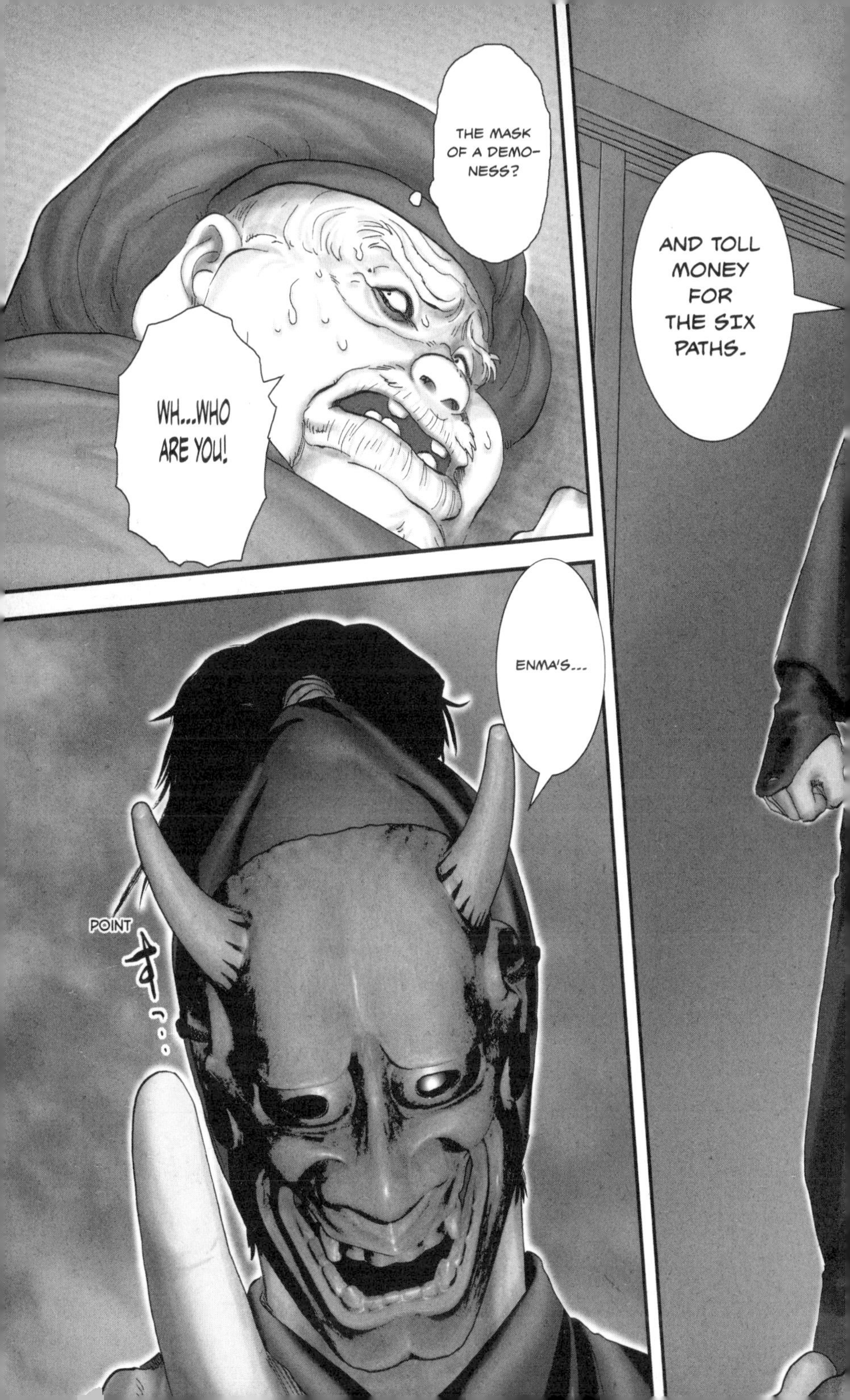
AND TOLL MONEY FOR THE SIX PATHS.
THE MASK OF A DEMONESS?
WH...WHO ARE YOU!
ENMA'S...
POINT

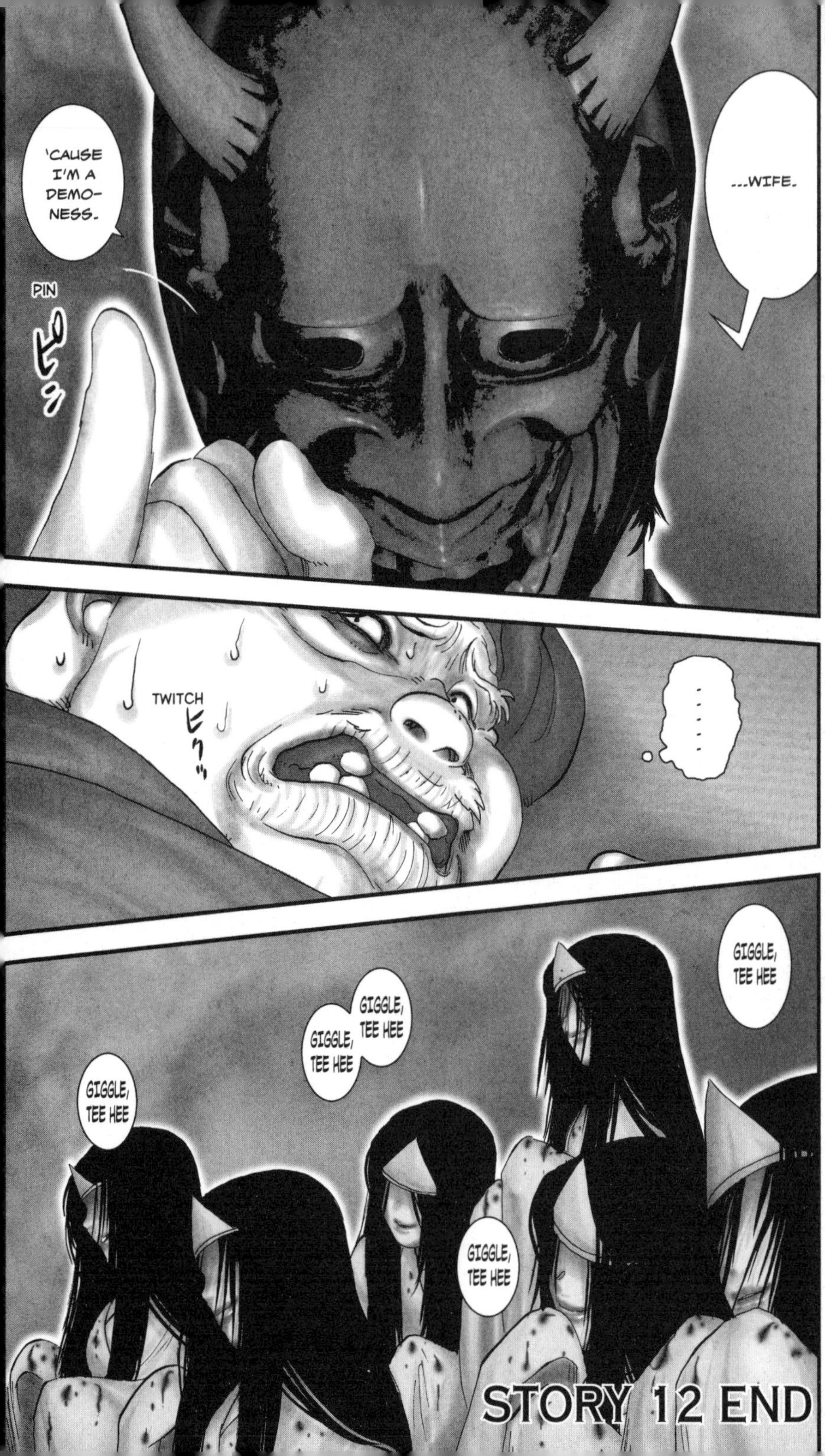
...WIFE.
'CAUSE I'M A DEMONESS.
PIN
ピッ
......
TWITCH
ビクッ
GIGGLE, TEE HEE
GIGGLE, TEE HEE
GIGGLE, TEE HEE
GIGGLE, TEE HEE
GIGGLE, TEE HEE
STORY 12 END

柳生十兵衛厳

YAGYU JYUBEI
MITSUYOSHI

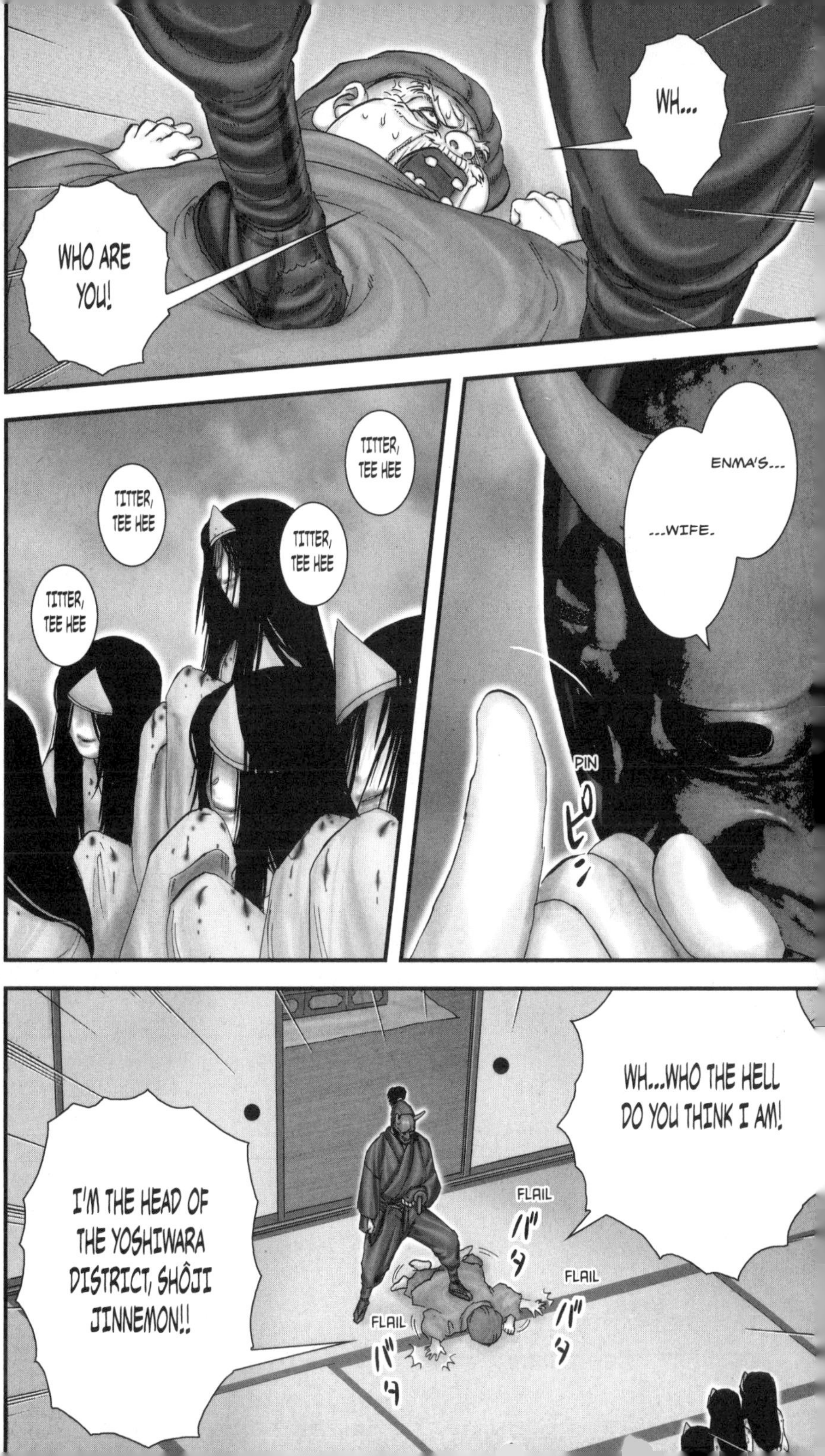
WH...
WHO ARE YOU!
ENMA'S...
...WIFE.
PIN
TITTER, TEE HEE
TITTER, TEE HEE
TITTER, TEE HEE
TITTER, TEE HEE
WH...WHO THE HELL DO YOU THINK I AM!
FLAIL
FLAIL
FLAIL
I'M THE HEAD OF THE YOSHIWARA DISTRICT, SHÔJI JINNEMON!!

STORY 13: THE BEARDED KYÔ DOLL

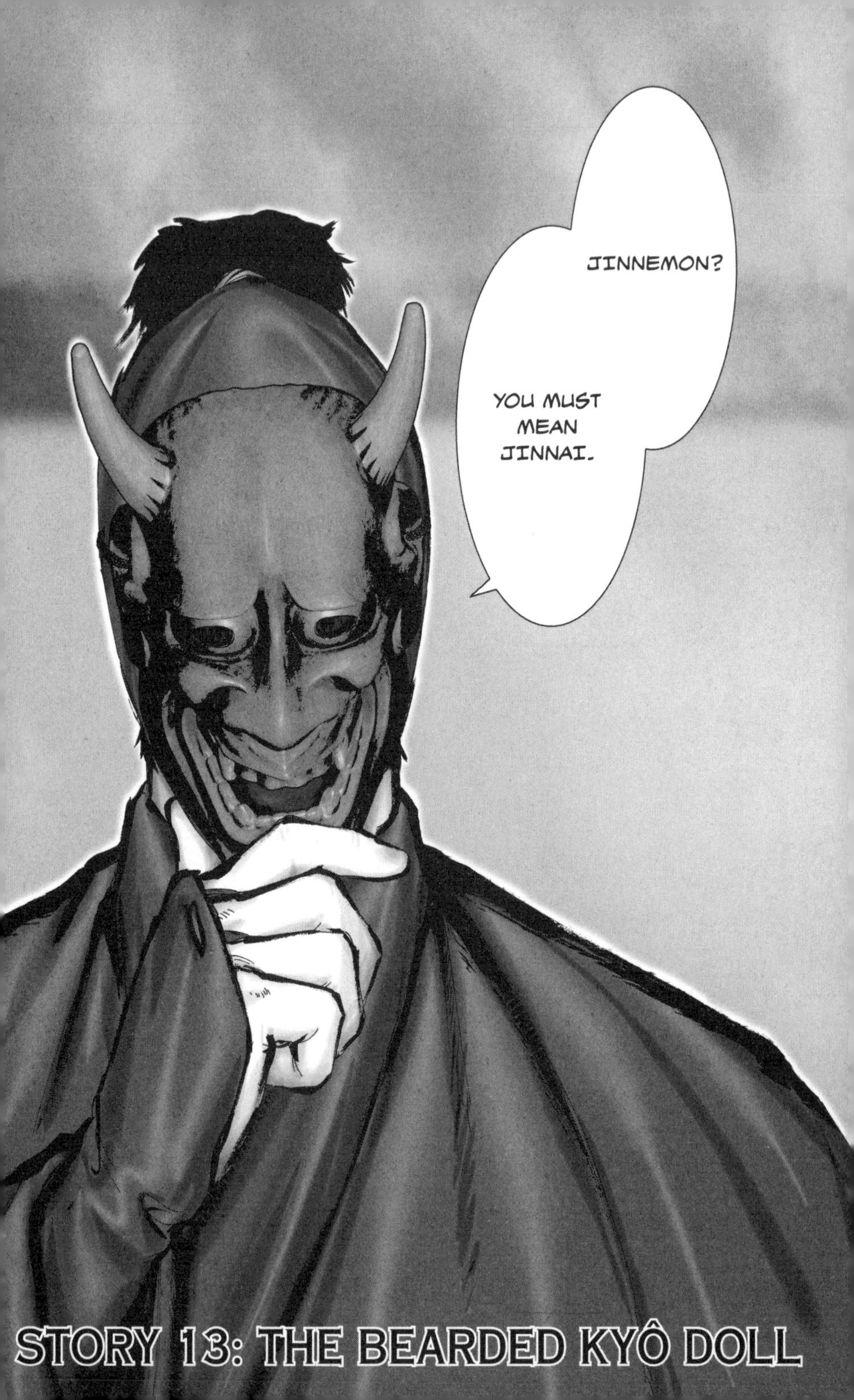
JINNEMON?
YOU MUST MEAN JINNAI.

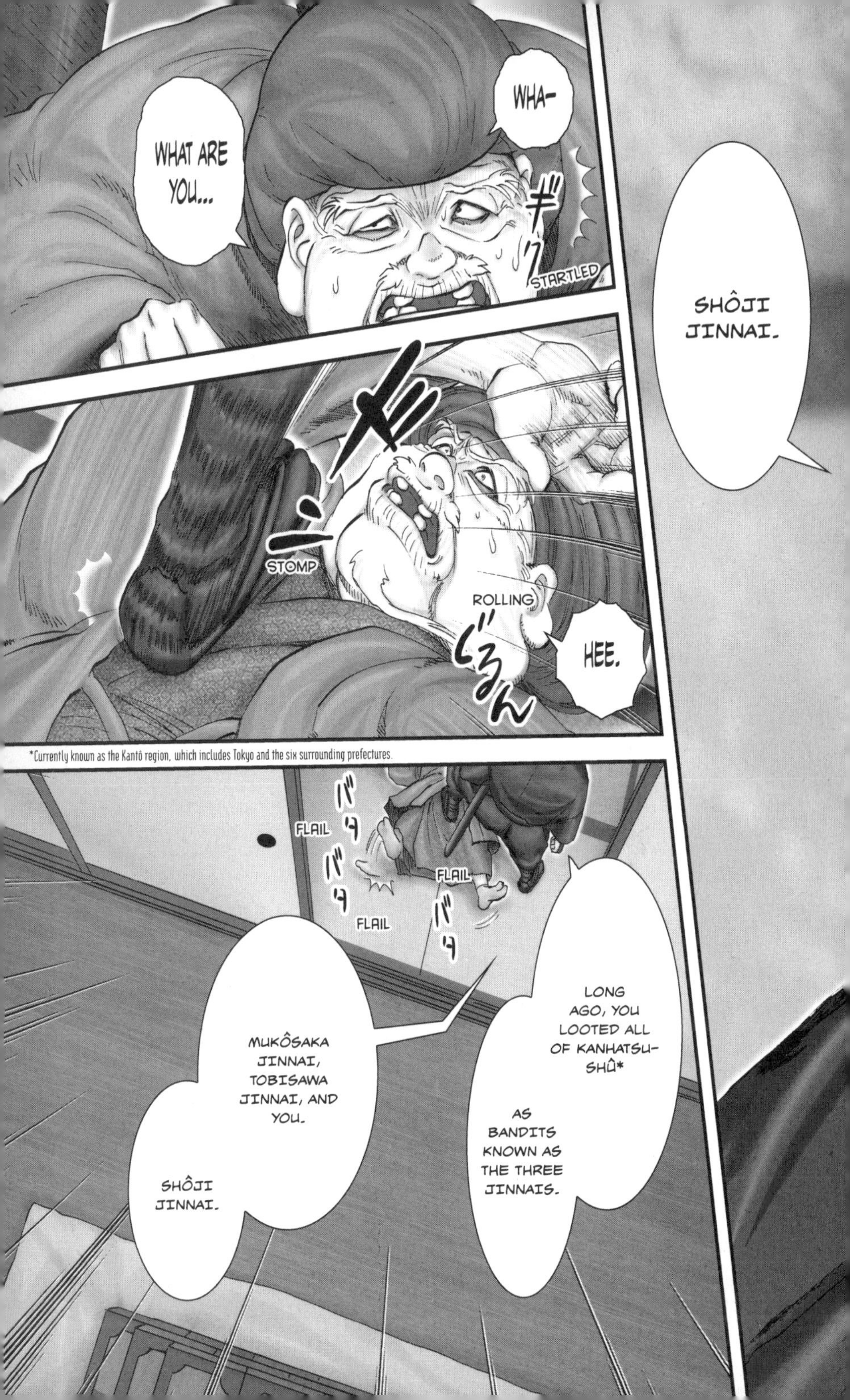
SHÔJI JINNAI.
WHA-
WHAT ARE YOU...
STARTLED
STOMP
ROLLING
HEE.
FLAIL
FLAIL
FLAIL
LONG AGO, YOU LOOTED ALL OF KANHATSU-SHÛ*
AS BANDITS KNOWN AS THE THREE JINNAIS.
MUKÔSAKA JINNAI, TOBISAWA JINNAI, AND YOU.
SHÔJI JINNAI.

*Currently known as the Kantô region, which includes Tokyo and the six surrounding prefectures.

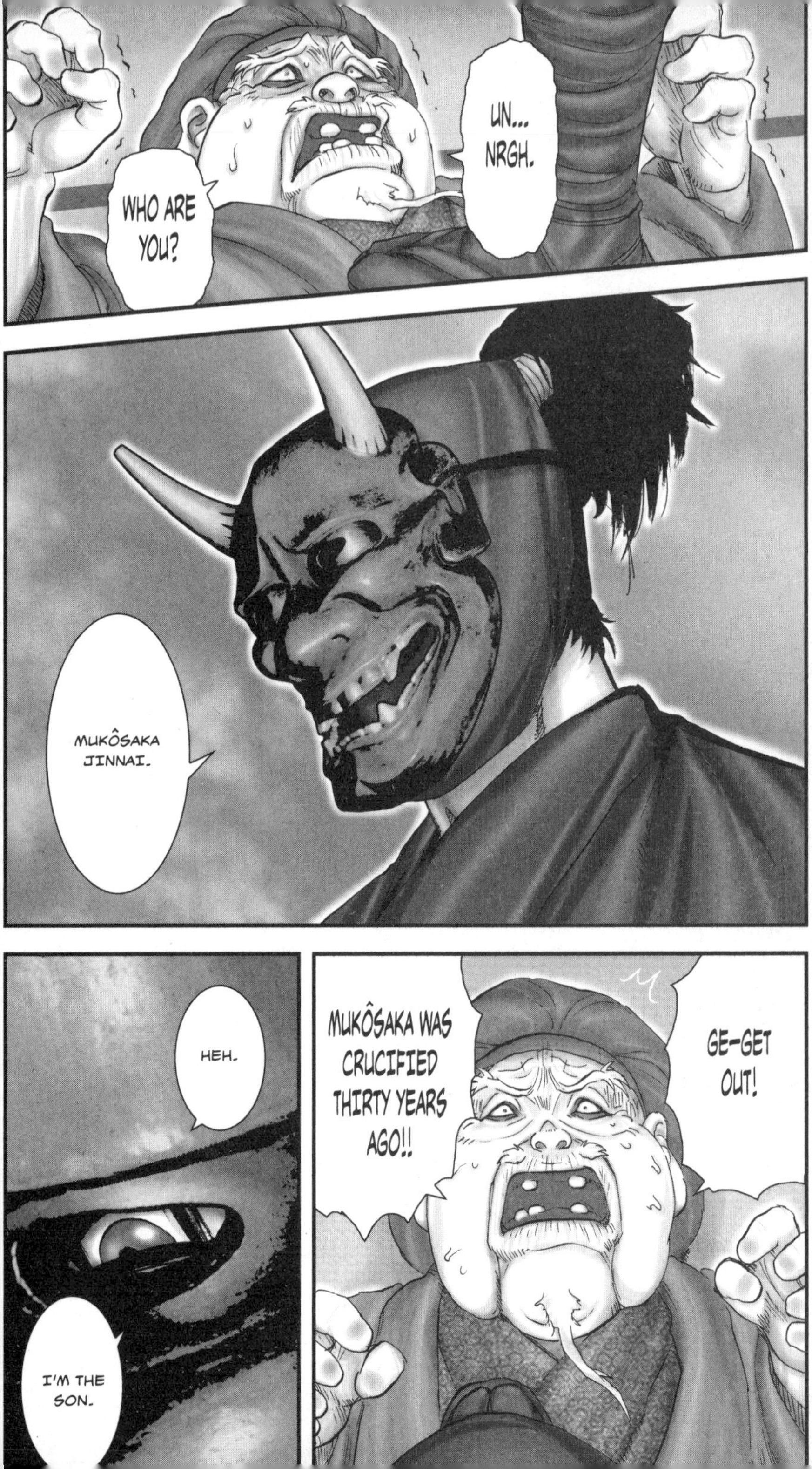
UN... NRGH.
WHO ARE YOU?
MUKÔSAKA JINNAI.
GE-GET OUT!
MUKÔSAKA WAS CRUCIFIED THIRTY YEARS AGO!!
HEH.
I'M THE SON.

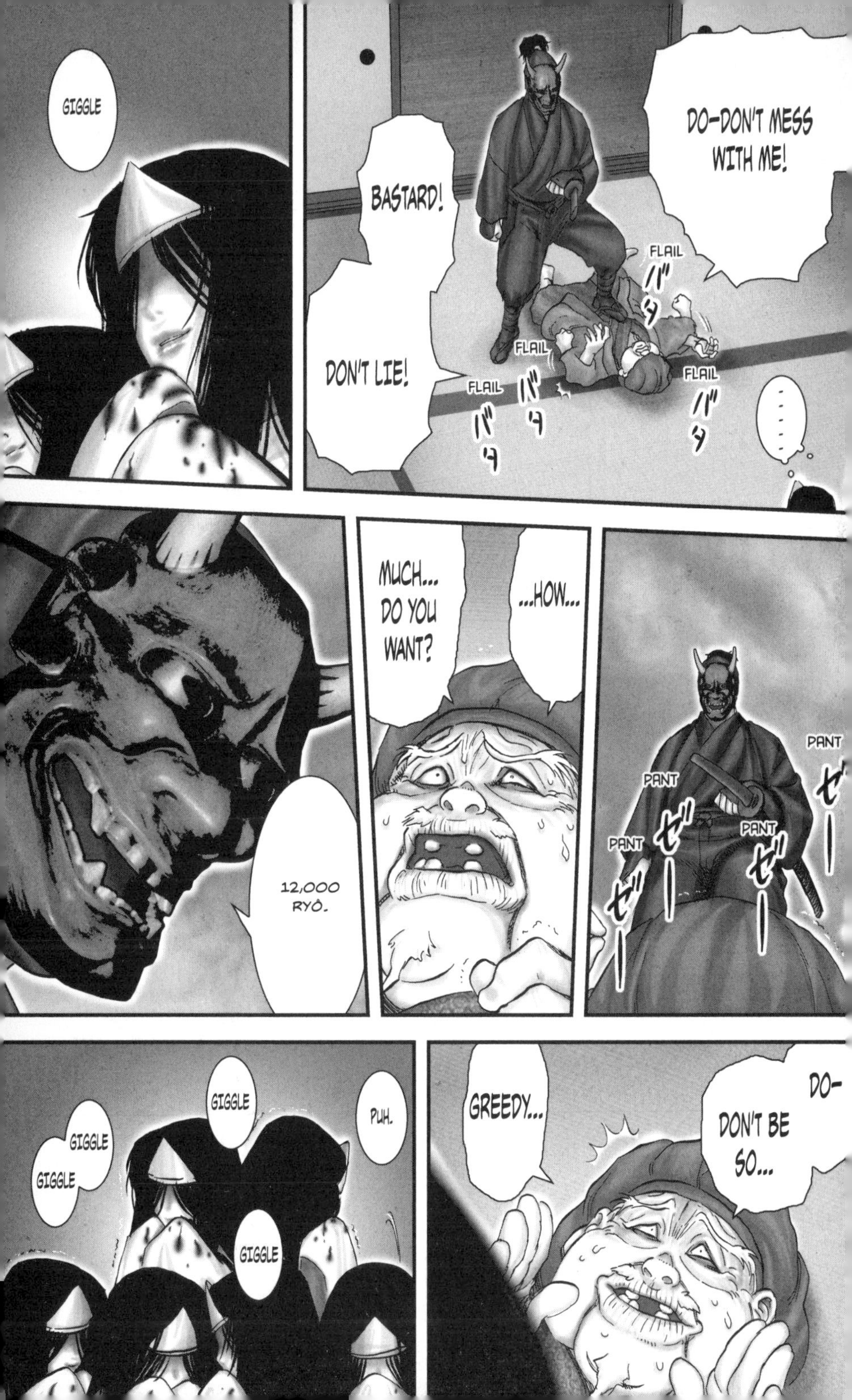
DO-DON'T MESS WITH ME!
BASTARD!
FLAIL
バタ
FLAIL
バタ
FLAIL
バタ
DON'T LIE!
FLAIL
バタ
......
GIGGLE
PANT
ゼー
PANT
ゼー
PANT
ゼー
PANT
ゼー
...HOW...
MUCH... DO YOU WANT?
12,000 RYŌ.
DO-DON'T BE SO...
GREEDY...
PUH.
GIGGLE
GIGGLE
GIGGLE
GIGGLE

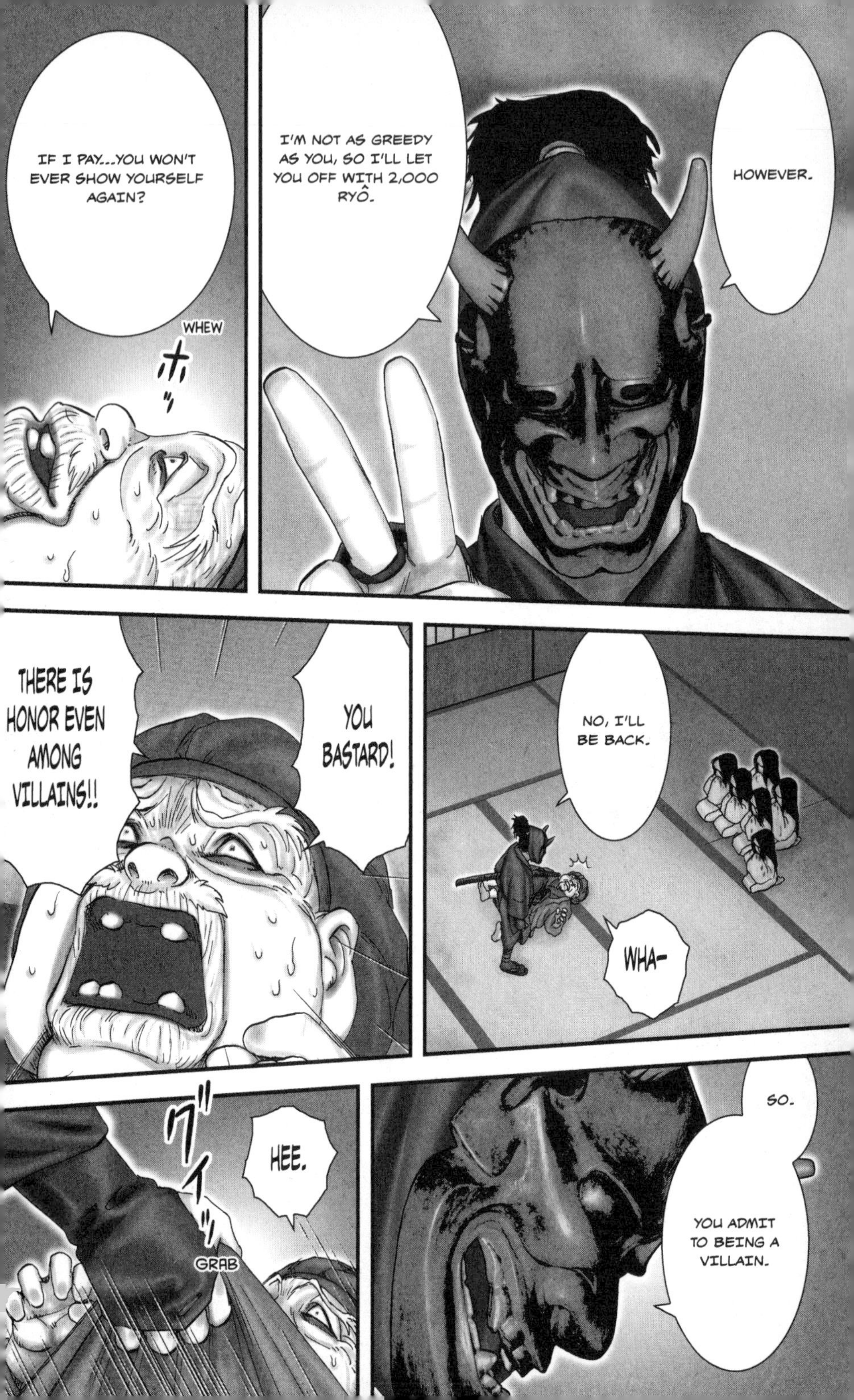
HOWEVER.
I'M NOT AS GREEDY AS YOU, SO I'LL LET YOU OFF WITH 2,000 RYÔ.
IF I PAY...YOU WON'T EVER SHOW YOURSELF AGAIN?
WHEW
NO, I'LL BE BACK.
WHA-
YOU BASTARD!
THERE IS HONOR EVEN AMONG VILLAINS!!
SO.
YOU ADMIT TO BEING A VILLAIN.
HEE.
GRAB

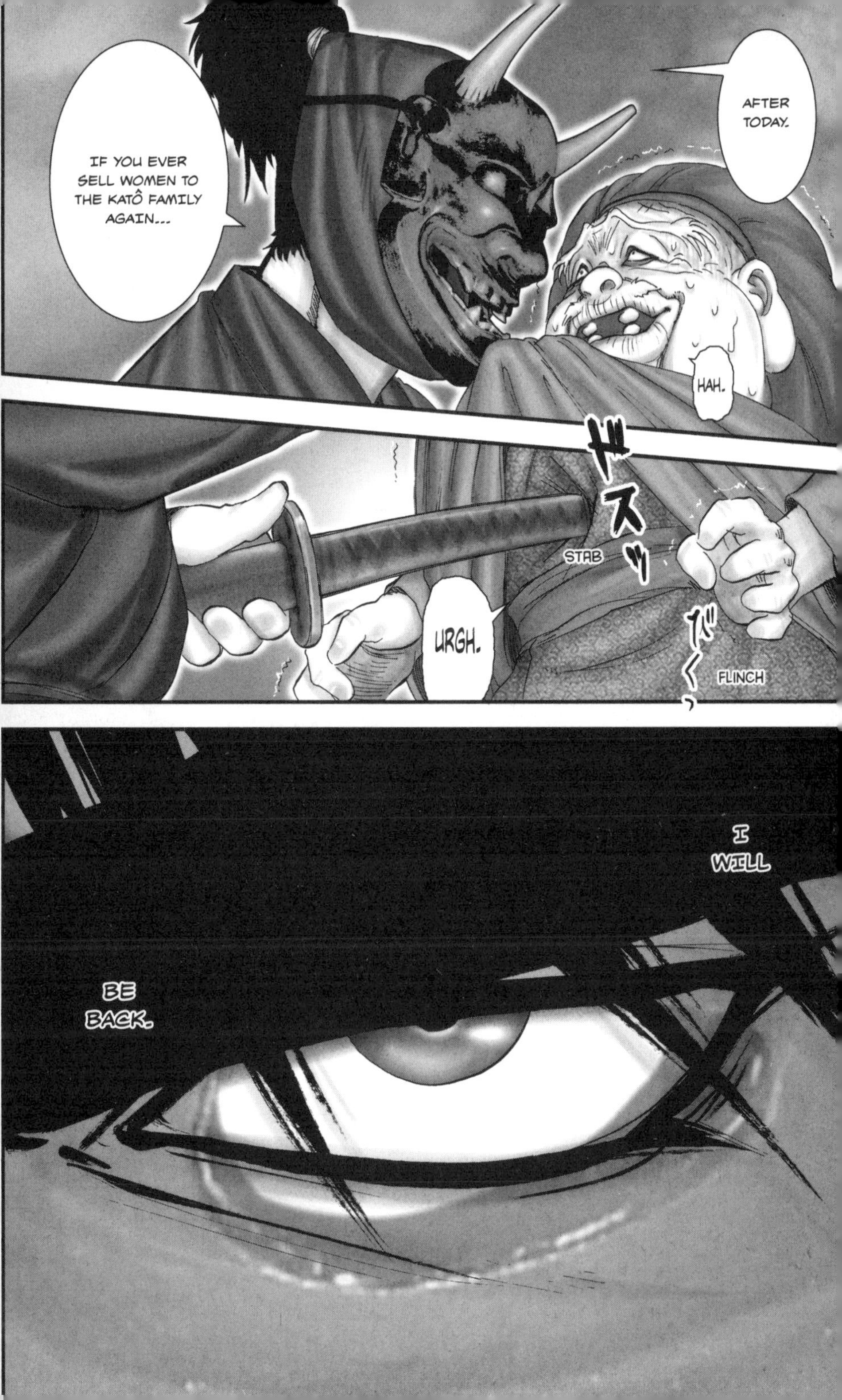
AFTER TODAY.
IF YOU EVER SELL WOMEN TO THE KATÔ FAMILY AGAIN...
HAH.
ズスッ
STAB
ビクッ
FLINCH
URGH.
I WILL
BE BACK.

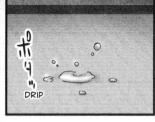

· · ·

JORRRRRRRR
ジョロロロロ

DRIP
ポタッ

AAH...

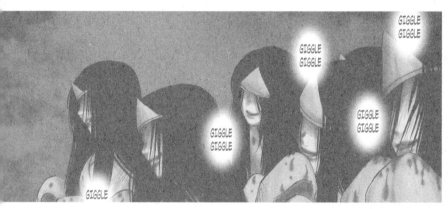

GIGGLE
GIGGLE

GIGGLE
GIGGLE

GIGGLE
GIGGLE

GIGGLE
GIGGLE

GIGGLE

· · ·

GULP...
ゴクッ…

PANT
ゼ゛

PANT
ゼ゛

PANT

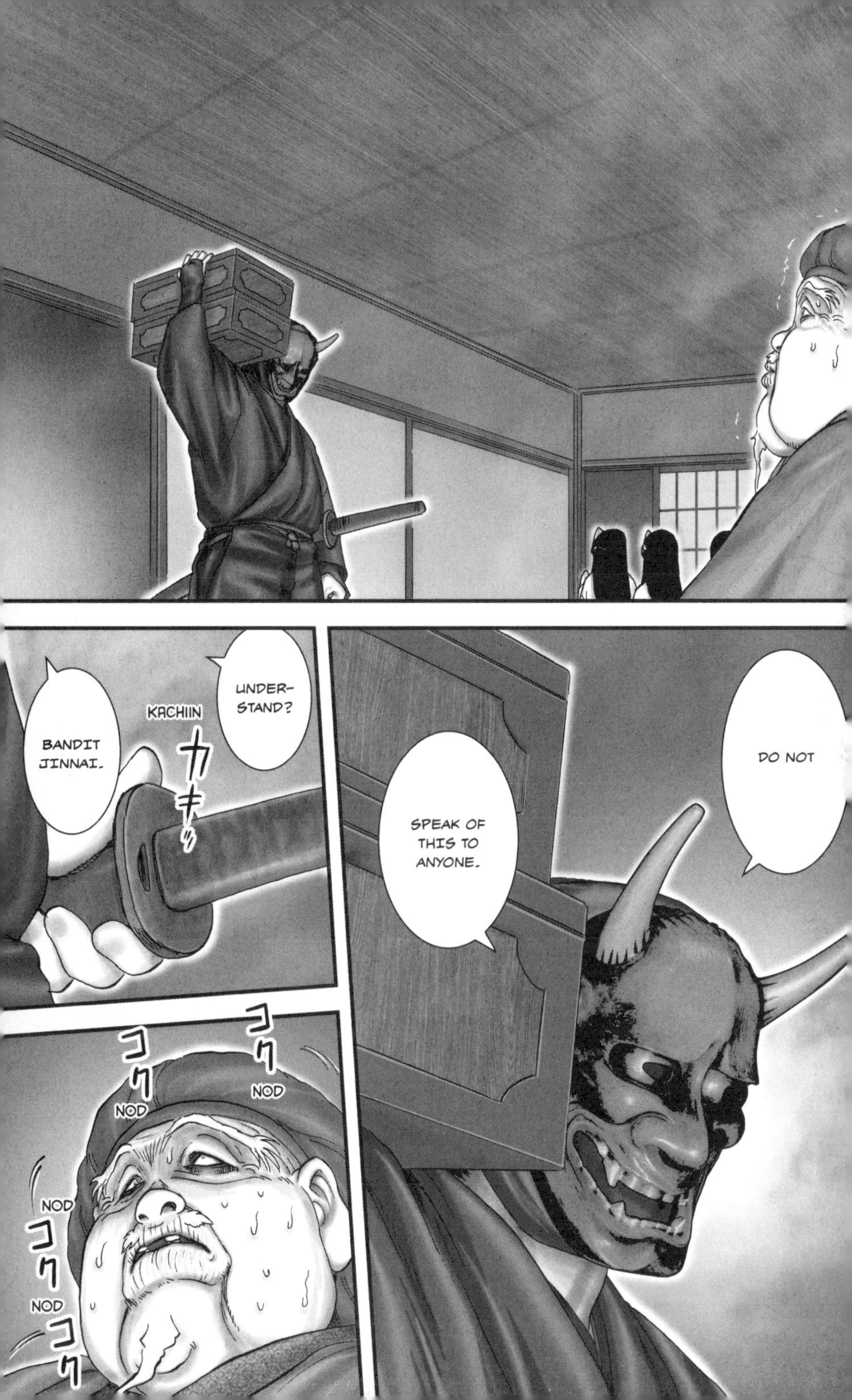
DO NOT
SPEAK OF THIS TO ANYONE.
UNDER-STAND?
KACHIIN
カキッ
BANDIT JINNAI.
コク
NOD
コク
NOD
NOD
コク
NOD
コク

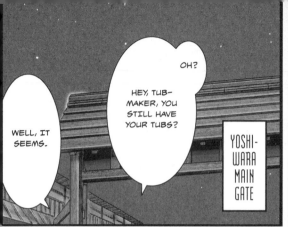

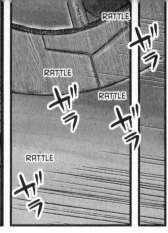

RATTLE
RATTLE
RATTLE
RATTLE
YOSHI-WARA MAIN GATE
OH?
HEY, TUB-MAKER, YOU STILL HAVE YOUR TUBS?
WELL, IT SEEMS.
THE BOSS AT NISHIDA-YA MADE A MISTAKE...
TURNS OUT HE HAD ENOUGH TUBS...YEP.
SHH.
GIGGLE
GIGGLE
GIGGLE
GIGGLE
RATTLE
RATTLE
RATTLE
HEH.
RATTLE

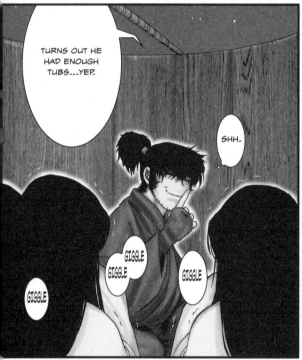

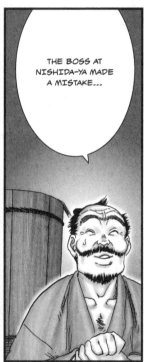

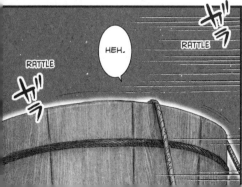

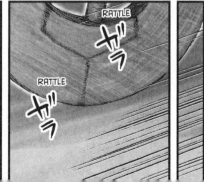

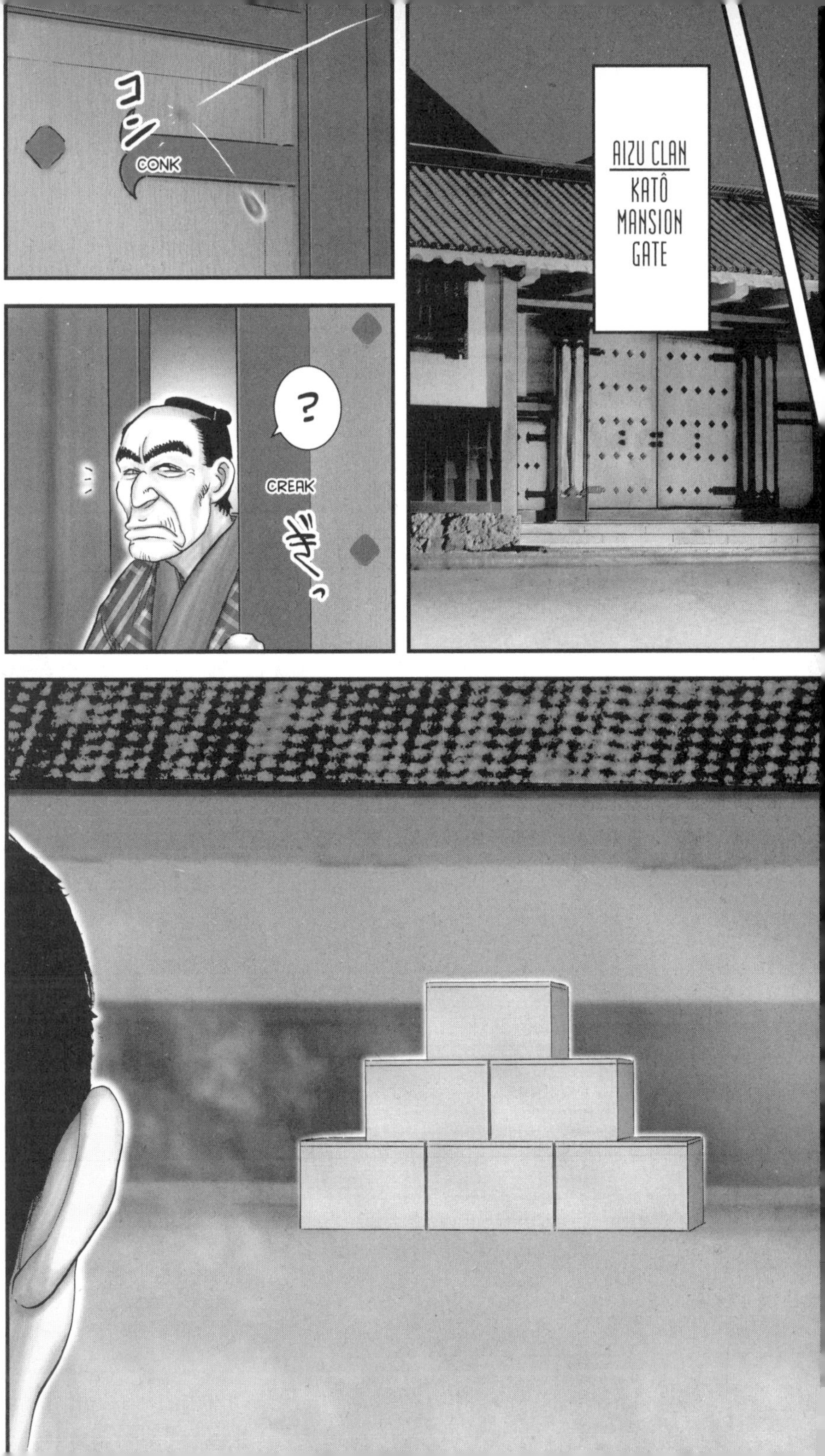
AIZU CLAN
KATÔ MANSION GATE
コン
CONK
?
CREAK
ぎぃっ

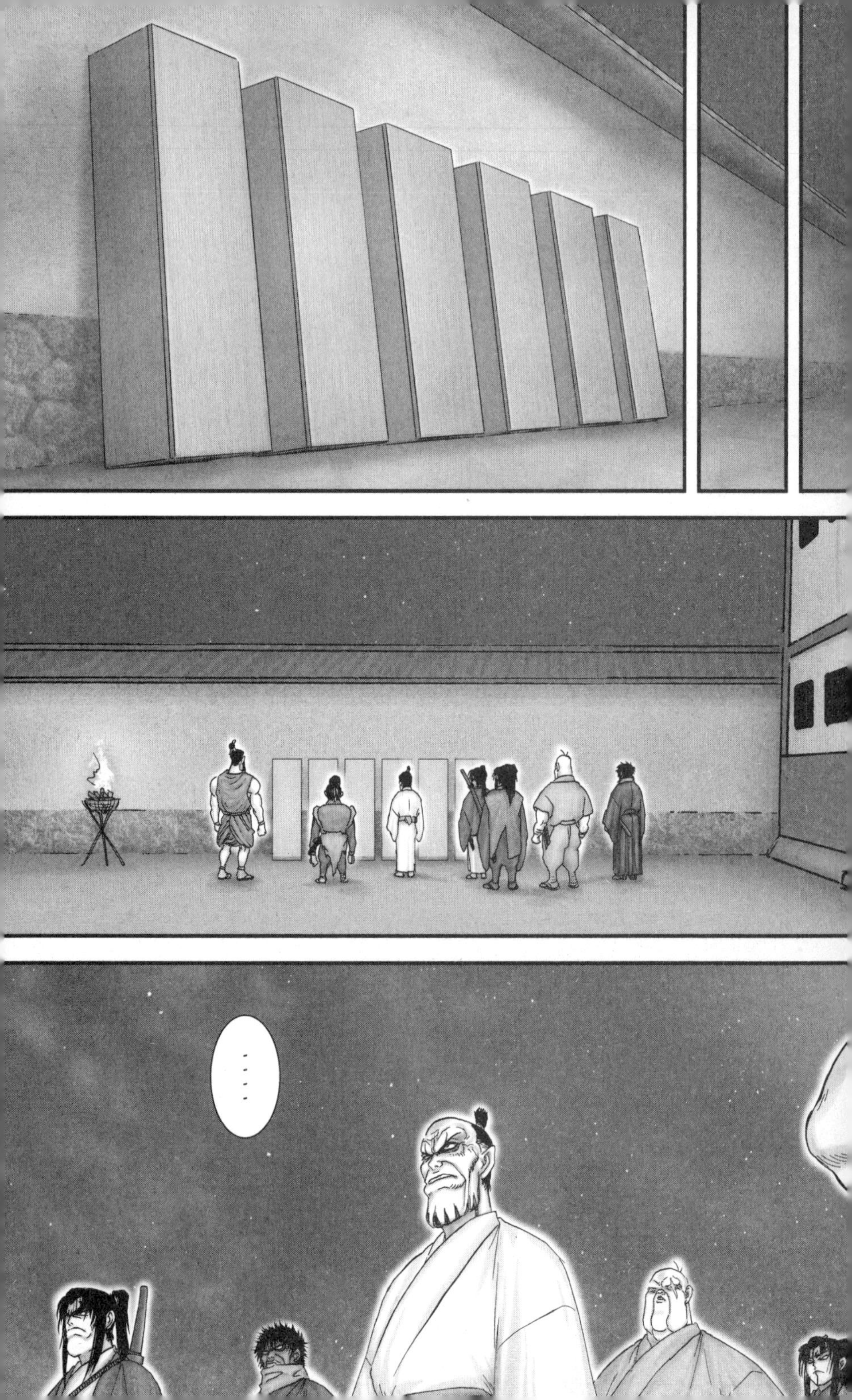
....

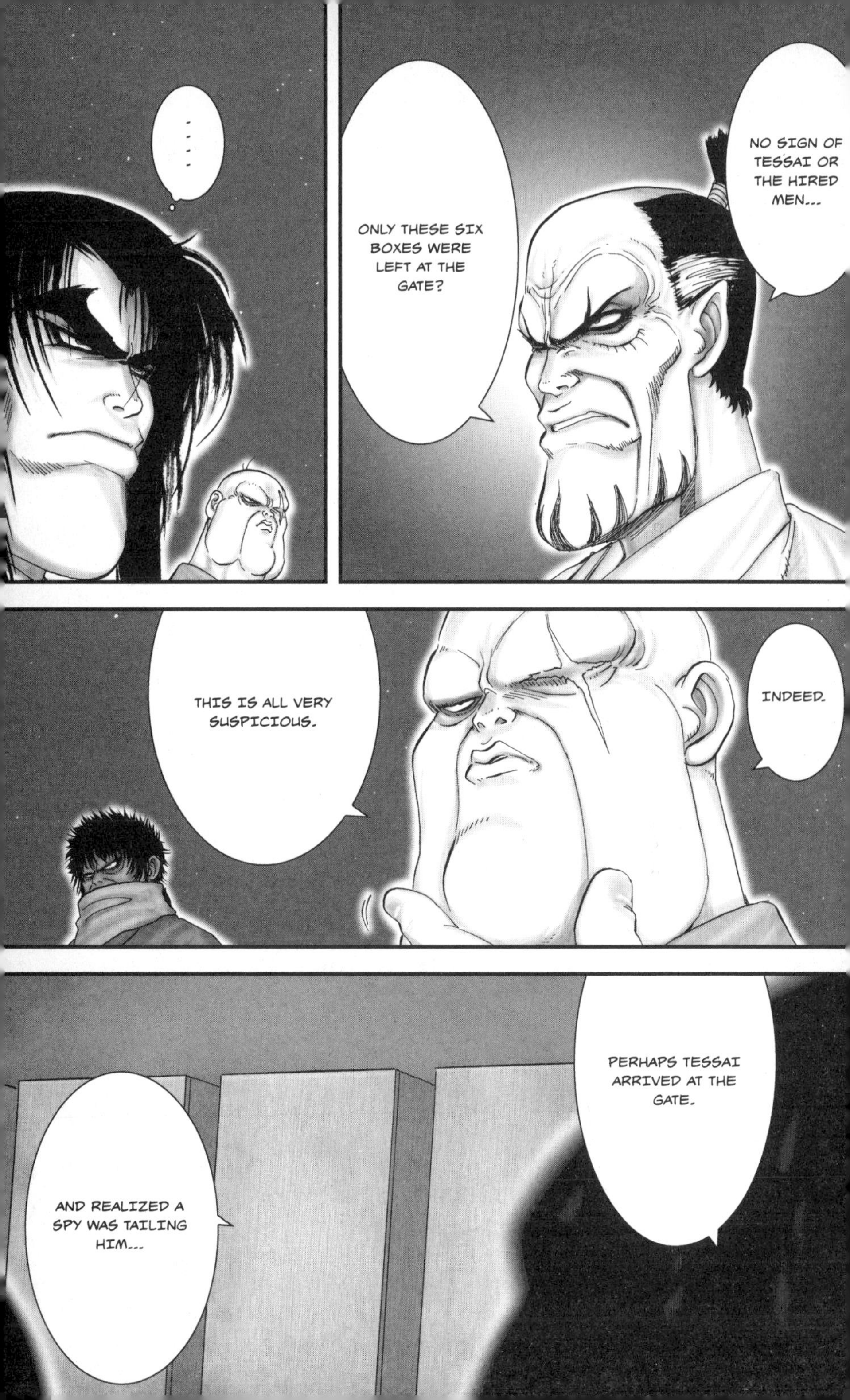
NO SIGN OF TESSAI OR THE HIRED MEN...
ONLY THESE SIX BOXES WERE LEFT AT THE GATE?
.....
INDEED.
THIS IS ALL VERY SUSPICIOUS.
PERHAPS TESSAI ARRIVED AT THE GATE.
AND REALIZED A SPY WAS TAILING HIM...

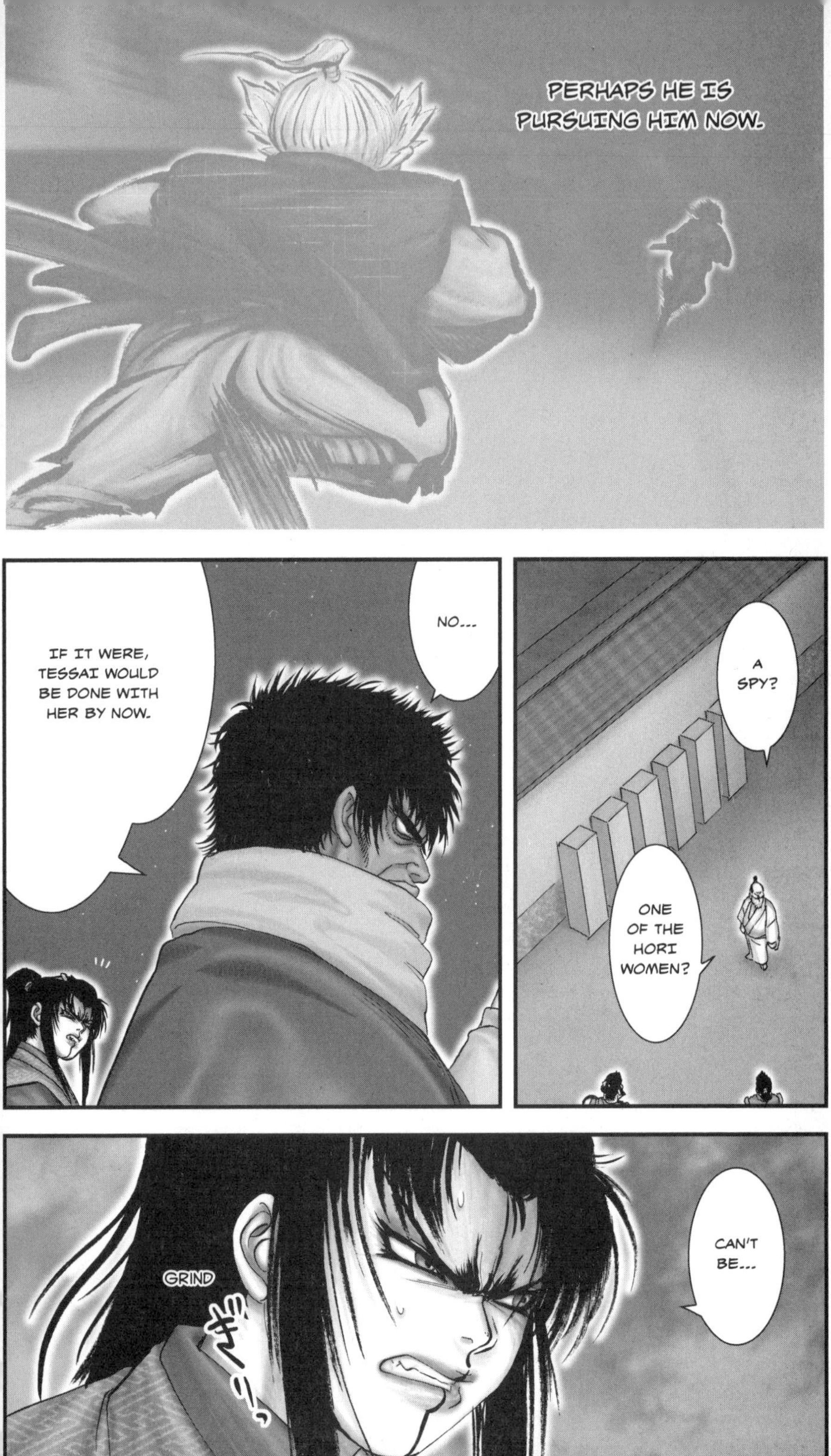
PERHAPS HE IS PURSUING HIM NOW.
A SPY?
ONE OF THE HORI WOMEN?
NO...
IF IT WERE, TESSAI WOULD BE DONE WITH HER BY NOW.
CAN'T BE...
GRIND

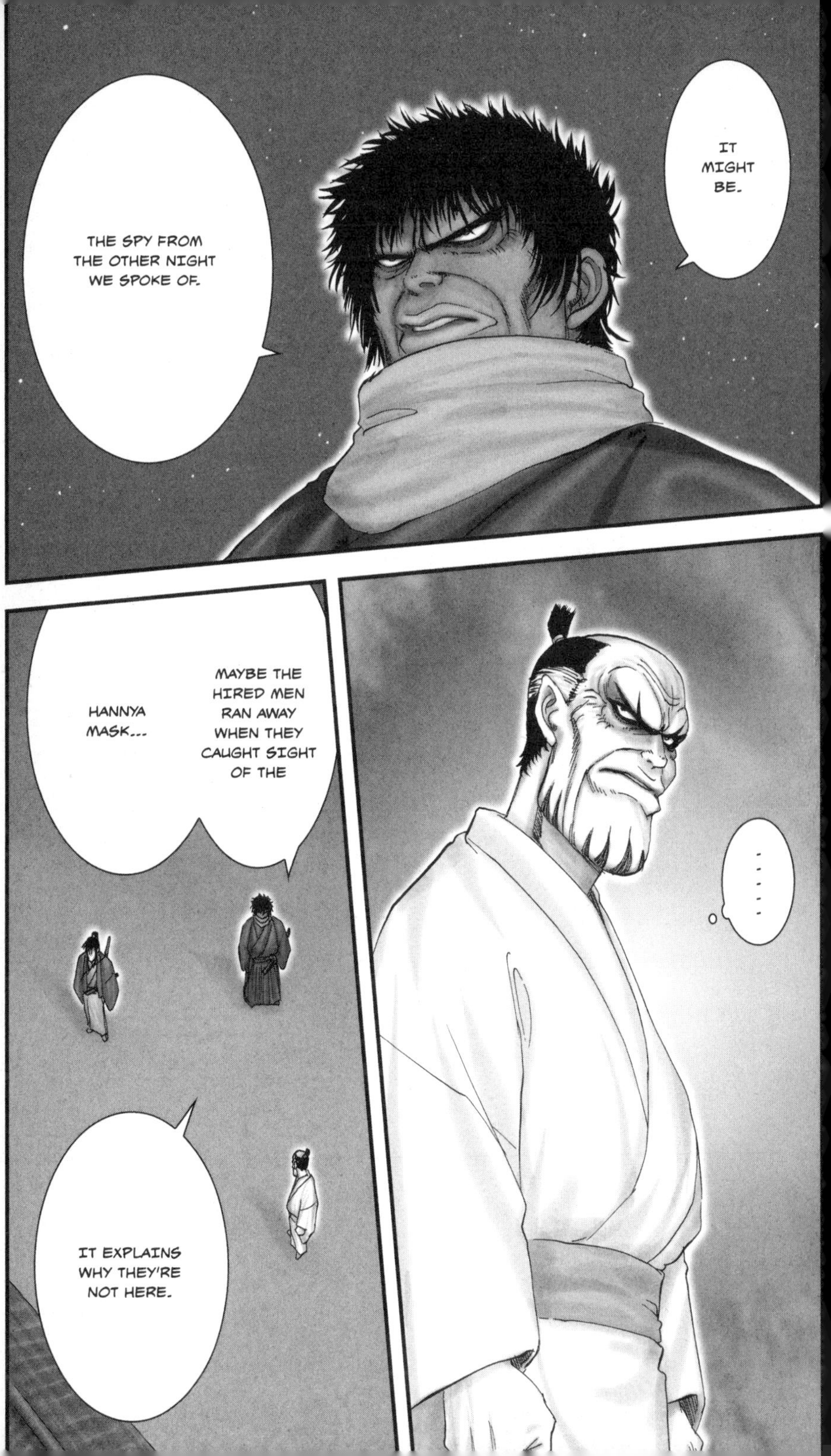
IT MIGHT BE.
THE SPY FROM THE OTHER NIGHT WE SPOKE OF.
......
MAYBE THE HIRED MEN RAN AWAY WHEN THEY CAUGHT SIGHT OF THE
HANNYA MASK...
IT EXPLAINS WHY THEY'RE NOT HERE.

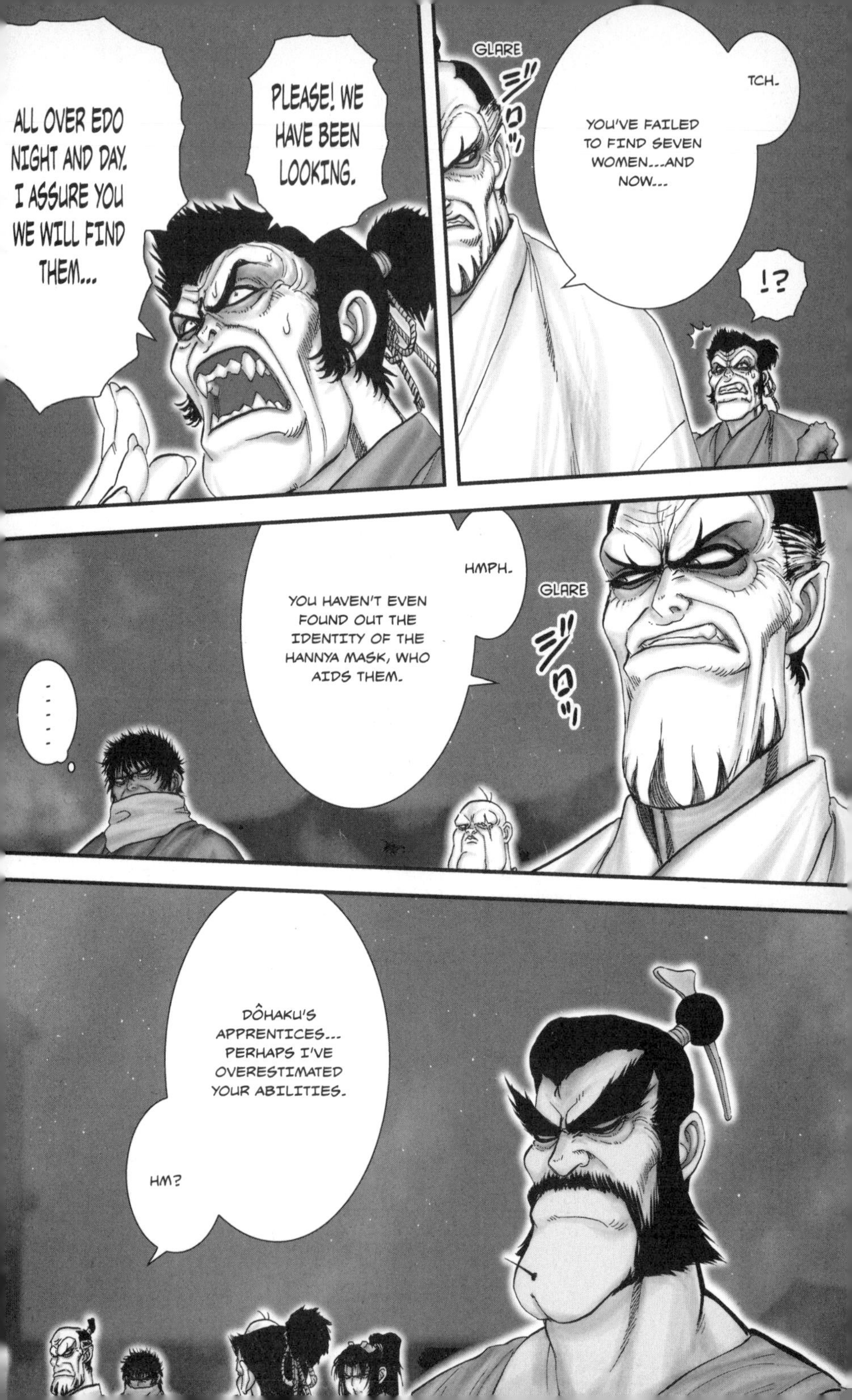
TCH.
GLARE
ジロッ
YOU'VE FAILED TO FIND SEVEN WOMEN...AND NOW...
!?
PLEASE! WE HAVE BEEN LOOKING.
ALL OVER EDO NIGHT AND DAY. I ASSURE YOU WE WILL FIND THEM...
HMPH.
GLARE
ジロッ
YOU HAVEN'T EVEN FOUND OUT THE IDENTITY OF THE HANNYA MASK, WHO AIDS THEM.
......
DÔHAKU'S APPRENTICES... PERHAPS I'VE OVERESTIMATED YOUR ABILITIES.
HM?

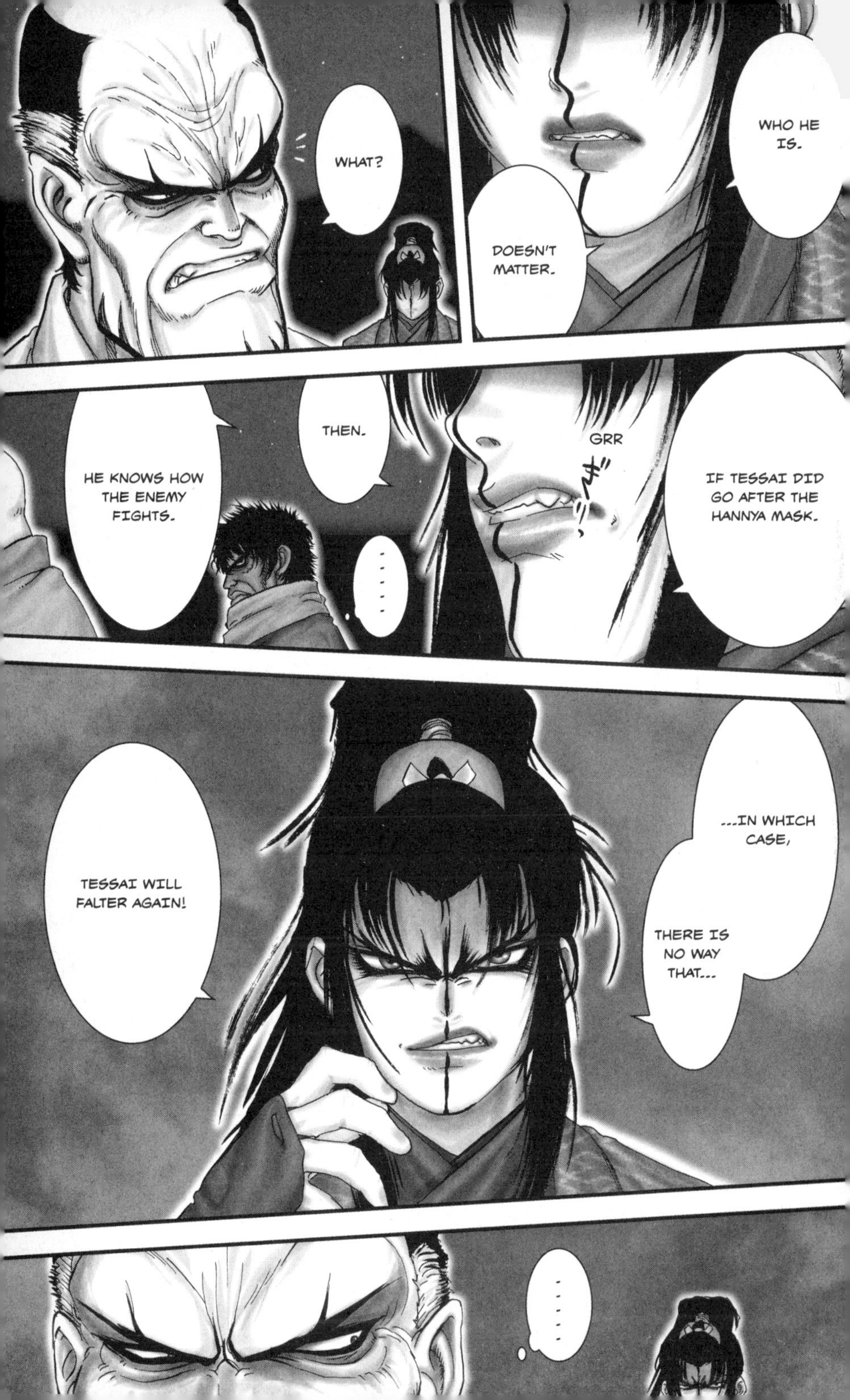
WHO HE IS.
DOESN'T MATTER.
WHAT?
IF TESSAI DID GO AFTER THE HANNYA MASK.
GRR
THEN.
HE KNOWS HOW THE ENEMY FIGHTS.
......
...IN WHICH CASE,
THERE IS NO WAY THAT...
TESSAI WILL FALTER AGAIN!
......

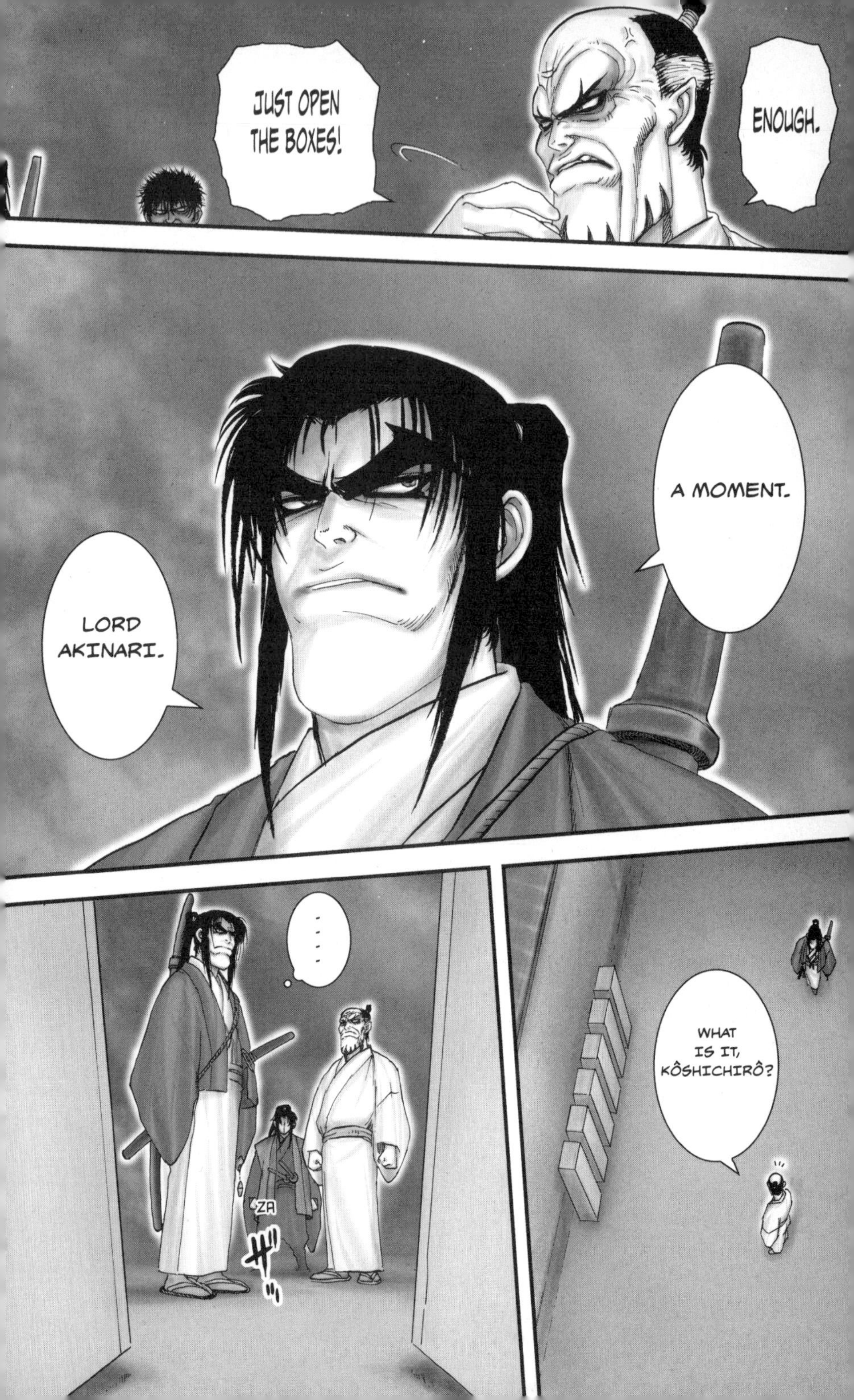
ENOUGH.
JUST OPEN THE BOXES!
A MOMENT.
LORD AKINARI.
WHAT IS IT, KÔSHICHIRÔ?
....
ZA

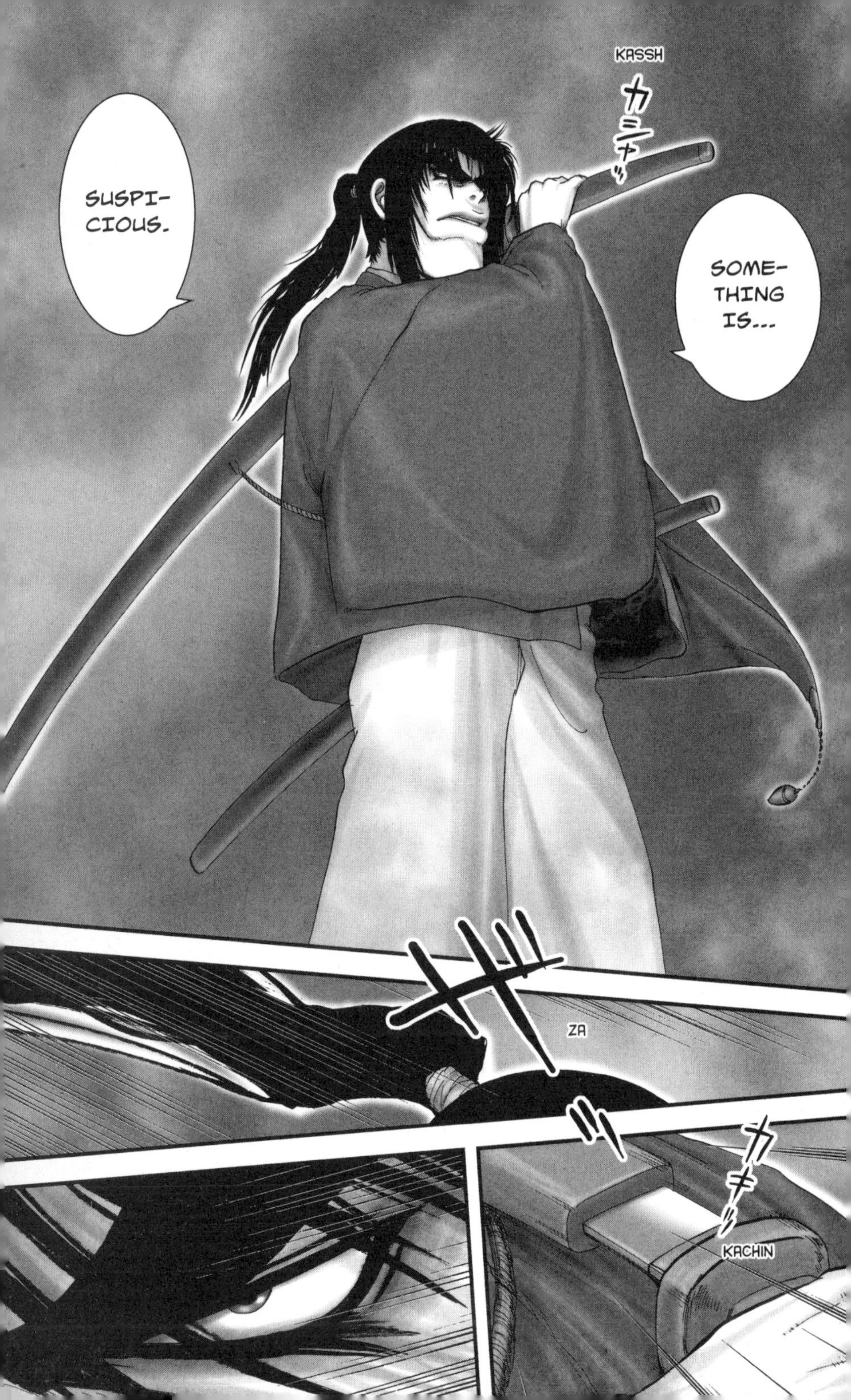
KASSH
SOME-THING IS...
SUSPI-CIOUS.
ZA
KACHIN

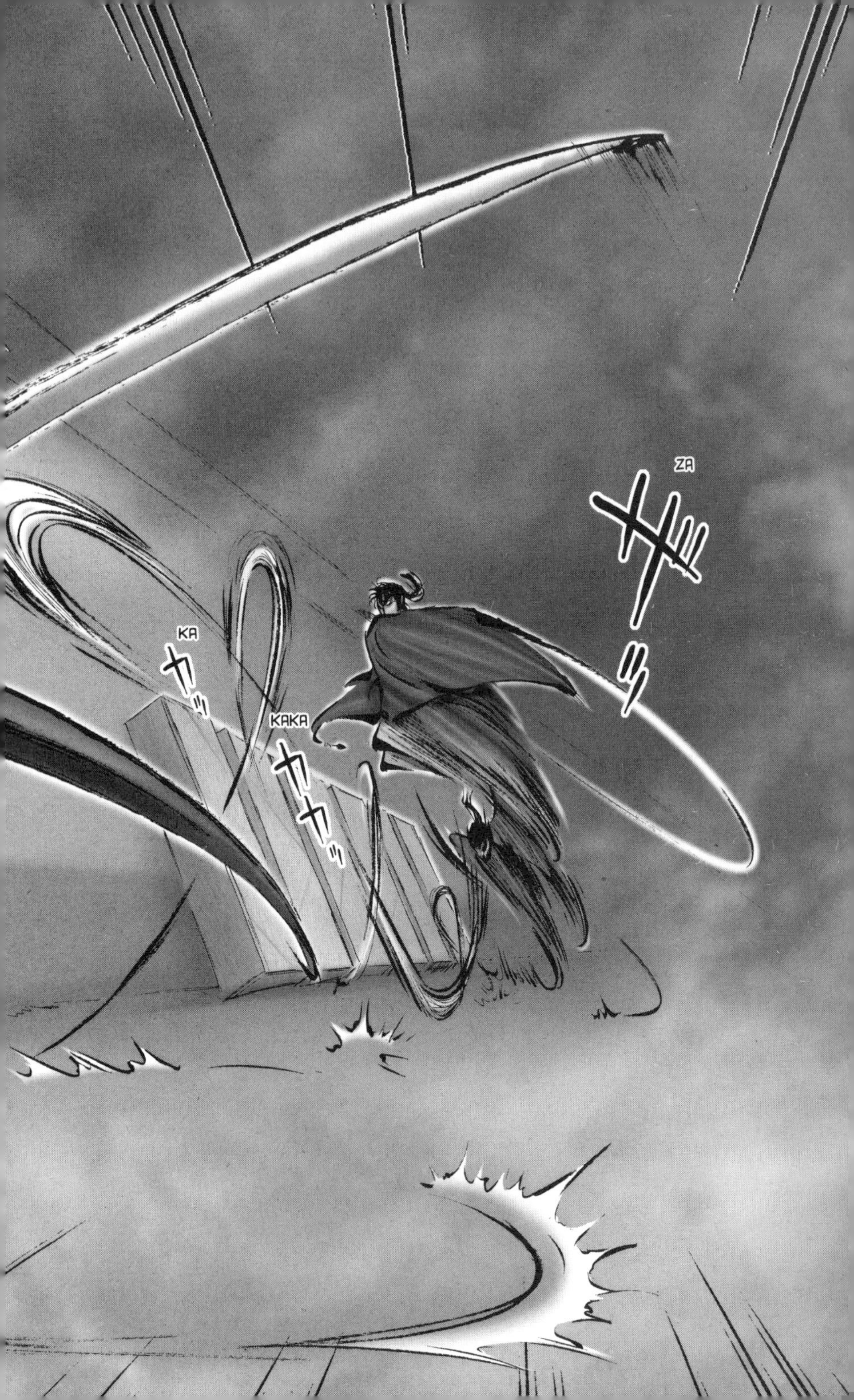
ZA
ザザッ
KA
カッ
KAKA
カカッ

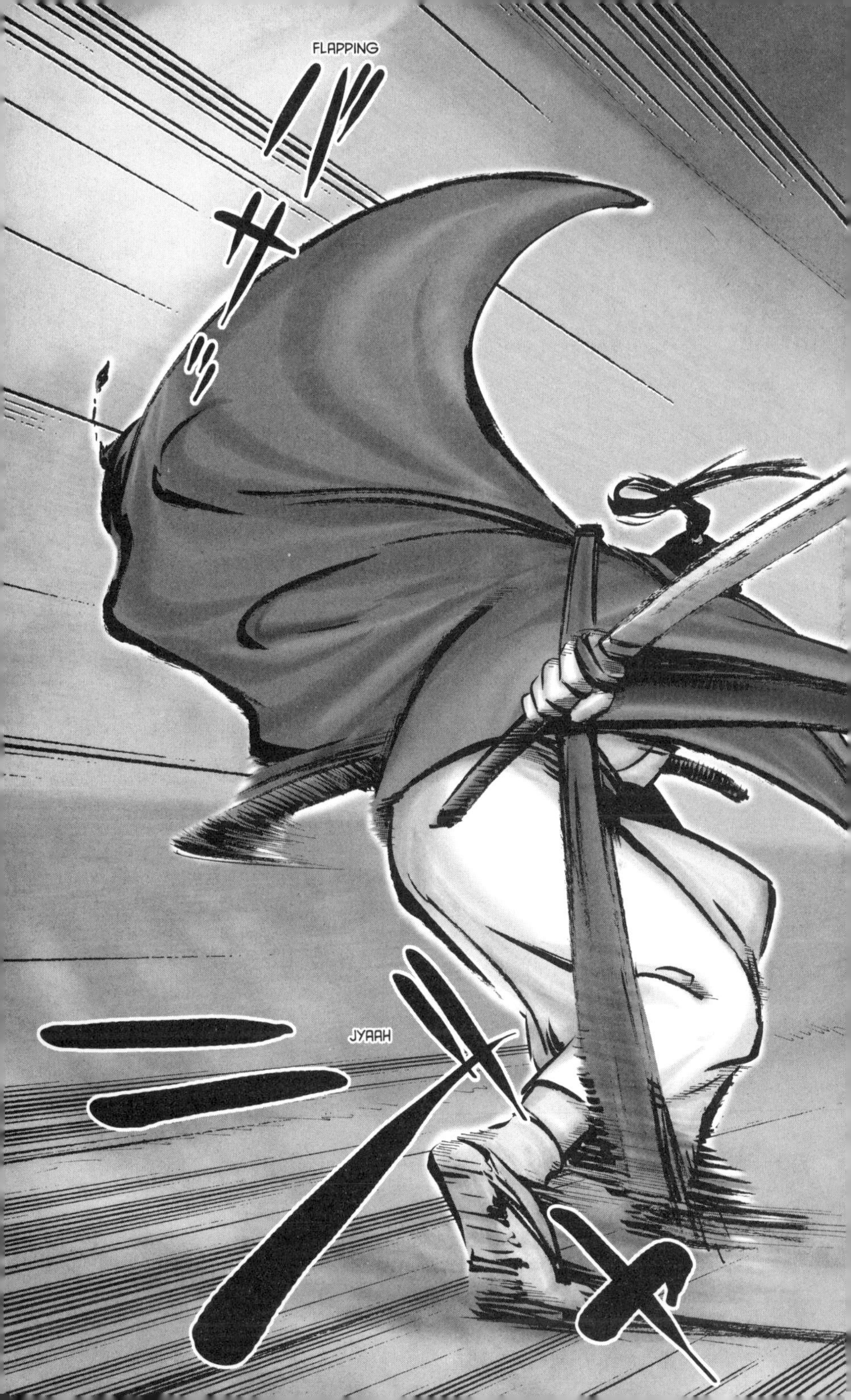
FLAPPING
JYAAH

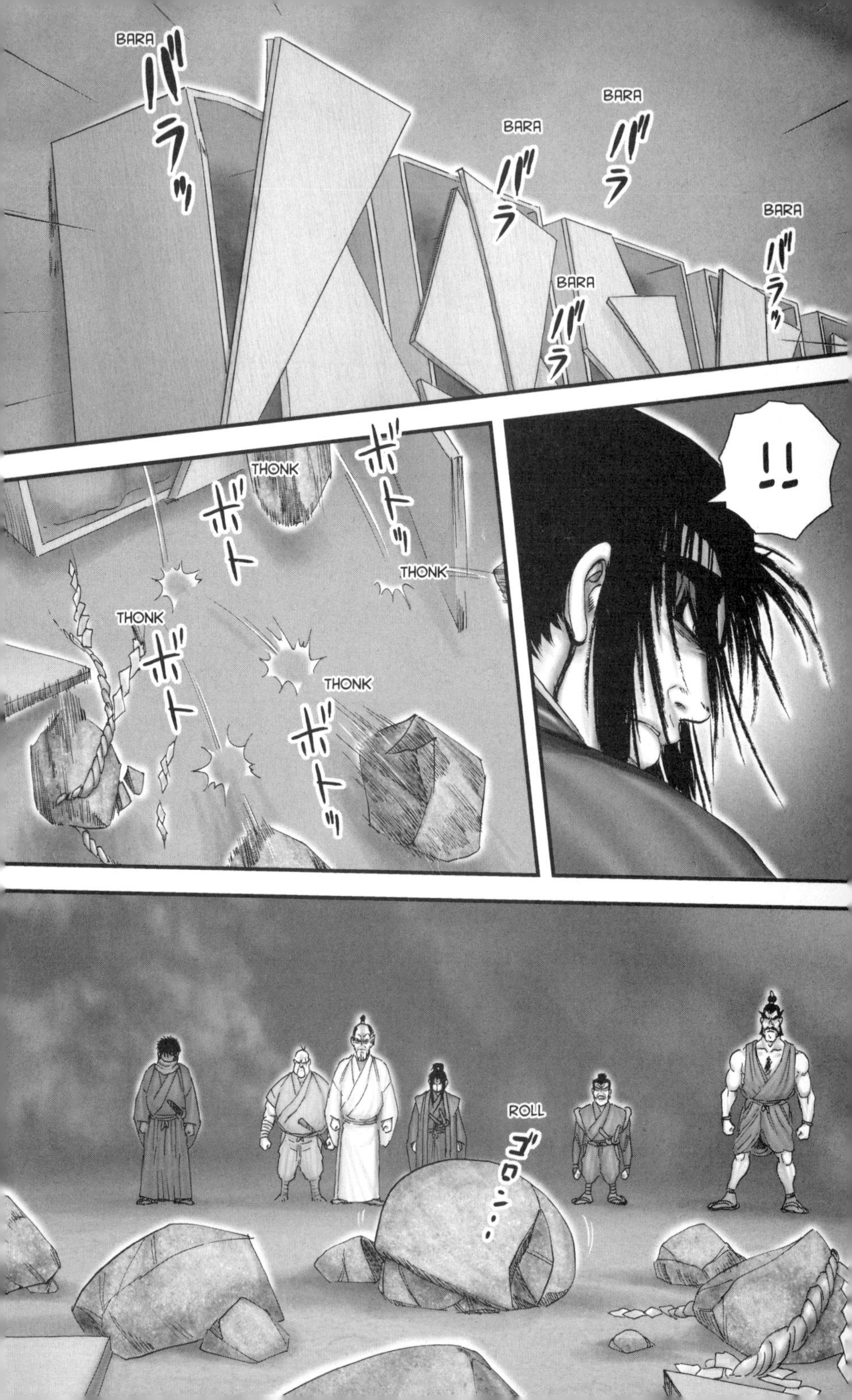
BARA
バラッ
BARA
バラ
BARA
バラ
BARA
バラ
BARA
バラッ
!!
ボトッ
THONK
THONK
ボト
THONK
ボトッ
THONK
THONK
ボト
ROLL
ゴロ…

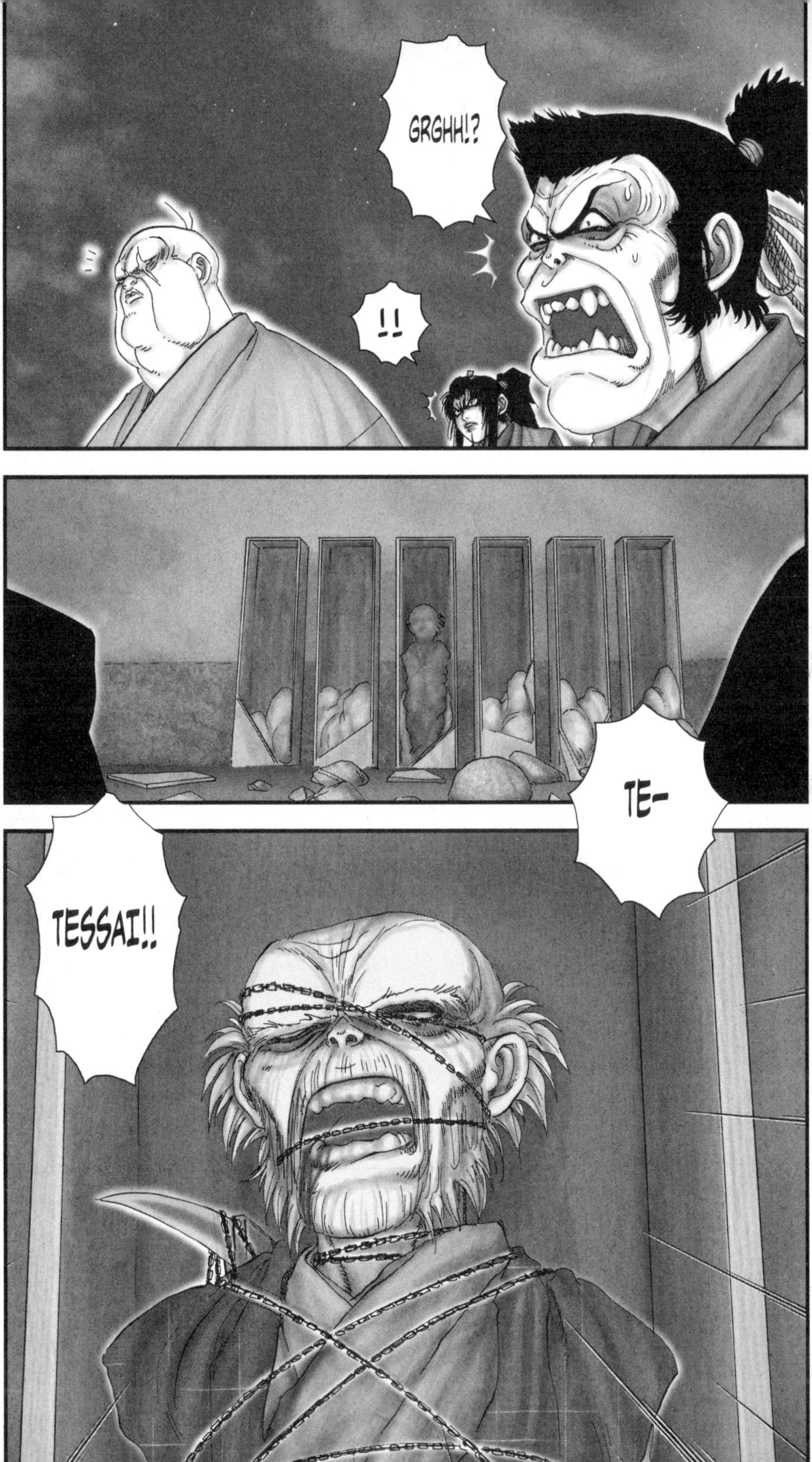
GRGHH!?
!!
TE-
TESSAI!!

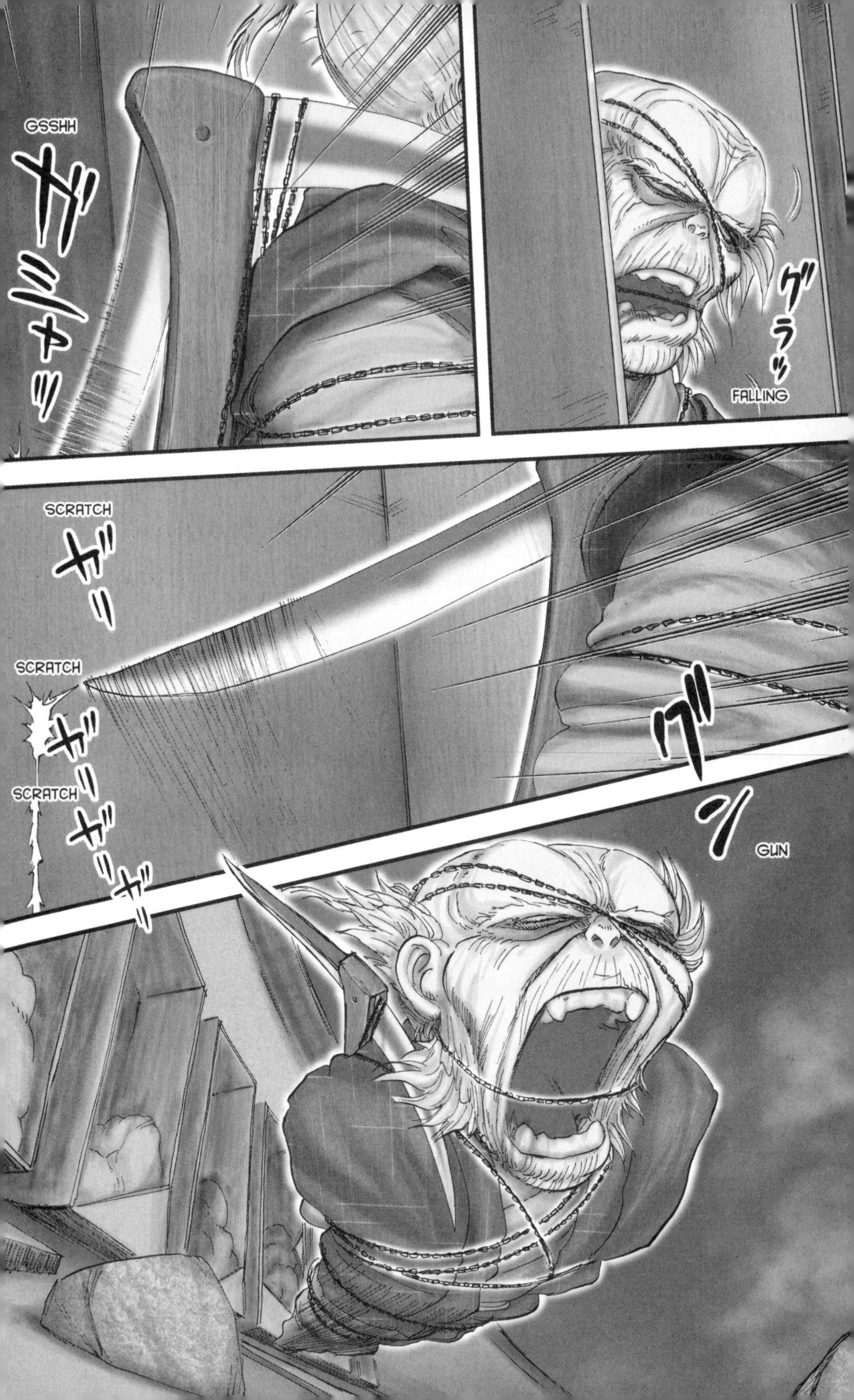
グラッ
FALLING
GSSHH
ガシャッ
SCRATCH
ガリ
SCRATCH
ガリ
SCRATCH
ガリガリ
グン
GUN

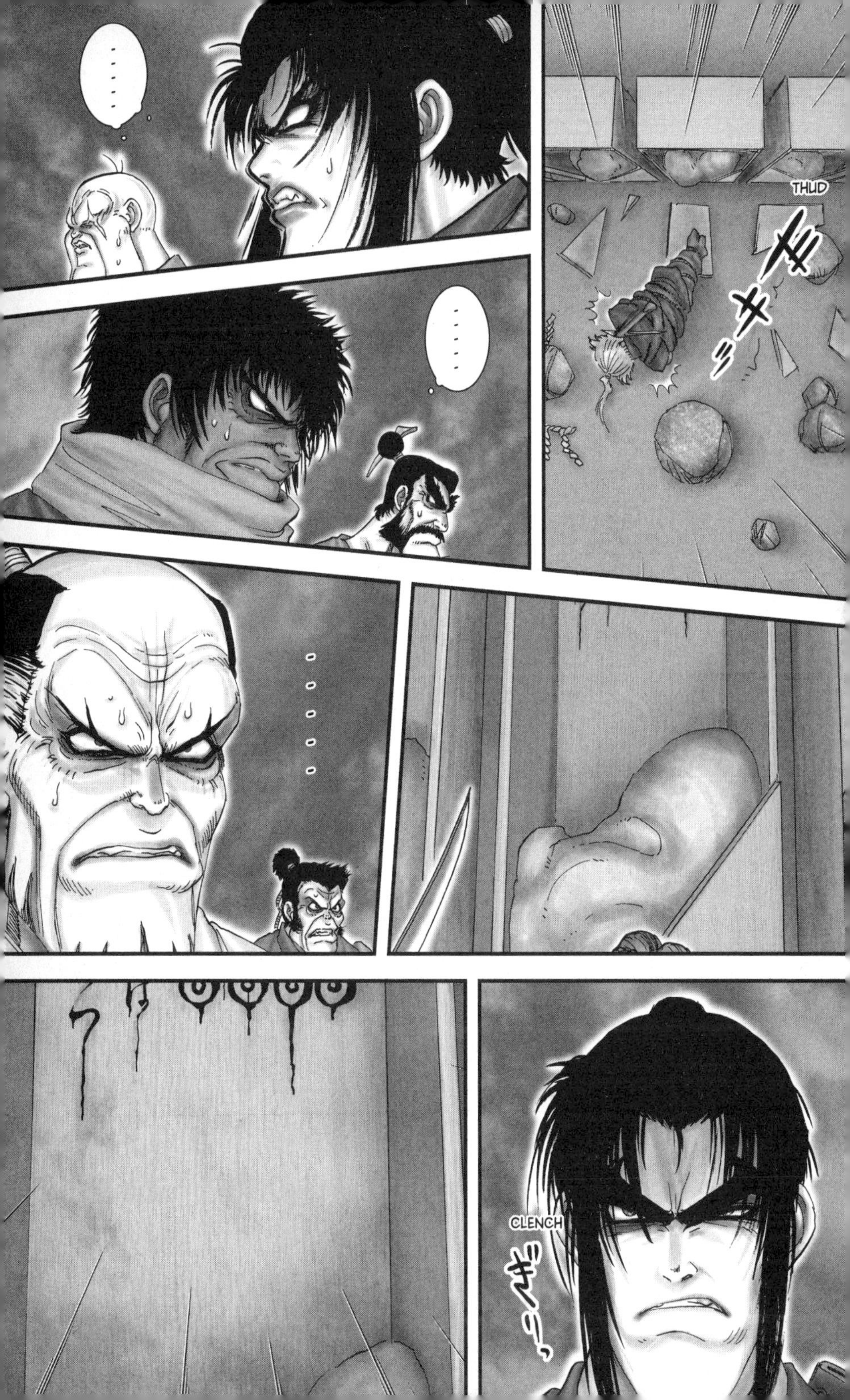
THUD
CLENCH

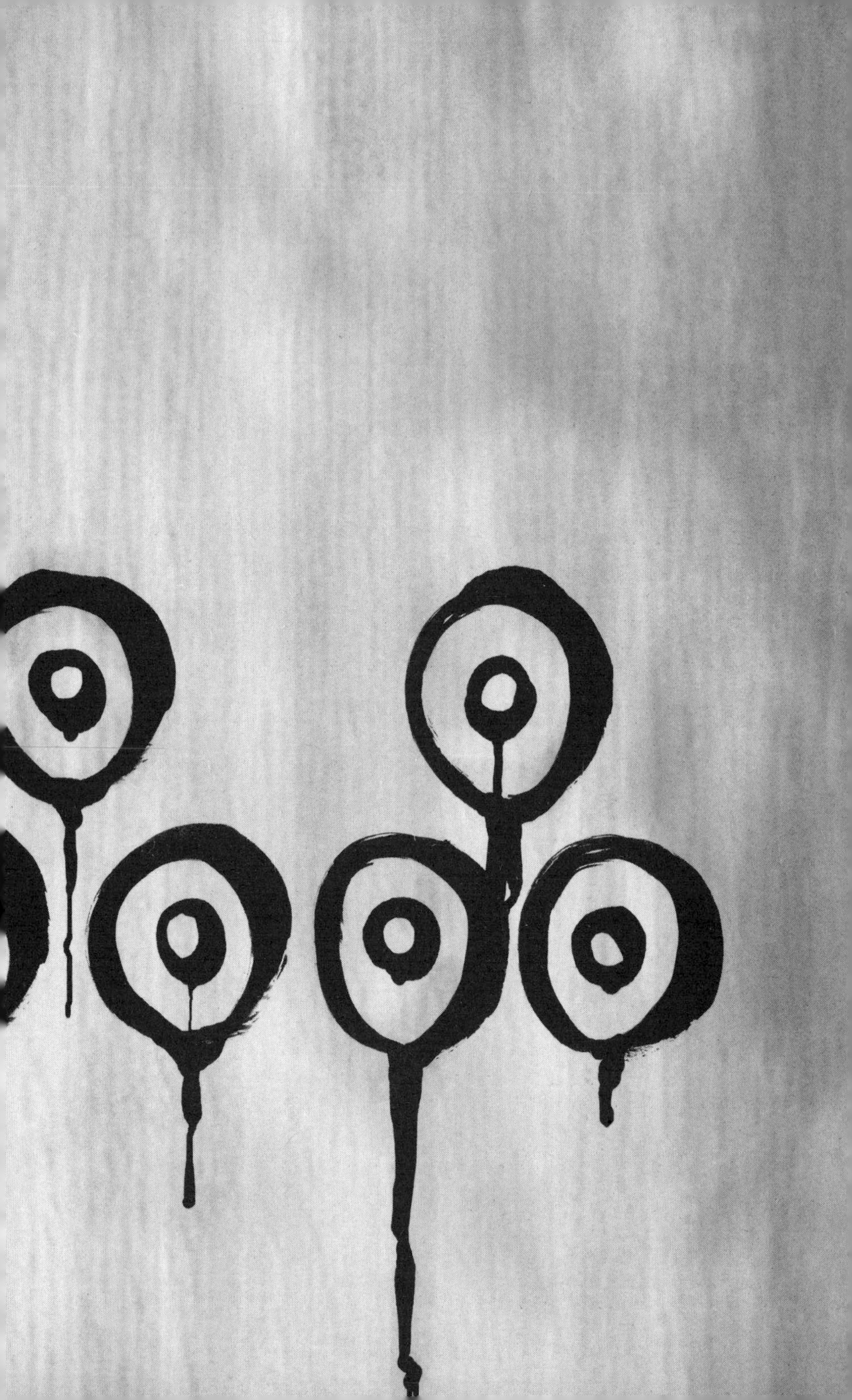

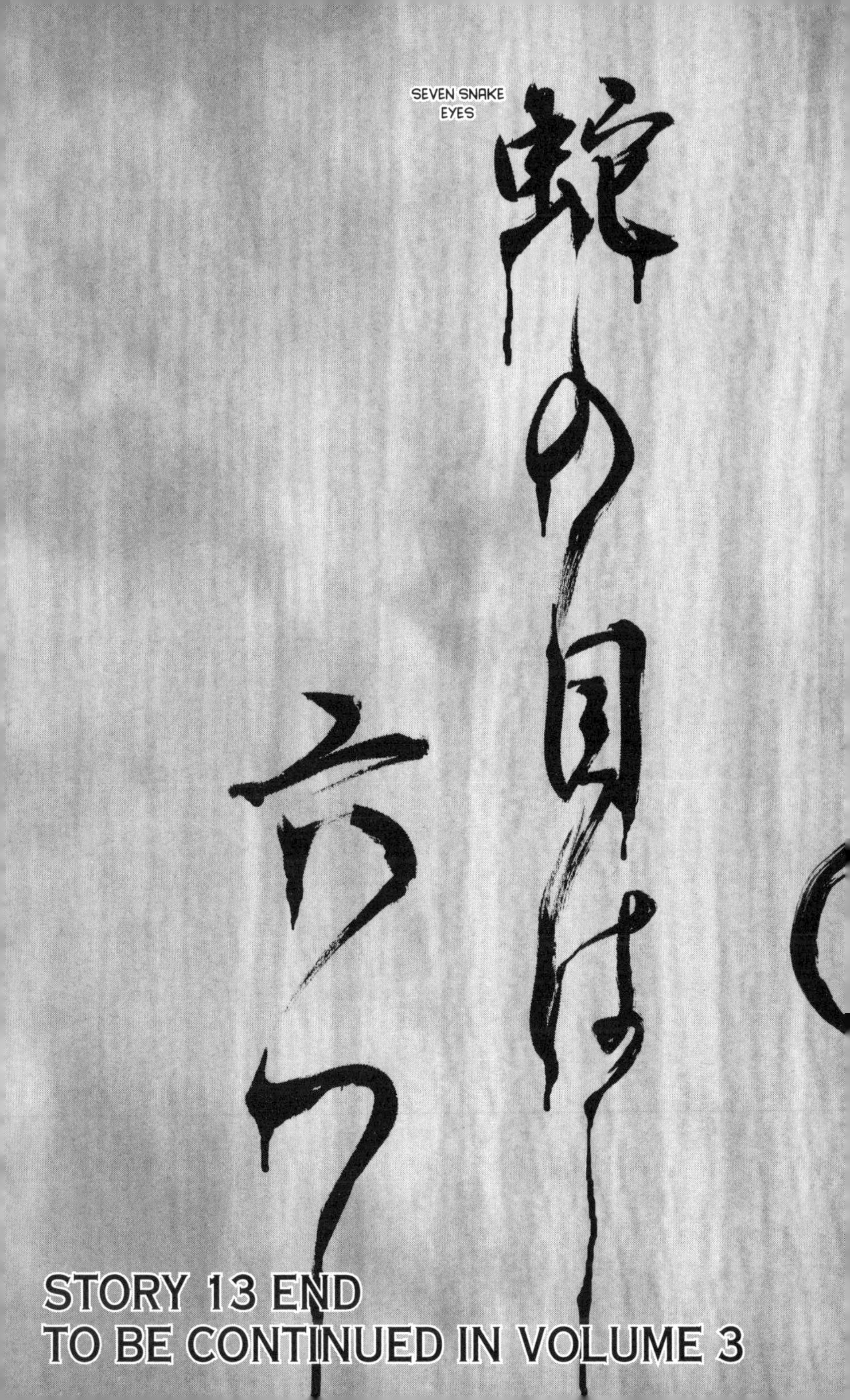
SEVEN SNAKE
EYES

STORY 13 END
TO BE CONTINUED IN VOLUME 3

about the authors

FŪTARO YAMADA

Born in 1922 in Hyogo Prefecture, Fūtaro Yamada made his debut as a novelist while still a student at Tokyo Medical University. Yamada was known for his mystery novels such as *Ganchuu No Akuma*. Later, his Ninja Scrolls series became wildly popular. He penned a wide body of literature, including the period piece *Makaitensei*, as well as several collections of essays such as *Ato Senkai No Banmeshi* and *Ningen Rinjyuu Zukan*. He passed away on July 28, 2001.

MASAKI SEGAWA

Masaki Segawa made his debut in 1997 with the series *Senma Monogatari,* which ran in the weekly comic *Morning*. In 1998, he began his long-running *Uppers* magazine series *Onigiri Jyuuzou,* which ended in the year 2000. This is his second-longest-running series and his first adaptation. He loves cats and watermelon. He currently resides in Funabashi.

Translation Notes

Japanese is a tricky language for most Westerners, and translation is often more an art than a science. For your edification and reading pleasure, here are notes on some of the places where we could have gone in a different direction or where a Japanese cultural reference is used.

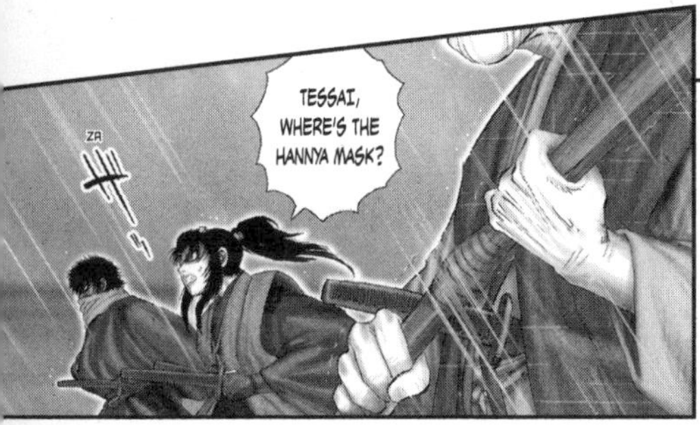
TESSAI, WHERE'S THE HANNYA MASK?
ZA

Hannya mask, page 25

Mask of a demoness, with horns and a face expressing a woman's jealousy, scorn, and pain.

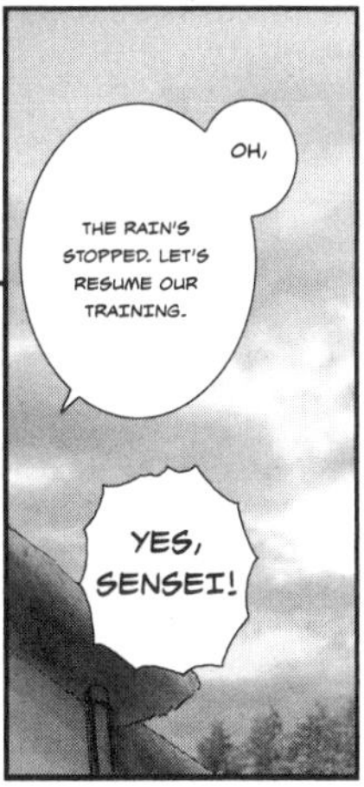
OH,
THE RAIN'S STOPPED. LET'S RESUME OUR TRAINING.
YES, SENSEI!

Sensei, page 62

Sensei is Japanese for teacher.

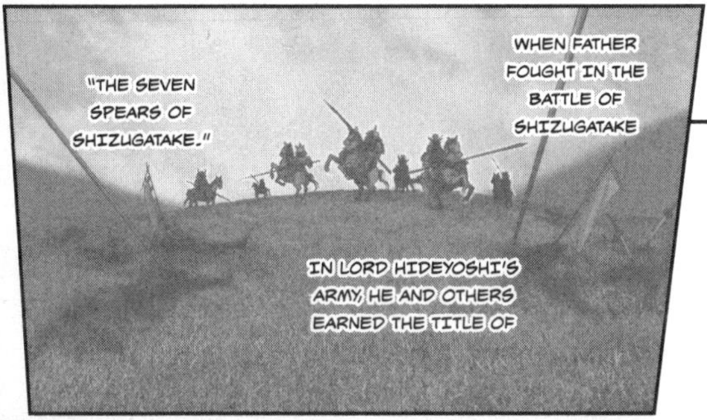
WHEN FATHER FOUGHT IN THE BATTLE OF SHIZUGATAKE
IN LORD HIDEYOSHI'S ARMY, HE AND OTHERS EARNED THE TITLE OF
"THE SEVEN SPEARS OF SHIZUGATAKE."

Lord Hideyoshi, page 64

Toyotomi Hideyoshi was the first person to unify the warring clans and to rule all of Japan.

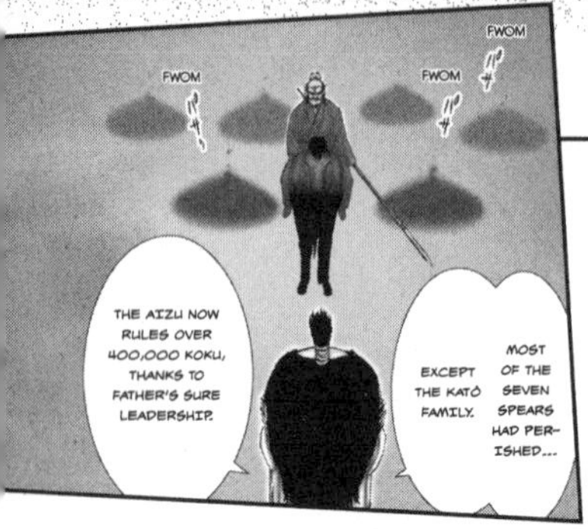
FWOM
FWOM
FWOM
MOST OF THE SEVEN SPEARS HAD PERISHED...
EXCEPT THE KATÔ FAMILY.
THE AIZU NOW RULES OVER 400,000 KOKU, THANKS TO FATHER'S SURE LEADERSHIP.

400,000 *koku,* page 65

A *koku* is a standard measurement of rice, but it's also used as a measurement of land ruled over by a lord. The Aizu clan rules over 400,000 *koku.* In other words, it rules over an area that could cultivate 400,000 *koku* of rice.

Kyô dolls, page 78

Dolls with long, black hair that were made to look like typical Kyoto women. In this case, the women are being likened to the dolls.

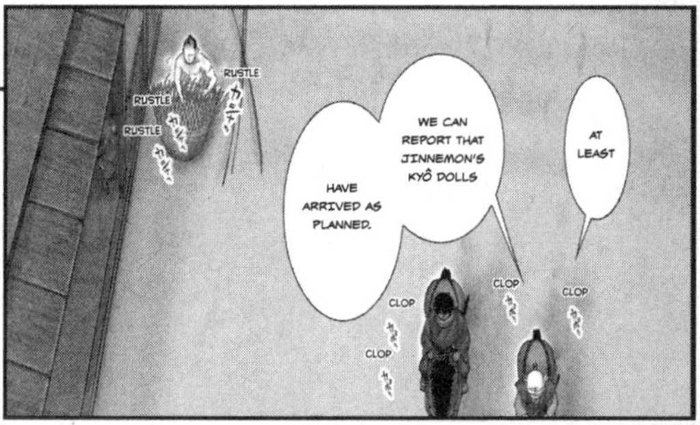
AT LEAST
WE CAN REPORT THAT JINNEMON'S KYÔ DOLLS
HAVE ARRIVED AS PLANNED.
RUSTLE
RUSTLE
RUSTLE
CLOP
CLOP
CLOP
CLOP

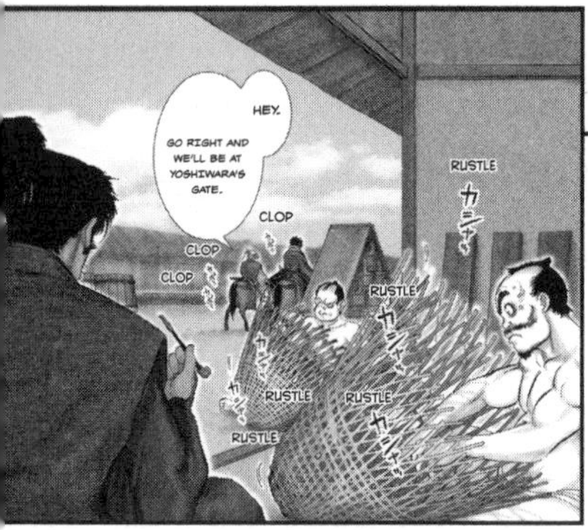
HEY.
GO RIGHT AND WE'LL BE AT YOSHIWARA'S GATE.
RUSTLE
CLOP
CLOP
CLOP
RUSTLE
RUSTLE
RUSTLE
RUSTLE

Yoshiwara, page 79

A brothel district recognized by the Edo shogunate.

Ama, page 112

Ama is the word for nun in Japanese. The seamstress's name is *ama* with an "o" in front to make it sound like a woman's name, e.g., Otori, Ochie, etc.

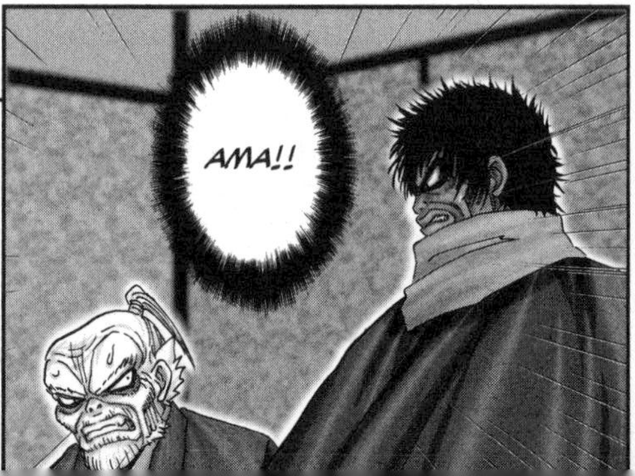
AMA!!

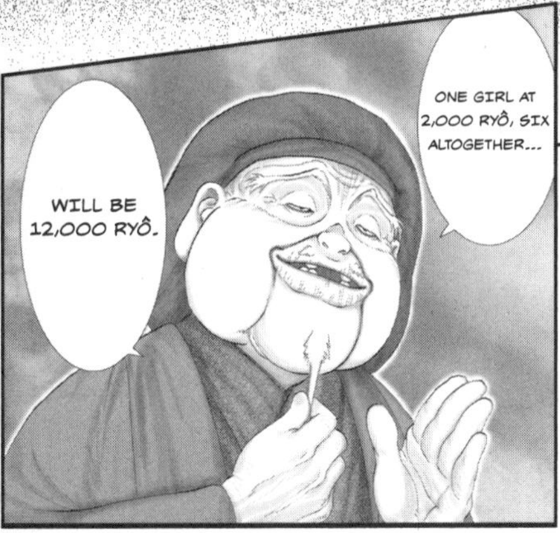
ONE GIRL AT 2,000 RYÔ, SIX ALTOGETHER...
WILL BE 12,000 RYÔ.

***Ryô*, page 113**

Ryô was the standard Japanese currency before the yen. One oval gold coin amounted to one *ryô*. Because the coin was made of gold, it would have been very heavy to transport 12,000 *ryô*.

Carriage, page 116

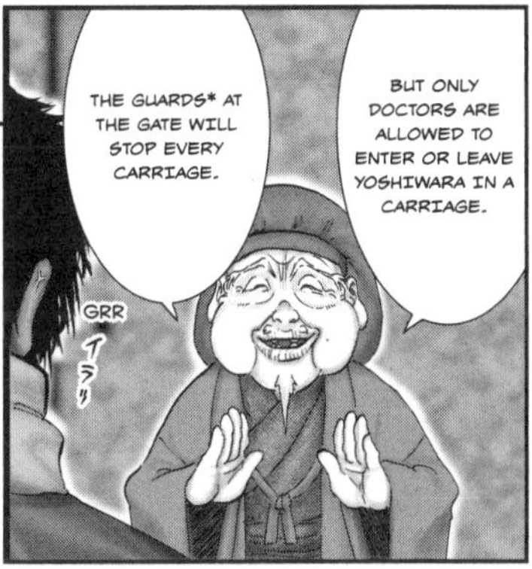
BUT ONLY DOCTORS ARE ALLOWED TO ENTER OR LEAVE YOSHIWARA IN A CARRIAGE.
THE GUARDS* AT THE GATE WILL STOP EVERY CARRIAGE.
GRR

A carriage or palanquin, usually carried by two men, was a mode of transportation reserved for people of high class and rank. Different types of carriages were used according to class and gender.

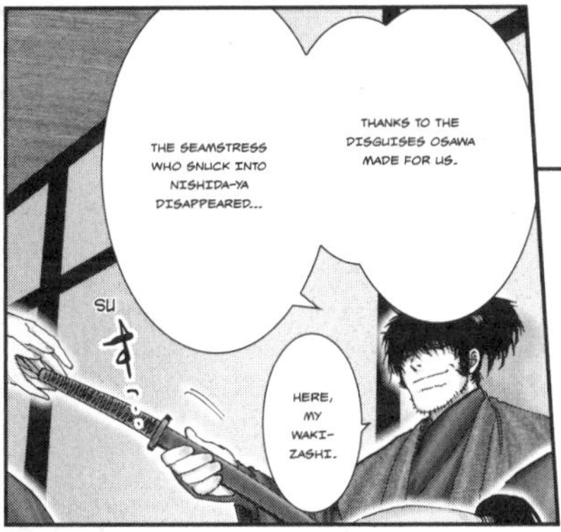
THANKS TO THE DISGUISES OSAWA MADE FOR US.
THE SEAMSTRESS WHO SNUCK INTO NISHIDA-YA DISAPPEARED...
SU
HERE, MY WAKI-ZASHI.

***Wakizashi*, page 124**

A *wakizashi* is a side sword. Samurai usually wore two swords on their left side (right if they're left-handed). One was the main long sword, and the other was a smaller sword called a *wakizashi*.

***Daimyô*, page 161**

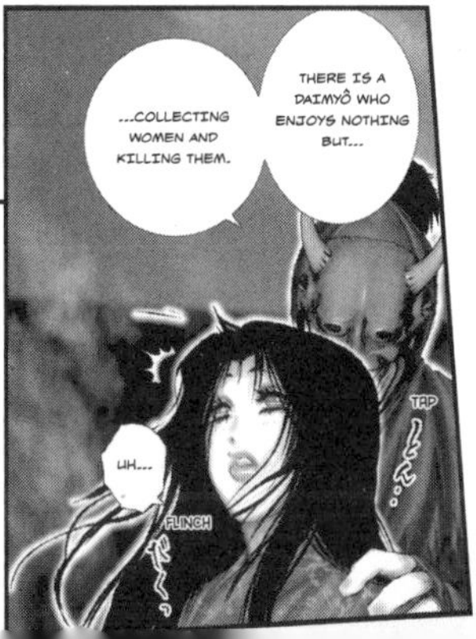
THERE IS A DAIMYÔ WHO ENJOYS NOTHING BUT...
...COLLECTING WOMEN AND KILLING THEM.
TAP
UH...
FLINCH

Daimyô means "feudal lord." A *daimyô* is the head of a clan. Lord Akinari is the *daimyô* of the Aizu clan.

INSIDE YOSHIWARA
EDO 1-CHÔME
RATTLE
RATTLE
RATTLE
RATTLE

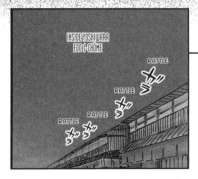

1-*chôme*, page 166

Chôme is a suffix roughly meaning "street."

WANDERING... AT THE CROSS-ROADS OF SIX PATHS*...
...TO THE... SANZU RIVER...
WAILING...

Sanzu River, page 170

Sanzu means "three crossings" because there are three crossings to get to the other side of the river. On the seventh day, the dead are said to cross this river into the afterlife. It is the Buddhist version of the River Styx.

ENMA'S...
POINT

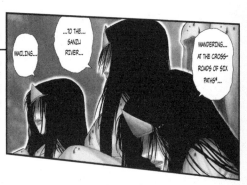

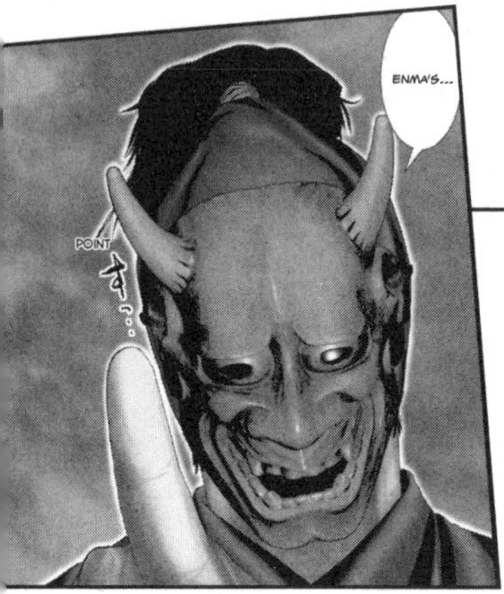

Enma, page 173

Enma is the great lord of the underworld, according to Buddhist belief.

...WIFE.
'CAUSE I'M A DEMONESS.
PIN

Pinky sticking up, page 174

This is a hand gesture that means "woman." For example, "Is she your…[raise pinky]?" Although a bit crass, it's a gesture that's still used today in conversation.

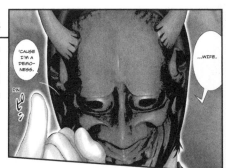

Preview of Volume 3

We are pleased to present you with a preview
of volume 3. Please check our website
(www.delreymanga.com) to see when this
volume will be available.

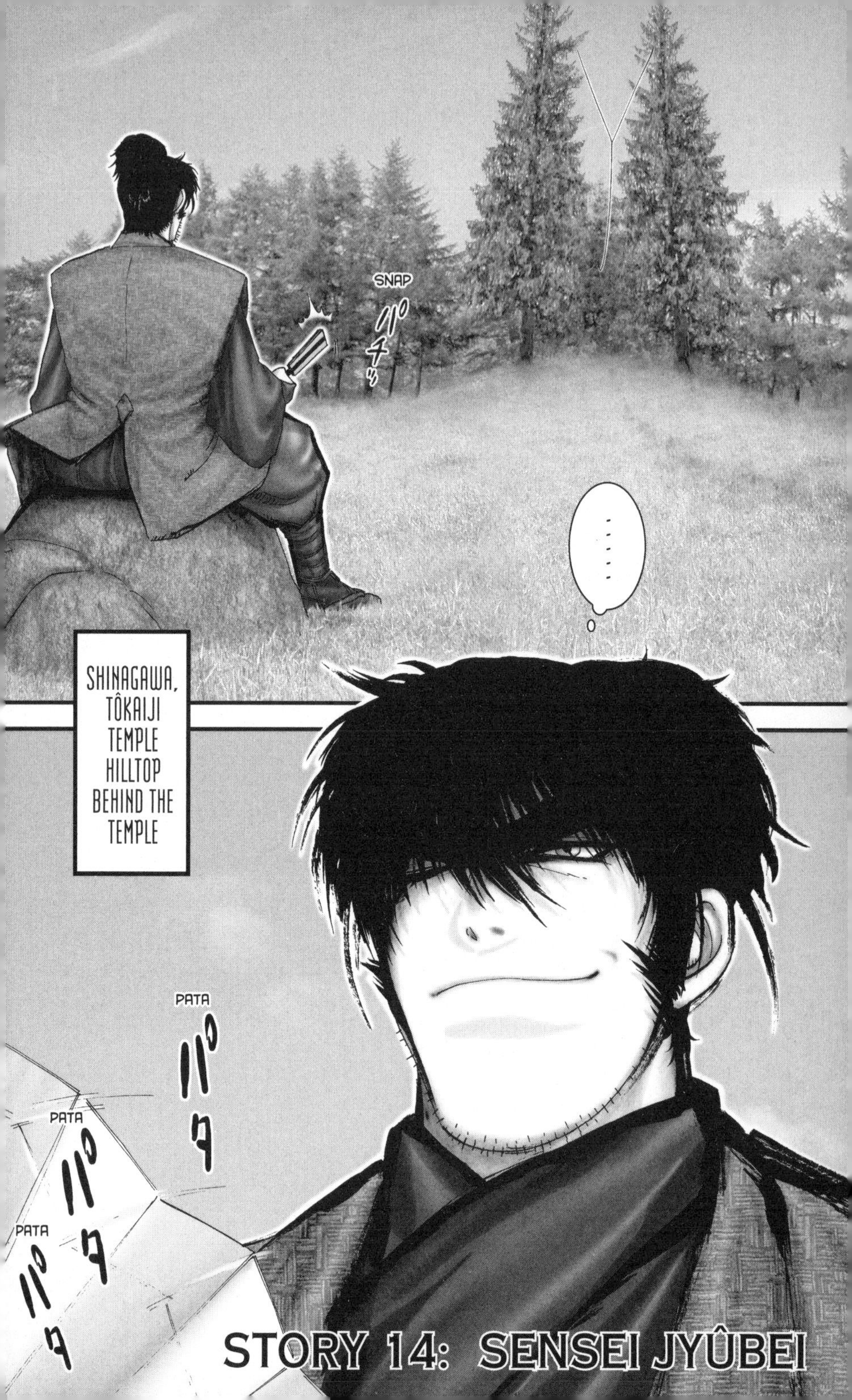
SNAP
パチッ
......
SHINAGAWA, TÔKAIJI TEMPLE HILLTOP BEHIND THE TEMPLE
PATA
パタ
PATA
パタ
PATA
パタ
STORY 14: SENSEI JYÛBEI

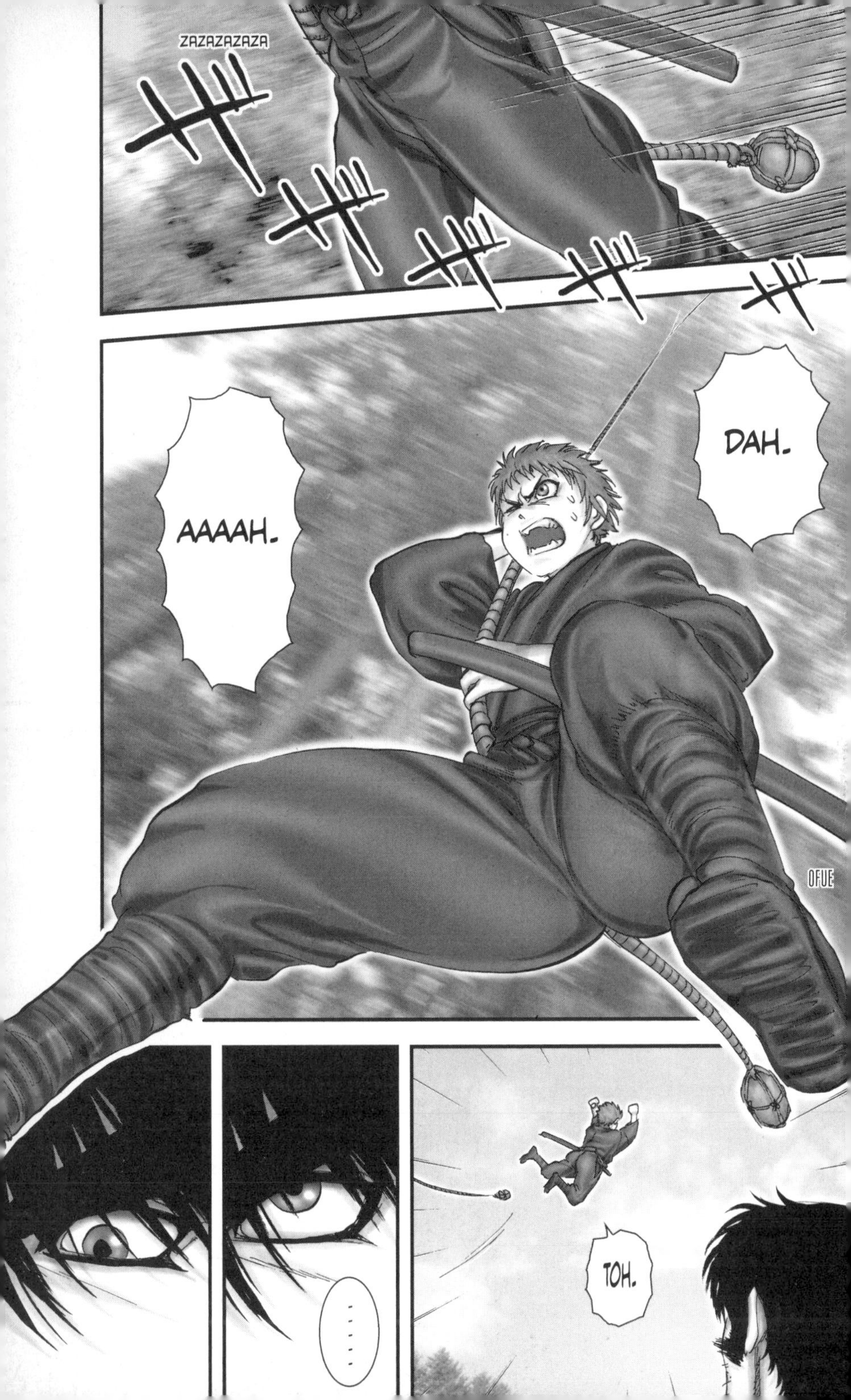
ZAZAZAZAZA
DAH.
AAAAH.
OFUE
TOH.
......

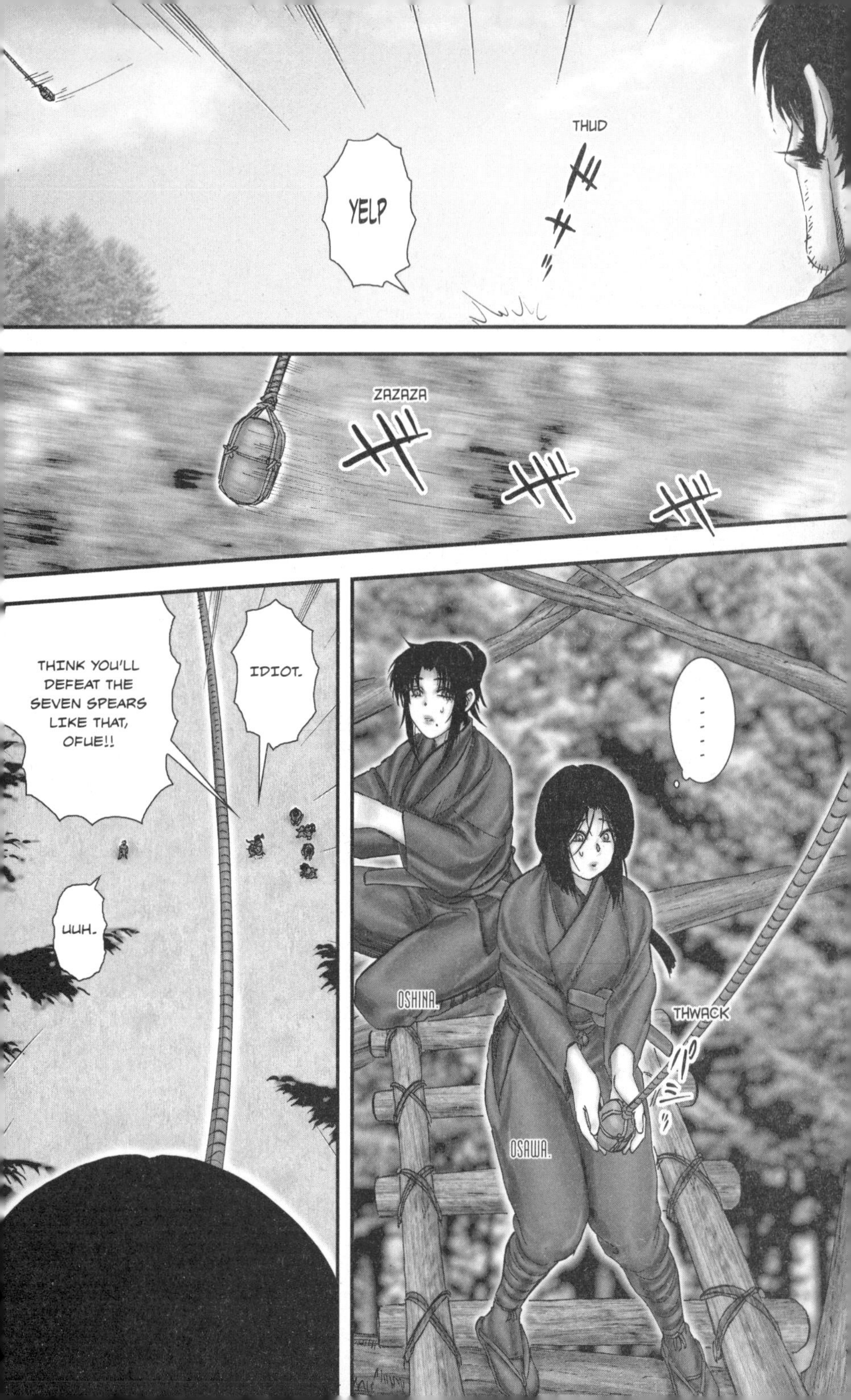
THUD
YELP
ZAZAZA
......
OSHINA.
THWACK
OSAWA.
IDIOT.
THINK YOU'LL DEFEAT THE SEVEN SPEARS LIKE THAT, OFUE!!
UUH.

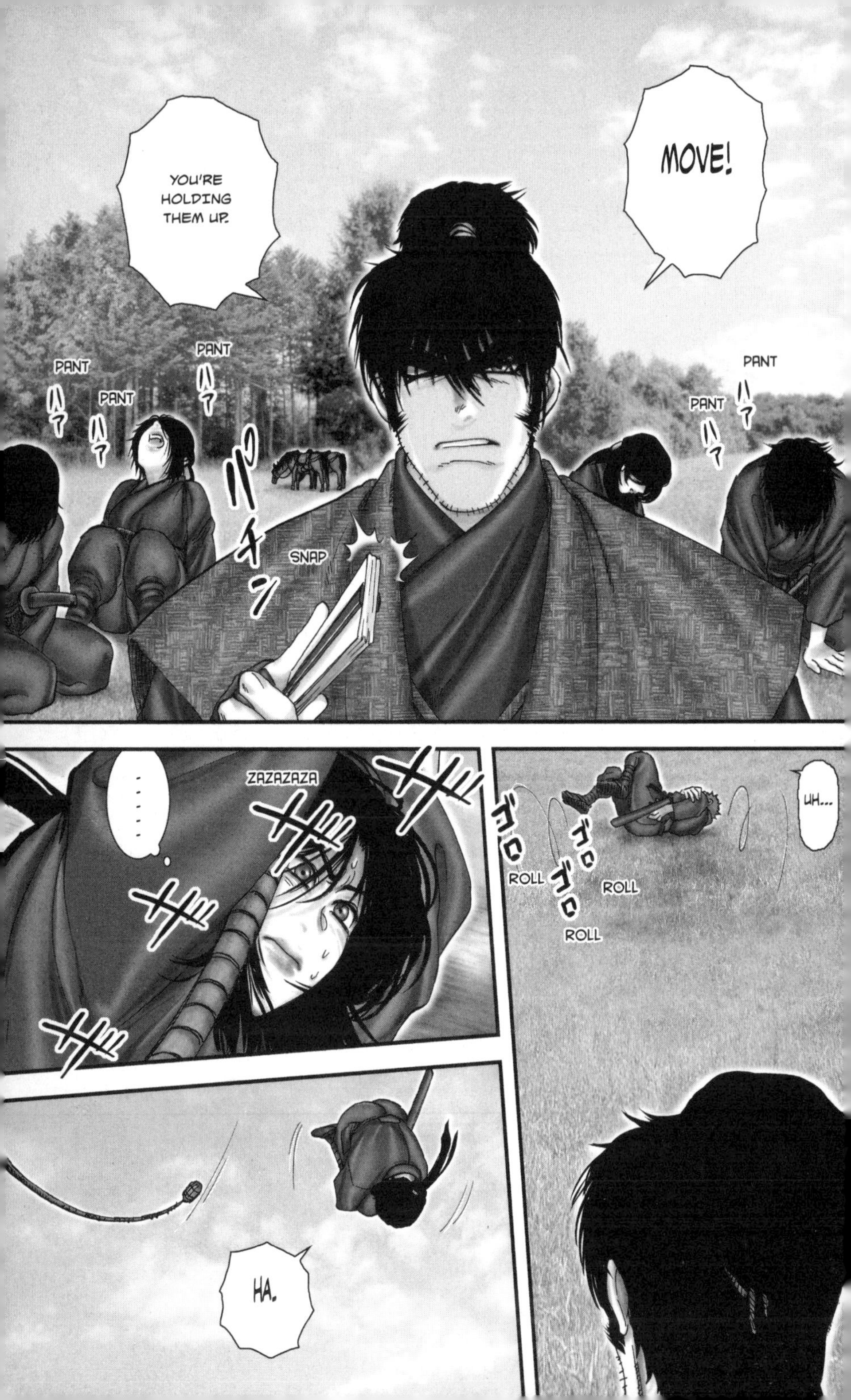
MOVE!
YOU'RE HOLDING THEM UP.
PANT
ハァ
PANT
ハァ
PANT
ハァ
PANT
ハァ
PANT
ハァ
SNAP
パキン
UH...
ゴロ
ROLL
ゴロ
ROLL
ゴロ
ROLL
ZAZAZAZA
......
HA.

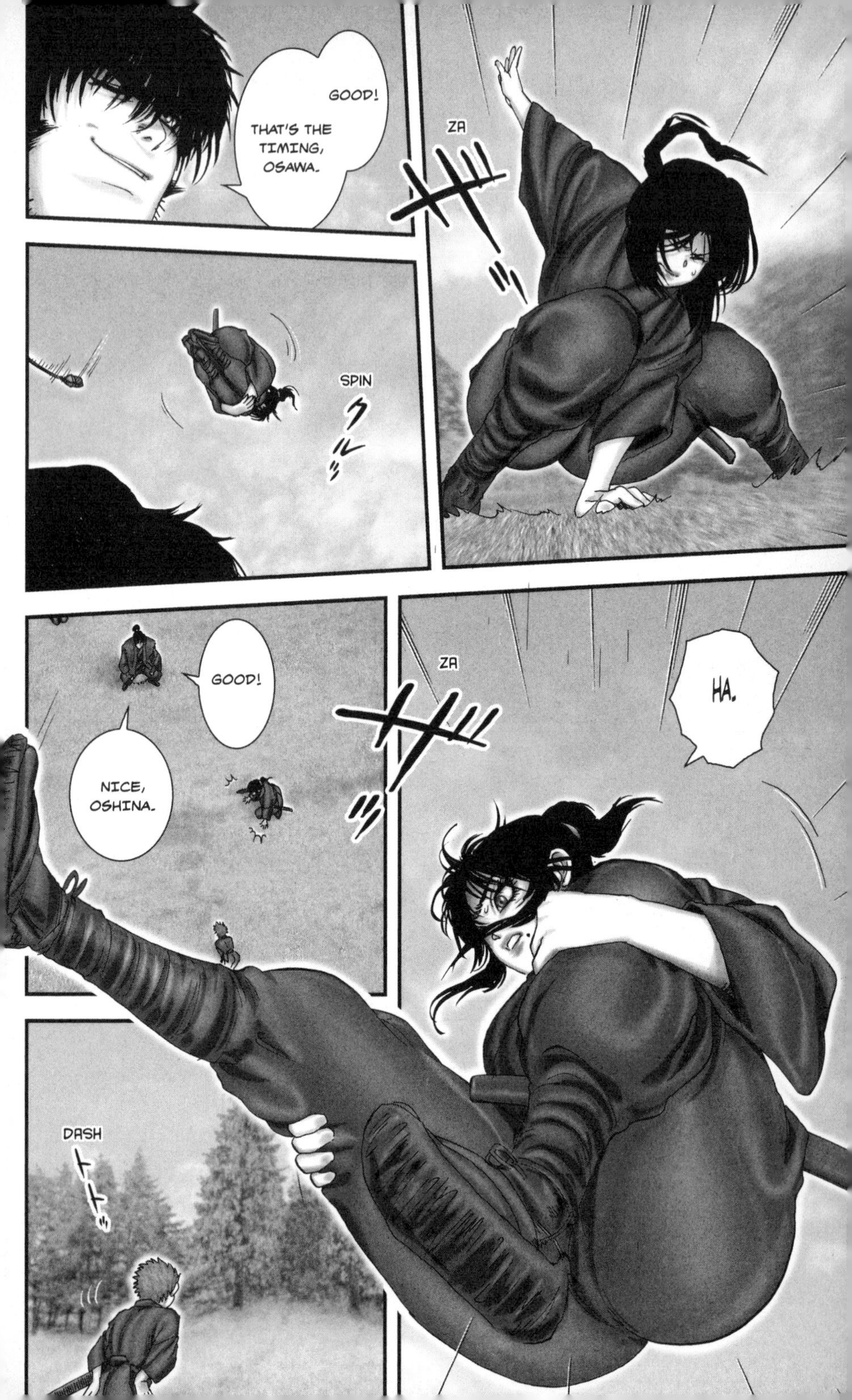
ZA
GOOD!
THAT'S THE TIMING, OSAWA.
SPIN
HA.
ZA
GOOD!
NICE, OSHINA.
DASH

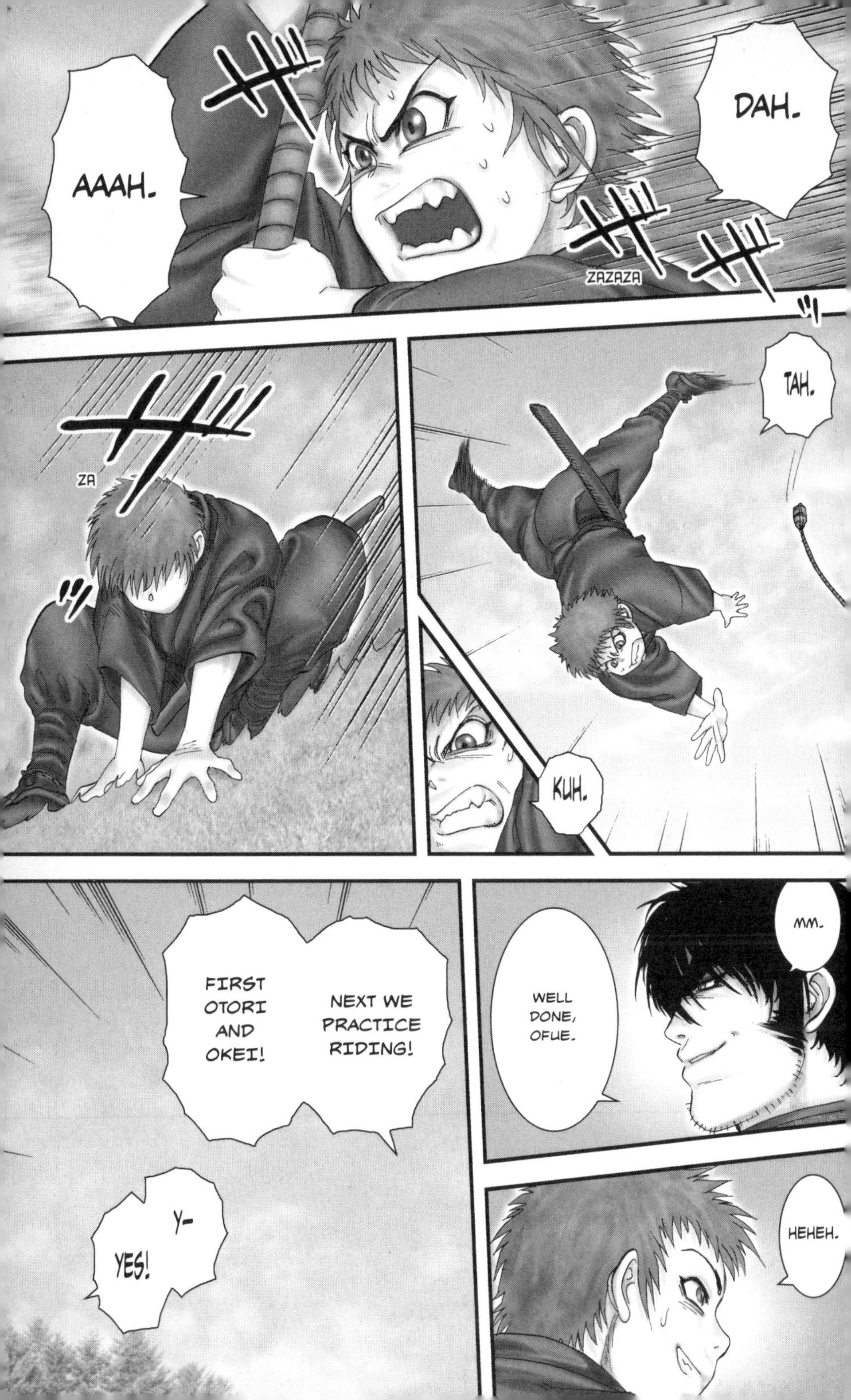
DAH.
ZAZAZA
AAAH.
TAH.
KUH.
ZA
MM.
WELL DONE, OFUE.
HEHEH.
NEXT WE PRACTICE RIDING!
FIRST OTORI AND OKEI!
Y-
YES!

SUZUKA

KOUJI SEO

SHE'S SO COOL

Yamato is ready for a fresh start. So when his aunt invites him to stay rent-free in her big-city boarding-house in hustling, bustling Tokyo, Yamato jumps at the chance. There's just one teensy-weensy catch: It's an all-girl housing complex and spa! Things get even more nerve-racking when Yamato meets his neighbor Suzuka, a beautiful track-and-field star. She's not just the cutest girl Yamato's ever met, she's also the coolest, the smartest, and the most intimidating. Can an ordinary guy like Yamato ever hope to win over a girl like Suzuka?

KOUJI SEO

Special extras in each volume! Read them all!

HIROYUKI TAMAKOSHI

JUST ONE OF THE GIRLS

A whole new Gacha Gacha story line begins! Akira Hatsushiba is just your typical, average high school kid . . . until a glitch in a Gacha Gacha video game changes his life forever. Now, every time Akira sneezes, his entire body undergoes a gender-bending switcheroo! That's right, Akira is always just an *achoo* away from getting in touch with his feminine side. But it's not all bad. Akira has had a crush on Yurika Sakuraba ever since he first laid eyes on her. He's always been too shy, but now that he can change into a girl, Akira finally has a chance to get close to Yurika. Being a girl certainly has its advantages!

Special extras in each volume! Read them all!

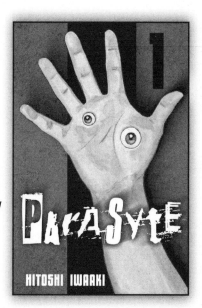

Le Chevalier d'Eon

STORY BY TOU UBUKATA
MANGA BY KIRIKO YUMEJI

DARKNESS FALLS ON PARIS

Amysterious cult is sacrificing beautiful young women to a demonic force that threatens the entire country. Only one man can save Paris from chaos and terror, the king's top secret agent: The Chevalier d'Eon.

• Available on DVD from ADV Films.

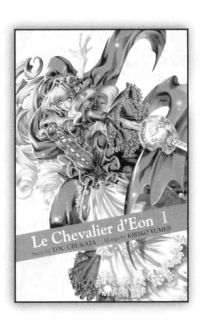

Special extras in each volume! Read them all!

Tomare!

STOP!

YOU'RE GOING THE WRONG WAY!

**MANGA IS A COMPLETELY DIFFERENT
TYPE OF READING EXPERIENCE.**

**TO START AT THE *BEGINNING*,
GO TO THE *END*!**

THAT'S RIGHT!

AUTHENTIC MANGA IS READ THE TRADITIONAL JAPANESE WAY—
FROM RIGHT TO LEFT, EAXACTLY THE *OPPOSITE* OF HOW AMERICAN
BOOKS ARE READ. IT'S EASY TO FOLLOW: JUST GO TO THE OTHER
END OF THE BOOK, AND READ EACH PAGE—AND EACH PANEL—
FROM RIGHT SIDE TO LEFT SIDE, STARTING AT THE TOP RIGHT.
NOW YOU'RE EXPERIENCING MANGA AS IT WAS MEANT TO BE.